Social Emotions in Nature and Artifact

OXFORD SERIES ON COGNITIVE MODELS AND ARCHITECTURES

Series Editor: Frank E. Ritter

Integrated Models of Cognitive Systems
Edited by Wayne D. Gray

In Order to Learn:
How the Sequence of Topics Influences Learning
Edited by Frank E. Ritter, Josef Nerb,
Erno Lehtinen, and Timothy O'Shea

How Can the Human Mind Occur
in the Physical Universe?
By John R. Anderson

Principles of Synthetic Intelligence PSI:
An Architecture of Motivated Cognition
By Joscha Bach

The Multitasking Mind
By David D. Salvucci and Niels A. Taatgen

How to Build a Brain:
A Neural Architecture for Biological Cognition
By Chris Eliasmith

Minding Norms:
Mechanisms and Dynamics of Social Order in Agent Societies
Edited by Rosaria Conte, Giulia Andrighetto, and Marco Campennì

Social Emotions in Nature and Artifact
Edited by Jonathan Gratch and Stacy Marsella

Social Emotions in Nature and Artifact

Edited by Jonathan Gratch and Stacy Marsella

OXFORD
UNIVERSITY PRESS

OXFORD
UNIVERSITY PRESS

Oxford University Press is a department of the University of Oxford.
It furthers the University's objective of excellence in research, scholarship,
and education by publishing worldwide.

Oxford New York
Auckland Cape Town Dar es Salaam Hong Kong Karachi
Kuala Lumpur Madrid Melbourne Mexico City Nairobi
New Delhi Shanghai Taipei Toronto

With offices in
Argentina Austria Brazil Chile Czech Republic France Greece
Guatemala Hungary Italy Japan Poland Portugal Singapore
South Korea Switzerland Thailand Turkey Ukraine Vietnam

Published in the United States of America by
Oxford University Press
198 Madison Avenue, New York, NY 10016

Library of Congress Cataloging-in-Publication Data

Social emotions in nature and artifact / edited by Jonathan Gratch, Stacy Marsella.
pages cm. – (Oxford series on cognitive models and architecture)
Includes bibliographical references and index.
ISBN 978–0–19–538764–3
1. Psychology—Computer simulation. 2. Emotions—Computer simulation. 3. Artificial intelligence. I. Gratch, Jonathan (Jonathan Matthew), 1963– II. Marsella, Stacy.

BF39.5.S63 2014
152.4—dc23
2013008884
9780195387643

Contents

Preface

Within emotion, social psychology and human–computer interaction research, there's been growing interest in the role of emotions in social interactions. Concepts like rapport, emotional contagion, or emergent emotions presuppose that people rapidly detect nonverbal affective cues, make inferences about the other party's mental state, and respond in ways that coconstruct an emotional trajectory between participants. Through this process, people can synchronize their thoughts and behaviors (promoting social bonds, enhancing trust, and increasing communicative efficiency), or desynchronize (establishing personal space and accentuating differences in status, power, or beliefs). Recent advances in biometrics and artificial intelligence are allowing computer systems to engage in this nonverbal dance, on the one hand opening a wealth of possibilities for human–machine systems, and on the other, creating powerful new tools for behavioral science research. This book reports on the state of the art in both social science theory and computational methods and illustrates how these two fields, together, can both facilitate and illuminate human social processes.

The book has several aims:

- Present current social science theories of social emotions from cognitive, biological, social, and developmental perspectives (Chapters 1–3, 10)
- Strengthen the theoretical foundation for building computational systems that coconstruct emotional trajectories with human participants (Chapters 4–9)
- Discuss computational models of social cognition that can represent and reason about the evolving relationship between interaction partners (Chapters 4–5)
- Present the current and future potential of sensing technology to reliably detect and classify affective nonverbal cues (Chapters 6–8)
- Discuss the potential of computational methods as tools for empirical research into human transactional processes (Chapter 4)
- Consider methodological approaches for assessing the social consequences of socioemotional systems (Chapters 10–11)

Intended Audience

The book has several relevant audiences. It is primarily addressed to researchers working at the intersection of social psychology and computing, including such scientific disciplines as affective computing, human–computer interaction, human–robot interaction, behavioral economics, cognitive modeling, computational social science, and artificial intelligence. It should also appeal to researchers in emotion and social psychology, especially those interested in using computer technology as a methodological tool for empirical research. The book capitalizes on recent interest in affective science.

Contributors

Marian Stewart Bartlett
Institute for Neural Computation
University of California
San Diego, CA

Jim Blascovich
Department of Psychological and Brain Sciences and Research Center for Virtual Environments and Behavior
University of California, Santa Barbara

Murtaza Bulut
Philips Research
Eindhoven, Netherlands

Carlos Busso
The University of Texas at Dallas

Steven Cadavid
Department of Electrical and Computer Engineering
University of Miami

Sy-Miin Chow
University of North Carolina
Chapel Hill, NC

Jeffrey F. Cohn
University of Pittsburgh and
Carnegie Mellon University
Pittsburgh, PA

Jonathan Gratch
Institute for Creative Technologies
University of Southern California
Los Angeles, CA

John D. Haltigan
University of North Carolina
Greensboro, NC

Sylwia Julia Hyniewska
Université de Genève, FPSE, and
TSI, Telecom ParisTech
Paris, France

Sin-Hwa Kang
Institute for Creative Technologies
University of Southern California
Los Angeles, CA

Leslie D. Kirby
Department of Psychology
Vanderbilt University
Nashville, TN

Mohammad H. Mahoor
Department of Electrical and Computer Engineering
University of Denver
Denver, CO

Stacy Marsella
Institute for Creative Technologies
University of Southern California
Los Angeles, CA

Daniel S. Messinger
University of Miami
Miami, FL

Louis-Phillippe Morency
Institute for Creative Technologies
University of Southern California
Los Angeles, CA

Javier R. Movellan
Institute for Neural Computation
University of California
San Diego, CA

Shrikanth Narayanan
Viterbi School of Engineering
University of Southern California
Los Angeles, CA

Radosław Niewiadomski
TSI, Telecom ParisTech
Paris, France

Brian Parkinson
University of Oxford
Oxford, UK

Catherine Pelachaud
CNRS—LTCI, Telecom ParisTech
Paris, France

David V. Pynadath
Institute for Creative Technologies
University of Southern California
Los Angeles, CA

Mei Si
Cognitive Science Department
Rensselaer Polytechnic Institute

Troy, NY
Institute for Creative Technologies
University of Southern California
Los Angeles, CA

Craig A. Smith
Department of Psychology and Human Development
Vanderbilt University
Nashville, TN

Ning Wang
Curious Lab LLC
Los Angeles, CA

Jacob Whitehill
University of California
San Diego, CA

Introduction

Toward an Information Processing Revolution in Social Emotions

Jonathan Gratch & Stacy Marsella

This book is aimed at advancing an interdisciplinary partnership between the social and computational sciences around the phenomena of social emotions. Emotions enjoy a rich tradition of scholarship for students of human psychology and intelligence, but they are an anathema to most students of intelligent artifacts. The computational sciences (and in this we include the decision sciences and, to some extent, cognitive science) have emphasized normative rational frameworks such as logic or Bayesian inference as the foundation for constructing intelligent systems. From this rationalist perspective, to the extent emotion is considered at all, it is cast as at best a heuristic but, more commonly, a harmful bias to proper decision making (Tversky & Kahneman, 1974). Recent scholarship in the social sciences has shaken this confidence in rational models, at least as currently conceived, as a basis for understanding and modeling intelligent behavior in both humans and artifacts. Clever studies in psychology and behavioral economics have clearly undermined the validity of rational models to describe human behavior, but more interestingly, they have begun to undermine their use as a foundation for artificial intelligence. Instead, evidence is mounting that emotions are best viewed as a form of information processing that serves a functional role in human cognition and social interactions. In this light, studies showing discrepancies between emotional and rational behavior may have less to say about the limits of human inference and more to say about the limits of current conceptions of rationality.[1]

The case for ignoring emotions is on its shakiest ground when it comes to social artifacts. One can debate whether emotions are rational, but regardless, people are emotional, and intentionally or not, technology is both a source and facilitator of human emotion: Bad technology design has long been a cause of human anger and frustration; interactive games and stories seek to evoke the full range of human emotional experience; and social media like Facebook and Twitter aim to facilitate emotional connections between us. Technology that purports to competently interact with people, or facilitate social interactions between people, must embody some understanding of human emotional experience. Often this understanding is implicit and guided by the intuitions of the designers. This book is predicated on the idea that advancements in both technology and our understanding of human emotion depend on making this connection explicit: that emotions perform important social functions, that these functions are best illuminated by an information processing perspective, that computer artifacts will be more effective when they incorporate these social functions, and that interactions between people and such social artifacts will provide unique insights into human behavior.

Computers in Cognitive Science Research

The partnership between the social and computational sciences has a long and productive tradition within the field of cognitive science, and these successes have important lessons for emotion research. In his 1969 book, *The Sciences of the Artificial*, Herb Simon articulated that computational scientists bring a unique and complementary perspective to the challenge of understanding human intelligence.

First, in contrast to the natural sciences, which seek to describe intelligence as it is found in nature, the "artificial sciences" seek to describe intelligence as it "ought to be in order to *attain goals*, and to *function*" (italics his). This normative emphasis often leads to serviceable abstractions that crisply capture the essence of a phenomenon while avoiding the messy details inherent in how these functions are implemented in biological organisms. Interestingly, although the terms *rational* and *normative* are often held up in opposition to emotion, this was not Simon's original intent. Rather, *rational* simply refers to an abstract characterization of function. If we posit that emotions serve important intra- and interpersonal functions, then they are subject to the sort of rational analysis Simon proposes. Indeed, some of his work emphasized that emotion serves important cognitive functions that would be required of any intelligent entity, be it natural or artificial (H. A. Simon, 1967).

Second, computational scientists approach the problem of achieving these goals and functions with a mind-set emphasizing *process*. Specifically, they conceptualize goal-directed behavior as an unfolding dynamic interaction between the intelligent artifact and its environment. Simon (1969) illustrated this point through his famous metaphor of an ant on the beach (p. 53):

> He moves ahead, angles to the right to ease his climb up a steep dunelet, detours around a pebble, stops for a moment to exchange information with a compatriot. Thus he makes his weaving, halting way back to his home.... Viewed as a geometric figure, the ant's path is irregular, complex and hard to describe. But its complexity is really a complexity in the surface of the beach, not a complexity in the ant.

The insight here is that apparent complex behavior can often be reduced to simple goal-directed processes interacting over time with a complex environment. And indeed, it is hard to imagine an "environment" more complex than the social landscape between two emotional people.

Finally, the ultimate aim of a computational scientist is to produce a working artifact that realizes this design. Once produced, this computational model serves as an "empirical object" in ways that more conventional paper-and-pencil theories cannot. For example, a designer might attempt to characterize an ant's cognitive processes in terms of a minimal number of abstract goals and functions. By building a program that realizes these processes, and simulating the interaction of this model with complex environments, the designer can empirically work out the implicit consequences of theoretical assumptions. This is particularly important in the context of social environments, where the presence of multiple sentient and adaptive entities can produce enormous complexity through their interactions.

As cognitive science has developed, computers have taken on other essential roles in the study of human cognition beyond what Simon originally anticipated. Continuing with the metaphor of the ant on the beach, computers are an increasingly important methodological tool for measuring and systematically manipulating the pebbles and dunelets. Controlling the environment is a central pillar of experimental research, and computers provide laboratory researchers with unprecedented control. Whether it is highly stylized stimuli such as Stroop task (but see MacLeod, 1991), computer "games," or fully immersive 3D virtual worlds (Loomis & Knapp, 2003), computer programs allow laboratory researchers to artificially design and systematically manipulate features of the environment in order to test theoretical assumptions about how cognition interactions with the outside world. A criticism of laboratory experiments is their artificiality (i.e., lack of ecological validity), but computers contribute here as well. Besides creating laboratory environments that mimic the real world, advances in mobile computing and surveillance technologies enable researchers to follow subjects "into the wild" and measure aspects of their everyday decision environments. Of course, the "natural" world is increasingly artificial as well, as people spend more and more time interacting through and with computational devices.

Information Processing Theory of Emotions

Despite the success of information processing theory in the study of cognition, this success has had only modest impact on the study of emotion. Early cognitive scientists argued that emotional influences that seem irrational on the surface have important cognitive functions that would be required by *any* intelligent system (see Oatley & Johnson-Laird, 1987; H. A. Simon, 1967; Sloman, 1987). Ironically, after arguing for the centrality of emotion in cognition, Simon and others in the cognitive science community went on to develop narrow, focused models of individual cognitive functions that assumed away many of the central control problems that emotion is purported to solve.

Only in the last two decades has there been a reemergence of sustained interest in emotion as a functional construct, largely centered on the cognitive, intrapersonal functions of emotion in adapting an organism to its environment, as opposed to emotion's roles in social interaction. According to this intrapersonal perspective, emotions evolved to achieve specific goals and functions that are required to survive in a dynamic, semipredictable, and social world, including the ability to rapidly sense external events; characterize how they relate to their internal needs (e.g., is this an opportunity or a threat?); consider potential responses (e.g., fight, flight, or plan); recruit the cognitive, physical, and social resources needed to adaptively respond; and monitor theses responses as they and the environment unfold over time. Progress in modeling such complex phenomena, according to the information processing perspective, depends on combining these functional theories with computational models that simulate how individual functions of emotion interoperate with each other and with other cognitive processes, how they can be controlled and directed to achieve adaptive goals in an uncertain changing environment.

There are now many attempts to translate intrapersonal theories of emotion into computational models (see Marsella, Gratch, & Petta, 2010, for a recent review). This work draws from a variety of theoretical traditions, and much of it falls outside the information processing perspective outlined above (for example, many computational models attempt to exhibit emotional behavior without consideration of its function and are directed at pragmatic goals, such as entertainment, rather than giving insight into human behavior). Nonetheless, there is a growing core of interdisciplinary research directed at incorporating the purported intrapersonal functions of emotion into working computational artifacts.

Computational work on emotion has drawn largely upon appraisal theories of emotion, not only because of their prominence in emotion research but also because they lend themselves naturally to an information processing perspective (Arnold, 1960; Frijda, 1987; Lazarus, 1991; Ortony, Clore, & Collins, 1988; Scherer, 1984). Appraisal theories argue for a close connection between emotional processes and the sort of individual cognitive processes traditionally explored in cognitive science. Emotion arises from inferential processes that compare internal beliefs, desires, and intentions with the external environment.[2] These inferences, referred to as *appraisals*, characterize specific functional aspects of the "person–environment relationship" (e.g., was this event expected in terms of my prior beliefs? is this event congruent with my goals? do I have the power to alter the consequences of this event?). From an information processing perspective, appraisals can be seen as features that help classify the state of the person–environment relationship (are things going well? does something need to change? can I effect change?). Further, these classifications help the organism recruit the appropriate cognitive and physiological resources needed to manage the current relationship with the environment. For example, through what many appraisal theorist refer to as *problem-focused coping*, a person–environment relationship that is appraised as desirable, or undesirable but controllable, will trigger approach-related emotions and action tendencies, and motivate the organism to act in the world to achieve its goals, fight to overcome obstacles, and so on. In contrast, a relationship that is seen as undesirable and uncontrollable will trigger *emotion-focused coping*: for example, withdrawal-related emotions and action tendencies such as goal distancing and resignation. These appraisals and action tendencies are argued to continuously unfold over time as actions unfold and the person–environment relationship evolves and to provide adaptive guidance.

Appraisal theory can be computationally modeled as a small number of processes that interact with each

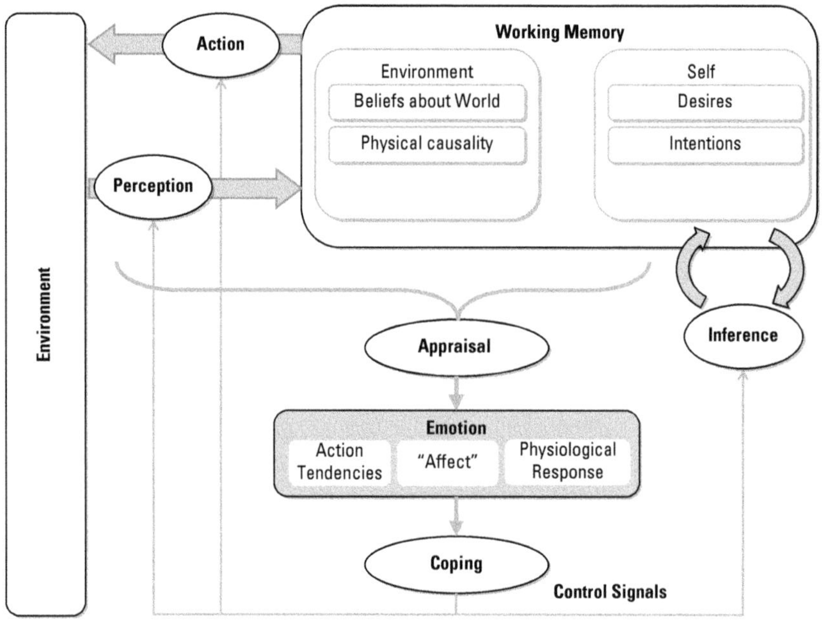

FIGURE 1. The architecture of a computational model of intrapersonal emotion.

other and the environment. For example, Figure 1 sketches the outlines of a computational model called EMA that we have developed in our research to investigate appraisal theories of emotion (see Chapter 4 for details). According to this model, appraisal is cast as a set of automatic pattern classifiers that calculate how events in the world relate to an agent's beliefs, desires, and intentions. These patterns motivate the model to act on the world or its mental state, depending on the nature of the agent–environment relationship.

The exercise of translating appraisal theory into a computational model has many of the important advantages outlined by Simon. Turning a paper-and-pencil psychological theory into a working computer program requires a reexamination and concretization of the assumptions underlying appraisal theory. EMA is just one of many such appraisal models. And once created, the model becomes an empirical artifact. Experimental scientists can use the model to generate specific predictions and then assess how these predictions fare in unfolding dynamic environments. We can then create artificial environments (e.g., computer games) and compare the behavior of people interacting with these landscapes with the behavior of the computer model (e.g., see Gratch & Marsella, 2005; Gratch, Marsella, Wang, & Stankovic, 2009; Marsella, Gratch, Wang, & Stankovic, 2009). Ideally this exercise—creating a abstract model and testing how it dynamically interacts with a complex environment—should give insight into not only our success in realizing theory but also the underlying theoretical assumptions: do the assumptions make sense from a design perspective (i.e., are they directed at achieving specific functions and goals), do the assumptions lead to predicted behavior, and more importantly, is the complexity of the model justified, or like Simon's ant, could this complexity be explained by even simpler models interacting with a complex environment?

Beyond Individual Cognition

Throughout its history, computer science research has emphasized individual and disembodied approaches to problem solving. Indeed, artificial intelligences are the quintessential "brain in a vat." But this is rapidly changing, and computers are beginning to enter the social world and are engaging people in natural ways. Computer programs are increasingly adept at sensing social cues such as speech and gestures. They routinely extract sentiment and opinions from blogs. They engage and assist people in complex social tasks. They even perform important social roles such as brokers or proxies. Nonetheless, as was the case for cognitive science in the 20th century, the theoretical foundations that underlie such systems rest largely on mathematical and logical frameworks developed for individual problem solving, and the growing interest in computational models of emotion has largely retained this intrapsychic focus. Could an information processing perspective on the *social* as well as cognitive functions of emotions transform how we conceive normative social models and social artifacts?

Clearly, emotions profoundly influence human social behavior, and it is increasingly accepted within the social sciences that these influences achieve important social functions that would be required by any entity (biological or artificial) that has to cooperate and compete in a social world. The *social functional view* of emotion emphasizes the utilitarian role of emotions in social cognition and communication (Keltner & Haidt, 1999). From this perspective, humans evolved to survive through social relationships, and emotions are a fundamental building block of effective social interactions. On the one hand, emotions are claimed to inform and direct cognitive processes in ways that help us successfully navigate social interactions. On the other, emotional displays influence the behaviors of others by transmitting coordinating information and eliciting adaptive social responses.

Several findings suggest that emotions help inform and motivate social decision making. It is generally accepted that emotions help inform the individual of personally significant events and recruit the cognitive and physical resources necessary to adaptively respond. Emotions such as love, guilt, shame, or anger inform us about the quality of our social relationships (Keltner & Haidt, 1999). For example, feelings of love signal our level of commitment to another, whereas anger informs us of threats to the righteousness of our own perspective (Clore & Storbeck, 2006). Beyond informing us of the quality of the interaction, social emotions also prepare our minds and bodies to respond to the social environment. For example, anger alters our social perceptions, sensitizing us to the injustices of others (Tiedens, 2001), and triggers physiological changes, moving blood from the internal organs toward the hands and arms in preparation for physical confrontation (Keltner & Haidt, 1999). Finally, emotions serve as rewards or punishments, reinforcing social behavior and promoting the formation of group bonds, loyalty, and identity. Trusting others actually feels good: Studies by Zak (2004) suggest that acts of trust, such as cooperating on simple social games such as the prisoner's dilemma, lead to the release of hormones implicated in the formation of social bonds—whereas harming others feels bad—anticipatory guilt and shame help enforce social norms (Barrett, 1995; Izard, 1977).

Whereas emotion may promote adaptive social decisions, displays of emotion often promote adaptive social responses in others. On the one hand, displays provide important coordinating information to other social partners (Parkinson, 2001; Spoor & Kelly, 2004). Our reactions to events convey important information about our interpretations of events—an undesired stimulus might result in a frown; an unexpected one might result in an expression of surprise—and thus indirectly convey information about how we are evaluating our situation vis-à-vis our current beliefs, desires, and intentions. They communicate our relationship with other social partners (e.g., through dominance or submission displays). On the other hand, displays of emotion seem to reflexively elicit adaptive social responses from others. Emotional behaviors are highly salient and, through affective priming (Klauer & Musch, 2003), automatically alter perceptions and judgments. Emotional displays further trigger behavioral responses. Anger, for example, can elicit fear-related responses even on subliminal presentation (Dimberg & Öhman, 1996) or serve as a demand for someone to change the course of his or interaction (Emde, Gaensbauer, & Harmon, 1976), distress can elicit sympathy (Eisenberg, Fabes, Schaller, & Miller, 1989), and joy seems to invite social interaction (Haviland & Lelwica, 1987). Many of these responses seem almost automatic and visceral and to have similar functions across a wide range of social animals (de Waal, 2006).

Toward an Information Processing Theory of Social Emotions

Computer systems may do well to incorporate the social functions of emotion posited by psychological theory, but computer models may further serve to deepen our understanding of these social functions. Social-functional theories of emotion are very much in line with Simon's design perspective on cognition and lend themselves to an information processing perspective on social emotions. These theories posit that emotions perform social functions and achieve social goals. Starting with such a theory, a computational scientist can consider how to design a serviceable abstraction to achieve such goals. Any discrepancies between this model and human behavior can give insight: it might suggest people are inherently irrational, it might suggest the theorist misrepresented emotion's function, or it might highlight the limits of the computational scientist's current abstract definitions of function. For example, Robert Franks' arguments for the social function of emotion were motivated in part by the observed discrepancy between human behavior on certain social dilemmas and the simulated behavior of "rational" models that, paradoxically, performed less efficiently than their supposedly irrationally emotional human counterparts (Frank, 1988).

But social artifacts can do far more than merely simulate human social behavior. By their nature as social artifacts, they can engage people in meaningful social interactions and thereby provide the means to systematically simulate and control the social landscape. Indeed, extensive research has documented that people exhibit social behavior to computers (Blascovich, 2002; Kraemer, 2008; Meltzoff, 2005; Reeves & Nass, 1996) (Chapter 3). People interacting with computers will try not to hurt the computer's feelings, they will attribute to it common human stereotypes, and most importantly for the perspective of this book, they will be influenced by synthetic displays of emotion. In this sense, computer simulations of human social behavior can serve as important methodological tools for studying human emotions. Just as social scientists use human confederates to test the hypothesized function of emotions in social interactions, computer models can serve as the perfect confederate, faithfully executing the social functions of emotion posited by a specific theory to a level of precision impossible by human laboratory assistants (see Bente, Kraemer, Petersen, & de Ruiter, 2001; Blascovich et al., 2002). Addressing discrepancies between how people treat each other and how they act toward such social artifacts can lead both to improved theories and improved software for a variety of applications.

Finally, by facilitating social interactions within the context of robots or digital media, social artifacts have become an important source of data to inform theories of social emotions. By nature of their operation, social artifacts increasingly are able to recognize and to some extent understand a rage of social-emotional signals including facial expressions, gestures, physiological signals and characteristics of voice quality. Understanding these cues is an important requirement to successfully engage people in social interactions, but as a by-product, such systems create vast quantities of data that can inform theories on the social functions of these cues.

Human social interaction is amazingly complex, but Simon's key insight in advancing information processing theory is that much of this complexity can be illusory. Simon's simple ant had to deal with a complex landscape of pebbles and dunelets, but just consider the landscape of human social relationships. Rather than navigate around inanimate pebbles, we have to navigate around sentient entities that are simultaneously trying to navigate around us. This complexity demands more mental machinery but perhaps not as much as simple observation might suggest. And as in cognitive science, the computational sciences have the potential to allow key advances. With respect to theory development, computational models can help concretize social theories and reasoning through their consequences by simulating the interaction of theoretical assumptions with dynamic multiagent environments. By their nature as social artifacts, these models become powerful tools for simulating and studying dynamic social environments, allowing people to interact with simulated social entities in order to further assess theoretical assumptions. And by systematically collecting and storing social data, they become rich grist for theory development.

Appraisal Theory as a Framework for Social Models

The chapters that follow can be seen advancing an information processing perspective on social emotions, both by adopting a design perspective on emotion's social function and using computer artifacts as methodological tools to inform understanding. And just as early work emphasized appraisal theory as a central theoretical construct for characterizing and modeling the intrapersonal functions of emotion, in this book we turn again to appraisal theory to begin to organize and model its social functions.

Following the metaphor of the ant on the beach, we argue that the complexity of social phenomena largely reflects the complexities of the social environment. Therefore, appraisal theories developed to address the intrapersonal function of emotion might require only modest extension if this additional complexity is properly considered (see also Chapters 1 and 2). Appraisal theory asserts that emotion is a relational construct: appraisal is a moment-to-moment assessment of an organism's goals vis-à-vis the environment that (1) mobilizes cognitive and physiological resources, (2) activates action tendencies, and (3) motivates actions (physical or mental) that maintain an adaptive relationship with the environment. In a social context, this relationship is more complex, but the adaptive needs remain the same. To maintain an adaptive relationship in the social world, an intelligent organism must not only understand how to shape the physical environment, but also learn to recognize, model, and shape the beliefs, desires, and intentions of other social actors (i.e., in needs to understand social causality). Some of this environmental complexity is directly available to the senses: so-called "social signals" (Vinciarelli, Pantic, Bourlard, & Pentland, 2008) such as actions, posture, or facial expressions can reveal fairly direct information about a social actor's dispositions, goals, and emotions. Other complexity is hidden and must be inferred from memory of past interactions and other contextual factors. Thus, a "social appraisal theory" retains the basic structure of appraisal theory illustrated in Figure 1 but includes richer representations and inferential processes to address the complexities of the social environment, as illustrated in Figure 2.

Of course, acknowledging that much of the complexity of social emotions resides in the environment does not mean we can use existing theories and computational models without any modification. Social entities must be sensed, and their beliefs, desires, and intentions must be inferred and, ideally, shaped. The chapters in this book outline how to extend conventional appraisal models with the social perceptions, actions, and inferences required to navigate a complex and dynamic social environment.

Social Perception and Action

Much of this new complexity is directly available to the human senses, and several chapters in this book discuss the partnership between the social and computational sciences around the physical manifestation of emotional signals. People are remarkably skilled at transmitting and decoding subtle cues. We communicate this information nonverbally, through facial expressions, speech prosody, postures, gestures, and physiological cues such as flushing or respiration; verbally through our words; and physically through our actions toward others or the environment. These signals do not simply communicate "emotion" but also reflect aspects of the relationship between the person and his or her environment. For example, facial displays are typically directed at objects or individuals in the environment, and these "contextual factors" (i.e., other environmental features that co-occur with the display) provide important clues to the nature of the social environment.

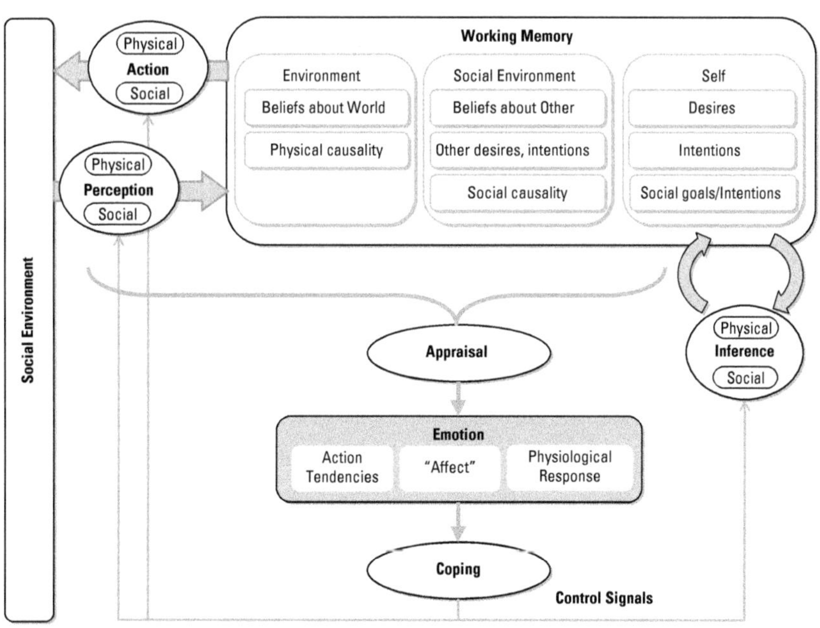

FIGURE 2. A possible computational model of social emotions.

Increasingly, researchers are incorporating these skills into computational artifacts. Computer vision techniques are becoming adept at tracking the location and movements of the body and face. Audio techniques detect subtle features of the voice that might predict emotional state. And while early work focused on recognizing emotional displays in isolation, techniques are beginning to attend to other contextual factors to help infer its meaning (see Chapter 6). Machines can transmit these signals as well. Robots and so-called "virtual humans" (computer-generated anthropomorphic characters) can communicate through synthetic facial expressions, gestures, speech, and speech intonation. This capability is important not only in creating social artifacts, but also in automatically gathering large quantities of human data to inform theory development.

Social Inference and Influence

Once perceived, expressions of emotion influence the nature of interaction in complex ways. They might directly provoke reactions but also inform our inferences about the social world. Several chapters discuss psychological and computational approaches to modeling, inferring, and accounting for these inferences and influences. Again, we argue that appraisal theory provides a framework for organizing how social signals and hidden states may influence emotions and social interaction. From a design perspective, we argue that these effects could occur at several levels of complexity, and it then becomes an empirical question, guided by computational models, as to which (if any) of these levels are required to satisfy social goals (see Figure 3).

Social Reactivity. At the most basic level, emotional signals might directly affect the actions of other social actors. For example, if we are walking down the street and a man comes toward us with an angry expression and raised fists, we may instinctively duck or run away. At this level, emotion expressions and behaviors are simply a feature of the environment that should be appraised and trigger certain action tendencies (e.g., run away). This is consistent with the view of Dimberg and Öhman (1996), who show that subliminal presentation of angry faces can elicit fear-related responses. Whether the are innate or learned from past associations, a design perspective would argue that any emotions signals that predict social actions should be used to inform behavior: in other words, they are salient features of the environment to which our "social ant" should react.

Social Inference. At a more sophistical level of analysis, entities can do more with emotional signals than trigger simple reflexes. According to appraisal theory, emotional signals reflect relational meaning. That

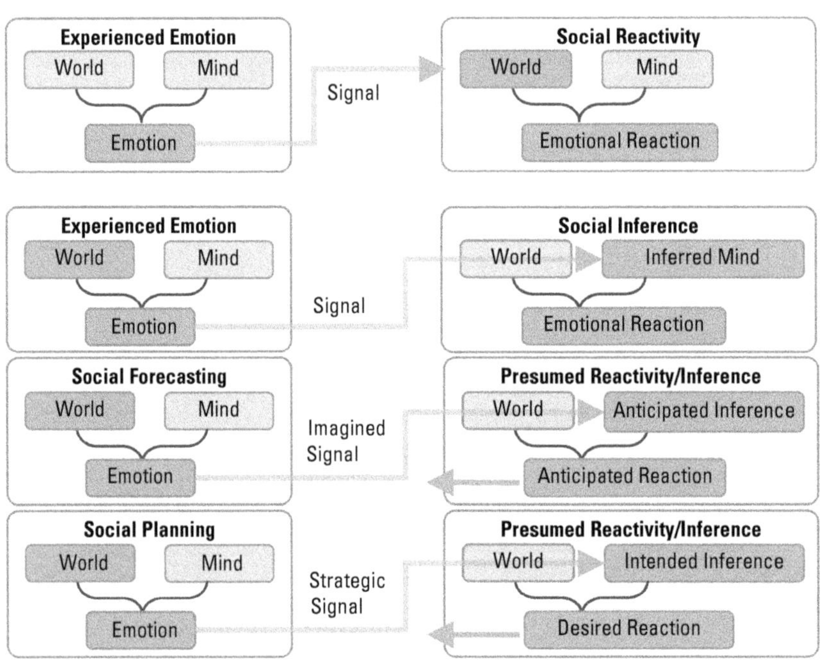

FIGURE 3. A taxonomy of social inference.

is, they communication information about how the organism views environmental events vis-à-vis its goals. Thus, if we see the aforementioned angry man, we might infer information about his goals (he wishes to cause us harm). Rather than simply react to the emotional display, we might instead appraise and react to this inferred mental state. In this way, through simple inferential processes on emotional signals, the mental state of other individuals can, in essence, become part of the social environment.

Hareli and Hess (2009) provide evidence that people can, from expressed emotion, make inferences about the character of the person displaying emotion (e.g., a person who reacted with anger to an accusation was perceived as more self-confident than one that reacted with sadness). We refer to this theory as *reverse appraisal*. Reverse appraisal can be seen as a form of theory of mind reasoning (Whiten, 1991), in that it involves inferring information about another's mental state from his or her appearance or behavior. Specifically, it proposes appraisal theory as a framework for how to infer information about another's mind from observable emotional behavior. As such, we posit it as both a mechanism that people could use to infer the mental state of other entities (including social artifacts that use appraisal theory to guide their actions), and as a framework that can guide a social artifact's understanding of human emotional decisions and behavior (thus, allowing it greater insight into the mind of people it interacts with). For example, imagine a social artifact and a person engaged in laboratory negotiation (e.g., de Melo, Carnevale, & Gratch, 2011). If the person makes an offer that falls well below the artifact's aspirations, it might appraise this negatively and express anger. Following reverse appraisal theory, we posit that the person observes this simulated display of anger and, running a simulation of appraisal in reverse, infers that the artifact has high aspirations. Thus, the artifact's "emotional" display not only enhances the realism of the agent (by displaying sensible behavior) but also further influences the nature of the social interaction by communicating specific information about the its beliefs, desires, and intentions. Similarly, if the human displays anger, the artifact might naturally infer that the human has high aspirations, guiding its own decision-making procedures on how to act next.

Social Forecasting. If we assume that other entities in the environment exploit emotional signals, either by simple reactions or more complex processes like reverse appraisal, then we could begin to anticipate how others might respond to our own emotional reactions. For example, imagine I'm playing a friendly game of poker with my friend and I draw a full house. If I express my joy, I could reasonably conclude he'll guess my good fortune and fold. This is a form of social forecasting—envisioning future responses of other entities to my own emotional displays.

Social forecasting is arguably at the heart of display rules (Ekman, 1972). Display rules are posited to explain why people either mask or accentuate emotional responses in certain social contexts. For example, if our significant other wears a particularly ugly outfit, we might smile politely rather than display our felt disgust to avoid the obvious anticipated emotional consequences. Although these may become cached as learned social conventions, display rules would "fall out" of any model that uses anticipated emotional reactions to modulate its own expressive behavior. In this sense, the anticipated emotional reactions of others can essentially become part of the social environment to which any intelligent entity should react.

Social Goals and Planning. Finally, at the most complex level of analysis (that we will consider here), the existence of social forecasting enables the possibility that entities use emotion to achieve specific social goals. Unlike the traditional instrumental goals studied by artificial intelligence and intrapersonal models of emotion (where the aim is to configure the physical environment in some desired way), social goals are aimed at configuring the beliefs, desires, and intentions of other agents in the environment (of course, this may be an intermediate step in obtaining longer term goals). For example, if I want my friend to fold his cards, because I'd drawn a particularly bad poker hand, I might choose to feign joy to influence belief about the quality of my hand. Social goals can be recursive—I want you to believe that I believe something. This is not to say that social goals are necessarily deceptive. Indeed, successful coordination requires an ability to efficiently understand the beliefs, desires, and intentions of other social entities (Grosz & Kraus, 1996; Levesque, Cohen, & Nunes, 1990; Marsella, Pynadath, & Read, 2004), and emotion signals, the underlying cognitive mechanisms for interpreting them, and the metacognitive mechanisms to attributing these interpretative processes to other entities could play a central role in promoting mutual cooperation and joint gain.

Many of the chapters explore how one or more of these levels of reasoning may explain social emotions and the behaviors that they motivate. From the psychological perspective, for example, Parkinson (Chapter 2, this volume) discusses how emotional displays communicate partial information about appraisals and intentions and that emotional meaning arises from a mutual and moment-to-moment appraisal and adjustment of the social relationship. Smith and Kirby (Chapter 1) discuss how appraisals are associated with expressive behaviors and how these behaviors might help achieve social goals. From a computational perspective, a model of social emotions involves extending the basic appraisal model in Figure 1 with some ability to sense social information, represent social goals, and make inferences about the social state. Such a model looks something like Figure 2. Marsella and Gratch (Chapter 4) discuss how the lack of theory of mind poses strong challenges to modeling social emotions in the EMA computational appraisal model. Finally, Pynadath and colleagues (Chapter 5) show how this form of appraisal and inference can be straightforwardly assimilated into computational models of theory-of-mind reasoning.

Social Artifacts

Given that computational techniques can begin to recognize, model, and transmit social-emotional signals, researchers can combine these pieces into social artifacts that can interact with people in real time. Software artifacts can be endowed with goals (e.g., negotiate a good deal on a new car), sense aspects of the environment, appraise the artifact–environment relationship, and select adaptive behaviors. By recognizing and projecting emotional cues, they can begin to understand and shape the social environment.

Such artifacts have pragmatic uses. They can improve the quality of social interactions with people by attending to and responding to their emotional needs (Wada, Shibata, Saito, & Tanie, 2004). They can also achieve specific social goals, such as managing negative emotions within the context of computer-supported learning (Conati, 2002; Elliott, Rickel, & Lester, 1999; Graesser et al., 2008; Heylen, Nijholt, & op den Aker, 2005; Whitehill, Bartlett, & Movellan, 2008). They can persuade people to improve their health through exercise or by adhering to medical advice (Bickmore, 2007; Bickmore, Gruber, & Picard, 2005; Marsella, Johnson, & LaBore, 2003). They can also have important theoretical uses as a methodological tool for studying human behavior, a theme to which we turn in the last chapters of the book.

Preview of the Book

The book is organized into three parts. Part I describes the theoretical foundations of social emotions. Part II describes computational methods, including methods for modeling social-emotional process as well as techniques for recognizing and synthesizing emotional cues. Finally, Part III closes the loop by showing how social artifacts that recognize, model, and synthesize social emotions can serve as methodological tools to guide theory development.

Theoretical Foundations

In the theoretical section, Smith and Kirby begin with an overview of appraisal theory, emphasizing that while it has largely been seen as an intrapersonal, self-centered process, social emotions are largely compatible with this theory. They begin with the evidence that appraisals are manifest in the environment through facial muscles and thus serve as a social signal. They then offer several suggestions for how appraisal theory should be developed to better account for interpersonal settings.

In the next chapter, Parkinson provides an overview of findings on how people apprehend the relational meaning of social situations and how much of the apparent complexity of social situations evaporates if one considers them as dynamic unfolding interactions with a rich social environment. He contrasts appraisal accounts with other theoretical approaches for explaining the functions. The central question raised here is whether appraisals are the cause of social emotions, as argued in appraisal theory, or whether they are the consequence, as suggested by what he calls *attributional approaches to emotion theorizing*. He aims at a synthesis by emphasizing the dynamic nature of social situations, arguing that appraisals are naturally seen as both the cause and consequence of emotion if one adopts a view of relational meaning arising from a close and unfolding interaction between and individual and other social actors in the environment.

Blascovich aims for a different sort of integration in the final chapter of the theory section. Leading us into the section on computational methods, he reviews research that people respond socially both to and through technology. His work on social motivation and on social influence within immersive virtual environments leads him to the conclusion that the distinction between natural and artificial is blurry at best, and that understanding social interactions within either physical or digital virtual environments demands an understanding of similar mechanisms: namely, how social cognitive processes, motivation, and emotion interact to produce behavior. In this chapter, he integrates insights from his biopsychosocial model of emotion with his findings on social interaction in virtual environments. The unifying perspective is that understanding social influence processes demands an understanding of the social and emotional motives that propel people to act in a social world.

Computational Methods

Part II considers computational techniques to sense, model, and simulate human social processes. The first two chapters in this section start with the mind. First, we describe EMA, a computational model based on appraisal theory. The model uses artificial intelligence techniques to represent and reason about the relationship between the self (i.e., an entity's desires, intentions, and beliefs about the self) and its subjective representation of the world (i.e., beliefs about the world and physical causality). Although broadly consistent with human data in several domains (Gratch & Marsella, 2005; Gratch et al., 2009; Mao & Gratch, 2006; Marsella et al., 2009), EMA has only been rigorously evaluated with respect to the intrapersonal antecedents and consequences of emotion. We argue that to adequately support social goals, forecasting, and planning, models like EMA must include some sort of general theory of mind capability (i.e., the ability to represent and make inferences about the beliefs, desires, and intentions of other social entities).

Pynadath and colleagues take this advice to heart and present an appraisal model built atop PsychSim (Marsella et al., 2004), an architecture for theory-of-mind reasoning. PsychSim is an implemented multiagent-based simulation tool for modeling social interaction and influence. Agents in this framework have their own decision-theoretic models of the physical and social environment, including not only beliefs about the world, but also recursive models of other agents' beliefs, desires, and intentions (recursive models support nested beliefs such as "I believe that you believe that I intend…). Using this framework, Pynadath and colleagues demonstrate the potential of this framework to concretize appraisal theories of emotion with a theory-of-mind context. The model of appraisal within PsychSim demonstrates the key role of a theory-of-mind capacity in appraisal and social emotions, as well as argues for a uniform process for emotion and cognition.

Modern computational techniques have moved well past the Descartian "brain-in-a-vat" criticisms of early artificial intelligence and cognitive science theories, and any viable cognitive model presumes a tight interconnection with techniques for sensing and acting on the environment. The next several chapters in Part II discuss how a social artifact can perceive and produce emotional behaviors from the social environment.

Whitehill, Bartlett, and Movellan (Chapter 6) review current computational approaches for automatic facial expression recognition, one of the most powerful ways humans communicate their mental states. They describe the basic challenges of characterizing facial movements—they adopt Ekman and Friesen's (1978) well-known Facial Action Coding System in their own work—and sketch the basic challenges and techniques for learning how to recognize these movements from data. Such a system has obvious scientific and practical applications and these are discussed as well. Emotions are also conveyed through the voice. Emotions are certainly communicated through words—a topic that we will not discuss here (Wilson, Wiebe, & Hwa, 2004)—but arguably they are more reliably conveyed through the manner in which these words are delivered (e.g., the intensity, tone, or prosody of the speech). In Chapter 7, Busson, Bulut, and Narayanan discuss some of the challenges and advances in automatically recognizing and synthesizing emotional speech.

As we argued above, emotional cues do not have intrinsic social meaning but, rather, reveal something about the relationship of the organism and its environment: a smile in response to a smile communicates something very different than a smile in response to a frown (see also Chapter 2). Ultimately, inferential processes such as reverse appraisal may be required to infer this meaning (e.g., he smiled after drawing his next poker card, so the card is probably good for him); however, some of this relational meaning is apparently directly from perception, or at least this is the argument made by Morency in Chapter 8. He argues that it is possible to significantly improve state-of-the-art recognition techniques by exploiting regularities in how people communicate that might reflect the underlying unobservable features of the social relationship. People do not provide affective feedback at random. Rather, they react to the current topic, previous utterances, and the speaker's current verbal and nonverbal behavior, and incorporating such dialogue context can improve recognition performance during human–robot interaction. His goal is to automatically discover these patterns using only easily observable features of human face-to-face interaction (e.g., prosodic features and eye gaze) and exploit them to improve recognition accuracy.

Besides sensing and modeling social-emotional processes, a social artifact should be able to project emotional signals into the social environment. Niewadomski and colleagues review techniques for conveying emotion through synthetic facial expressions and gestures. They discuss the impact of different theoretical perspectives of emotion on this generation process (e.g., dimensional theories of emotion suggest different generation schemes than appraisal theories) and emphasize the importance of expression dynamics in conveying meaning—something often overlooked in psychological studies that emphasize static pictures as experimental stimuli.

Closing the Loop

Finally, we conclude the book with two chapters that use computational methods to inform theory development. In his chapter on the development of social competency in infants, Messinger and colleagues draw on computer vision techniques to study early emotional communication. Chapter 10 reports on two studies. The first examines microinteractions between mother and infant and provides evidence of changing emotional dynamics during the course of the interaction. The second study describes methods for formally modeling these dynamic processes. The chapter illustrates how computational methods can give novel and fundamental insights into human social processes.

In the final chapter, Wang and colleagues illustrate the potential of social artifacts as methodological tools for studying human social-emotional processes. They describe a series of studies using the "rapport agent." This is an interactive computational system that recognizes human nonverbal cues and, in a sense, reflects them back to establish a nonverbal sense of rapport or synchrony. The system is able to provide subtle nonverbal feedback (e.g., head nods and postural mimicry) in a fashion consistent with psychological theories of rapport (Tickle-Degnen & Rosenthal, 1990). They are then able to show that, by systematically manipulating components of this theory, the nature of the social interaction changes in fundamental ways. The results lend insights into the role of emotional behaviors in interpersonal communication and have important practical application to domains such as negotiation or health care.

Concluding Thoughts

The cognitive science revolution transformed the science of the human mind but left emotions as a footnote. Decades later, the tide has begun to shift. An information processing revolution is afoot in emotion research. Researchers have carefully documented the important influences, functions, and cognitive mechanisms of emotion processes, and computational models are increasingly used to inform theory and experimental design. At present, social emotions remain something of a footnote but this is rapidly changing.

This book argues for an information processing revolution in social emotions. By revisiting the original inspiration behind information processing theory, we have tried to highlight the benefits of a partnership between the social and computational sciences. On the one hand, emotions serve important functions that would be needed by any intelligent social entity and can expand the narrow rational basis for current intelligent system design. On the other hand, computational models can play an essential role in guiding theory development, in teasing apart complexity in the world versus complexity in cognition. They serve as "empirical objects" that, via simulation, can reveal unanticipated consequences of theoretical assumptions. They serve as "social artifacts" that can instantiate social theories as virtual confederates, allowing unprecedented tools for experimentation. They serve as patient observers that can vacuum up and label vast quantities of social information. Finally, they serve as ends in themselves—artificial tools that can more intelligently navigate and hopefully benefit the human social world.

Notes

1. Our criticism of rational models touches on controversies over dual-process theories of cognition popular in cognitive science (Evans, 2008; Kahneman

& Frederick, 2002), but we are emphasizing a different distinction. In dual-process theories, the mind is "implemented" as two systems: one fast, automatic, and biased (if not irrational), the other slow, deliberate and (approximately) rational, with emotion invariably placed in the former category. Instead, we are arguing that the conception of what constitutes rational behavior (as formalized from the information processing perspective) is impoverished and can be enriched by a functional analysis of emotion processes. Whether emotions are "implemented" as fast or slow systems is an important but separate distinction.

2. Here we adopt the perspective and terminology common in artificial intelligence wherein an entity's mental state can be profitably characterized in terms of beliefs, desires, and intentions (BDI for short), representing, respectively, its informational, motivational, and deliberative states (Rao & Georgeff, 1995).

References

Arnold, M. (1960). *Emotion and personality*. New York: Columbia University Press.

Barrett, K. C. (1995). A functionalist approach to shame and guilt. In J. P. Tangney & K. W. Fischer (Eds.), *Self-conscious emotions: The psychology of shame, guilt, embarrassment, and pride* (pp. 25–63). New York: Guilford Publications.

Bente, G., Kraemer, N. C., Petersen, A., & de Ruiter, J. P. (2001). Computer animated movement and person perception: Methodological advances in nonverbal behavior research. *Journal of Nonverbal Behavior, 25*(3), 151–166.

Bickmore, T. (2007). Long-term interactions with pedagogical agents. *Educational Technology, 47*(1), 47–50.

Bickmore, T., Gruber, A., & Picard, R. W. (2005). Establishing the computer-patient working alliance in automated health behavior change interventions. *Patient Education and Counseling, 59*(1), 21–30.

Blascovich, J. (2002). Social influence within immersive virtual environments. In R. Schroeder (Ed.), *The social life of avatars* (pp. 127–145). Springer-Verlag, London.

Blascovich, J., Loomis, J., Beall, A., Swinth, K., Hoyt, C., & Bailenson, J. N. (2002). Immersive virtual environment technology as a methodological tool for social psychology. *Psychological Inquiry, 13*, 103–124.

Clore, G., & Storbeck, J. (2006). Affect as information about liking, efficacy, and importance. In J. Forgas (Ed.), *Affective influences on social behavior*. New York: Psychology Press.

Conati, C. (2002). Probabilistic assessment of user's emotions in educational games. *Journal of Applied Artificial Intelligence, special issue on "Merging Cognition and Affect in HCI," 16*(7–8), 555–575.

de Melo, C., Carnevale, P. J., & Gratch, J. (2011, May). *The effect of expression of anger and happiness in computer agents on negotiations with humans*. Paper presented at the the Tenth International Conference on Autonomous Agents and Multiagent Systems, Taipei, Taiwan.

de Waal, F. (2006). *Primates and philosophers: How morality evolved*. Princeton, NJ: Princeton University Press.

Dimberg, U., & Öhman, A. (1996). Beyond the wrath: Psychophysiological responses to facial stimuli. *Motivation and Emotion, 20*, 149–182.

Eisenberg, N., Fabes, R. A., Schaller, M., & Miller, P. A. (1989). Sympathy and personal distress: Development, gender differences, and interrelations of indexes. In N. Eisenberg (Ed.), *Empathy and related emotional responses* (Vol. 44, pp. 107–126). San Francisco: Jossey-Bass.

Ekman, P. (1972). Universals and cultural differences in facial expressions of emotions. In J. Cole (Ed.), *Nebraska symposium on motivation* (pp. 207–283). Lincoln: University of Nebraska Press.

Ekman, P., & Friesen, W. (1978). *Facial Action Coding System: A technique for the measurement of facial movement*. Palo Alto, CA: Consulting Psychologists Press.

Elliott, C., Rickel, J., & Lester, J. (1999). Lifelike pedagogical agents and affective computing: An exploratory synthesis. In M. Wooldridge & M. Veloso (Eds.), *Artificial intelligence today: Recent trends and developments* (pp. 195–212). Berlin/Heidelberg: Springer.

Emde, R. N., Gaensbauer, T. J., & Harmon, R. J. (1976). Emotional expression in infancy: A behavioral study. , *Psychological Issues, 10*(1, Monograph No. 37), New York: International Universities Press.

Evans, J. (2008). Dual-processing accounts of reasoning, judgment, and social cognition. *Annual Review of Psychology, 59*, 255–278.

Frank, R. (1988). *Passions with reason: The strategic role of the emotions*. New York: W. W. Norton.

Frijda, N. (1987). Emotion, cognitive structure, and action tendency. *Cognition and Emotion, 1*, 115–143.

Graesser, A. C., D'Mello, S. K., Craig, S. D., Witherspoon, A., Sullins, J., McDaniel, B., et al. (2008). The relationship between affect states and dialogue patterns during interactions with AutoTutor. *Journal of Interactive Learning Research, 19*, 293–312.

Gratch, J., & Marsella, S. (2005). Evaluating a computational model of emotion. *Journal of Autonomous Agents and Multiagent Systems, 11*(1), 23–43.

Gratch, J., Marsella, S., Wang, N., & Stankovic, B. (2009, September). *Assessing the validity of appraisal-based models of emotion*. Paper presented at the International Conference on Affective Computing and Intelligent Interaction, Amsterdam.

Grosz, B., & Kraus, S. (1996). Collaborative plans for complex group action. *Artificial Intelligence, 86*(2), 269–357.

Hareli, S., & Hess, U. (2009). What emotional reactions can tell us about the nature of others: An appraisal perspective on person perception. *Cognition and Emotion, 24*(1), 128–140.

Haviland, J. M., & Lelwica, M. (1987). The induced affect response: 10-week-old infants' responses to three emotion expressions. *Developmental Psychology, 23*, 97–104.

Heylen, D., Nijholt, A., & op den Aker, R. (2005). Affect in tutoring dialogues. *Applied Artificial Intelligence, special issue on "Educational Agents – Beyond Virtual Tutors."*

Izard, C. (1977). *Human emotion*. New York: Plenum.

Kahneman, D., & Frederick, S. (2002). Representativeness revisited: Attribute substitution in intuitive judgment. In T. Gilovich, D. Griffin, & D. Kahneman (Eds.), *Heuristics of intuitive judgment: Extensions and applications*. New York: Cambridge University Press.

Keltner, D., & Haidt, J. (1999). Social functions of emotions at four levels of anysis. *Cognition and Emotion, 13*(5), 505–521.

Klauer, K. C., & Musch, J. (2003). Affective priming: Findings and theories. In K. C. Klauer, J. Musch, & N. J. Mahwah (Eds.), *The psychology of evaluation: Affective processes in cognition and emotion* (pp. 7–49). Mahwah, NJ: Lawrence Erlbaum.

Kraemer, N. (2008, September). *Social effects of virtual assistants. A review of empirical results with regard to communication*. Paper presented at the Proceedings of the 8th International Conference on Intelligent Virtual Agents, Tokyo.

Lazarus, R. (1991). *Emotion and adaptation*. New York: Oxford University Press.

Levesque, H. J., Cohen, P. R., & Nunes, J. H. T. (1990). *On acting together*. Menlo Park, CA: AI Center, SRI International.

Loomis, J., & Knapp, J. (2003). Visual perception of egocentric distance in real and virtual environments. In L. J. Hettinger & M. W. Haas (Eds.), *Virtual and adaptive environments: Applications, implications, and human performance issues*. (pp. 21–46). Mahwah, NJ: Lawrence Erlbaum Associates Publishers.

MacLeod, C. M. (1991). Half a century of research on the Stroop effect: An integrative review. *Psychological Bulletin, 109*, 163–203.

Mao, W., & Gratch, J. (2006, May). *Evaluating a computational model of social causality and responsibility*. Paper presented at the 5th International Joint Conference on Autonomous Agents and Multiagent Systems, Hakodate, Japan.

Marsella, S., Gratch, J., & Petta, P. (2010). Computational models of emotion. In K. R. Scherer, T. Bänziger, & E. Roesch (Eds.), *A blueprint for affective computing: A sourcebook and manual*. New York: Oxford University Press.

Marsella, S., Gratch, J., Wang, N., & Stankovic, B. (2009, September). *Assessing the validity of a computational model of emotional coping*. Paper presented at the International Conference on Affective Computing and Intelligent Interaction, Amsterdam.

Marsella, S., Johnson, W. L., & LaBore, C. (2003, July). *Interactive pedagogical drama for health interventions*. Paper presented at the Conference on Artificial Intelligence in Education, Sydney, Australia.

Marsella, S., Pynadath, D., & Read, S. (2004, August). *PsychSim: Agent-based modeling of social interactions and influence*. Paper presented at the International Conference on Cognitive Modeling Pittsburg, PA.

Meltzoff, A. N. (2005). Imitation and other minds: the "like me" hypothesis. In S. Hurley & N. Chater (Eds.), *Perspectives on imitation: From neuroscience to social science*. Cambridge, MA: MIT Press.

Oatley, K., & Johnson-Laird, P. N. (1987). Towards a cognitive theory of emotions. *Cognition and Emotion, 1*(1), 29–50.

Ortony, A., Clore, G., & Collins, A. (1988). *The cognitive structure of emotions*. Melbourne, Australia: Cambridge University Press.

Parkinson, B. (2001). Putting appraisal in context. In K. Scherer, A. Schorr. & T. Johnstone (Eds.), *Appraisal processes in emotion: Theory, methods, research* (pp. 173–186). London: Oxford University Press.

Rao, A. S., & Georgeff, M. P. (1995, June). *BDI agents: From theory to practice*. Paper presented at the 1st International Conference on Multiagent Systems, San Francisco.

Reeves, B., & Nass, C. (1996). *The media equation: How people treat computers, television, and new media like real people and places*. Cambridge University Press, New York.

Scherer, K. (1984). On the nature and function of emotion: A component process approach. In K. R. Scherer & P. Ekman (Eds.), *Approaches to emotion* (pp. 293–317). Hillsdale, NJ: Lawrence Erlbaum.

Simon, H. (1969). *The sciences of the artificial*. Cambridge, MA: MIT Press.

Simon, H. A. (1967). Motivational and emotional controls of cognition. *Psychological Review, 74*, 29–39.

Sloman, A. (1987). Motives, mechanisms and emotions. *Cognition and Emotion, 1*, 217–234.

Spoor, J. R., & Kelly, J. R. (2004). The evolutionary significance of affect in groups: Communication and group bonding. *Group Processes and Intergroup Prelations*, 7(4), 398–412.

Tickle-Degnen, L., & Rosenthal, R. (1990). The nature of rapport and its nonverbal correlates. *Psychological Inquiry, 1*(4), 285–293.

Tiedens, L. Z. (2001). The effect of anger on the hostile inferences of aggressive and nonaggressive people: Specific emotions, cognitive processing, and chronic accessibility. *Motivation and Emotion, 25*(3), 233–251.

Tversky, A., & Kahneman, D. (1974). Judgment under uncertainty: Heuristics and biases. *Science, 185*, 1124–1131.

Vinciarelli, A., Pantic, M., Bourlard, H., & Pentland, A. (2008, October). *Social signals, their function, and automatic analysis: A survey*. Paper presented at the Proceedings of the 10th International Conference on Multimodal Interfaces, Chania, Crete, Greece.

Wada, K., Shibata, T., Saito, T., & Tanie, K. (2004). Effects of robot-assisted activity for elderly people and nurses at a day service center. *IEEE*, 92(11), 1780–1788.

Whitehill, J., Bartlett, M. S., & Movellan, J. R. (2008, June). *Automatic facial expression recognition for intelligent tutoring systems*. Paper presented at the CVPR 2008 Workshop on Human Communicative Behavior Analysis, Anchorage, Alaska.

Whiten, A. (Ed.). (1991). *Natural theories of mind*. Oxford, UK: Basil Blackwell.

Wilson, T., Wiebe, J., & Hwa, R. (2004, July). *Just how mad are you? Finding strong and weak opinion clauses*. Paper presented at the Proceedings of the 19th National Conference on Artifical Intelligence, San Jose, CA.

Zak, P. J. (2004). Neuroeconomics. *Philosophical Transactions of the Royal Society Biology, 359*, 1737–1748.

1

On the Sociality of Emotion-Eliciting Appraisals: Two Aspects

Craig A. Smith & Leslie D. Kirby

On the Sociality of Emotion-Eliciting Appraisals: Two Aspects.

There is considerable tension within current emotion theory concerning the sociality of human emotions. As the contributions to this volume clearly indicate, emotions are highly social. One of the basic functions long ascribed to emotion (e.g., Buck, Savin, Miller, & Caul, 1972; Scherer, 1984) is that of *social communication*. Through their observable, expressive manifestations (postural, facial, vocal, etc.), emotions are thought to communicate much to others in the social environment about the emotional person's thoughts, feelings, and likely behaviors—for instance, whether the person is likely to strike out in anger, or to give up and withdraw in sadness, or is perceiving a serious danger in fear, and so on. This information can then be used by the perceiver to regulate his or her actions to both the expressive individual and the affect-eliciting circumstances—to apologize to the angry person, to offer support and comfort to the sad one, to become more vigilant to potential danger in the fear-inducing circumstances, and so forth. However, within *appraisal theory*—currently the dominant theoretical perspective concerned with the antecedents of emotion—the elicitation of emotions is viewed as a largely *intrapersonal, self-centered* process. On this view, emotions are elicited by appraisals, or evaluations of what one's circumstances imply for *personal* well-being (see Smith & Lazarus, 1990). How one's circumstances are appraised is hypothesized to determine one's emotional state, with different appraisals leading to the experience of different emotions. Thus, emotions are elicited on the basis of an evaluation that is conducted within a person's own head, and that is concerned with the person's own well-being. The self-centered, seemingly nonsocial nature of appraisal as an emotion elicitor, as depicted in appraisal theory, has been roundly criticized (e.g., Manstead & Tetlock, 1989; Parkinson, 1997; Parkinson & Manstead, 1992).

Much of the research conducted to date on appraisal theory has maintained the seemingly self-centered focus described above. This is because the bulk of this research has been focused on developing and testing what we have referred to as *structural models* of appraisal (e.g., Frijda, Kuipers, & ter Schure, 1989; Kuppens, Van Mechelen, Smits, & De Boek, 2003; Lazarus, 1991; Roseman, 1991, 2001; Roseman, Spindel, & Jose, 1990; Scherer, 1984, 1997, 2001; Smith & Ellsworth, 1985; Smith & Lazarus, 1990, 1993; Tong et al., 2007). These models attempt to describe the specific evaluations that are made in appraisal as well as how these evaluations differentiate emotional experience (that is, to describe the appraisals that elicit anger vs. sadness vs. fear, etc.). These structural models and the research examining them have maintained a rather tight focus on how appraisals, once elicited, relate to the experience of particular emotions. This work has not been terribly concerned with how the emotion-eliciting appraisals themselves are generated. With this focus, this work, indeed, has had a strongly intraindividual flavor, perhaps at the expense of considering social factors that might be important in the generation of appraisal (e.g., Manstead & Fischer, 2001; Manstead & Tetlock, 1989; Parkinson & Manstead, 1992).

However, the scope of appraisal theory extends far beyond a focus on the relations between appraisal and emotional experience. To the contrary, from early on appraisal theory has attempted to provide a fairly comprehensive account of human emotion (Frijda, 1986; Lazarus, 1968, 1991; Scherer, 1984; Smith & Lazarus, 1990) and both theoretically and empirically has broached such topics as: the patterning of physiological activity, both autonomic and facial, in emotion (Lazarus, 1968; Smith, 1989); the role of emotion in motivating coping behavior and adjustment (Lazarus, 1991; Smith & Kirby, 2011); and the situational and dispositional antecedents of appraisal (Smith & Kirby, 2009). As these additional aspects of appraisal theory are considered, the potential for appraisal theory to capture a number of the interpersonal aspects of emotion becomes evident. For instance, as will be detailed below, appraisal theorists (e.g., Scherer, 1984, 1992; Smith, 1989; Smith & Scott, 1997) have already made headway in changing and enriching our understanding of the information encoded in emotional facial expressions, which is thus likely to be communicated to others. Moreover, as research on appraisal theory expands beyond a consideration of the specific linkages between appraisal and emotion to considerations of both the antecedent processes that give rise to the appraisals (e.g., Smith & Kirby, 2009) and the roles that emotions serve in coping and adaptation (e.g. Lazarus, 1991; Smith & Kirby, 2011), there is considerable potential, and, in fact, need, to explicitly incorporate social factors into appraisal theory (see, e.g., Manstead & Fischer, 2001).

In the present chapter, we will examine both of these potential aspects of sociality in appraisal theory. First, we will examine what appraisal theory has to say about the informational structure of emotional facial expression. We will review the theoretical claims that appraisal theory makes about this structure and briefly review the existing evidence in support of these claims. Second, in a more agenda-setting fashion, we will consider several ways in which appraisal might be further developed to better capture the interpersonal nature of appraisal and emotion.

The Informational Structure of the Facial Expression of Emotion

The face, through emotional facial expression, is widely recognized as an important channel of social communication. However, what are the major messages communicated through this channel, and how are they encoded? As a starting point, there is considerable evidence (reviewed in Ekman, Friesen, & Ellsworth, 1982) indicating distinct, prototypical facial signals that across a variety of cultures can be reliably recognized as corresponding to at least six different emotions (happiness, sadness, surprise, disgust, anger, and fear), and possibly others, including interest, shame (Izard, 1971), and contempt (Ekman & Friesen, 1986; Izard, 1971; Izard & Haynes, 1988). However, what is the information conveyed through these facial expressions, and how is this information organized? More specifically, do the facial expressions for various emotions systematically encode information about the person's emotional state beyond the emotion's categorical identity, and if so, how is this information encoded?

In pursuing this issue, it is helpful to contrast two distinct models. First, although it may be something of a straw person that few have explicitly embraced, much of the existing literature appears to be consistent with a model that might be termed the *purely categorical model*. Within this model, emotional facial expressions are conceptualized as comprising a primitive, nonverbal "language" (e.g., Fridlund, 1994; Mandler, 1980, 1984) in which individual expressions are the basic units of meaning, analogous to words in spoken language. In this language, the meanings conveyed by facial expressions consist of the categorical identities of the various emotions. Just as most words are arbitrary symbols whose meanings are determined by convention or historical accident, facial expressions are arbitrarily structured symbols that are imbued with meaning through learned cultural conventions governing relationships between specific expressions and the emotions they represent. The fact that expressions for some emotions (e.g., fear and surprise) appear more similar to one another than others (e.g., fear and happiness), and that this similarity is due to shared facial actions (here, raised eyebrows and widely opened eyes), is coincidental and noninformative. Taken by themselves, the individual facial actions (or components) that contribute to the expressions are essentially meaningless. This is the same as the case with the fact that the English words *dog* and *door* both start with the letters *d* and *o*. The fact that those particular letters contribute to the spelling of those particular words tells us nothing about what the words mean.

Starting in part with observations made by Darwin (1872/1965), appraisal theorists have tended to reject the idea that the muscle patterning associated with various facial expressions is arbitrary or meaningless. Instead they have tended to believe that the physiological changes associated with various emotions are systematically organized, and that, as Lazarus (1968, p. 206) argued early on, "The physiological patterns should be associated with the different adaptive tasks which the appraisals leading to the different emotions seem to require." In other words, many appraisal theorists have shared the expectation that physiological activities in emotion, including facial activities, are in some way organized around the appraisal meanings giving rise to those emotions. Building upon this general idea, both Scherer (1984, 1992) and Smith (1989; Smith & Scott, 1997) have proposed *componential models* that go beyond the purely categorical model, and hypothesize that, rather than being arbitrary and meaningless, at least some of the individual components contributing to a given facial expression are inherently meaningful. That is, emotional expressions have a systematic, coherent, and meaningful structure, and consideration of the individual components that contribute to that structure can directly reveal much about the underlying properties of the emotion being expressed. For example, the fact that the prototypical expressions of fear and surprise share raised eyebrows and widely opened eyes indicates something about the properties that these states share—possibly that the person experiencing either emotion is uncertain about some aspect of his or her circumstances and is actively attending to the environment in an attempt to reduce that uncertainty (see the following paragraphs).

It should be noted that componential models are not inherently incompatible with the chief claim of the categorical model that the overall pattern of facial activity in an expression captures the emotion's categorical identity (but see Ortony & Turner, 1990, for a componential model that is incompatible with this claim). Instead, the chief point of conflict between the two models concerns whether the individual muscle actions (facial components) contributing to the overall pattern are themselves meaningful or arbitrary, with the componential models asserting that individual components carry meaning that goes beyond categorical identity.

In fact, appraisal-based componential models make some fairly strong assumptions regarding the directness and strength of the relations between particular appraisals and the individual components of facial activity that are associated with them. Specifically, at least some facial components contributing to emotional facial expressions are assumed to directly reflect the appraisals an individual is making at any given moment. For instance, Scherer (2009) has hypothesized that a careful analysis of the timing and patterning of a sequence of facial actions contributing to an emotional expression can be used to make inferences regarding sequencing of the appraisals giving rise to that emotion (e.g., Delplanque et al., 2009).

The prototypical expressions corresponding to a range of emotions have been well described in the literature (Darwin, 1872/1965; Ekman & Friesen, 1978; Frois-Wittmann, 1930; Izard, 1971; reviewed in Smith & Scott, 1997), and from these descriptions several things are evident that make the central distinction between these two models potentially quite important. First, emotions are not signaled through single muscle movements, but rather, through coordinated patterns of muscle activity, involving multiple facial muscles (Ekman et al., 1982; Frois-Wittmann, 1930). Thus, for instance, there is no single "anger muscle" to unambiguously signal anger; the anger expression is a coordinated pattern of muscle activity, which typically includes: drawing the eyebrows together and down into a frown through the contraction of the *corrugator supercilii*, a raised upper eyelid through the contraction of the *levator palpebrae superioris*, a raised or tightened lower eyelid through the contraction of the *orbicularis occuli*, and often a tightened mouth through the contraction of the *orbicularis oris* (see Smith & Scott, 1997).

Second, individual facial actions often contribute to multiple facial expressions. For example, as noted previously, expressions of surprise and fear both share raised eyebrows (due to contraction of the *frontalis*) and widened eyes (due to raised upper eyelids). The raised eyebrows, at least in the central part of the forehead (due to the contraction of the *medial frontalis*), are also shared by expressions of sadness, and as just noted, the raised upper eyelids are also evident in expressions of anger. Similarly, in addition to both being evident in anger, the eyebrow frown is also shared by expressions of sadness, fear, and disgust, whereas a raised/tightened lower eyelid is also shared by expressions of happiness (the "Duchenne smile," Ekman, Davidson, & Friesen, 1990) and disgust (see Smith & Scott, 1997). The key question asked by componential models of facial expression, which is not addressed by the purely categorical model, is whether these shared expressive components reveal anything about the underlying properties of the emotions being expressed.

Answering this question is important, in part, because if the individual components of facial expression carry meaning, then the face could serve as an effective channel of social communication, via the activity of individual facial components, even under conditions in which the categorical expression of an emotion breaks down. Notably, although there is currently very little data concerning the frequency with which the prototypical patterns carrying the emotions' categorical identities are displayed (Fernandez-Dols & Ruiz-Beldo, 1997; Russell, 1994), the data that do exist suggest that there might be a broad array of conditions under which the categorical facial expression of emotion is quite rare. For instance, as often noted (e.g., Ekman & Friesen, 1969), spontaneous expressions of emotion may be constrained by cultural or personal display rules that prescribe whether and under what conditions certain emotions may be freely expressed. For example, it appears that individuals are generally less expressive in the presence of strangers than when among friends (e.g., Buck, Losow, Murphy, & Costanzo, 1992; Wagner & Smith, 1991), and there appears to be a pervasive norm, practiced to the extreme by some individuals, to minimize the expression of negative emotion in the presence of others (e.g., Buck et al., 1992; Smith, McHugo, & Lanzetta, 1986). Although the operation of such display rules may often prevent the full, categorical expression of one's emotional state, to the extent to which individual facial actions associated with that emotion are still activated, at least some information about that emotional state can still be communicated to the point at which those facial actions, themselves, carry meaning.

There is also considerable evidence suggesting that it is rare for most individuals to experience strong feelings of a single, isolated emotion. Instead, across a variety of emotionally evocative contexts, it is common for individuals to report the subjective experience of complex blends of multiple emotions (e.g., Ellsworth & Smith, 1988; Folkman & Lazarus, 1985; Schwartz & Weinberger, 1980; Smith & Ellsworth, 1987). Although there have been attempts to describe the facial expressions characteristic of a limited number of emotional blends (Ekman & Friesen, 1975), the principles by which such blended expressions are produced have not yet been articulated. In any event, it is likely that the resulting composite patterns of facial activity would obscure the identities of the individual emotions contributing to the blends. A categorical system could handle some degree of blending if it treated the expressions characteristic of specific blends as distinct expressive categories. However, such a system would quickly become unwieldy because the number of distinct blends that can be produced by combinations of several emotions, each at varying levels of intensity, is dauntingly large. On the other hand, if the individual expressive components carried meaning, even in very complicated displays, those meanings would still be readily available.

Based on their review of a number of sources, including Andrew (1965), Darwin (1872/1965), Duchenne (1862/1990), Frijda (1969), Scherer (1984, 1992), and Smith (1989), Smith & Scott, 1997) have articulated a number of hypotheses regarding the meanings potentially carried by individual facial-expressive components, while noting that these hypotheses are very unlikely to represent an exhaustive listing of the meanings potentially encoded in various facial actions. Among their hypotheses, Smith & Scott (1997) have argued that there may be two distinct clusters of facial actions, each of which provides information along a broad dimension of meaning. One cluster, which includes the eyebrow frown and a variety of activities involving the mouth, is proposed to encode information about the subjective pleasantness of the emotional state. Thus, raising the lip corners into a smile has been hypothesized to represented subjective pleasantness, as has the presence of an open mouth; conversely, the eyebrow frown has been widely hypothesized to signal subjective unpleasantness, as have lowered lip corners (due to contraction of the *depressor anguli oris*), a tightened mouth, and a raised chin (due to contraction of the *mentalis*).

A second cluster of facial activities appears to encode information related to the type of attentional activity associated with the emotional state (Smith & Scott, 1997). Both an open mouth and a raised upper eyelid are proposed to reflect efforts to increase one's attention to the environment. Raised eyebrows are also placed in this cluster, although there have been some different proposals regarding its exact significance. Whereas Darwin (1972/1965) viewed raised eyebrows, like a raised upper eyelid, as reflecting an increase of attentional activity, Smith (1989) has proposed that the raised eyebrows reflect uncertainty about one's circumstances, and Scherer (1984) has proposed that both raised eyebrows and raised upper eyelids reflect the detection of novelty in the environment. Also included in this cluster is a tightened lower eyelid, which Smith (1989) has hypothesized reflects a sense of certainty about one's circumstances.

Additional meanings have been proposed for a number of the above facial actions. First, those facial actions proposed to be associated with increased attentional activity (i.e., raised eyebrows, raised upper eyelids, and an open mouth), have also been proposed to be associated with low levels of personal agency or control. In addition, a meaning beyond subjective unpleasantness has been proposed for the eyebrow frown, but there has been disagreement about what this meaning is. Specifically, Darwin (1872/1965, p. 220) associated the eyebrow frown with "reflection with an effort, or with the perception of something difficult or disagreeable," and he noted (p. 221) that "a man may be absorbed in the deepest thought, and his brow will remain smooth until he encounters some obstacle in his train of reasoning, or is interrupted by some disturbance, and then a frown passes like a shadow over his brow." Scherer (1984) translated Darwin's observations into a proposal that the eyebrow frown is associated with the perception of some type of discrepancy between one's needs or goals and one's actual circumstances. In contrast, Smith (1989) interpreted Darwin's statements as implying that the frown was associated with anticipating the need to expend effort to cope with one's situation.

One important thing to note about these hypotheses is that in a number of cases there is unlikely to be a simple one-to-one mapping between single components of facial activity and specific meanings. Rather, certain types of information may be encoded by multiple facial actions, and a single facial action may encode several distinct types of information. That multiple components may encode similar meanings simply implies that there is some redundancy in the communication system. In general, such redundancy increases the system's resiliency because it provides multiple ways for a given piece of information to be communicated. The possibility that a single component may carry multiple meanings is potentially problematic, though, because it creates ambiguity as to the meaning of particular facial components when they are viewed in isolation. However, the degree of ambiguity involved is not great because in virtually every instance, the multiple meanings hypothesized to be encoded by a single component are related. Thus, unpleasant experiences often involve goal discrepancies and expenditure of effort. Similarly, uncertainty about one's circumstances, perceptions of novelty, and/or feelings of not being in control are often associated with attempts to attend closely to one's environment. Nonetheless, given that these related constructs are not identical, to the extent that individual components are found to encode multiple constructs, it is important to investigate the degree to which the specific meaning encoded by a particular component can be disambiguated contextually.

To date, only a couple of the hypotheses noted above have been evaluated empirically. First, a large body of data demonstrates that the eyebrow frown is associated with subjective unpleasantness (e.g., Cacioppo, Martzke, Petty, & Tassinary, 1988; Cacioppo, Petty, Losch, & Kim, 1986) and that raising one's lip corners into a smile is associated with subjective pleasantness (e.g., Cacioppo et al., 1986; Ekman, Friesen, & Ancoli, 1980). In addition, in accord with Darwin's observations, there have been suggestions that something distinct from unpleasantness, often interpreted as "concentration," is associated with the eyebrow frown (Cacioppo, Petty, & Morris, 1985).

Smith (1989) and Pope and Smith (1994) have built upon this latter evidence and have conducted two studies designed to examine the significance of the eyebrow frown and to differentiate among the various hypotheses that have been advanced for this muscle action. Both studies involved monitoring muscle activity in the eyebrow and cheek regions (corresponding to activity of the *corrugator* and *zygomatic* muscles, respectively) using surface electromyography (EMG) while subjects engaged in directed imagery.

The first study (Smith, 1989) controlled for the eyebrow frown's documented relation to unpleasantness by focusing exclusively on pleasant situations. Participants imagined themselves in hypothetical situations in which the combined appraisals of anticipated effort and perceived goal obstacles (i.e., specific goal discrepancies) were manipulated. In a between-subjects design, subjects imagined themselves in situations that either did or did not involve the presence of a goal obstacle and the expenditure of effort (e.g., trying to beat a friend in a foot race versus having a relaxing picnic lunch with friends in a meadow). In addition, in a within-subject manipulation, participants first imagined their reactions to the global situation, and then their attention was drawn (in counterbalanced order) to the pleasant aspects of the situation, and, separately, to the aspects of the situation that involved high or low levels of effort and/or goal obstacles.

Consistent with the hypotheses advanced for the eyebrow frown, activity in the eyebrow region, but not the cheek region, was observed to increase significantly with the combined evaluations of anticipated effort and perceived goal obstacles. These increases were largest when the participant's attention was specifically focused on the effort and/or obstacle-related aspects of their imagined situations. Thus, these findings directly support the hypotheses advanced by Darwin (1872/1965), Scherer (1984), and Smith (1989) that the eyebrow frown encodes information distinguishable from subjective pleasantness that concerns individuals' perceptions of goal obstacles and/or anticipated effort.

Follow-up analyses suggested the eyebrow frown is more closely related to perceived goal obstacles than to anticipated effort, thereby supporting Scherer's (1984) interpretation of the meaning of this component over Smith's (1989). Although the experimental design intentionally confounded evaluations of anticipated effort and perceived goal obstacles, participants serendipitously dissociated these two evaluations across the experimental scenarios. A series of regression analyses indicated that the relation between goal obstacles and the eyebrow frown was more direct than that between anticipated effort and the eyebrow frown; statistically controlling for the perception of goal obstacles eliminated the observed relation between anticipated effort and the eyebrow frown, but controlling for anticipated effort did not eliminate the relation between the eyebrow frown and the perception of goal obstacles.

This latter finding was conceptually replicated by Pope and Smith (1994). In their study, using a within-subjects design, participants imagined themselves in a variety of pleasant and unpleasant situations in which goal discrepancies and anticipated effort varied freely (these situations ranged from receiving an "A" on a midterm exam to learning that a friend had been in a serious car accident). In response to the imagined situations, subjects provided self-reports of subjective pleasantness, perceived goal obstacles, the presence of goal discrepancies more generally, and anticipated effort. In this study, no evidence was obtained for a relation between anticipated effort and the eyebrow frown, but brow region activity was found to be positively correlated with perceived goal obstacles and goal discrepancies and negatively correlated with subjective pleasantness. In contrast, cheek region activity was negatively correlated with perceived goal obstacles and goal discrepancies and was positively correlated with subjective pleasantness. Importantly, even though the subjects' self-reports of subjective pleasantness and goal discrepancies were themselves highly correlated (approximately .90, an uncharacteristically high value for this relation; see Pope & Smith, 1994), regression analyses indicated that brow activity (reflecting the eyebrow frown) was most directly related to the perceived presence of goal discrepancies, whereas cheek activity (reflecting the raising of the lip corners in a smile) was most directly related to subjective pleasantness.

Thus, the existing evidence suggests that, as most investigators have hypothesized, raising the lip corners primarily encodes feelings of subjective pleasantness, and that, in line with Scherer's (1984) hypothesis, the eyebrow frown most directly encodes appraisals related to the perception of need–goal discrepancies—appraisals that are correlated with subjective unpleasantness but are nonetheless distinguishable from it.

That both the smile and the eyebrow frown have been demonstrated to encode relatively specific information related to one's emotional state, not involving the emotion's categorical identity, lends considerable support to the componential approach to understanding facial expression and illustrates nicely how appraisal theory, from which the componential approach has been advanced, has enriched our theoretical perspective on the information socially communicated through emotional facial activity. Nonetheless, it is still the case that only a small subset of the proposed relations between individual components and specific meanings has received direct empirical attention. Thus, the work reported represents a mere start to the development and testing of the componential approach. To conclude this section on the componential approach, we would like to simply point to three potential lines of research that we believe have considerable promise for the further development of this approach.

First, an obvious necessary step in this development is to test the validity of the additional hypotheses that have been proposed. In addition, building on the assumption, noted previously, that the links between appraisals and facial actions are strong and direct (Scherer, 2009), we believe that attempts to draw on the componential approach to study the sequencing of appraisals (e.g., Delplanque et al., 2009) are especially valuable, as they hold considerable promise to both validate key assumptions of the componential model and reveal much about the processes underlying appraisal. Finally, we think there is considerable value to combining work along both these lines with efforts to use the componential approach to develop computational models of facial expression that can be used to drive the facial behavior of virtual characters (e.g., Courgeon, Clavel, & Martin, 2009; Malatesta, Raouzaiou, Karpouzis, & Kollias, 2009). In addition to having a number of applications in their own right, efforts to develop such models can be very useful in highlighting areas in which specific models derived from the componential approach are underspecified, as well as in evaluating the plausibility of various theoretical assumptions associated with the approach.

On Increasing the Sociality of Appraisal Theory More Directly

Thus far we have focused on some implications of appraisal theory for how we understand emotional facial expressions and the information they potentially communicate to others in the social environment. Although this treatment has illustrated an important contribution that appraisal theory has made to our understanding of the social nature of emotion, it does not directly address the criticism (e.g., Parkinson, 1997; Parkinson & Manstead, 1992) that appraisal theory's depiction of its central construct of *appraisal* is largely asocial. In the remainder of this chapter, we would like to address this issue. We will do this both by highlighting the often-overlooked sociality already present in appraisal theories, and by briefly considering some ways that we believe appraisal theory can and should be further developed, so that the theory can better capture the social nature of emotion. Although we believe that the theoretical depiction of appraisal as self-centered is largely accurate, it is also clear that these appraisals do not occur in a social vacuum. For modern humans, many, if not most, emotion-eliciting situations are social creations, and often highly interpersonal. Even deeply personal events, such as losing one's job, or learning that one has a serious chronic illness, have important, wide-ranging interpersonal implications. Therefore, we believe that in its future development, it is vital that appraisal theory more explicitly embrace the highly social nature of both appraisal and emotion.

Inherently Interpersonal Appraisals and Emotions Already Handled by Appraisal Theory: Anger and Guilt. At least two of the emotions commonly considered by appraisal theory—anger and guilt—are associated with appraisals that are inherently interpersonal. Both emotions are associated with an evaluation of who is responsible for an undesired situation: If someone else is held responsible, then anger results, whereas if one holds oneself responsible, guilt results (Smith & Lazarus, 1990, 1993). The social nature of these two emotions and their antecedent appraisals are further highlighted if one considers the functions posited to be served by these emotions (e.g., Ellsworth & Smith, 1988; Izard, 1977; Plutchik, 1980; Smith & Lazarus, 1990; Tomkins, 1963). The function commonly proposed for anger is to remove an external source of harm (i.e., the person appraised as responsible for the problem) from the environment, and to undo the harm if possible; in guilt the focus is on the self, who has been appraised as responsible, and the proposed function of guilt is to motivate the person to make reparations for harm that he or she has caused, and more generally, to motivate prosocial behavior. In both cases, the appraisal of responsibility serves to identify a social target toward whom to direct one's emotion-related behaviors, whether it be to get someone else to stop their harmful behavior in anger, or toward oneself to make amends to others for perceived wrongs that one has committed.

Although we feel that appraisal theory has more of a social orientation than may at first appear to be the case, it is nonetheless true that appraisal models need to be extended to better take the social context of emotional experience into account. One way to accomplish this is to increase the range of emotions addressed by structural appraisal models.

Accounting for Differences Among Guilt, Shame, Embarrassment: The Need to Extend Appraisal Models. Consider the emotions of guilt, shame, and embarrassment. All three emotions are often referred to as "self-conscious" emotions (e.g., Tangney, 1990, 1992), and all three arise in negative circumstances appraised as having been brought about by oneself. Thus, all three emotions share some strong "family resemblances." In fact, historically, shame and guilt have often been treated as synonyms referring to the same underlying emotion, and there is a long tradition of considering embarrassment to be a mild form of shame (e.g., Borg, Staufenbiel, & Scherer, 1988; Tomkins, 1987). However, although the exact differences among these emotions remain somewhat controversial, there is a growing theoretical consensus emerging regarding the key differences among them (e.g., Parkinson, Fischer, & Manstead, 2005; Sabini, Garvey, & Hall, 2001; Sabini & Silver, 1997; Tangney, 1990, 1992).

First, there is a fair degree of consensus that guilt focuses on a specific event or transgression committed by the person that violates internal standards (e.g., Tangney, 1990), whereas in shame the focus appears to be more on a more general problem regarding the self—often a perceived character flaw (e.g., Parkinson et al., 2005; Tangney, 1990). Second, in both shame and embarrassment there appears to be a focus on the evaluation of the (flawed) self by others that does not seem to characterize guilt (Parkinson et al., 2005; Sabini et al., 2001; Tangney, 1990). However, in shame the negative evaluation by others need not have occurred but can be simply anticipated if others were to find out about the perceived flaw (Parkinson et al., 2005; Tangney, 1990). In contrast, in embarrassment actual public exposure of the perceived flaw is more central (Parkinson et al., 2005). In addition, in shame the person believes that the flaw he or she is concerned about revealing is real and reflects a true shortcoming in his or her character, whereas in embarrassment the person views the perceived flaw as something that might lower his or her esteem in the eyes of observers, but which in his or her own eyes does not reflect a true personal shortcoming (Sabini et al., 2001; Sabini & Silver, 1997). For example, a woman who trips while walking across a stage to receive an award will likely feel embarrassed, but not ashamed, because although worried that the audience might think she is clumsy, she knows this is not the case, and that it was a momentary distraction, not general clumsiness, that led her to trip.

In general, as currently proposed, none of the current major appraisal models (i.e., Roseman, 1984, 1991, 2001; Scherer, 1984, 2001; Smith & Lazarus, 1990) do a terribly good job of capturing the differences among these three emotions. None of the models even consider embarrassment. In addition, although some appraisal models (e.g., Roseman, 1984, 1991, 2001; Scherer, 1984, 2001) do make some fairly minor distinctions between the appraisals associated with shame versus guilt, none of them have available the constructs needed to adequately capture the concern, seemingly central to both shame and embarrassment, that one may be, or is in the process of being, judged by others and that one is likely to be found lacking. We are not yet sure of the best way to build such an evaluation into any of these appraisal models without giving the models too much of an ad hoc feel. However, we believe that efforts to do so will reflect an important extension to appraisal theory that will increase the theory's ability to account for the social aspects of emotional experience, and we are currently pursuing this avenue ourselves (e.g., Krumeich, Smith, & Kirby, 2006).

Appraisal As a Social Process. A second way that appraisal theory can be extended to better take the social context of appraisal and emotion into account is to begin to consider appraisal as a social process, rather than as a purely intrapersonal one. Although consideration of the descriptions of existing appraisal models might lead one to suspect that most emotion-eliciting appraisals are made by lone individuals with little or no input from others in the social environment, this clearly is not the case. We are a gregarious species, and we talk to one another about the important things that are happening in our lives (and which are likely to be accompanied by considerable emotion). The information we extract from such conversations very likely systematically influences and shapes the appraisals, and hence the emotions, we experience. To date, to our knowledge, very few appraisal theorists have considered how input from the social environment might affect appraisal. As a clear start in this direction, Manstead and Fischer (2001) have introduced the construct of "social appraisal" and have argued that how a person appraises his or her own circumstances can often be influenced by both how others are appraising and responding to similar circumstances, and how that person perceives or anticipates others appraising his or her circumstances and behaviors. For example, in the face of a potentially threatening event (e.g., an upcoming important exam), how anxious one becomes may often be influenced by how others are responding to the event: To the extent to which others are expressing high levels of anxiety, one's own anxiety is likely to be heightened, whereas to the extent to which others seem calm and nonchalant, one's anxiety is likely to be minimized.

This emphasis on social appraisal represents an important and promising start toward conceptualizing appraisal as a much more social process than has traditionally been depicted. Nonetheless, we believe that it is important for appraisal theory to develop considerably further in this direction. Next, we highlight three literatures that we believe provide important leads as to how appraisals are likely to be influenced through social interaction.

First, *seeking social support* is a common coping response to stressful events (Carver, Scheier, & Weintraub, 1989; Dunkel-Schetter, Folkman, & Lazarus, 1987; Ptacek, Smith, & Dodge, 1994). In addition to seeking help, or instrumental support, individuals often also seek informational and emotional support. That is, they talk with their friends about the stressful events, gaining information about them that might change their appraisals of, and hence their emotional reactions to, those events.

A very similar theme can be found in the literature on the *social sharing of emotion*, advanced by Rimé and colleagues (e.g., Luminet, Bouts, Delie, Manstead, & Rimé, 2000; Rimé, Mesquita, Philippot, & Boca, 1991). An extremely common, almost ubiquitous response to strong emotional experiences is to seek out opportunities to talk about the emotional experience with others in one's social environment. In these conversations the person will talk about the circumstances leading up to the emotional reaction, his or her feelings in the situation, and his or her reactions to the experience more generally. In reviewing their work on the social sharing of emotion, Rimé, Corsini, and Herbette (2002) note that this sharing appears to be related to a need to "search for meaning" and/or to come to terms with the emotional event. In other words, it appears that through this social sharing others in the social environment help the person to shape and validate his or her appraisals of emotionally significant events.

In the third literature, Snyder and colleagues (e.g., Snyder, 1989; Snyder & Higgins, 1988, 1997) have examined the role of excuses in a process that they refer to as "*reality negotiation*." They have found that when caught in a situation involving a personal transgression (i.e., a situation that should elicit guilt or shame), individuals will engage in a "negotiation" with others in the social environment, in which, through the use of excuses, they seek to minimize the negative impact of the situation on themselves. Notably the excuses that are proffered are typically designed to reduce the perceived seriousness of the transgression (referred to as "valence-of-act" by the authors, but essentially the degree of appraised goal discrepancies in the situation), or the person's perceived responsibility for the situation (referred to by the authors as "linkage-to-act"; e.g., Snyder & Higgins, 1997). Thus, through the excuses, the person who committed the transgression seeks to minimize the appraisals leading to shame or guilt. The investigators note that the persons in the social environment often serve as active coconspirators in the reality negotiation process and often work with the person to support the modified appraisals meant to be produced through the offered excuses (Snyder & Higgins, 1988).

Together, these three literatures indicate that emotional experiences are very social in a way that must strongly influence the person's appraisals of emotion-eliciting circumstances, however self-centered those appraisals may be. Whether it is conceptualized as support seeking, emotional sharing, or reality negotiation, individuals appear to talk extensively with others in their social environment about their emotional experiences, and it appears that these emotion-related discussions serve to help shape the person's appraisals of the emotion-eliciting event. Thus, it appears that a very important and promising direction for the development of appraisal theory is to make more meaningful contact with the literatures alluded to above, and to begin to explicitly model the influences of the social environment on the appraisal process.

Social Extensions to the Self and Self-Interest. Although, as we have been arguing thus far, both the contents and processes of appraisal are more socially oriented than current appraisal models suggest, it is still the case that, ultimately, we agree with the theoretical characterization of appraisal as highly self-centered, in that appraisal is an evaluation of what one's circumstances imply for *personal* well-being. However, in this final section, we want to argue that even this self-centeredness can be subject to considerable social influence.

First, our sense of self does not develop in a vacuum, but rather in a social context. We come to identify with certain individuals and groups and to differentiate ourselves from others. This identification process can have profound effects on our self-concept, and thus on how we appraise our social environment. It is now generally accepted that people's identities are shaped in part through their relationships with others (Aron & McLaughlin-Volpe, 2001; Hogg, 2001; Lancaster & Foddy, 1988; Sedikides & Brewer, 2001; Smith, Coats, & Walling, 1999). As individuals enter into close relationships with others, these relationships help the individual to define his or her goals, values, and expectations in ways that help determine what the individual will appraise as important, what he or she will appraise as good or bad, what is blameworthy, and so on. And thus, by helping to shape the individual's identity and beliefs, these sources of social influence also help to shape the individual's personal appraisals and emotions.

Second, our self-interest is not purely about our own individual self (see, for example, Lazarus' 1991 discussion of "ego-identity"). Instead, when we are in very close relationships, and when we strongly identify with another person or group, we can incorporate these others into our self-concept, such that their well-being becomes an extension of our own personal well-being. Specifically, it appears that the boundaries of one's self-concept can be expanded to incorporate certain others, such that their interests become one's own self-interest as well. As noted by Smith et al. (1999), "close relationships and group membership both involve some sort of merging of self and of other" and "this process may deeply influence cognition, affect, and behavior in relationships and group contexts" (p. 881). Aron and McLaughlin-Volpe (2001) note that this merging of oneself with another entails that people to some degree assume their close other's motives and cognitions. Thus, in appraising the relevance of one's circumstances for personal well-being, the concerns of the other explicitly can be taken into account.

The boundaries of the self also can be extended to encompass others through the social roles we assume (Lancaster & Foddy, 1988). These roles are almost always connected to a significant *role-other*: mothers have children, husbands have a wife, graduate mentors have a graduate student, and so on. Often in the eyes of the social environment, due to the role relationship, the way in which the role-other behaves is in part perceived as the responsibility of the actor. For example, a young child's behavior in public is often seen as being the responsibility of the child's parents. Thus, when the child acts out in public (e.g., by throwing a tantrum in a grocery store), the parent is often viewed with disapproval. Thus, it becomes part of the parent's direct self-interest to help the child to successfully navigate the particular public encounter. There are numerous social roles that a person might assume (parent, teacher, caregiver, etc.), in which by taking on the role, the person becomes directly responsible for another's well being. In such cases it is very natural and adaptive for the self-interests of the parties involved in the role relationships to become heavily merged.

Thus, it appears that the definition of the "self" that provides the basis of one's self-interest in appraisal is itself rather socially defined and quite interpersonal in nature. Expanding the scope of appraisal theory so that it more explicitly takes into account the social, interpersonal nature of the self represents an important future direction for appraisal theorists.

Summary and Conclusions

Appraisal theory represents an important and influential approach to understanding emotion. Given this, and given that, as noted, the theory aspires to provide a fairly comprehensive account of human emotion (e.g., Frijda, 1986; Lazarus, 1968, 1991; Scherer, 1984), it is crucial that it capture the important social/interpersonal facets of emotional experience. In the present chapter, we have considered two distinct ways in which appraisal theory is being developed, or might be developed, to increase the sociality of the appraisal construct. First, we have reviewed how appraisal theory has promoted the development of a theoretical approach, the componential approach, which is enriching our understanding of the information socially communicated through emotional facial expressions. Second, we have highlighted the importance of extending the theory to better capture the social nature of appraisal itself. We have made the case that, although nominally focused on one's personal self-interest, appraisals are highly social in several respects: individuals often discuss with others their emotional experiences, and these discussions almost certainly help define the individual's appraisals of those experiences; one's self-concept is in part defined by significant others in the social environment; and the boundaries of the self-concept can be expanded to incorporate the interests and concerns of others who are sufficiently important to the person. As a result, however self-centered appraisals might be, they are often far from selfish. It appears that appraisals, although based on one's self-interest, are, in fact, every bit as interpersonal and social as the emotions they elicit. We hope that the directions and issues we have pointed to here will be a help in further developing appraisal theory to better capture this sociality.

References

Andrew, R. J. (1965). The origins of facial expressions. *Scientific American, 213*, 88–94.

Aron, A., & McLaughlin-Volpe, T. (2001). Including others in the self. In C. Sedikides & M. B. Brewer (Eds.), *Individual self, relational self, collective self* (pp. 89–108). Philadelphia: Psychology Press.

Borg, I., Staufenbiel, T., & Scherer, K. R. (1988). On the symbolic basis of shame. In K. R. Scherer (Ed.), *Facets of emotion: Recent research* (pp. 79–98). Hillsdale, NJ: Lawrence Erlbaum.

Buck, R., Losow, J. I., Murphy, M. M, & Costanzo, P. (1992). Social facilitation and inhibition of emotional expression and communication. *Journal of Personality and Social Psychology, 63*, 962–968.

Buck, R. W., Savin, V. J., Miller, R. E., & Caul, W. F. (1972). Communication of affect through facial expressions in humans. *Journal of Personality and Social Psychology, 23*, 362–371.

Cacioppo, J. T., Martzke, J. S., Petty, R E., & Tassinary, L. G. (1988). Specific forms of facial EMG response index emotions during an interview: From Darwin to the continuous flow hypothesis of affect-laden information processing. *Journal of Personality and Social Psychology, 54*, 592–604.

Cacioppo, J. T., Petty, R E., Losch, M. E., & Kim, H. S. (1986). Electromyographic activity over facial muscle regions can differentiate the valence and intensity of affective reactions. *Journal of Personality and Social Psychology, 50*, 260–268.

Cacioppo, J. T., Petty, R E., & Morris, K. J. (1985). Semantic, evaluative, and self-referent processing: Memory, cognitive effort, and somatovisceral activity. *Psychophysiology, 22*, 371–384.

Carver, C. S., Scheier, M. F., & Weintraub, J. K. (1989). Assessing coping strategies: A theoretically-based approach. *Journal of Personality and Social Psychology, 56*, 267–283.

Courgeon, M., Clavel, C., & Martin, L.-C. (2009). Appraising emotional events during a real-time interactive game. *Proceedings of the International Workshop on Affective-Aware Virtual Agents and Social Robots* (Article # 7). New York: Association for Computing Machinery. DOI: 10.1145/1655260.1655267

Darwin, C. (1965). *The expression of the emotions in man and animals*. Chicago: University of Chicago Press. (Original work published 1872)

Delplanque, S., Grandjean, D., Chrea, C., Coppin, G., Aymard, L., Cayeux, I., Margot, C., Velazco, M., Sander, D., & Scherer, K. R. (2009). Sequential unfolding of novelty and pleasantness appraisals of odors: Evidence from facial electromyography and autonomic reactions. *Emotion, 9*, 316–328. DOI: 10.1037/a0015369

Duchenne, G. B. (1990). *The mechanism of human facial expression* (R A. Cuthbertson, Ed. and Trans.). Cambridge, UK: Cambridge University Press. (Original work published 1862)

Dunkel-Schetter, C., Folkman, S., & Lazarus, R. S. (1987). Correlates of social support receipt. *Journal of Personality and Social Psychology, 53*, 71–80.

Ekman, P., Davidson, R. J., & Friesen, W. V. (1990). The Duchenne smile: Emotional expression and brain physiology II. *Journal of Personality and Social Psychology, 58*, 342–353.

Ekman, P., & Friesen, W. V. (1969). The repertoire of nonverbal behavior—Categories, origins, usage and coding. *Semiotica, 1*, 49–98.

Ekman, P., & Friesen, W. V. (1975). *Unmasking the face: A guide to recognizing emotions from facial clues*. Englewood Cliffs, NJ: Prentice-Hall.

Ekman, P., & Friesen, W. V. (1978). *Investigator's guide to the Facial Action Coding System*. Palo Alto, CA: Consulting Psychologists Press.

Ekman, P., & Friesen, W. V. (1986). A new pan-cultural facial expression of emotion. *Motivation and Emotion, 10*, 159–168.

Ekman, P., Friesen, W. V., & Ancoli, S. (1980). Facial signs of emotional experience. *Journal of Personality and Social Psychology, 39*, 1125–1134.

Ekman, P., Friesen, W. V., & Ellsworth, P. (1982). Research foundations. In P. Ekman (Ed.), *Emotion in the human face* (2nd ed., pp. 1–143). New York: Cambridge University Press.

Ellsworth, P. C., & Smith, C. A. (1988). From appraisal to emotion: Differences among unpleasant feelings. *Motivation and Emotion, 12*, 271–302.

Fernández-Dols, J. M., & Ruiz-Belda, M. A. (1997). Spontaneous facial behavior during intense emotional episodes: Artistic truth and optical truth. In J. A. Russell & J. M. Fernández-Dols (Eds.), *The psychology of facial expression* (pp. 255–274). New York: Cambridge University Press.

Folkman, S., & Lazarus, R. S. (1985). If it changes it must be a process: Study of emotion and coping during three stages of a college examination. *Journal of Personality and Social Psychology, 48*, 150–170.

Fridlund, A. J. (1994). *Human facial expression: An evolutionary view*. San Diego, CA: Academic Press.

Frijda, N. H. (1969). Recognition of emotion. In L. Berkowitz (Ed.), *Advances in experimental social psychology* (Vol. 4, pp. 167–223). New York: Academic Press.

Frijda, N. H. (1986). *The emotions*. New York: Cambridge University Press.

Frijda, N. H., Kuipers, P., & ter Schure, E. (1989) Relations among emotion, appraisal, and emotional action readiness. *Journal of Personality and Social Psychology*, 57, 212–228.

Frois-Wittmann, J. (1930). The judgment of facial expression. *Journal of Experimental Psychology*, *13*, 113–151.

Hogg, M. A. (2001). Social identity and the sovereignty of the group: A psychology of belonging. In C. Sedikides & M. B. Brewer (Eds.), *Individual self, relational self, collective self* (pp. 125–146). Philadelphia: Psychology Press.

Izard, C. E. (1971). *The face of emotion*. New York: Appleton-Century-Crofts.

Izard, C. E. (1977). *Human emotions*. New York: Plenum.

Izard, C. E., & Haynes, O. M. (1988). On the form and universality of the contempt expression: A challenge to Ekman and Friesen's claim of discovery. *Motivation and Emotion*, *12*, 1–16.

Krumeich, M. E., Smith, C., & Kirby, L. D. (August, 2006). *Making appraisal theory more social: Appraisal-related differences in shame and embarrassment*. Atlanta, GA: Meeting of the International Society for Research on Emotions.

Kuppens, P., Van Mechelen, I., Smits, D. J. M., & De Boek, P. (2003). The appraisal basis of anger: Specificity, necessity, and sufficiency of components. *Emotion*, 3, 254–269.

Lancaster, S., & Foddy, M. (1988). Self-extensions: A conceptualization. *Journal for the theory of social behavior*, *18*, 77–94.

Lazarus, R. S. (1968). Emotions and adaptation: Conceptual and empirical relations. In W. J. Arnold (Ed.), *Nebraska symposium on motivation* (Vol. 16, pp. 175–266). Lincoln: University of Nebraska Press.

Lazarus, R. S. (1991). *Emotion and adaptation*. New York: Oxford University Press.

Luminet, O., Bouts, P., Delie, R., Manstead, A. S. R., & Rimé, B. (2000). Social sharing of emotion following exposure to a negatively valenced situation. *Cognition and Emotion*, *14*, 661–688.

Malatesta, L., Raouzalou, A., Karpouzis, K., & Kollias, S. (2009). Towards modeling embodied conversational agent character profiles using appraisal theory predictions in expression synthesis. *Applied Intelligence*, *30*, 58–64. DOI: 10.1007/s10489-007-0076-9

Mandler, G. (1980). The generation of emotion: A psychological theory. In R. Plutchik & H. Kellerman (Eds.), *Emotion: Theory, research, and experience: Vol. 1. Theories of emotion* (pp. 219–243). New York: Academic Press.

Mandler, G. (1984). *Mind and body*. New York: Norton.

Manstead, A. S. R., & Fischer, A. H. (2001). Social appraisal: The social world as object of and influence on appraisal processes. In K. R. Scherer, A. Schorr, & T. Johnstone (Eds.). *Appraisal processes in emotion: Theory, methods, research* (pp. 221–232). New York: Oxford University Press.

Manstead, A. S. R., & Tetlock, P. E. (1989). Cognitive appraisals and emotional experience: Further evidence. *Cognition and Emotion*, 3, 225–239.

Ortony, A., & Turner, T. J. (1990). What's basic about basic emotions? *Psychological Review*, 97, 315–331.

Parkinson, B. (1997). Untangling the appraisal-emotion connection. *Personality and Social Psychology Review*, *1*, 72–79.

Parkinson, B., Fischer, A. H., & Manstead, A. S. R. (2005). *Emotion in social relations: Cultural, group, and interpersonal processes*. New York: Psychology Press.

Parkinson, B., & Manstead, A. S. R. (1992). Appraisal as a cause of emotion. In M. S. Clark (Ed.), *Review of personality and social psychology, Vol 13: Emotion* (pp. 122–149). Newbury Park, CA: Sage.

Plutchik, R. (1980). *Emotion: A psychoevolutionary synthesis*. New York: Harper & Row.

Pope, L. K, & Smith, C. A. (1994). On the distinct meanings of smiles and frowns. *Cognition and Emotion*, 8, 65–72.

Ptacek, J. T., Smith, R. E., & Dodge, K. L. (1994). Gender differences in coping with stress: When stressor and appraisals do not differ. *Personality and Social Psychology Bulletin*, *20*, 421–430.

Rimé, B., Corsini, S., & Herbette, G. (2002). Emotion, verbal expression, and the social sharing of emotion. In S. R. Fussell (Ed.), *The verbal communication of emotions: Interdisciplinary perspectives* (pp. 185–208). Mahwah, NJ: Lawrence Erlbaum Associates.

Rimé, B., Mesquita, B., Philippot, P., & Boca, S. (1991). Beyond the emotional event: Six studies on the social sharing of emotion. *Cognition and Emotion*, 5, 435–465.

Roseman, I. J. (1984). Cognitive determinants of emotion: A structural theory. In P. Shaver (Ed.), *Review of personality and social psychology: Vol. 5. Emotions, relationships, and health* (pp. 11–36). Beverly Hills, CA: Sage.

Roseman, I. J. (1991). Appraisal determinants of discrete emotions. *Cognition and Emotion*, 5, 161–200.

Roseman, I. J. (2001). A model of appraisal in the emotion system: Integrating theory, research, and applications. In K. R. Scherer, A. Schorr, & T. Johnstone (Eds.). *Appraisal processes in emotion: Theory, methods, research* (pp. 68–91). New York: Oxford University Press.

Roseman, I. J., Spindel, M. S., & Jose, P. E. (1990). Appraisals of emotion-eliciting events: Testing a theory of discrete emotions. *Journal of Personality and Social Psychology*, 59, 899–915.

Russell, J. A. (1994). Is there universal recognition of emotion from facial expression? A review of the cross-cultural studies. *Psychological Bulletin, 115*, 102–141.

Sabini, J., Garvey, B., & Hall, A. L. (2001). Shame and embarrassment revisited. *Personality and Social Psychology Review*, 27, 104–117.

Sabini, J., & Silver, M. (1997). In defense of shame: Shame in the context of guilt and embarrassment. *Journal for the Theory of Social Behavior*, 27, 1–15.

Scherer, K R. (1984). On the nature and function of emotion: A component process approach. In K. R. Scherer & P. Ekman (Eds.), *Approaches to emotion* (pp. 293–317). Hillsdale, NJ: Erlbaum.

Scherer, K. R. (1992). What does a facial expression express? In K. T. Strongman (Ed.), *International review of studies of emotion* (Vol. 2, pp. 139–165). New York: Wiley.

Scherer, K. R. (1997). Profiles of emotion-antecedent appraisal: Testing theoretical predictions across cultures. *Cognition and Emotion, 11*, 113–150.

Scherer, K. R. (2001). Appraisal considered as a process of multilevel sequential checking. In K. R. Scherer, A. Schorr, & T. Johnstone (Eds.), *Appraisal processes in emotion: Theory, methods, research* (pp. 92–120). New York: Oxford University Press.

Scherer, K. R. (2009). The dynamic architecture of emotion: Evidence for the componential process model. *Cognition and Emotion*, 23, 1307–1351. DOI: 10.1080/02699930902928969

Schwartz, G. E., & Weinberger, D. A. (1980). Patterns of emotional responses to affective situations: Relations among happiness, sadness, anger, fear, depression, and anxiety. *Motivation and Emotion*, 4, 175–191.

Sedikides C., & Brewer, M. B. (2001). Individual self, relational self and collective self: Partners, opponents or strangers? In C. Sedikides & M. B. Brewer (Eds.), *Individual self, relational self, collective self* (pp. 1–6). Philadelphia: Psychology Press.

Smith, C. A. (1989). Dimensions of appraisal and physiological response in emotion. *Journal of Personality and Social Psychology*, 56, 339–353.

Smith, C. A., & Ellsworth, P. C. (1985). Patterns of cognitive appraisal in emotion. *Journal of Personality and Social Psychology*, 48, 813–838.

Smith, C. A., & Ellsworth, P. C. (1987). Patterns of appraisal and emotion related to taking an exam. *Journal of Personality and Social Psychology*, 52, 475–488.

Smith, C. A., & Kirby, L. D. (2009). Putting appraisal in context: Toward a relational model of appraisal and emotion. *Cognition and Emotion*, 23, 1352–1372. DOI: 10.1080/20699930902860386

Smith, C. A., & Kirby, L. D. (2011). The role of appraisal and emotion in coping and adaptation. In R. J. Contrada & A. Baum (Eds.), *Handbook of stress science: Biology, psychology, and health* (pp. 195–208). New York: Springer.

Smith, C. A., & Lazarus, R. S. (1990). Emotion and adaptation. In L. A. Pervin (Ed.), *Handbook of personality: Theory and research* (pp. 609–637). New York: Guilford.

Smith, C. A., & Lazarus, R. S. (1993). Appraisal components, core relational themes, and the emotions. *Cognition and Emotion*, 7, 233–269.

Smith, C. A., McHugo, G. J., & Lanzetta, J. T. (1986). The facial muscle patterning of posed and imagery-induced expressions of emotion by expressive and nonexpressive posers. *Motivation and Emotion, 10*, 133–157.

Smith, C. A., & Scott, H. S. (1997). A componential approach to the meaning of facial expressions. In J. A. Russell & J. M. Fernández-Dols (Eds.), *The psychology of facial expression* (pp. 229–254). New York: Cambridge University Press.

Smith, E. R., Coats, S. & Walling, D. (1999). Overlapping mental representations of self, in-group and partner: Further response time evidence and a connectionist model. *Personality and Social Psychology Bulletin*, 25, 873–882.

Snyder, C. R. (1989). Reality negotiation: From excuses to hope and beyond. *Journal of Social and Clinical Psychology*, 8, 130–157.

Snyder, C. R., & Higgins, R. L. (1988). Excuses: Their effective role in the negotiation of reality. *Psychological Bulletin, 104*, 23–35.

Snyder, C. R., & Higgins, R. L. (1997). Reality negotiation: Governing one's self and being governed by others. *Review of General Psychology, 1*, 336–350.

Tangney, J. P. (1990). Sharing shame and guilt: Another social clinical interface. *Contemporary Social Psychology, 14*, 83–88.

Tangney, J. P. (1992). Situational determinants of shame and guilt in young adulthood. *Personality and Social Psychology Bulletin*, 18, 199–206.

Tomkins, S. S. (1963). *Affect, imagery, consciousness: Vol. 2. The negative affects*. New York: Springer.

Tomkins, S. S. (1987). Shame. In D. Nathanson (Ed.), *The many faces of shame* (pp. 133–161). New York: Guilford.

Tong, E. M. W., Bishop, G. D., Enklemann, H. C., Why, Y. P., Diong, S. M., Khader, M. A., & Ang, J. C. H. (2007). Emotion and appraisal: A study using ecological momentary assessment. *Cognition and Emotion, 21*, 1361–1381. doi: 10.1080/02699930701202012

Wagner, H. L., & Smith, J. (1991). Facial expression in the presence of friends and strangers. *Journal of Nonverbal Behavior, 15*, 201–214.

2

Processes of Emotional Meaning and Response Coordination

Brian Parkinson

Introduction

Emotions have meanings, communicate meanings, and relate to meaningful situations. Sometimes these three kinds of emotional meaning are consistent and continuous. My anger may imply that I blame you, convey my blame to you, and depend on believing that you are to blame (respectively). They may also follow a simple sequence running from interpretation and evaluation of situational meaning to meaningful emotion to communication of this meaning to other people. My sense that you are to blame (appraisal) leads to a pattern of responses that I recognize as angry blame (meaning of emotion) and communicates the same meaning to you (communicative meaning).

The present chapter argues that emotions also emerge in responsive social environments in other ways. For example, your increasingly defensive response may push me into a corresponding angry stance, or my need to find someone to blame may lead to my presentation of anger. In the first case, your assignment of emotional meaning to my actions shapes my emotional response. In the second case, communicative meaning shapes both personal appraisals of the situation and the other person's ascription of meaning (attribution). Although meaning still takes priority in both cases, it is produced by interpersonal rather than purely intrapsychic processes.

This chapter also suggests that emotions need not be guided by any of these meaning processes: They may emerge more directly as part of transactions with the dynamic social environment. Meaningful emotions do not always depend on anyone recognizing or communicating their meaning in advance. The fact that anger communicates blame and relates to blameworthy situations need not imply prior intentions to communicate blame or antecedent appraisal of the blame attached to someone else's actions.

The assumption that meaning precedes emotion is a form of the so-called "cognitive fallacy": the assumption that we should explain someone's reaction to anything in terms of how that person worked out how to react to it. According to this assumption, people respond because they decide to respond, so explanation requires identification of the grounds for that decision. But is explaining how someone reached a decision to respond any easier than explaining the response itself? And when we have explained how the decision was reached, does that really explain the reaction itself or only the decision that prompted it? Explaining the decision to respond emotionally may be even more problematic because emotions are not self-evidently thought-out or preplanned responses. Knowing the meanings is not enough. We also need to know how the meanings assemble or are constructed, and to be sure about how they relate to the emotions we are trying to explain.

Because modelers are typically concerned with how information must be processed in order to generate coherent, differentiated emotions, it makes sense for them to consult psychological theories that attempt to uncover an underlying generative grammar, emphasizing rule-based extraction of meaning from a structured situation (cf. Ortony, Clore, & Collins, 1988). Such an approach may also fall victim to the cognitive fallacy. Emotions are viewed as a direct function of the appraised relationship between personal goals and individually perceived environmental cues relevant to those goals. Although this provides a good way of mapping emotions to relational meanings, it does not address processes whereby emotions and meanings emerge in real-time embodied transactions with the practical and social environment, where the information value of what is happening may not be the only relevant consideration. Further, modelers often treat emotions as encapsulated outputs or states rather than as dynamic, continually adjusting modes of active engagement with unfolding events. The present review of approaches to relational and emotional meaning may permit a clearer fix on their production, construction, and formulation, and how these processes might be addressed by modelers.

This chapter will consider the advantages and disadvantages of a range of previous approaches to the issue of emotional meaning. These approaches vary in their assumptions about what role meaning plays in the emotion process and whether it is cause, content, consequence, or side effect of the emotional action. A simplified classification of their assumptions is presented in Table 2.1. First, agnostic approaches argue that meaning is something that is attributed to experience and plays no necessary role in activating or regulating feeling states or emotional response syndromes. According to these accounts, researchers should not assume that terms such as "anger" or "embarrassment" correspond to real psychological objects. These representations are imposed on experience by perceivers and do not necessarily reflect its intrinsic structure. Second, appraisal accounts explain the activation of emotion response syndromes in terms of the processes whereby the meaning of the current situation (or person–environment transaction) is interpreted and evaluated. In this view, genuine emotional responses are coordinated by prior meaning extraction processes. Communicative accounts, by contrast, argue that emotions convey meanings to others without necessarily depending on prior apprehension of the meanings they convey. Emotion is seen as a social-influence strategy attuned to actual and anticipated consequences. Finally, transactional approaches see meaning as an emergent phenomenon that may or may not coalesce as emotion develops in real time. Meaning is a function of response consolidation rather than a prior condition of this consolidation.

TABLE 2.1 Approaches to Emotional Meaning and Response Coordination

	At what stage is meaning registered?	*What role does meaning play?*	*Coherence of response syndrome*
Attributional	Often after the fact	Perception and interpretation of affective experience	No intrinsic interconnections between components Response integrity in the eye of the perceiver
Appraisal	Prior to emotional response	Selection of adaptive responses	Loosely coupled syndromes coordinated by appraisals
Communicative	After emotional response if at all (by others, self, or both)	Determination of others' responses to emotion	Functional rather than (consistent) structural coherence
Transactional	During emotional response if at all	No central role in response consolidation	Dynamic self-organization

According to these four accounts, emotions are meanings applied to experience, responses to meanings of transactions, ways of communicating meanings, or processes whereby meanings are constructed. Each of these approaches brings important insights, but none can fully accommodate the range of processes whereby emotions and emotional meanings unfold in the dynamic social environment. A more plural and flexible account of emotion may be the only realistic option.

Explaining Emotions or "Emotions"? Agnostic Attributional Approaches

Although psychologists continue to disagree about what emotions are (e.g., Bard & Cornelius, 2007; Kleinginna & Kleinginna, 1981), they mostly assume that there are definable things in the psychological world that loosely correspond to everyday emotion categories from ordinary language. Partly for this reason, psychological researchers usually ask people to describe or rate their own experience (self-report) as a way of "measuring" emotion. We take participants' word for it when they say they are experiencing or have experienced a certain level of anger, embarrassment, or guilt. However, emotion words are used in a variety of senses and for a range of purposes in everyday life, so it is a mistake to see them as transparent windows revealing an internal realm of feelings (e.g., Edwards, 1999; Parkinson, 1998). Saying that "I am angry" does not necessarily describe my current experience; it also serves to direct blame externally, and to discipline, chide, or threaten someone. An additional issue is that many English-language nouns and adjectives commonly used to describe or present emotional meanings cannot be precisely translated into other languages (see Parkinson, Fischer, & Manstead, 2005), casting doubt on their direct correspondence with any universal set of distinctive subjective states.

To address these issues, Russell (2003) developed a principled account of emotion categories as cognitive scripts that shape the interpretation of affective experience. For him, the mental substance underlying so-called emotions is "core affect"—a combination of current levels of pleasure and arousal with dimensional rather than categorical structure. The apparent intactness and separability of distinct emotions arises partly as an artifact of sense making using culturally supplied categorical concepts. Just as we see stellar constellations when observing the nighttime sky rather than a space mapped out by topographical distances, so too we perceive affective states as connected with conventional antecedents and consequences organized in a cognitive narrative (script). Emotion representations are thus akin to the lines and pictures superimposed on indeterminate scatterings of stars in astrological illustrations. Emotions are meanings applied to experience rather than the raw material of experience itself.

If Russell is correct, then it is a mistake to look for control processes that coordinate emotional responses because coordination, in fact, occurs at the level of emotion perception rather than emotion production. Similarly, emotional meaning is often applied to responses after the fact rather than shape those responses in advance.

Russell's (2003) model has antecedents in earlier accounts of emotion. Following James (1898), many researchers began to assume that emotional experience derives directly or indirectly from perception or interpretation of bodily responses of various kinds. For example, Schachter's (1964) two-factor theory proposed that emotion is experienced when the individual believes that feelings associated with physiological arousal (release of metabolic energy) are caused by emotionally relevant features of the environment (a process of "attribution" of arousal to an emotional situation). Thus, anger is constituted by the perception that arousal is due to someone else's provocative actions. However, arousal need not be genuinely caused by the perceived provocation for the experience to count as anger: It might equally well be a response to a strong cup of coffee or a surreptitious adrenaline injection (Schachter & Singer, 1962).

The main difference between Russell's model and these earlier accounts concerns the status of an individual's conclusions about his or her emotional state (self-attribution of emotion). For Schachter, labeling your own emotion was equivalent to being in an emotional state and affected behavior accordingly (see also Barrett, 2006, and further in this chapter). For Russell, self-attribution has no further consequences for emotional state (which is partly a cultural fiction anyway). However, categorizing yourself as being in a particular emotional state may bring less direct consequences further downstream. For example, the conclusion that you are "angry" may lead to various attempts to calm yourself down (self-regulation).

Although these theories offer principled accounts of the direct causes of emotional self-attributions, their focus does not fall directly on the processes that activate the responses that provide the material for these attributions in the first place (e.g., Dewey, 1895). For James, the bodily responses perceived as emotion were simply direct consequences of some "exciting fact." For Schachter, the interpretation (or appraisal) of the emotional situation was typically (but not always) the genuine as well as the perceived cause of the physiological reaction. For Russell, there is no single process that can account for all the response components integrated in the emotion concept. In his view, trying to provide any general explanation for patterned responses in emotion is a mistake because there is no consistent patterning to explain in the first place.

Indeed, there is little clear evidence for coherent response profiles corresponding to distinct emotions (see Barrett, 2006, for a review). Although some studies do find moderate correlations between response components such as autonomic responses and facial expressions under certain circumstances (e.g., Mauss et al., 2005), others find little evidence for consistent patterning (e.g, Reisenzein, 2000; Reisenzein et al., 2006). If emotions are coupled systems, their coupling seems to be loose and indeterminate. Responses may become synchronized because of the simultaneous effects of several separate processes (e.g., Ortony & Turner, 1990) rather than being coordinated by any executive mechanism (see Scherer, 2001).

Like Russell, I doubt that all episodes classified under the heading of any specific emotion term such as "anger" share common and distinctive response patterns. However, it also seems unlikely that the consistencies in response features represented in prototypical scripts for each emotion (e.g., Rimé, Philippot, & Cisamolo, 1990; Russell & Fehr, 1994) bear no relation to the realities of emotional response, or that there is no structure whatsoever to our emotional experiences. One reason why emotion categories are associated with distinctive prototypes is that responses do fall into coherent patterns in specific relational situations that are perceived to be closely associated with the emotion in question. For example, although I often get angry without shouting or clenching teeth and fists, anger in direct physical confrontations often genuinely is associated with these responses at certain key moments (cf. Cacioppo et al., 1993). The fact that prototypical anger actually occurs in these defining situations partly accounts for the presence of these features in the anger script.

Partial response coherence in emotion-defining situations arises because their specific challenges and threats impose simultaneous functional demands on different response systems. Although "components" (such as facial expressions, bodily changes, and behavioral impulses) often serve functions that are not *intrinsically* emotional (e.g., attention, energy mobilization, signaling), each may also be implicated in a broader process of emotional engagement. Events that attract visual attention and its corresponding facial movements often also require vigilance and associated autonomic activation. Warding off an antagonist not only involves warnings communicated on the face but also physical preparation for attack. Neither emotions nor appraisals are consistently associated with specific behaviors of either kind, but there may still be context-dependent patterning of responses when the practical and communicative requirements of the current transaction are congruent.

The central issue is not whether responses are patterned but how closely any patterns are aligned with cultural emotion categories such as anger, fear, and embarrassment. Russell emphasizes both lack of coherence and lack of consistency across different classified instances of any given emotion, but the prototypic representation of the emotion still implies some level of internal organization (both over time: diachronically; and at any given moment in time: synchronically). Indeed, why would the cultural evolution of these scripts proceed in an arbitrary and autistic manner? Instead, prototypical scripts for emotions are often based on directly experienced situations that provide a developmental template for adopting and communicating emotions in a culturally readable way. Thus, there are intrinsic connections between emotion categories and response patterns, but these response patterns only occur in instances that are given special emphasis within a culture (i.e., *hypercognized* instances, Levy, 1973) and not across all possible cases of any given emotion.

Although attributional approaches can never provide a comprehensive account of all possible emotion processes, their distinctive contribution lies in the recognition that emotion representations should not be confused with empirical emotion processes (see also Parkinson, 1995, 1997). Further, by treating emotion representation as a topic in its own right, Russell (2003) correctly draws attention to the perceptual and regulatory effects exerted when emotion scripts are applied to experience. Indeed, regardless of whether self-attributions correspond to the nature of underlying emotion, their explicit articulation may still transform its enactment and expression. People can relate to the world in an emotional way without recognizing the fact (e.g.,

Frijda, 2005), but knowing that you are emotional can bring consequences that go beyond unselfconscious, prereflective experience (cf. Lambie & Marcel, 2002).

Emotion as Categorization

Deriving from the attributional accounts described above, an alternative approach to the relation between emotion representation and reality is provided by Barrett's (2006) view of emotions as conceptual acts. Like Russell, Barrett believes that the basis for emotion is "core affect" consisting of sensations of pleasure and (possibly) arousal (or related behavior). However, for her, the representation process has a more direct impact on the nature of subjective experience. In particular, core affect is transformed into a discrete emotion when it is categorized in more specific terms using socialized knowledge that links it to particular object or occurrence. To have an emotion, in this view, is to feel that affect has a particular focus on events, but these events need not be implicated in its actual causation (cf. Schachter, 1964).

Barrett's ideas about how individuals represent their own core affect also differ from Russell's. In her view, emotion categorization does not depend on resemblance to an abstractly defined prototypical script, but on context-specific sensory representations derived from previous experiences that have been labeled using the same emotion label (e.g., during cultural learning of emotion word meanings).

In Barrett's (2006) terms, emotion is a conceptual act, and not any kind of motivating force or mode of engagement with the environment (although categorizing yourself as emotional may set priorities for action and regulation). Like Schachter's theory, such an account treats emotion as equivalent to emotion labeling. However, in my view, having an emotion, acting emotionally, or being in an emotional state are conceptually and practically distinct from thinking that one is in an emotional state. Even an implicit, embodied registration of emotional quality is not identical to emotion itself. For example, philosophers often point out that the last person to notice the presence of jealousy is the jealous person himself or herself (e.g., Bedford, 1957).

People often respond to the environment in an emotional way and see the world from an emotional perspective without registering the fact that they are emotional at all. In this respect, Frijda (1986; see also Sartre, 1962) notes that the content of emotional experience is often the perception of the environment as having certain affective characteristics rather than the perception of oneself as being emotional. When angry, we often feel that another person is behaving unconscionably and not that we are angry with them. For Barrett (2006) these experiences of prereflective (Parkinson, 2008) or world-focused (Lambie & Marcel, 2002) emotion simply indicate that core affect is operating in the background rather than being the focus of consciousness. However, other theorists (e.g., Parkinson, Fischer, & Manstead, 2005) consider taking an evaluatively loaded relational stance toward the environment to be the most basic and central form of emotion, with articulated or self-conscious emotional experiences being secondary derivatives of this primary phenomenon. Although Barrett's theory can deal with perceptions of the world that are drenched with core affect (e.g., finding something pleasant or arousing), it is not well equipped to explain experiences in which more specific orientations, attunements, and action tendencies are operating.

Meaning Comes First: Appraisal Approaches

For Russell and Barrett, meaning is something that is imposed on affective experience following its original activation. By contrast, appraisal theories focus on the processes whereby the detection of situational (or transactional) meanings activates emotional responses in the first place. Barrett's theory implies that what needs explaining is the identification of an affective experience (e.g., a pleasant or an unpleasant feeling) as an instance of a particular emotion. In appraisal theory, the focus shifts backward in time to explaining how person–environment transactions are identified as relevant occasions for emotion.

Another difference between the two theoretical traditions is that many appraisal theorists see the emotion itself as a form of relational activity or action readiness (Frijda, 1986) rather than a subjective mental state. From this angle, the functionality of the particular action readiness mode depends on it being appropriately attuned to the adaptive demands of what is happening. Appraisal is the process whereby these adaptive demands are registered and evaluated so that emotion can serve its purposes.

Based on this reasoning, Smith and Lazarus (1993) argued that recognizing the core relational meaning of a person–environment transaction, whether consciously or unconsciously, is a necessary and sufficient precondition for becoming emotional. After all, if the cognitive system had not arrived at the conclusion that someone else was to blame at some level, how would it be able to determine whether anger was the appropriate response?

Early appraisal theorists focused on the content of the relational meanings associated with different emotions in an attempt to explain emotion differentiation (e.g., Roseman, 1979; Smith & Ellsworth, 1985). The central issue was "What meanings activate which emotions?" Subsequently, attention turned to the processes producing emotional meanings. However, many appraisal theorists still believe that the output of these processes rather than the processes themselves plays the key role in determining what emotion is experienced. As Lazarus (1991, p. 160) wrote, "it is meaning that counts in emotion, not how that meaning is achieved." Similarly, Smith and Kirby (2000) argue that individuals may arrive at the "core relational theme" (appraisal pattern) that characterizes any given emotion as a result of either conditioned associations or deliberative processes, but in either case, the quality of that emotion stays the same. Recognizing (at either an implicit or explicit level) that a transaction requires an angry reaction, for example, depends on registering another person's (or agent's) accountability for some event that conflicts with current concerns, and recognizing that a transaction requires a guilty reaction depends on registering one's own accountability. In short, these kinds of appraisal theory (appraisal content theories) contend that relational meanings take priority in the emotion process and lead to generation of emotion response components. Meanings precede and cause emotional responses rather than being imposed on those responses after the fact.

One problem for these theories lies in establishing that emotions genuinely are preceded by apprehension of relational meaning at some level. There is little disagreement that they *sometimes* can be (Roseman & Evdokas, 2004). For example, you may only work out that a remark was insulting after thinking about it afterward. Further, appraisals clearly often make a difference to how an already developing emotion unfolds (Lazarus & Alfert, 1964). For example, your reaction to the insulting remark will differ if you believe that it was specifically intended to upset you. However, the real question is whether such examples are representative of the full range of experienced emotions.

Can emotions be activated without prior appraisal? Different appraisal theorists disagree on this point. For example, Roseman (e.g., 2001) readily acknowledges that drugs may directly induce emotions in ways that bypass appraisal processes. By contrast, Smith and Lazarus (1993; see also Smith & Kirby, 2004) explicitly contend that appraisal is both a necessary and sufficient condition for emotion: without appraisal, no emotion is possible; with appropriate appraisals, emotion is inevitable. Clearly, generating comprehensive confirmatory evidence for such a hypothesis is a practical impossibility because it would require exhaustively cataloguing all possible instances of emotions and appraisals. However, as Lazarus (1991) has emphasized, the uncompromising nature of the appraisal necessity hypothesis does make it eminently susceptible to falsification.

Subsequent evidence apparently yields precisely this falsification. For example, Nezlek and colleagues (2008) found that associations between reported appraisals and ratings and six different emotions were not consistent across different individuals, leading the authors to conclude that there is no one-to-one correspondence between appraisals and emotions in everyday life. Similarly, Parkinson and Illingworth (2009) found that ratings of guilt were closely related to perceived self-blame when someone else's blame was perceived as reasonable but not when it was perceived as unreasonable, and Parkinson, Roper, and Simons (2009) found that reasonable anger was more closely related to other-blame appraisals than unreasonable anger (see also Parkinson, 1999). Kuppens and his colleagues' (2003) research led them to conclude that relations between appraisals and emotions vary depending both on the person and situation.

However, like most of the evidence supporting appraisal theory, this unsupportive evidence relies almost entirely on correlating self-reports of appraisals with self-reports of emotions. Appraisal necessity theorists are therefore entitled to explain apparent cases of appraisal-independent emotion by reference to nonconscious, implicit, or otherwise unmeasured appraisal processes, or to mistaken self-attributions of emotion. Although research participants sometimes fail to report other-blame appraisals in connection with reported anger, for example, they may still have perceived other blame at some level (e.g., unconsciously?), or may have mislabeled their emotion as "anger" when it was actually mere frustration. Resolving these issues requires the development of more valid measures indicating the presence of appraisals and emotions. Even then, the problem of temporal resolution still remains, making it difficult to establish, for example, whether any implicit tendency toward other-blame genuinely preceded and activated the associated implicitly detected anger response. Some theorists (e.g., Scherer, 1993) believe that neurological measures may ultimately permit such precision, but current conceptual formulations of appraisals and emotion have not been convincingly located in particular topographic regions within the brain (e.g., Barrett & Wager, 2006), let alone tracked in real time.

Without evidence of these kinds, the belief that emotion requires prior appraisal begins to seem more like an article of faith than an empirically substantiated hypothesis (e.g., Zajonc, 1984). In my view, clinging on to appraisal necessity accounts is partly motivated by subscription to the cognitive fallacy outlined previously. Indeed, cognitive theories typically reframe psychological explanations in terms of what information is required by the mental system in order to select the appropriate response. When this metaphor is not taken too literally, it often remains relatively harmless. However, it risks ironing out differences between causal processes that depend on perception, attention, interpretation, and rationalization, and deflects emphasis from any energetic or interpersonal processes driving emotional engagement. In what sense do people really arrive at a conclusion about a transaction's relational meaning before the emotion process begins? What kind of entity is the core relational theme that supposedly coordinates emotional response if its meaning is not represented explicitly even to the person holding it? Indeed, does the unconscious form of other-blame apparently associated with anger amount to anything more than the implicit communicative meaning of the emotion itself? Do I really need to have arrived at the conclusion that someone else is to blame, before I can enter the relational blaming mode that we usually refer to as anger? These questions might equally be directed at computer models using rules or algorithms to extract meaning from situational input in order to generate appropriate emotions.

Emotions Convey Relational Meanings: Communicative Approaches

Another way to explain associations between relational meanings and emotions is to argue that one function of some or all emotions is to communicate relational meanings to others. In this view, anger is an act of blaming rather than a response to perceiving someone else as to blame for some unwanted event. There are even occasions when anger is adopted self-consciously as a strategic move to direct or redirect blame. We may put on a show of being angry in order to deny an accusation. However, more commonly, an angry orientation develops moment by moment in response to unfolding pressures from the interpersonal environment and is experienced as authentic rather than dissimulated. At a more general level, becoming emotional communicates appraisals about what is happening to others even when the emotional person has not personally arrived at those appraisals in advance.

In line with these ideas, Parkinson (2001a) suggested that anger occurs relatively commonly among drivers partly because the usual face-to-face channels for indicating disapproval do not work in their usual way in traffic situations. If anger serves the function of communicating blame, then it should persist or intensify until the other person gets the message. However, when driving, the other person is usually some distance away and insulated from vocal signals both by the vehicle's shell and by the background noise from other vehicles. Furthermore, given competing demands on attention, the other driver may not even be looking in the right direction to pick up any transmitted visual signal. To get through to them, it is necessary to escalate your angry presentation using other means such as honking the horn or getting so close to the other car that you can no longer be ignored. To the other driver, such acts may seem disproportionate even if the misdemeanor is acknowledged. Thus, the second driver's reaction will often be intensified and will face similar problems getting back to the first driver. Consistent with such an account, Parkinson (2001a) reported data indicating that factors relating to the desire to communicate anger and delay in perceived receipt of anger communication predicted anger intensity even when effects of other-blame appraisals were statistically removed.

Leary, Landel, and Patton (1996) obtained analogous findings for embarrassment rather than anger. In their study, participants recorded their own rendition of the cheesy ballad "Feelings." Those given an opportunity to communicate their subsequent embarrassment ended up less embarrassed especially when the experimenter had clearly registered their expression of this emotion. Embarrassment seemed to become unnecessary once it had served the function of indicating to the audience that the singer was aware of the limitations of the performance.

Turning from the communicator to the recipient of emotional presentations, research into "social referencing" demonstrates that posed facial expressions can regulate another person's behavior toward an object. For example, Sorce and colleagues (1985) placed 1-year-old toddlers (individually) at the opposite side of a visual cliff (a high step covered with thick glass) from their mothers, who had been instructed to show either a fear expression or a smile on their faces. About three quarters of infants ventured over the apparent precipice if their mother was smiling, but none crossed if their mother put on a fear face. Thus, expressing fear indicates to someone else that an object is dangerous whereas displaying happiness conveys safety.

Many of these communicative effects may be explained by arguing that people use explicit verbal and nonverbal symbols strategically to communicate appraisals to others. For example, we may pull an "angry" face or say that we are angry as a way of warning someone else to back down. In such cases, the other person's understanding of the meaning and implications of (prototypical) anger allows him or her to anticipate how the episode is likely to unfold and make appropriate adjustments to behavior. In other words, actors may draw on shared understandings in order to influence others using emotion presentation. However, this process need not be preplanned. Because the roles of communicator and message recipient apply equally to both parties to the interaction, their respective emotional stances develop in continuous attunement to each other rather than being cooked up in advance by either party.

If emotions are communications, why are these communications delivered emotionally rather than as simple verbal statements? One answer is that emotional presentation carries certain advantages such as permitting messages that are dynamically attuned to events that unfold in real time (using continuous movements of the body and face). Further, emotion conveys the person's level of involvement directly because of its embodiment (Sarbin, 1986). Finally, emotion can address issues that cannot easily be resolved using a simple logic of argumentation. Emotions are oriented to relational issues concerning which there is no defensible right answer: issues of taste, faith, prejudice, right and wrong, or where different social norms are brought into conflict (Averill, 1980).

For example, a female participant in one of our studies described the following emotional incident:

> One of my best friends was arguing with some of our male friends about which place in Portugal was best. It was very petty. Our male friends were winding her up by disagreeing with her. They were joking about, but she took it seriously and was getting heated. She shouted at them and called them abusive names. I said to her, smiling, that there was no need and it was just a joke. She got angry and wouldn't speak to me. It was like we were 5 years old.

Although it may not be immediately obvious, the narrator of this story is describing a time when she felt intensely guilty (at a level of 9 on a scale running from 0 to 10). However, her rating of self-accountability was at 0. So if the experienced guilt did not relate to appraising herself as personally responsible for her friend's suffering, how did it come about? The narrator describes trying to placate her friend with reason, but this only induces anger. From her friend's perspective, the issue is not that the narrator is to blame for the taunting she is suffering but that she appears to be siding with her male tormentors rather than with herself as a female friend. The friend's evident suffering and the implied blame conveyed by her anger coupled with the narrator's desire to put things right with this friend ultimately produces a guilty response. Guilt serves as an emergent tactic for repairing the relationship with the close friend and reestablishes their solidarity based on a shared gender identity (despite other possible allegiances).

More generally, our recent studies demonstrate that people sometimes report guilt in response to being blamed by a close other even in the absence of reported self-accountability (Parkinson & Illingworth, 2009), helping to explain the dissociations between appraisal and emotion described earlier. The emotion serves to communicate an identity claim to someone else rather than simply reflect an individual apprehension of relational meaning (Parkinson, 1995).

According to the communicative account, emotions and relational meanings are intrinsically interconnected but not because individuals need to understand the personal significance of what is happening in order to generate an appropriate emotion (cf. Lazarus, 1984). Relational meanings are just that: meanings that characterize relations between people (and between people and objects). They may or may not be registered by the person before, during, or after getting emotional. Often the message is clear to others but not always. Further, the way the message is delivered is highly context dependent and uses whatever channels are available and appropriate to the current encounter (thus explaining the lack of structural coherence of response components). In all cases, however, relations between people (or between people and objects) are modified when someone gets emotional.

Emergence of Meaningful Emotions: Transactional Approaches

Both appraisal theories and communicative theories tend to focus more on the relational meanings associated with emotions than the factors that directly impact on response components (such as facial expressions, bodily changes, action impulses). Appraisal content theories typically assume that response components are activated by implicit or explicit processes of meaning apprehension without specifying precise mechanisms. Correspondingly, communicative theories typically assume that the voice, face, and body are channels whereby social influence is exerted but say relatively little about how these channels are selected or serve their communicative functions.

Transactional approaches, by contrast, specifically attempt to explain response components and their interrelations. Instead of investigating the meanings associated with emotions, they focus on how patterns of responses are pieced together, potentially leading to meaningful emotion syndromes. The basic idea is that coordinated environmental inputs bring low-level response processes online simultaneously (e.g., Ortony & Turner, 1990). Further, mutual constraints imposed by components on one another leads to emergent patterning in real time (e.g., Fogel, 1993). For example, try raising the corners of your lips into a smile while opening your eyes as wide as they will go. Repeated experience of the consequently co-occurring components leads to the development of associations between them (Camras, 1992). Thus, patterned response syndromes emerge from bottom-up processes without any executive integrating mechanism or prior extraction of meaning (e.g., Fogel, 1993; Parkinson, 2001b).

Such ideas are not entirely alien to appraisal theory. For example, Smith and Kirby (2000) argue that emotions are sometimes activated by low-level associations, raising the possibility that separate emotion components are triggered individually as conditioned responses to different events in the environment, instead of being coordinated by higher level meaning structures. However, their model still maintains that any activated meaning component needs to be integrated within a broader core relational theme before the emotion is generated.

Scherer's (e.g., 2001) theory comes closer to the dynamic systems account outlined above. In his view, appraisal involves a rapidly cycling sequence of stimulus evaluation checks (SECs) whose complexity progressively increases (like a radar scanning for changes). In each sweep, the system first detects novelty, then intrinsic pleasantness, goal/need significance, and so on, until further downstream, assessments of event aspects such as norm compatibility are made. In addition, Scherer assumes that the emotion itself develops cumulatively as these checks run off, with response components consolidating as the appraisals become more complex over time. In other words, although meaning still comes first in Scherer's model, it need not be integrated into a coherent relational pattern before the emotion process begins. Emotions are not generated as the end result of some metaphorical decision process but, rather, emerge flexibly in response to the vicissitudes of unfolding situations.

However, even Scherer's model may be overrestrictive in its specification of the structure and content of mental mediation. The SECs follow a fixed sequence, and each picks up an abstractly defined feature of the current situation before outputting an appropriate functional adjustment to the individual's physical and mental system. Thus, the emotion process is articulated as a series of discrete hierarchically organized states based on interchanges between the individual and a separable environment.

A more radical transactional approach would argue that emotions require no extraction of abstract information from unfolding situations even at this piecemeal level. In such a view, there is no necessary consistency in the mechanisms of information registration or in the nature of their output to the emotion process. Local and specific adjustments in the course of action are made in continuous attunement to the unfolding context within which action is embedded. Further, the impact of context on action does not entirely depend on its registration by predefined appraisals or stimulus evaluation checks. Instead of emotions being guided by central mechanisms detecting classes of relevant cues, they adjust responsively to incoming feedback whose nature depends on the characteristics of the current situated action. For example, face-to face interactions involve mutual attunements of facial and gestural movements over time (e.g., Bernieri, Reznick, & Rosenthal, 1988; Grammer, Kruck, & Magnusson,

1998), which may lead to emergent complementary or contrasting emotional stances.

Distinguishing Approaches to Emotion, Meaning, and Response Coordination

This section summarizes distinctions between the four approaches to emotion and relational meaning set out in the preceding sections to pave the way for the integrative approach presented in the following section.

First, *attributional approaches* argue that the association of "emotions" with relational meaning is a largely contingent matter. Perceivers infer emotions in themselves partly on the basis of information about their relation to the current situation. The integrity of differentiated emotional response syndromes is a perceptual phenomenon telling us about how "emotions" are represented and not (directly) about how putative emotion-relevant processes interrelate in reality. Emotional meaning is imposed on fortuitously associated processes that may or may not implicate apprehension of relational meaning.

By contrast, *appraisal-content approaches* assume that emotions are coordinated responses to detected or inferred relational meanings. Implicitly or explicitly recognizing the particular personal significance of a current transaction leads to the activation of an integrated response syndrome designed to address the identified challenge or threat. Outputs are organized on the basis of agendas set by appraisals. Thus, relational meaning takes priority in the generation and patterning of emotional responses.

Communicative approaches emphasize the priority of the social functions of emotions, and their orientation to actual or imagined effects on someone else. Although emotions convey relational meanings to others, they need not be based on any prior apprehension of these meanings. What drives emotion is the unfolding, coconstructed, relational agenda rather than how that relational agenda is appraised by any individual interactant.

Finally, according to *transactional approaches*, the coherence of emotional response syndromes emerges bottom-up rather than being imposed top-down by coordinative meaning-based processes. Separate emotion components adjust online to changing local demands and to the effects of other components. Response patterns depend both on parallel effects of different aspects of the unfolding, structured situation and on the mutual constraints imposed by component processes. Although these emergent response patterns are meaningfully related to the practical and social environment, their relational meaning need not be registered at any level by the individual undergoing the emotion.

Emotion As Relation Alignment

None of the approaches to emotion, emotional meaning, and response coordination mentioned in previous sections offer a comprehensive account of these interrelated phenomena that applies across all circumstances. However, each can explain certain kinds of emotion-related phenomena in delimited situations. One problem facing any all-purpose emotion theory is precisely the need to accommodate a very wide range of processes, so that different explanations apply differentially depending on other factors. However, the points of convergence across different emotion theories suggest that an overarching approach might at least orient researchers and modelers to the possible connections between separate sectors of the bigger picture.

With this aim in mind, I want to argue that all phenomena falling under the conventional heading of "emotion" are examples of *relation alignment* (see also Frijda, 1986). Emotions align relations between the emotional person and the thing that their emotion is about (the "object" of the emotion, which is often also another person), between the emotional person and other people who are also oriented to the emotional object, and between the respective person–object relations of the emotional person and these other people. For example, my anger about your insult not only aligns the relations between me and you and between you, me, and your insult, but also presents my orientation to your behavior as insulting to others present, thus aligning their relations with you, me, and the insult.

The approaches distinguished in previous sections of this chapter focus selectively on different aspects of this relation alignment process. Attribution approaches focus on how the emotional person uses relational information to infer that the episode is an instance of anger. Appraisal approaches focus on how relations between the emotional person and the emotion object are evaluated and interpreted. Communicative approaches focus on how the emotional person's orientation toward the emotion object influences the orientations of others who are present. Finally, transactional approaches focus on how specific aspects of the relational situation activate the various responses that constitute and communicate the emotion.

Integrating these aspects requires attention to how transactional information is processed by the emotional person, how responses are generated, how meaning is attributed to these responses by the emotional person and others present, and how the relational process is regulated by the emotional person's goals and by online feedback from others. Additionally, explanations for the emergence of interconnections between these processes need to focus not only on the real-time unfolding of the transaction but also on the process of individual development over a much longer timescale.

In particular, it is worth considering how emotions come to carry relational meanings as babies develop into children and, ultimately, adults. Many emotions start out already having communicative meanings, at least to those who respond to them. Early life involves an intense relationship in which the infant's smallest push or pull, glance, or blink solicits direct and often exaggerated immediate feedback from the caregiver (e.g., Gergely & Watson, 1999). States of communion and breaks in interpersonal contact carry relational significance that registers in others' responses, and these responses in turn regulate ongoing emotion presentation. Children too young to understand concepts of self or accountability rapidly come to engage with others in ways that bear close resemblance to more articulated appraisal-relevant emotions.

For example, Reddy (2000) observed 3-month-old infants producing "coy smiles" as common responses to sustained attentional contact with mothers, experimenters, or themselves as reflected in a mirror. This pattern of movement involved turning away the eyes or head while a smile developed. Uninformed observers of the videotape spontaneously labeled this reaction as coyness, bashfulness, or embarrassment (Draghi-Lorenz, Reddy, & Morris, 2005), and indeed the observed dynamic pattern of facial expression corresponds closely to the specifications of an adult embarrassment display outlined by Keltner (1995).

These specific movements serve both practical and communicative functions. Turning away immediately breaks attentional contact, thus discontinuing exposure to the other person's uncomfortably persistent gaze. Furthermore, the other person can easily pick up the signal that attentional contact is no longer desired. Finally, the simultaneous smile communicates that withdrawal should not be seen as undermining the continuing affiliative relationship between caregiver and infant.

One interpretation of these findings is that infants regulate other people's attention using innately programmed displays. However, it seems more likely that the pattern of adjustments quickly consolidates as a function of coregulated activity between infant and caregiver in accordance with transactional approaches. Withdrawal of attention is directly reinforced and rapidly learned. Smiling rapidly becomes attuned to certain modes of interpersonal contact. The specific combination of these movements arises partly because of the simultaneous presence of communion and arousal-regulating needs, and partly because of sensitivity to feedback from the caregiver.

Later in development, such patterns of response also take on a more abstract meaning based on cultural representations and norms. They come to stand for specific hypercognized situations in which others' attention is unwanted. In many Western societies, for example, displays of this kind are considered appropriate and legitimate when some temporary faux pas has been committed or there is an unintended disruption of a performance that should have been more poised and fluid. The message transmitted to others is an elaboration or articulation of the original functional basis of the patterned activity. As well as maintaining an affiliative relationship despite a temporary disruption of attentional exposure, it serves to communicate an acknowledgment of faulty but correctable conduct. Only at this stage does the facial response may become coordinated with articulated relational meaning structures (e.g., appraisals).

Communicating embarrassment does not necessarily involve producing the precisely timed movements associated with coy smiles. Depending on the mode of contact with the other person and the channels available for communication, it may involve other forms of withdrawal from public gaze or more explicit indications of emotional state using language (as in Leary, Landel, & Patton's 1996 study). However, the core meaning of these relational patterns is laid down at an early age as a function of direct experience with attention-regulating alignments of relations between infants and caregivers.

The fact that adult embarrassment is represented in terms of more basic dynamics of affiliation and attention regulation means that people may sometimes misperceive their own experience in terms of physical reactions that have actually not occurred. They know that they are in a relational mode corresponding to embarrassment and therefore assume that its conventionalized nonverbal signal pattern is also present (cf. Gilovich, Savitsky, & Medvec, 1998). For example, most participants in Reisenzein et al.'s (2006) study of facial expressions accompanying surprise reported showing the stereotypical surprise expression despite its actual absence (cf. Gilovich, Savitsky, & Medvec, 1998). Thus, at least part of the coherence of response patterning in emotions may depend on perception (or somatovisceral illusion; Cacioppo et al., 1993) rather than reality (e.g., Barrett, 2006; Russell, 2003).

According to the relation alignment approach, emotions can be activated as emergent patterns of prereflective, coregulated activity (in accordance with transactionalist approaches) or as articulated (though often automatized) means of making identity claims or communicating appraisals (in accordance with the communicative approach). The latter kind of emotion partly derives its form from cultural representations, and its enactment is shaped by cultural norms and prescriptions, but still bears the trace of the more basic dynamics of its original form. Further, the development of articulated, culturally drenched emotion episodes does not render prereflective emotions obsolete. Adults continue to experience emotions in the prereflective mode throughout their lives.

What role do attributions and appraisals play in the relation alignment process? First, an emotion's interpersonal effects depend on the meaning attributed to each of its response components. The script-based representations applied to a facial expression or a gesture partly determine the other's expectations about the future trajectory of the emotional person's line of action and shape interpersonal responses. For example, interpreting your gaze as an angry stare may induce me to back off or to adopt an antagonistic stance intended to make you back down. Correspondingly, response components specified in scripted representations may be used to convey the emotional meaning and to encourage the other to respond to one's emotion presentation as an instance of anger. Thus, the communicative power of an emotion display may derive from its attributed meaning as well as from the direct adjustments it may provoke at the transactional level.

Turning to appraisal, entering a mode of relation alignment often depends on the appraised meaning of the precipitating situation. Believing at some level that the other person is to blame is one of the most frequent reasons for blaming him or her in an angry way. However, other-blame may consolidate gradually over the course of an unfolding transaction instead of coordinating responses wholly in advance. Further, there are times when relations are angry because of the coregulated mutual adjustments of two parties in interaction, neither of whom registers other-blame at any level until afterward, if at all.

Conclusions: Meaning and Emotion

Although each emotion has a distinctive relational meaning, this does not imply that an individual person needs to represent this meaning internally before getting emotional. Advance appraisal is simply one of the routes whereby the emotional process can be activated or modified. Indeed, as argued elsewhere (Parkinson, 1997), the evidence for this route being central and primary is mainly based on self-report studies in which participants have to account for their emotional experiences, or make them seem reasonable to the experimenter. Relational meanings may also emerge from an ongoing transaction with the practical and social environment without being integrated by either party to the exchange. Individuals may represent their experience in emotional terms in the absence of a coordinated response pattern, and emotional representation can affect subsequent processes of regulation and communication in emotionally relevant ways. Finally, emotions may also be used to convey relational meanings to others.

Linking all of these ideas is the notion that emotions serve to align or realign relations with objects and other people. Anger is a struggle against some resistant force or an act of blaming an agent of some kind. Embarrassment is a means of deflecting interpersonal attention without breaking contact irrevocably, or a communicated acknowledgment of faulty performance. In each case, arriving at the relational stance that achieves such alignments need not involve individually recognizing the need for alignment either in advance or during the encounter. Instead, the emotion process may respond moment-by-moment to the unfolding pulls and pushes of the dynamic environment. People can get backed into emotional corners or dragged forward by the force of events and can take on emotional positions for more strategic ends.

Implications for Modeling

In a realistic emotion model, the agent needs to be embedded in a continually responsive environment and to be oriented from the outset to the relational positions of other agents (see also Gratch, 2008). Further, the emotion should be specified as part of the process of active adjustment to other agents and the environment, and not simply as an indirect side-effect of these transactions. In principle, much of this may be achievable by implementing interlocking dynamic feedback systems at several levels, and by specifying when and how top-down monitoring and regulation need to kick in or out. The nature of this regulation may be shaped by cultural descriptions of, and prescriptions about, emotional state and is open to modification as a function of learning.

Alternatively, an extended appraisal-based model incorporating additional dimensions of relational meaning and conditional context-based rules specifying alternative prerequisites for similar emotions may be sufficient for certain purposes, especially if there is no requirement for real-time responsiveness. At one level, there is no doubt that it is possible to specify emotions in terms of cues that shape their emergence and rules whereby those cues are transformed into meanings. However, it is important to acknowledge that real-world embodied emotions are often attuned to anticipated consequences in addition to unfolding and responsive dynamic feedback and that the extraction of relational meaning does not always represent the sole driving force behind the emotion process.

References

Averill, J. R. (1980). A constructivist view of emotion. In R. Plutchik & H. Kellerman (Eds.), *Theories of emotion* (pp. 305–340). New York: Academic Press.

Bard, K., & Cornelius, R. (Eds.) (2007). *Emotion researcher: The definition issue* (Vol. 22, 1–2). Poughkeepsie, NY: International Society for Research on Emotions.

Barrett, L. F. (2006). Solving the emotion paradox: Categorisation and the experience of emotion. *Personality and Social Psychology Review, 10,* 20–46.

Barrett, L. F., & Wager, T. D. (2006). The structure of emotion: Evidence from neuroimaging studies. *Current Directions in Psychological Science, 15,* 79–83.

Bedford, E. (1957). Emotions. *Proceedings of the Aristotelian Society, 57,* 281–304.

Bernieri, F., Reznick, J. S., & Rosenthal, R. (1988). Synchrony, pseudo-synchrony, and dissynchrony: Measuring the entrainment process in mother-infant interactions. *Journal of Personality and Social Psychology, 54,* 243–353.

Cacioppo, J. T., Klein, D. J., Berntson, G. G., & Hatfield, E. (1993). The psychophysiology of emotion. In M. Lewis & J. M. Haviland (Eds.), *Handbook of emotions* (pp. 119–142). New York: Guilford.

Camras, L. A. (1992). Expressive development and basic emotions. *Cognition and Emotion, 6,* 269–283.

Dewey, J. (1895). The theory of emotion II: The significance of emotional attitudes. *Psychological Review, 2,* 13–32.

Draghi-Lorenz, R., Reddy, V., & Morris, P. (2005). Young infants can be perceived as shy, coy, bashful, embarrassed. *Infant and Child Development, 14,* 63–83.

Edwards, D. (1999). Emotion discourse. *Cultural Psychology, 5,* 271–291.

Fogel, A. (1993). *Developing through relationships: Origins of communication, self, and culture.* Chicago: University of Chicago Press.

Frijda, N. H. (1986). *The emotions.* Cambridge: Cambridge University Press.

Frijda, N. H. (2005). Emotion experience. *Cognition and Emotion, 19,* 473–497.

Gergely, G., & Watson, J. S. (1999). Early socio-emotional development: Contingency perception and the social-biofeedback model. In P. Rochat (Ed.), *Early social cognition: Understanding others in the first months of life* (pp. 101–136). Mahwah, NJ: Lawrence Erlbaum Associates.

Gilovich, T., Savitsky, K., & Medvec, V. H. (1998). The Illusion of Transparency: Biased assessments of others' ability to read one's emotional states. *Journal of Personality and Social Psychology, 75,* 332–346.

Grammer, K., Kruck, K. B., & Magnusson, M. S. (1998). The courtship dance: Patterns of nonverbal synchronization in opposite-sex encounters. *Journal of Nonverbal Behavior, 22,* 3–29.

Gratch, J. (2008). True emotion vs. social intentions in nonverbal communication: Towards a synthesis for embodied conversational agents. In I. Wachsmuth & G. Knoblich (Eds.), *Lecture notes in artificial intelligence 4930: Modelling communication with robots and virtual humans* (pp. 181–197). Berlin: Springer.

James, W. (1898). *The principles of psychology* (Vol. 2). London: Macmillan.

Keltner, D. (1995). Signs of appeasement: Evidence for the distinct displays of embarrassment, amusement, and shame. *Journal of Personality and Social Psychology, 68,* 441–454.

Kleinginna, P. R., & Kleinginna, A. M. (1981). A categorized list of emotion definitions, with suggestions for a consensual definition. *Motivation and Emotion, 5,* 345–379.

Kuppens, P., Van Mechelen, I., Smits, D. J. M., & De Boeck, P. (2003). The appraisal basis of anger: Specificity, necessity and sufficiency of components. *Emotion*, 3, 254–269.

Lambie, J. A., & Marcel, A. J. (2002). Consciousness and the varieties of emotion experience: A theoretical framework. *Psychological Review*, *109*, 219–259.

Lazarus, R. S. (1984). On the primacy of cognition. *American Psychologist*, 39, 124–129.

Lazarus, R. S. (1991). Emotion and adaptation. New York: Oxford University Press.

Lazarus, R. S., & Alfert, E. (1964). Short circuiting of threat by experimentally altering cognitive appraisal. *Journal of Abnormal and Social Psychology*, *69*, 195–205.

Leary, M. R, Landel, J. L., & Patton, K. M. (1996). The motivated expression of embarrassment following a self-presentational predicament. *Journal of Personality*, *64*, 619–636.

Levy, R. (1973). *Tahitians*. Chicago: Chicago University Press.

Mauss, I. B., Levenson, R. W., McCarter, L., Wilhelm, F. L., & Gross, J. J. (2005). The tie that binds? Coherence among emotion experience, behavior, and physiology. *Emotion*, 5, 175–190.

Nezlek, J. B., Vansteelandt, K., Van Mechelen, I., & Kuppens, P. (2008). Appraisal-emotion relationships in everyday life. *Emotion*, 8, 145–150.

Ortony, A., Clore, G., & Collins, A. (1988). *The Cognitive Structure of Emotions*. Melbourne, Australia: Cambridge University Press.

Ortony, A., & Turner, T. J. (1990). What's basic about basic emotions? *Psychological Review*, 97, 315–331.

Parkinson, B. (1995). *Ideas and realities of emotion*. London: Routledge.

Parkinson, B. (1997). Untangling the appraisal-emotion connection. *Personality and Social Psychology Review*, *1*, 62–79.

Parkinson, B. (1998). What we think about when we think about emotions. *Cognition and Emotion*, *12*, 615–624.

Parkinson, B. (1999). Relations and dissociations between appraisal and emotion ratings in reasonable and unreasonable anger and guilt. *Cognition and Emotion*, *13*, 347–385.

Parkinson, B. (2001a). Anger on and off the road. *British Journal of Psychology*, 92, 507–526.

Parkinson, B. (2001b). Putting appraisal in context. In K. R. Scherer, A. Schorr, & T. Johnstone (Eds.), *Appraisal processes in emotion: Theory, research, application* (pp. 173–186). New York: Oxford University Press.

Parkinson, B. (2008). Emotions in direct and remote social interaction: Getting through the spaces between us. *Computers in Human Behavior*, *24*, 1510–1529.

Parkinson, B., Fischer, A., & Manstead, A. S. R. (2005). *Emotion in social relations: Cultural, group, and interpersonal processes*. Philadelphia: Psychology Press.

Parkinson, B., & Illingworth, S. (2009). Guilt in response to blame from others. *Cognition and Emotion*, *23*, 1589–1614.

Parkinson, B., Roper, A., & Simons, G. (2009). Appraisal ratings in diary reports of reasonable and unreasonable anger. *European Journal of Social Psychology*, 39, 82–87.

Reddy, V. (2000). Coyness in early infancy. *Developmental Science*, 3, 186–192.

Reisenzein, R. (2000). Exploring the strength of association between the components of emotion syndromes: The case of surprise. *Cognition and Emotion*, *14*, 1–38.

Reisenzein, R., Bördgen, S., Holtbernd, T., & Matz, D. (2006). Evidence for strong dissociation between emotion and facial displays: The case of surprise. *Journal of Personality and Social Psychology*, *91*, 295–315.

Rimé, B., Philippot, P., & Cisamolo, D. (1990). Social schemata of peripheral changes in emotion. *Journal of Personality and Social Psychology*, 59, 38–49.

Roseman, I. J. (1979, September). *Cognitive aspects of emotion and emotional behavior.* Paper presented at the 87th Annual Convention of the American Psychological Association, New York City.

Roseman, I. J. (2001). A model of appraisal in the emotion system: Integrating theory, research, and applications. In K. R. Scherer, A. Schorr, & T. Johnstone (Eds.), *Appraisal processes in emotion: Theory, methods, research* (pp. 68–91). London: Oxford University Press.

Roseman, I. J., & Evdokas, A. (2004). Appraisals cause experienced emotions: Experimental evidence. *Cognition and Emotion*, *18*, 1–28.

Russell, J. A. (2003). Core affect and the psychological construction of emotion. *Psychological Review*, *110*, 145–172.

Russell, J. A., & Fehr, B. (1994). Fuzzy concepts in a fuzzy hierarchy: Varieties of anger. *Journal of Personality and Social Psychology*, *67*, 186–205.

Sarbin, T. R. (1986). Emotion and act: Roles and rhetoric. In R. Harré (Ed.), *The social construction of emotions* (pp. 83–97). Oxford, UK: Blackwell.

Sartre, J.-P. (1962). Sketch for a Theory of the Emotions, trans. *P. Mairet. London: Methuen.*

Schachter, S. (1964). The interaction of cognitive and physiological determinants of emotional state. In L. Festinger (Ed.), *Advances in experimental social psychology* (Vol. 1, pp. 49–80). New York: Academic Press.

Schachter, S., & Singer, J. E. (1962). Cognitive, social, and physiological determinants of emotional state. *Psychological Review*, *69*, 379–399.

Scherer, K. R. (1993). Neuroscience projections to current debates in emotion psychology. *Cognition and Emotion*, *7*, 1–41.

Scherer, K. R. (2001). The nature and study of appraisal: A review of the issues. In K. R. Scherer, A. Schorr, & T. Johnstone (Eds.), *Appraisal processes in emotion: Theory, methods, research* (pp. 369–392). New York: Oxford University Press.

Smith, C. A., & Ellsworth, P. C. (1985). Patterns of cognitive appraisal in emotion. *Journal of Personality and Social Psychology*, *48*, 813–838.

Smith, C. A., & Kirby, L. D. (2000). Consequences require antecedents: Toward a process model of emotion elicitation. In J. Forgas (Ed.), *Feeling and thinking: The role of affect in social cognition* (pp. 83–106). New York: Cambridge University Press.

Smith, C. A., & Kirby, L. D. (2004). Appraisal as a pervasive determinant of anger. *Emotion*, *4*, 133–138.

Smith, C. A., & Lazarus, R. S. (1993). Appraisal components, core relational themes, and the emotions. *Cognition and Emotion*, *7*, 233–269.

Sorce, J. F., Emde, R. N., Campos, J., & Klinnert, M. D. (1985). Maternal emotional signaling: Its effect on the visual cliff behavior of 1 year olds. *Developmental Psychology*, *21*, 195–200.

Zajonc, R. B. (1984). On the primacy of affect. *American Psychologist*, *39*, 117–123.

3

Challenge, Threat, and Social Influence in Digital Immersive Virtual Environments

Jim Blascovich

Social influence is at the center of the field of social psychology. Social psychologists seek understanding of how and in what ways people are influenced by the presence of others, whether face-to-face (i.e., actual), thought about (i.e., implied), or even conjured (i.e., imagined). Over a century of theory and research has led to an understanding of fundamental social influence effects on people's thoughts, feelings, and motives.

Until relatively recently, very little attention has been directed toward determining whether the actual, implied, and imagined presence of others have similar or distinctive effects on people. However, for those of us interested in the social psychology of virtual social interaction, such determinations are critical. In this chapter, we begin to remedy this deficit by marrying a theoretical model of human motivation, including affective and cognitive components, developed wholly outside of virtual technology–mediated social interaction with a structural model of social influence developed wholly within it.

Over the last two decades, the "biopsychosocial [BPS] model of challenge and threat" (Blascovich, 2008; Blascovich & Mendes; 2000; Blascovich & Tomaka, 1996) has become an increasingly powerful causal explanatory model of motivation as the BPS itself has become more elaborated, associated neurophysiological indexes of the banner motivational states have been validated, and evidence supporting the model has accrued. Similarly, over the last decade, the threshold model of social influence within immersive virtual environments (Blascovich et al., 2002a, 2002b; Blascovich & Bailenson, 2011) has proven effective via its elaboration, testing, and application within digital immersive virtual environments. This chapter describes and reviews both theoretical frameworks and describes how both models can inform the development of digital immersive virtual social environments.

Much work in social psychology and related fields during the last quarter or so of the 20th century focused on important but relatively narrowly defined and operationalized cognitive processes underlying hypothetical social psychological constructs such as attitudes, the self, decision making, stereotypes, and so on. Importantly, a major conclusion that can be drawn from work on social cognition is that much of social influence is driven by so-called unconscious or automatic processes (cf. Hassin, Uleman, & Bargh, 2005).

Arguably, during the ascendance of social cognition in social psychology, work on emotion and motivation took a back seat. However, more recent times have witnessed a reemergence of work on emotion and motivation including among social cognition researchers (e.g., Elliot, 2008; Mackie & Smith, 1998), indicating the importance of the latter constructs for understanding social influence.

Our work on social motivation and on social influence within immersive virtual environments has led us to conclude that understanding social interactions within either physical or digital virtual environments, especially digitally immersive ones, requires not only knowledge of social cognitive processes but also of motivational and emotional ones. Furthermore, we have found it important to recognize that cognition, motivation, and emotion do not operate independently as separate, parallel processes but, rather, in a temporally parallel and interactive fashion in almost if not all psychosocial situations.

We believe that the most pragmatic perspective for understanding social influence processes within (and outside of) digital immersive virtual environments is to determine and understand what propels people to act in the ways that they do. Hence, we focus on people's "motivation" to act, but without filtering out the effects of emotional and cognitive processes on such motivation.

The Biopsychosocial Model of Challenge and Threat

The biopsychosocial model of challenge and threat fits within the more generic approach and avoidance category of motivation theories (Elliot, 2006). Elliot and Trash (2002) define approach motivation classically, that is, as the energization of behavior directed toward positive or desirable stimuli or situations, and avoidance motivation as the energization of behavior directed away from negative or undesirable stimuli or situations. Blascovich (2008) points out that there are two other logical possibilities for the combination of energization and direction, including energization or movement toward negative stimuli and energization or movement away from positive stimuli.

What may energize people toward or away from hedonically mismatched situations (i.e., movement away from positive stimuli or movement toward negative stimuli) has more to do with the value of long-range (i.e., distal or superordinate) goals rather than the value of near-term (i.e., proximal or subordinate) goals. To be more specific, movement toward a positive long-range goal (e.g., getting a certain job) often requires approaching a negative subordinate proximal goal (e.g., undergoing taxing training). And, movement away from a negative short-term goal (e.g., losing one's driving license) can require avoiding a positive near-term goal (e.g., drinking before driving). The point is that motivational hierarchies must be taken into account; that is, the valence of near-term goals can be at odds with the valence of long-term goals and delayed gratification can prevail.

The BPS model was originally developed to explain people's performances in potentially stressful or threatening performance situations. The model specifies that *challenge* motivation occurs when a person's evaluated resources outweigh evaluated situational demands and *threat* occurs when evaluated situational demands outweigh a person's evaluated resources. Neither of these evaluations need be conscious or deliberate; that is, they can occur automatically or unconsciously.

In order to reach a valued superordinate or distal goal, an individual may "approach" subordinate goals (e.g., exams) that may be threatening even though the individual's evaluated resources do not outweigh evaluated situational demands. In such a situation, the individual is motivated to approach a negative performance situation because the superordinate goal is perceived as valuable enough for the individual to approach a necessary but negative subordinate goal and perform in what he or she evaluates as threatening situations.

According to the BPS model, both challenge and threat can motivate psychological, physiological, and overt physical movement toward a goal-relevant situation. Additionally, however, threat includes psychological, physiological, and sometimes physical movement away from a goal. Because both challenge and threat motivation, as the BPS model defines them, involve approach, they can be thought of as ends on a bipolar continuum anchored by pure approach at one end and equivalent approach/avoidance on the other. So defined, challenge maps onto approach motivation and threat maps onto approach–avoidance motivation.

For the BPS model, task disengagement is regarded as avoidance motivation.

As its nomenclature suggests, the BPS model integrates processes across three levels of analysis: social-environmental, psychological, and biological. At the social-environmental level, the BPS model takes into account that people's motives are influenced by the actual, imagined, and/or implied presence of others interacting within the environments or contexts in which they find themselves. At the psychological level, the BPS incorporates cognitive and affective processes as well as motivational ones. At the biological level, the BPS examines the interplay between autonomic and endocrine influences on the cardiovascular system.

In sum, according to the BPS model, challenge–threat motivation is rooted in all three levels of analysis (social-environmental, psychological, and biological) including the interplay among them. Hence, challenge and threat are person/situation-evoked motivational states with affective, cognitive, and physiological antecedents and consequences.

Biological Component. The biopsychosocial model is rooted in Dienstbier's (1989) neuroendocrine theory of "physiological toughness." Reviewing animal studies, Dienstbier noted differing patterns of peripheral physiological responses, specifically cardiovascular responses, in potentially dangerous foraging situations (i.e., in the vicinities of predators) that were associated with differences in both foraging performance and long-term survival. Dienstbier delineated central nervous system–controlled peripheral neural and endocrine processes that underlie differing cardiovascular response patterns in potentially threatening but goal-relevant performance situations—one for animals that thrive during and following performance and one for animals that do not.

Dienstbier labeled the positive pattern "physiological toughness," and implied that the opposite, negative pattern is one of physiological weakness. In terms of neuroendocrine processes, both patterns involve sympathetic neural and adrenal medullary (SAM) axis activation. The SAM axis activation elevates sympathetic neural stimulation, thereby increasing heart rate (HR) as well as contractility of the left ventricle of the heart (VC), that is, how hard the left ventricle contracts to pump blood, dispersing it against the pressure of the body's vasculature. According to Dienstbier, the SAM axis causes elevations in adrenal medullary activation, resulting in increased epinephrine in the bloodstream that both increases HR and dilates the arteries, creating a decline in total peripheral vascular resistance (TPR). The SAM action results in notable increases in blood flow as indexed by cardiac output (CO).

In "physiologically weak" animals, activation of the hypothalamic pituitary adrenal (HPA) axis occurs in tandem with SAM activation. Specifically, HPA activation creates continuous adrenal cortical release of cortisol, thereby attenuating SAM effects, and sometimes actually increasing TPR and thereby decreasing CO.

Dientbier's theory, based on the interaction of the SAM and HPA axes, denoted patterns of cardiovascular responses (VC, HR, CO, and TPR) that distinguish functional and dysfunctional responses during goal-relevant task performance situations in animals. In the early and mid-1990s (see Blascovich & Mendes, 2010; Blascovich & Seery, 2007, for reviews), we experimentally determined that these patterns also clearly distinguished functionality from relative dysfunctionality in humans during goal-relevant task performance situations.

Psychological Component. At the psychological level, the BPS model is a type of appraisal theory historically rooted in Lazarus & Folkman's (1984) cognitive appraisal theory. Taking into account convincing evidence of the role of nonconscious or automatic processes or unconscious processes in "appraisals," particularly those related to affect in human behavior (cf. Blascovich & Mendes, 2000), we concluded that the determining processes were often less conscious than the label "cognitive appraisal" implied. Hence, we replaced the term "cognitive appraisal" with "evaluation" in the BPS model, a change in nomenclature that we believe has less conscious and cognitivistic connotations, and, importantly, allows for the incorporation of affective and emotional influences on motivation.

Nevertheless, it was Lazarus and Folkman's appraisal model (1984) that suggested to us that human "physiological toughness" and "weakness" involved evaluations of situational goal relevance as well as performance demands and resources. We reasoned that if resource and demand evaluations in humans were associated with Dienstbier's peripheral neurophysiological patterns of toughness and weakness responses in animals, then the biological and psychological aspects of performance motivation could be unified.

Specifically, we hypothesized that when evaluated resources meet or exceed performance demands in a goal-relevant, motivated performance situation, a positive-approach motivational state that we labeled "challenge" would result, and such individuals would exhibit the physiological toughness cardiovascular pattern identified by Dienstbier in rodents (i.e., increased HR, VC, and CO, and decreased TPR). We also hypothesized that when evaluated resources do not meet or exceed performance demands, a negative motivational state would result that we labeled "threat" and that such individuals would exhibit the physiological weakness cardiovascular pattern identified by Dienstbier (i.e., increased HR and VC, and little change or a decrease in CO and little change or an increase in TRP).

Our validational studies (e.g., Tomaka, Blascovich, Kelsey & Leiten, 1993; Tomaka, Blascovich, Kibler, & Ernst, 1997; see Blascovich & Mendes, 2010, for a review) centered on laboratory-based motivated performance tasks that are goal relevant and task engaging and that require instrumental cognitive responses, in other words, active coping tasks (Obrist, 1981). The validational studies included vocal serial subtraction (i.e., "mental arithmetic") and giving speeches, typical "stressors" used by psychological stress researchers. We performed correlational, experimental, and predictive validational studies while recording cardiovascular response patterns involving electrocardiographic, impedance cardiographic, and hemodynamic (i.e., blood pressure) measurement technologies described elsewhere (see Blascovich & Seery, 2007, for details). This paradigm allowed us to assess the cardiovascular response patterns (i.e., changes from baseline resting levels) of VC, HR, CO, and TPR based on Dienstbier's model in humans (see Figure 3.1).

The results of all of our validational experiments (more than a dozen) verified the patterns, thereby confirming that the challenge and threat motivational states delineated in the BPS involve the same or, at least, very similar neuroendocrine processes as described in Dienstbier's model. Importantly, in the context of this chapter, these neurophysiological indexes provide important methodological advantages. They are impervious to measurement errors associated with self-report measures such as impression management concerns. They have the advantages of being continuous and collected online in real time. In addition, these indexes can and have been used to test motivational aspects of a wide range of social influence theories, not only informing these theories, but also providing further convergent validation of the indexes themselves (see Blascovich and Mendes, 2010, for a review).

Figure 3.2 formally depicts the major components of the BPS model. The model summarizes the

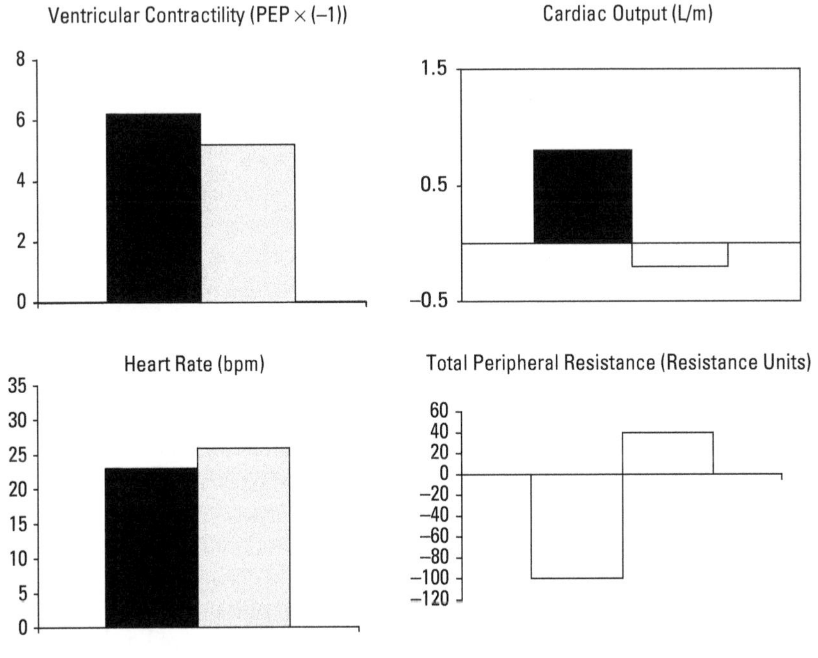

FIGURE 3.1 Tomaka et al.'s (1993) validational patterns of cardiovascular reactivity (i.e., changes from baseline resting levels) during challenge and threat in humans.

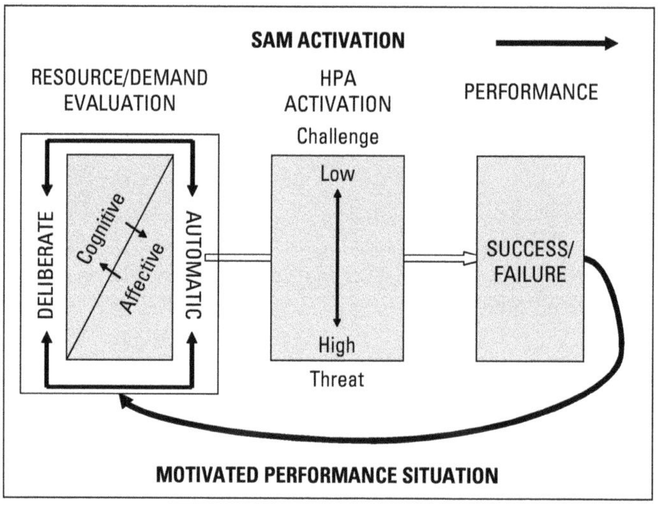

FIGURE 3.2 General components of the biopsychosocial model of challenge and threat.

processes theoretically underlying the emergence of challenge/threat motivational states. As depicted, the challenge/threat motivational process begins when individuals become task engaged in a personally goal-relevant performance situation inducing resource and demand evaluations based on both cognitions and affect or emotion, at least on an unconscious level, that result in energizing the individual for performance in ways consistent with either challenge or threat.

Once an individual is task engaged as indexed by increased VC and HR, a cybernetic evaluation feedback process ensues that modulates challenge/threat motivation. Given increased VC and increased HR performance, this modulation can be indexed by changes in HPA axis influences on CO and TPR. Increased CO and decreased TPR indicate challenge while decreased or static CO and static or increased TPR indicate threat (see Figure 3.1). Individuals continuously reevaluate resources and demands as they experience successes and failures during the performance task itself. It should be noted that if resource and demand evaluations result in unreasonably high or low "ratios" of resources to demands, disengagement will result because the task loses meaning or goal relevance for the individual, an argument paralleling the one underlying the Yerkes-Dodson law (Yerkes & Dodson, 1908).

Resource/demand evaluations can be very complex because they can involve many interrelated factors, most of which are quite subjective in nature. Recent versions of the BPS model (e.g., Blascovich, 2008) take into account that almost any identifiable related factor has implications for both resources and demands. These factors are represented as bipolar dimensions with regard to their effects on resource and demand evaluations and include among others: psychological and/or physical danger/safety, uncertainty/certainty, novelty/familiarity, required effort, abilities and knowledge, the presence of others, affective cues, and attitudes and beliefs. Hence, many more dimensions than those directly related to task performance influence resource and demand evaluations. For example, serially subtracting "3's" from a three- or four-place number should hardly be threatening for most American college students. However, it can be a very different story in a psychology experiment in which the subtractions are vocal and monitored by "highly evaluative" others such as psychologists. In addition, levels of contributions of any of the resource or demand factors to overall evaluations are influenced by intrapersonal differences in temperament, dispositional traits and states, and quality of self-knowledge.

Finally, according to the BPS model, performance generally reflects the resource/demand ratio such that a challenge ratio (greater resources relative to demands) is typically associated with better performance than a threat ratio (greater demands relative to resources). Nonetheless, challenge and threat states are both highly motivational. In most cases, performance during challenge may exceed performance during threat, but in some cases threat appears to be related to better performance (e.g., on vigilance tasks, Hunter, 2001).

The Threshold Model of Social Influence Within Digital Immersive Virtual Environments

Although humans are endogenously equipped to "travel virtually" to imaginary or "unreal" places, our species has also developed exogenous tools to do so. The history of communication media ranging from storytelling, cave art, theater, and manuscripts to printed books, photography, and cinematography to broadband radio, television, and the Internet, and now digital immersive virtual environment technology (immersive virtual environment) is a history of some of the exogenous tools humans have developed for such virtual travel.

Humans' virtual wanderings typically include visual and auditory images of "others" whether or not those others are actually known to exist in physical or grounded reality. Not surprisingly, the content of humans' virtual wanderings involves social interactions with virtual human representations (i.e., "others"), thereby initiating social influences. In general, *social influence* refers to the effects that people have on one another, including classic ones such as: persuasion, conformity, social facilitation, social inhibition, group identity, and antisocial and prosocial behaviors, to name a few.

The answer to the question, "Does social influence occur in immersive virtual environment–mediated virtual environments?" is an unequivocal "Yes!" But, *how* social influence occurs in digital immersive virtual environments is another question. During the decade or so during in which we have studied social interaction using digital immersive virtual environment technology, we have developed and expanded a theoretical model addressing the "how" question that we labeled *the threshold model of social influence within digital immersive virtual environments* (Blascovich et al., 2002a, 2002b). Digital immersive virtual environments are ones that facilitate engagement or immersion in a virtual world by perceptually surrounding "inhabitants" visually and aurally, typically but not necessarily via head-mounted displays or CAVE display technology.

The threshold model involves interactions among five major dimensions or factors including: *Agency*, *Communicative Realism*, *Response System*, *Self-Relevance*, and *Context*. Here, we describe the model from the perspective of a single human user, though there can be many users interacting within it.

Agency involves a user's theory of mind regarding other human representations within the digital immersive virtual environment. More specifically, the agency dimension involves the perceived human sentience (e.g., attributions of consciousness and free will) of other representations and ranges from nonsentient (nonhuman) to sentient (human; see the abscissa in the graphs in Figure 3.3). Our convention (Bailenson & Blascovich, 2004) defines an agent as a digital representation that may be more or less human in appearance but that is driven and controlled completely by system algorithms. The same convention defines an avatar as a digital representation of an actual person in real time that may appear more or less in human form and that is controlled by that individual's tracked and rendered behaviors. Anything "in between" combining features of agents (i.e., computer algorithms) and avatars (i.e., actual human-controlled actions) is defined as a *cyborg*. It is important to note that neither agents nor avatars need to have all possible human actions or algorithms, respectively, depicted in digital virtual worlds.

Assumption and deduction are two ways in which user attributions of agency can be made. Assumed attributions are those a user learns to be the case via externally provided information before or during an immersive virtual environment experience. For example, information from any number of sources (e.g., an investigator or operator; cf. Hoyt, Blascovich, & Swinth, 2003) can inform users that a digital representation is

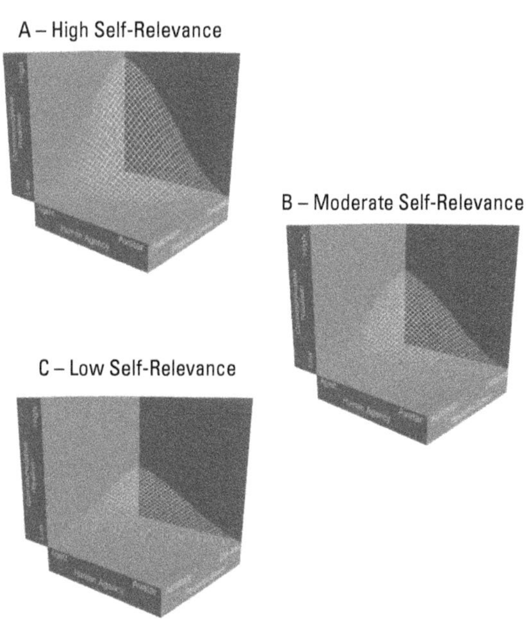

FIGURE 3.3 The threshold model of social influence.

that of a computer algorithm (i.e., an agent) or that the digital human representation is that of a person in real time and, thus, an avatar, though such information need not be veridical.

If there is no external basis for a sentience assumption, then any agency attributions are typically deduced from the actions of the representations within the immersive virtual environment. For example, in a digital immersive virtual environment, if a human representation speaks to or moves toward a user or when a user speaks to or moves toward digital human representations, the user can look for auditory and visual signs that help him or her make an agency or theory of mind (i.e., sentient or nonsentient) attribution. This is a sort of *Turing test* that users can employ consciously. Whether arrived at via assumption or deduction, the belief that a person holds about a human representation is important for agency attributions in digital immersive virtual environments. If a user believes a representation is an avatar, he or she will consciously treat it as an avatar whether or not it is.

Communicative Realism refers to the human-like signal quality of communicative acts. Within digital immersive virtual environments, communicative realism varies from low to high (the ordinate in the graphs in Figure 3.3). While not essential for representations that digital immersive virtual environment users assume are avatars, communicative realism is a very important aspect of representations that users don't know are avatars or assume are agents (i.e., computer algorithms). In the latter situations, communicative realism can be a powerful influence on users' automatic or unconscious processing. That is, even though immersive virtual environment users may believe that a representation is an agent, unconscious or bottom-up processes can attenuate the implications of such conscious knowledge on social influence within digital immersive virtual environments.

According to our five-factor model, communicative realism is a latent variable that is based on three decreasingly important manifest communication variables. In the model, the most important manifest variable is movement realism (e.g., proxemic behaviors, postures, gestures, facial expressions) followed closely by anthropometric realism (human-like appearance and articulation of body joints) and distantly by photographic realism (the fidelity of recognizable individuals). Anthropometric realism is often necessary in service of movement realism in the sense that human movements can not be made by a digital human representation without apparent human body parts such as joints, arms, legs, faces, and so on. Somewhat surprisingly to many, photographic realism in digital immersive virtual environments serves mainly and perhaps only to connote personal and group identity. Notably, even high photographic fidelity is unnecessary to communicate personal identity as even "cartoonized" or caricatured representations of actual people are often enough to communicate their personal identity.

Human movements give rise to low-level brain processes involving mirror neurons that project to areas of the brain controlling various mental processes that predispose people to treat others, even those known to be agents (e.g., physical robots), as sentient at some level, perhaps even unknowingly (see Rizzolatti & Sinigaglia, 2010). Agents' and avatars' movement realism can compensate for some lack of anthropometric and photorealism, something people often experience while viewing animations such as those produced by cartoonists.

Our model's third dimension is *Response System Level*, which varies from automatic to deliberate (see z-dimension in the graphs in Figure 3.3). Social influence can affect uncontrolled or automatic behaviors as well as controlled or deliberate ones. As previously reviewed, social psychologists have noted the ubiquity and strength of "implicit" or automatic social influence effects. This is true for social influences whether they occur in physical or virtual reality. We argue that unconscious social influence processes are similar within or outside of immersive virtual environments. If a digital agent smiles, users smile back, as they would in grounded reality (e.g., Bailenson & Yee, 2005). If a digital agent makes a loud noise, users exhibit a startle response, just as they would in grounded reality.

Figure 3.3a depicts theoretical relationships among agency, communicative realism, and response system level in a highly self-relevant context for an immersive virtual environment user while Figures 3.3b and 3.3c depict such theoretical relationships in moderately self-relevant and low self-relevant contexts, respectively. The surface within the three-dimensional framework is termed the "threshold of social influence." This threshold predicts the likely occurrence of social influence effects as a function of the three factors discussed above. At or above the surface, social influence effects are more likely to occur. Below the surface, they are not.

To illustrate, if agency is high (i.e., the representation is believed to be an avatar), then neither high communicative realism nor deliberate response system level are necessary for social influence effects to occur. Hence, an avatar representation that is merely a "frowning face" can elicit negative affect as evidenced by automatic user behaviors such as a returned frown or in terms of a consciously delivered user response such as a "Thank you!" On the other hand, if agency is low (i.e., the user believes the representation is an agent), then social influence will occur as a function of communicative realism (e.g., high movement realism) for deliberate user responses such as occur during conversation. High levels of communicative realism are not necessary for automatic or unconscious user responses even to an agent.

Self-Relevance is the fourth factor in our model. Self-relevance ranges from high to low and can be thought of simply as the personal meaningfulness of a social interaction. This is as true in physical or grounded reality as in digital immersive virtual environments. Some social interactions are casual or are relatively unimportant transactions. Some are more important, especially when they invite evaluations by others such as task performances. Some are very important; for example, the development of a romantic relationship. Figures 3.3b and 3.3c depict the lower surfaced thresholds of social influence for moderate and low self-relevant contexts.

Finally, the fifth factor in our model is *Context* (not depicted). Factors underlying context include ecological complexity and behavioral options. These factors help determine directly the minimum level of communicative realism that is necessary for the kind of social interaction appropriate to the context, and, hence, the level of social influence within it. For example, if one plays games in an immersive virtual environment, communicative realism, at least in terms of anthropometric and photographic realism, can be low, and players will still become quite immersed because the information exchange and the movements one can make are typically delimited.

A "gedanken" experiment helps make this clear. Suppose one entered an immersive digital virtual room with six sides (four walls, a floor, and a ceiling) furnished like a typical family room. The purpose of being in this digital immersive virtual environment is to play the game of "hot" and "cold." A digital human representation tells the person to find an object that it is thinking about and explains the rule that you cannot talk or ask questions. While searching for the target object in the room by moving about, the person hears the agent's voice telling her that she is getting "warm," "warmer," "hot," and so on, or "cold," "colder," "freezing", and so on, as she gets closer to or farther away from the target object. In this situation, one could easily create an agent that would be indistinguishable from an avatar because both the context and the behavioral options are limited. However, if the immersive virtual environment context is more complex, say a business meeting, it would be quite unlikely, given current artificial intelligence technology, that an agent could be created that would pass muster; that is, as an avatar.

Challenge and Threat Motivation Within Immersive Virtual Environments

We believe that there is substantial value in assessing motivation via the BPS-based cardiovascular indexes within many types of digital immersive virtual environment contexts. Heretofore, most immersive virtual environments have been designed and programmed as motivated performance situations; that is, ones that are goal relevant to intended users and that require instrumental responses or performance on their part. Such immersive virtual environments are exemplified, for example, by digital simulations such as those created for military training purposes (e.g., Traum, Marsella, Gratch, & Lee, 2008). Others are created for clinical purposes such as the diagnosis of attention deficit and hyperactivity disorder (Parsons et al., 2007) and treatment of psychological disorders such as phobias (Wiederhold & Wiederhold, 2000) and posttraumatic stress disorders (Rizzo et al., 2009). Still others can be created for personnel selection purposes (cf. Aginas, Henle, & Beaty, 2001). And, digital immersive virtual environment "classrooms" have been built and used to investigate questions related to learning (e.g., McCall, Bunyan, Bailenson, Blascovich, & Beall, 2009). At present, more immersive virtual environment technology, such as Nintendo's Wii and Microsoft's Kinect tracking systems, is finding its way into the recreational games and fitness arenas.

All of these examples, and the kinds of immersive virtual environments they involve, easily fit the criteria for motivated performance situations. More specifically, users have to perform some task in an evaluative situation. Because we can index challenge and threat motivational states within motivated performance situations, it is feasible to assess whether users are challenged or threatened by the virtual situation and whether they become less or more so over time by using the validated cardiovascular patterns associated with the BPS. Though one can think of many more;

here we suggest three such categorical usages: specifically, as indexes of immersion, personnel selection, and simulation training efficacy.

Immersion. One way in which we have combined the BPS, including its cardiovascular measures of challenge and threat motivational states, and our threshold model of social influence within immersive virtual environments is to assess immersion. It is known from research in our social neuroscience laboratory that when a nonstigmatized person interacts, even cooperatively in a motivated performance situation, with a "stigmatized other," such as a person with a facial birthmark, the nonstigmatized person will exhibit a threat pattern of cardiovascular responses as described above (e.g., Blascovich, Mendes, Hunter, Lickel, & Kowai-Bell, 2001; Mendes, Blascovich, Lickel, & Hunter, 2002) but without necessarily being aware that they were threatened. Furthermore, we know that the cardiovascular threat (and challenge) patterns are often driven unconsciously or automatically (Weisbuch-Remington, Mendes, Seery, & Blascovich, 2005). We reasoned that if users were immersed in a digital immersive virtual environment, they would exhibit the same automatic cardiovascular response patterns indicative of threat when they interacted with stigmatized avatars representing individuals who, themselves, weren't physically stigmatized.

During our experiment (see Blascovich and McCall, 2010), participants met with another "participant" (actually a confederate employed by us), when they physically showed up at our lab. The confederate either bore or did not physically bear a facial stigma (i.e., a "port wine" facial birthmark). After meeting, the participant and confederate entered a shared digital immersive virtual environment. They sat at a virtual table and played a cooperative word-finding game. The experimental manipulation was whether or not the confederate's avatar bore the facial birthmark in the virtual world independently of whether she bore it in the physical world, thereby completely crossing whether or not the confederate bore the stigma physically with whether or not the avatar bore it.

The cardiovascular response patterns of participants revealed that during the first minute of playing the word-finding game in the immersive virtual environment, participants were threatened only if the confederate had borne the birthmark physically, that is, outside of the immersive virtual environment. However, by the fourth task minute, participants were threatened only if the confederate's avatar bore the birthmark digitally, that is, in the immersive virtual environment. As one might expect, during the first part of the cooperative game play, the confederates' facial feature (i.e., the birthmark) in physical or grounded reality took precedence. But, by the fourth minute, the confederates' facial feature in the immersive virtual environment took precedence.

We argue that these results, that is, the crossover of challenge/threat cardiovascular response patterns in the first few minutes of the digital immersive environmental experience, provided a strong index of immersion within it. Hence, we conclude that the BPS-based cardiovascular measures can be used to determine how immersed a person is in a digital immersive virtual environment. The question of immersion is an important one that is determined in large part by immersive virtual environment design and functionality and users' susceptibility to them. Hence, one can determine the immersive properties of either the immersive virtual environment design or the susceptibility of the user by experimentally varying the other.

Personnel Selection. We have also demonstrated that there is predictive value in assessing the BPS-based cardiovascular indexes of challenge and threat while having individuals virtually imagine themselves in a motivated performance situation while giving a speech about how they would perform in that situation. The cardiovascular data recorded during the speech is predictive of their future performance in the actual situation (unimaginary) they gave the speech about.

One study involved an athletic performance situation, playing baseball. Blascovich, Seery, Mugridge, Weisbuch, & Norris, (2004) had baseball players (hitters) on the University of California, Santa Barbara, baseball and softball teams give a speech about how they would perform when coming to bat with two outs in the last half of the last inning with runners on second and third base and their team trailing by a run. A unitary challenge/threat index was computed from the cardiovascular measures. That index reliably predicted the baseball and softball players' offensive baseball statistics, such as batting average and runs–generated index, during the varsity baseball and softball seasons 6 months after they gave the speeches. Similarly, Seery, Weisbuch, and Blascovich (2010) used the cardiovascular challenge and threat indexes based on speeches about upcoming course performance by college students. Again the cardiovascular index predicted the grades they eventually received in that course.

We argue that if the cardiovascular indexes are as powerful as suggested by these two studies with participants only being in an imaginary virtual situation, they can be much more powerful when participants are immersed in a digital immersive virtual environment. One could easily think about creating digital immersive virtual environments appropriate to personnel performance tasks (e.g., air traffic control operations) to select candidates for training and eventual job placement.

Simulation Training Efficacy. Many immersive virtual environments are created for training purposes for military and paramilitary operations. Consider the creation of digital immersive virtual environments for training personnel in counterterrorism strikes. We would expect such training simulations to be highly self-relevant and, therefore, highly task engaging motivationally and particularly immersive for those who have this dangerous duty.

Given that in nearly all types of motivated performance tasks in prior BPS research, better performance occurs among individuals who are challenged compared with individuals who are threatened, we would expect at the end of training within these highly self-relevant digital training immersive virtual environments that successful trainees would be challenged within the simulations, as could be assessed using ambulatory cardiovascular measuring equipment. Those who are not challenged might be retrained or reassigned to other duties.

Finally, although challenge and threat are generally always with positive and negative emotion, such a pairing is not necessarily always the case. For example, Tomaka et al. (1999) have shown that anger is associated with challenge. Additionally, challenge and threat are not always associated with better and worse performance. Hunter (2001) has shown that vigilance is associated with threat. Hence, one must take care to ferret out the inconsistent cases. Hence, one cannot necessarily predict performance with perfect accuracy from identifying the motivational or emotional state alone.

Summary

In summary, we have reviewed two theoretical models. One is *the biopsychosocial model of challenge and threat* that involves ratios of resource evaluations to demand evaluations for performance that moderate overall approach-like motivational states and that vary on a continuum from challenge to threat. Furthermore, we have specified and reviewed the patterns of cardiovascular responses that index these motivational states. The other model is *the threshold model of social influence within digital immersive virtual environments*. This model is predictive of social interaction–produced influences based on the interaction of up to five factors including: Theory of Mind, Communicative Realism, Response System Level, Self-Relevance, and Context. Because many digital immersive virtual environments involve motivated performance situations (e.g., for training, games, instruction, negotiation, etc.), there is value in determining the utility of such worlds on the basis of the challenge–threat motivational states of users via those cardiovascular indexes.

References

Aguinas, H., Henle, C. C. & Beaty, J. C. (2001). Virtual reality technology: A new tool for personnel selection. *International Journal of Selection and Assessment*, 9, 70–83.

Bailenson, J. N., & Blascovich, J. (2004). *Avatars*. Paper presented at the Encyclopedia of Human-Computer Interaction, Berkshire Publishing Group.

Bailenson, J. N. & Yee, N. (2005). Digital chameleons: Automatic assimilation of nonverbal gestures in immersive virtual environments. *Psychological Science*, *16*, 814–819.

Blascovich, J. (2008). Challenge and threat. In A. J. Elliot (Ed.) *Handbook of approach and avoidance motivation* (pp. 431–446). New York: Erlbaum.

Blascovich, J. & Bailenson, J. (2011). *Infinite realty: Avatars, eternal life, new worlds and the dawn of the virtual revolution*. New York: William Morrow.

Blascovich, J., Loomis, J., Beall, A., Swinth, K., Hoyt, C., & Bailenson, J. (2002a). Immersive virtual environment technology as a research tool for social psychology. *Psychological Inquiry*, *13*, 103–125.

Blascovich, J., Loomis, J., Beall, A., Swinth, K., Hoyt, C., & Bailenson, J. (2002b). Immersive virtual environment technology: Not just another research tool for social psychology. *Psychological Inquiry*, *13*, 146–149.

Blascovich, J., & McCall, C. (2010). Attitudes in virtual reality. In J. Forgas, W. Crano, & J. Cooper (Eds), *Attitudes and persuasion* (pp. 283–298). New York: Psychology Press.

Blascovich, J., & Mendes, W. B. (2000). Challenge and threat appraisals: The role of affective cues. In J. Forgas (Ed.), *Feeling and thinking: The role of affect in social cognition* (pp. 59–82). Cambridge, UK: Cambridge University Press.

Blascovich, J., & Mendes, W. B. (2010). Social psychophysiology and embodiment. In S. B. Fiske, D. T. Gilbert, & G. Lindzey (Eds.), *Handbook of social psychology* (Vol. 1, 5th ed., pp. 194–227). New York: Wiley.

Blascovich, J. Mendes, W. B., Hunter, S. B., Lickel, B., & Kowai-Bell, N. (2001). Perceiver threat in social interactions with stigmatized others. *Journal of Personality and Social Psychology*, *80*, 253–267.

Blascovich, J., Mendes, W. B., & Seery, M. (2002). Intergroup encounters and threat: A multi-method approach. In D. Mackie & E. Smith (Eds.), *From prejudice to intergroup emotions: Differentiated reactions to social groups* (pp. 89–110). New York: Psychology Press.

Blascovich, J., & Seery, M. D. (2007). Visceral and somatic indexes of social psychological constructs. In A. Kruglanski & E. T. Higgins (Eds.), *Social psychology: Handbook of basic principles* (2nd ed., pp. 19–38). New York: Guilford.

Blascovich, J., Seery, M., Mugridge, C., Weisbuch, M., & Norris, K. (2004). Predicting athletic performance from cardiovascular indicators of challenge and threat. *Journal of Experimental Social Psychology*, *40*, 683–688.

Blascovich, J., & Tomaka, J. (1996). The biopsychosocial model of arousal regulation. In M. Zanna (Ed.), *Advances in experimental social psychology* (Vol. 28, pp. 1–51). New York: Academic Press.

Dienstbier, R. A. (1989). Arousal and physiological toughness: Implications for mental and physical health. *Psychological Review*, *96*, 84–100.

Elliot, A. J. (2006). The hierarchical model of approach-avoidance motivation. *Motivation and Emotion*, *30*, 111–116.

Elliot, A. J. (2008) (Ed.). *Handbook of approach and avoidance motivation*. New York: Erlbaum.

Elliot, A. J., & Trash, T. M. (2002). Approach-avoidance motivation in personality: Approach and avoidance temperaments and goals. *Journal of Personality and Social Psychology*, 82(5), 804–818.

Hassan, R. R., Uleman J., & Bargh J. A. (Eds). (2005). *The new unconscious*. New York: Oxford University Press.

Hoyt, C., Blascovich, J., Swinth, K. (2003). Social inhibition in immersive virtual environments. *Presence: Teleoperators and virtual environments*, *12*, 183–195.

Hunter, S. B. (2001). Performance under pressure: The impact of challenge and threat states on information processing. Unpublished doctoral dissertation, University of California, Santa Barbara.

Lazarus, R. S., & Folkman, S. (1984). *Stress, appraisal, and coping*. New York: Springer.

Mackie, D. M., & Smith, E. R. (1998). Intergroup relations: Insights from a theoretically integrative approach. *Psychological Review*, *105*, 499–529.

McCall, C., Bunyan, D. P., Bailenson, J. B., Blascovich, J., & Beall, A. (2009). Leveraging collaborative virtual environment technology for inter-population research on persuasion in a classroom setting. *PRESENCE: Teleoperators and Virtual Environments*, *18*, 361–369.

Obrist, P. (1981). *Cardiovascular psychophysiology: A perspective*. New York: Plenum.

Mendes, W. B., Blascovich, J., Lickel, B., & Hunter, S. (2002). Challenge and threat during interactions with White and Black men. *Personality and Social Psychology Bulletin*, 28, 939–952.

Parsons, T. D., Bowerly, T., Buckwalter, J. G., & Rizzo, A. A. (2007). A controlled clinical comparison of attention performance in children with ADHD in a virtual reality classroom compared to standard neuropsychological methods. *Neuropsychology, development, and cognition. Section C, Child neuropsychology*, *13*, 363–

Rizzo, A., Newman, B., Parsons, T., Reger, G., Difede, J., Rothbaum, B. O., Mclay, R. N., Holloway, K., Graap, K., Newman, B., et al. (2009). Development and clinical results from the Virtual Iraq Exposure Therapy Application for PTSD. *IEEE Explore: Virtual Rehabilitation* (pp. 8–15).

Rizzolatti, G., & Sinigaglia, C. (2010). The functional role of the parieto-frontal mirror circuit: Interpretations and misinterpretations. *Nature Reviews Neuroscience* *11*, 264–274.

Seery, M. D., Weisbuch, M., & Blascovich, J. (2010). Cardiovascular measures independently predict performance in a university course. *Psychophysiology*, *47*(3), 535–539.

Tomaka, J., Blascovich, J., Kelsey, R. M., & Leitten, C. L. (1993). Subjective, physiological, and behavioral effects of threat and challenge appraisal. *Journal of Personality and Social Psychology*, *65*, 248–260.

Tomaka, J., Blascovich, J., Kibler, J., & Ernst, J. M. (1997). Cognitive and physiological antecedents of threat and challenge appraisal. *Journal of Personality and Social Psychology*, 73, 63–72.

Tomaka, J., Palacios, R., Schneider, K. T., Colotla, M., Concha, J. B., & Herrald, M. (1999). Assertiveness predicts threat and challenge reactions to potential stress among women. *Journal of Personality and Social Psychology*, *76*, 1008–1021.

Traum, D. R., Marsella, S., Gratch, J., & Lee, J. (2008). *Multi-party, multi-issue, multi-strategy negotiation for multi-modal virtual agents*. 8th International Conference on Intelligent Virtual Agents, Tokyo, Japan. Weisbuch-Remington, M., Mendes, W. B., Seery, M. D., & Blascovich, J. (2005). The non-conscious influence of religious symbols in motivated performance situations. *Personality and Social Psychology Bulletin*, *31*, 1203–1216.

Wiederhold, B. K., & Wiederhold, M. D. (2000). Lessons learned from 600 virtual reality sessions. *CyberPsychology & Behavior*, 3, 393–400.

Yerkes, R. M., & Dodson, J. D. (1908). The relation of strength of stimulus to rapidity of habit-formation. *Journal of Comparative Neurology*, *18*, 459–482.

4

Requirements for a Process Model of Appraisal From a Social Functional Perspective

Stacy Marsella & Jonathan Gratch

Introduction

Research on computational models of human emotional processes has grown rapidly over the last decade, due to their potential in basic research on emotion as well as their use in an ever increasing range of applications (Marsella, Gratch, & Petta, 2010). Much of the work on computational models of emotion has relied on appraisal theories as the basis for the model. However, there is an ongoing debate as to whether appraisal theories, and by extension the computational models based on appraisal, do a good accounting of the social phenomena that are integral to human emotional processes (e.g., Parkinson, 2001; Parkinson, Chapter 3, this volume). In particular, it has been argued that traditional appraisal theories focus on the individual and largely ignore the influence of the social environment both on how events are appraised, how events impact social goals, and how emotions are regulated and expressed (Manstead & Fischer, 2001). Smith and Kirby (Chapter 1, this volume) specifically argues that appraisal checks of current appraisal theories do not adequately explain the differences between the social emotions of guilt, shame, and embarrassment.

Clearly, a failure to account for the social environment is a significant criticism of appraisal theories. Emotions often arise in a social context out of a social concern. Embarrassment arises out of an impression management goal, a concern that some act may negatively impact others' impression of self. Further, emotions serve a social function. Anger can coerce responses in others and enforce social norms, guilt can induce acts of atonement for transgressions and displays of guilt can elicit reconciliation, distress can be seen as a way of recruiting social support, and displays of joy or pity are a way of signaling such support to others.

Given that computational models of emotion have largely been based on appraisal theory, the question of appraisal theory's ability to model the social/interactional aspects of emotions extends directly to these computational models. The question is especially relevant given that a major, arguably the most common, use of computational models of emotion is in human–computer interaction and specifically the creation of virtual characters that can socially interact with human users.

We investigate this question using our own work on EMA (*em*otion and *a*daptation), a computational process model of appraisal. We begin in the next section by laying out the challenges that have been raised by various authors that need to be addressed for a social functional perspective on emotion processes and the requirements that such a perspective presupposes.

Then, we discuss EMA, laying out its design. EMA has been discussed and evaluated elsewhere (Gratch & Marsella, 2004; Gratch, Marsella, Wang, & Stankovic, 2009; Marsella & Gratch, 2009;Marsella, Gratch, Wang, & Stankovic, 2009). We use EMA as a frame against which we can assess the requirements for modeling human social emotions in a computational model of appraisal theory. To that end, we go on to critique EMA from the perspective of social/transactional emotions, laying out what are the basic requirements on a computational model of appraisal for it to delineate the social influences and consequences on emotional processes. Finally, we conclude with a proposal for a social-emotional appraisal process that addresses many of these requirements through incorporation of theory-of-mind reasoning.

Challenges and Requirements for a Social Functional Account

The social functional account of emotions (Keltner & Haidt, 1999) is a claim that emotions serve a social function; that emotions arise from, and attempt to solve, social problems. Specifically, social functional accounts start from the basis that people are social animals who must effectively deal with social problems arising from their interactions and relations to others. Emotions are evoked in response to problems such as perceived injustices, the need to form and maintain relations, and coordinating/cooperating/competing with others. The resulting emotional response serve to address those social problems, by changing the individual's behavior or signaling others in ways that change their behavior. Finally, emotions are dynamic, interactional processes that mediate the individual's relation to the changing social environment (Lazarus, 1991).

Working from an appraisal theory perspective, we can identify several ways that a social functional account presents challenges to the processes that appraisal theory postulates.

Social Goals and Threats

Different social emotions arise due to different social goals and patterns of threats to these goals. Smith and Kirby (Chapter 1, this volume) illustrate this point by considering the problems for appraisal theories raised by social emotions such as embarrassment, shame, and guilt. Research has emphasized important differences regarding when shame and embarrassment are elicited and the social functions the display of these emotions seem to serve. Guilt seems to involve transgressions that violate internal standards whereas shame and embarrassment seem to arise from the perceived negative evaluations of self by others. Shame and embarrassment seem further distinguished in that shame involves situations in which both self and other agree that the transgression represents a fundamental character flaw, whereas embarrassment involves a temporary condition that might be (mis)perceived by others as a more fundamental flaw.

For example, an individual might find it difficult to sing in public, and feel embarrassment that his or her poor performance might be viewed as an inherent defect in singing ability. These displays seem to be strategically employed. For example, Leary, Landel, and Patton (1996) showed that participants exhibited less embarrassment and reported feeling less embarrassed after singing aloud in public when they believed that the experimenter already knew they were uncomfortable. Adopting an appraisal perspective, Smith and Kirby (Chapter 1, this volume) argue that distinctions between emotions such as shame and embarrassment can be handled within appraisal theory with greater attention to social goals and social inferences. For instance, embarrassment involves the appraisal of a particular social goal, in effect, reputation or self-presentation, which may or may not be threatened, depending on the inferences formed by others.

Thus, appraisal theory, and computational models of appraisal theories, must distinguish between the type of goal being threatened (and consequently, what is perceived as a threat to it). Lazarus makes a similar point when he argues that shame is a threat to a goal that is part of the individual's ego ideal while guilt is a threat to a moral standard (Lazarus, 1999, pp. 239–240).

Social Influences on Appraisal Processes

In addition to threats to different social goals leading to different social emotions, there is the issue of whether the social environment impacts the appraisal process itself, for example the determination of whether something is a threat to one's reputation. In other words, the social environment also may impact how inferences associated with appraisal unfold. Work on social referencing (Campos, 1983; Campos et al., 2003) and social comparison theory (Fetinger, 1954) have long argued that the social environment influences how we assess ourselves. *Social appraisal theory* (Manstead & Fischer, 2001) argues specifically that not only do we appraise ourselves as social entities with social roles and goals but also that those appraisals are impacted by how others have appraised a situation—how others react emotionally—and furthermore, the subsequent expression of emotion will be mediated by how the individual imagines others will appraise that expression.

This implies that the individual has some way of inferring how others appraise a situation and, further, that the individual has some way of inferring how others appraisals will be impacted by one's own emotional expression. The work of Hareli and Hess (2009) on reverse-engineered appraisal suggests one mechanism for this; arguing that people could infer others' appraisals of a situation by reverse-engineering those appraisals from the others' emotional expressions. We will argue in latter sections that in general this presupposes that an individual can model the mental constructs and processes of others, and that reverse-engineered appraisal can be viewed as a form of theory-of-mind reasoning (Premack & Woodruff, 1978).

Socioemotive Behavior

As social appraisal theory argues, the social environment also impacts the behavioral consequences of emotions, including how emotions are regulated and expressed in behaviors, including expressions. In particular, as noted above, the expression of emotion will be mediated by how the individual imagines others will appraise that expression. This suggests a form of impression management. For instance, Leary et al. (1996) argues that embarrassment serves self-presentational ends and therefore ceases to be necessary once these ends are fulfilled. Related to this, Ekman talks of display rules (Ekman & Freisen, 1975) that seek to suppress expressions or mask them with other expressions.

Another way social factors influence appraisal concerns is how coping processes, such as seeking information, shifting blame, or seeking social support, might be recruited to help influence one's own as well as others' beliefs and appraisal about a situation. See Smith and Kirby's discussion in Chapter 1 of this volume of reality negotiation (Snyder, 1989; Snyder & Higgins, 1997).

Such coping strategies raise issues both in terms of modeling how they are elicited as well as modeling what the incentive is for the individual to use the strategy, what the impact is on the individual and the social environment. Note that these impacts also presuppose some form of implicit or explicit theory of mind reasoning. For instance, how seeking social support or shifting blame will alter the beliefs and behaviors of others.

Social Interaction

That the expression of emotion may in turn impact others' appraisals essentially closes the social connection. Individuals are aware that others are appraising the situation, and those appraisals not only influence their own appraisals but also lead them to try to manage appraisals by others through management of their own responses. One view of this interaction is that emotion meaning essentially emerges from the social interaction (see Parkinson, Chapter 3, this volume). For example, consider two people interacting. One person leans forward (with the expectation that the other will lean back). If the other instead leans forward as well, it may change the person's beliefs of the other party's mental beliefs/action tendencies and perceptions of control, creating an appraisal of threat that didn't exist before, perhaps evoking anger. Thus, anger "emerges" from the social interaction.

This connection is made even more explicitly apparent in coping behaviors (Folkman & Moskowitz, 2004). Coping responses are often taken in social environments that may support, sanction, or impact the effectiveness of those actions. The actions themselves may in principle be social actions, such as seeking emotional or instrumental support or trying to establish dominance in the face of threat. As these responses unfold, they will impact subsequent appraisals by self and others.

This interaction over time in a social environment blurs self and other as constructors of emotional meaning. However, the self still remains distinct and central. Shame and embarrassment illustrate the point—whether the individual sees the behavior as a meaningful flaw and how others perceive it clearly separate the self from other in the construction of emotional meaning.

Requirements

To summarize, a social functional view argues for several requirements on an appraisal model. First, distinguishing between social emotions requires distinguishing type of goals, who ascribes to the importance of that goal, and whether it is self or other who perceives the goal being threatened. Second, the individual's appraisal may be influenced by how it infers others appraise the situation—and that in turn may be based on inferring others' appraisals from their emotional reactions. Third, an individual's emotional behavior, either emotional expressions or coping strategies, influences others, and that will factor into how the individual responds. And finally, these various influences may operate within a social interaction that unfolds over time.

Although we have laid out these various requirements as distinct, they are closely interlinked. The need to regulate socioemotive behavior, for example, by employing display rules, can be viewed as a by-product of having a social goal of impression management—a concern for what others believe about self. In fact, a recurring theme that ties these requirements together is the importance of the self's beliefs about others' mental states, including what others appraise, what others believe, what others believe about the self, and what others see as moral standards for behavior.

These requirements raise specific challenges for a computational model of appraisal. Before we assess the EMA model's ability to address these challenges, we first lay out EMA in detail.

EMA

A computational model of emotion should address how emotions arise in, and impact, a range of eliciting situations, not only simple physical events but also more complex social scenarios.

In this section, we first lay out the theoretical and process assumptions that inform our approach toward the computational modeling of emotions, and then describe the current incarnation EMA, a general computational framework for modeling emotion processes.

Theoretical Requirements

In our computational model, we adopt the central tenets shared by appraisal theories of emotion: Appraisal is a process of interpreting a person's relationship with his or her environment; this interpretation can be characterized in terms of a set of criteria (variously called *appraisal dimensions*, *appraisal variables*, or *appraisal checks*), and specific emotions are associated with certain configurations of these criteria. In addition, appraisal theories posit specific appraisal dimensions and coping strategies that impose representational and inferential requirements on any system that hopes to accurately model the computation of these appraisals, as well as their consequences on cognition and behavior.

Review of EMA (EMotion and Adaptation)

We define a computational model of a mental process as a model of a process or processes operating on representations. A computational model of appraisal consists of a set of processes that interpret a representation of the person–environment relationship in terms of a set of posited appraisal variables, and a set of processes (i.e., coping strategies) that manipulate this representation in response to the appraised interpretation.

To address those requirements, EMA uses a representation built on the causal representations developed for decision-theoretic planning, augmented by the explicit representation of intentions and beliefs. Planning representations capture a number of essential distinctions required for computing appraisals, including causal reasoning, the ability to detect future benefits and threats, and the ability to represent the causal agents associated with these benefits and threats. The decision-theoretic notions of probability and utility allow EMA to compute the appraisals of desirability and likelihood. Finally, explicit representations of intentions and beliefs are also critical for distinguishing merely contemplated actions from those an agent is committed to perform, an important distinction for computing attributions of blame and responsibility. Finally, explicit representations of beliefs and intentions are important for modeling coping strategies, especially emotion-focused coping (e.g., abandoning a commitment to a goal, or wishing away a belief).

Knowledge Representation

In EMA, the agent's interpretation of its "agent–environment relationship" is reified in an explicit representation of beliefs, desires, intentions, plans, and probabilities, which we refer to as the causal interpretation to emphasize the importance of causal reasoning as well as the interpretative (subjective) character of the appraisal process. The causal interpretation (corresponding to the agent's working memory) encodes the input, intermediate results, and output of inferential processes that mediate between the agent's goals and its physical and social environment (e.g., perception, planning, explanation, and natural language processing).

The causal interpretation represents a snapshot of the agent's current view of the agent–environment relationship, and this representation changes moment to moment in response to internal and external changes. For example, the agent's actions or actions of other social actors change the environment, and these effects are reflected in the causal interpretation as soon as they are perceived by the agent's senses. Further, the mere act of thinking can change the perceived agent–environment relationship. For example, as the agent develops plans or forms intentions, these are also reflected as changes in the casual interpretation. In this sense the causal interpretation changes moment to moment in response to observation or inference.

Appraisal Process

Appraisal theories characterize emotion-eliciting events in terms of a set of specific appraisal variables, but most theories are vague with respect to the processes that underlie these judgments. We assume that appraisal is fast, parallel, and automatic. This is achieved by modeling appraisal as a set of continuously active feature detectors that map features of the causal interpretation into appraisal variables. All significant features in the causal interpretation are appraised separately, simultaneously, and automatically. For example, if the causal interpretation encodes an action with two consequences, one good and one bad, each consequence is appraised in parallel, and any factors that influence the desirability or likelihood of these consequences are automatically reflected in these appraisals as soon as these factors are recorded in the causal interpretation. In this sense, appraisals do not change the causal interpretation but provide a continuously updated "affective summary" of its contents.

The appraisal process in EMA associates a data structure, called an *appraisal frame*, with each proposition. The appraisal frame maintains a continuously updated set of appraisal values associated with each proposition. These variables include:

- *Relevance:* A proposition is judged to be relevant if it has nonzero utility for some agent. This includes not only propositions that have intrinsic utility for the agent but also propositions that have extrinsic utility by virtue of causally impacting a proposition that has utility.
- *Perspective*: The viewpoint from which the proposition is judged. EMA can appraise events not only from its own perspective but also ostensibly from the perspective of other agents. However, this capacity is limited significantly by the fact that the causal interpretation cannot model the agent's beliefs about other agents' beliefs. Rather, it assumes that a common set of beliefs is shared between agents.
- *Desirability*: This characterizes the value of the proposition to the agent (e.g., does it causally advance or inhibit a state of utility for the agent?). Desirability can be positive or negative. As in the case of relevance, desirability may be intrinsic or extrinsic.
- *Likelihood*: This is a measure of the likelihood of propositions. If the state is in the past or present, this will be 0 or 1, indicating if the state is true or false (EMA assumes at present that propositions are fully observable—i.e., there is no uncertainty about the current state of the world). If the state is in the future, this indexes the likelihood that it will occur, derived from the decision-theoretic plan.
- *Expectedness*: This the extent to which a state could have been predicted from the causal interpretation.
- *Causal attribution*: Who deserves credit/blame. This currently depends on what agent was responsible for executing the action, but could potentially involve considerations of intention, foreknowledge, and coercion (see Mao & Gratch, 2005, and Pynadath, Si, & Marsella, Chapter 5, this volume).
- *Controllability*: Can the outcome be altered by actions under control of the agent?
- *Changeability*: Can the outcome be altered by some other causal agent?

Each appraised event is mapped into an emotion instance of some type and intensity, as we discuss next.

Emotion, Focus of Attention and Mood

In EMA, we support a two-level notion of emotional state—appraisal and mood—that can account for some of the indirect effects of emotion documented in empirical research. The appraisal level determines the agent's coping response, but this is biased by an overall mood state. Mood acts as a proxy for certain subsymbolic (brain or bodily) processes (in the sense of Zajonc, 1980) that we don't yet know how to model but that are important for reconciling appraisal models with empirical observations such as affect-as-information (Clore, Schwarz, & Conway, 1994) and core affect (Barrett, 2006). Our theoretical perspective on mood is that the initial appraisal of a situation leads to the recruitment of brain and bodily resources that facilitate certain mental and physical activities and thereby change the subsequent appraisal of the situation. For example, if the body is in a high state of arousal, it may be easier to cope with physical threats as certain responses are already "energized." However, EMA does not explicitly model such bodily consequences of appraisal.

At the appraisal level, EMA maintains multiple appraisal frames (one for each proposition in the causal interpretation), each of which is labeled with a specific emotion type and intensity, and each competing to determine the agent's coping response. We assign symbolic labels (e.g., hope, joy, fear) to appraisal frames; however, the label is primarily a convenience (e.g., it facilitates the mapping of appraisal patterns to facial expressions), and the specific configuration of appraisal variables determines the agent's coping responses. For example, an undesirable and uncontrollable future state would be labeled as fear eliciting and this appraisal pattern leads to avoidance coping. In some cases, the same frame might generate multiple emotion labels. For example, an unexpected and beneficial outcome would elicit both joy and surprise.

At the mood level, individual appraisal frames (and their associated intensities) are also aggregated into a higher level *mood*. We refer to this aggregate state as the agent's mood because it (a) represents a summary of various appraised events, (b) is disassociated from the original eliciting event (i.e., it is not intentional), and (c) tends to change slowly over time as appraisal frames are added or removed in response to changes in the causal interpretation. The representation of the mood state is currently represented as a set of emotion labels (e.g., Hope, Joy, Fear, etc.) with an [0..1] intensity that is a function of all appraisal frames with the corresponding type. For example, if EMA has several appraisal frames labeled with Hope, the intensity of these frames is added and passed through a sigmoid function to map it into the range of 0 to 1 and serves as the hope component of the mood state. The mood state has an indirect effect on appraisal in that EMA applies a mood adjustment to individual appraisal frames. For example, if an appraisal frame is labeled with Hope and has an intensity of X, the mood-adjusted intensity of this frame is X+*Mood*(hope). In this sense mood essentially "bleeds over" into the appraisal process.

EMA's moment-to-moment coping response is determined by a simple activation-based, focus-of-attention model that incorporates both appraisal and mood. Specifically, the appraisal frame that determines coping is the most recently accessed appraisal frame with the highest mood-adjusted intensity. This pattern of appraisal variables associated with this frame determines the agent's expression and its next coping response. The fact that the appraisal frame is mood adjusted allows for indirect emotional effects. For example, if an event is appraised as equally hope- and fear provoking, the agent will focus on its fears if its mood state contains more fear than hope.

Coping Process

Finally, EMA includes a computational model of coping integrated with the appraisal process (according to Lazarus's theory). Coping determines, moment-to-moment, how the agent responds to the appraised significance of events. Within EMA, coping strategies are proposed to maintain desirable or overturn undesirable in-focus events (appraisal instances). Coping strategies essentially work in the reverse direction of the appraisal that motivates them, by identifying features of the causal interpretation that produced the appraisal and that should be maintained or altered (e.g., beliefs, desires, intentions, and expectations).

In EMA, coping strategies can be seen as control signals that enable or suppress the cognitive processes that operate on the causal interpretation. These include sensing unknown state features, avoiding a threat, refining a plan, or adding/dropping goals and intentions. Coping acts as a sequential gatekeeper that sanctions the action congruent with the current appraisal pattern. We organize strategies in terms of their impact on the agent's focus of attention, beliefs, desires, or intentions:

Attention-related coping: Certain coping strategies seek to modulate the agent's attention to features of the environment.

- *Seek information:* Form a positive intention to monitor the pending, unexpected, or uncertain state that produced the appraisal frame. Seek information is preferred if the truth value of the state is uncertain, if it changed unexpectedly, and if appraised controllability is high.
- *Suppress information*: Form a negative intention to monitor the pending, unexpected, or uncertain state that produced the appraisal frame. Suppress information is preferred if the truth value is unambiguous or if appraised controllability is low.

Belief-related coping:

- *Shift responsibility*: Shift an attribution of blame/credit from (toward) the self and toward (from) some other agent. The agents to whom responsibility is shifted must have some causal relationship to the event (e.g., they facilitated or inhibited the appraised consequence). Shift responsibility is preferred if the consequence has low appraised controllability.
- *Wishful thinking*: Increase (lower) the probability of a pending desirable (undesirable) outcome or assume some intervening act or actor will improve desirability. For example, if the appraisal frame is associated with a future action with an undesirable outcome, wishful thinking will lower the perceived probability that this effect will occur. Wishful thinking is preferred if the appraised controllability of the outcome is low.

Desire-related coping:

- *Distance/mental disengagement*: Lower utility attributed to a desired but threatened state. For example, if an agent's plan for achieving a goal has a low probability of success, the consequence of distancing is that the agent will come to care less about this goal. Distancing is preferred if the appraised controllability of the appraised outcome is low.
- *Positive reinterpretation/silver lining*: Increase utility of a positive side effect of some action with a negative outcome. For example, if the appraisal frame refers to an undesired outcome of a future action but the action has another outcome that is desirable, this positive outcome will achieve greater importance for the agent. Positive reinterpretation is preferred if the appraised controllability of the appraised outcome is low.

Intention-related coping:

- *Planning/action selection*: Form an intention to perform some external action that improves an appraised negative outcome. For example, if a goal is currently unachieved, the agent will form an intention to execute some action that achieves the goal. If the action is not immediately executable, this will trigger a search for possible actions that can satisfy the precondition of this action. This strategy is preferred when the agent has some control over the appraised outcome (i.e., controllability is medium or high).
- *Seek instrumental support*: Form an intention to get someone else to perform an external action that changes the agent–environment relationship. For example, if a goal is currently unachieved and the only action that achieves it can be executed by another agent, this will trigger communicative acts (e.g., order or request another party to execute the intended action). This strategy is preferred if the action in question is likely to succeed (i.e., controllability is medium or high).
- *Make amends:* Form an intention to redress a wrong. For example, if the agent performed an action that harms another (i.e., desirability is low for the other and causal attribution is the self), it may seek to make amends (and mitigate the resulting feelings of guilt) by performing an action that reverses the harm. This strategy is preferred if the action in question is likely to succeed (i.e., controllability is medium or high).
- *Procrastination*: Defer an intention to some time in the future. For example, if a goal is currently unsatisfiable, but there is reason to believe that circumstances will change in the future, and then wait for an external event to change the current circumstances. This strategy is preferred if the situation is appraised as having moderate or low controllability but high changeability.
- *Resignation:* Drop an intention to achieve a desired state. For example, if a goal is appraised as essentially unachievable, the agent may abandon this goal. This strategy is preferred if the agent has little appraised control over the state
- *Avoidance:* Take an action that attempts to remove the agent from a looming threat. Avoidance is preferred if the threat is appraised as uncontrollable.

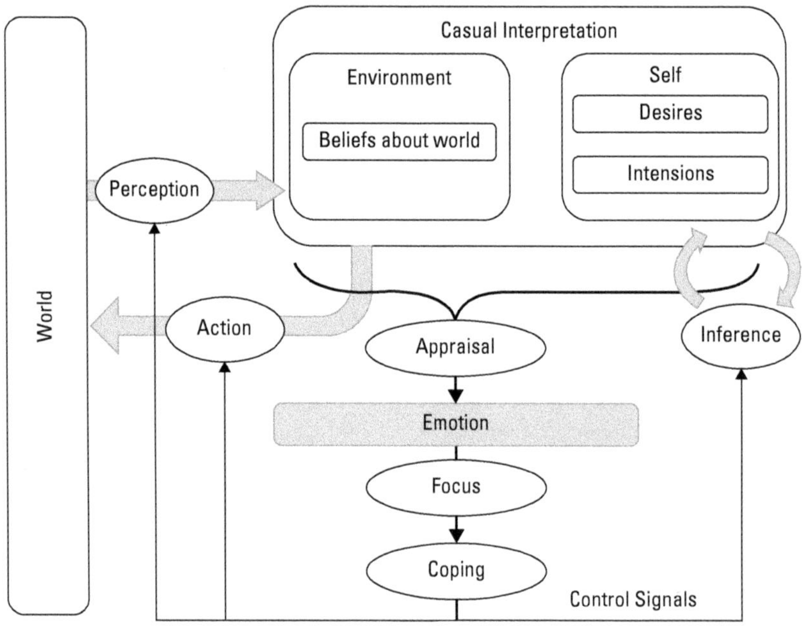

FIGURE 4.1 EMA's appraisal, coping, and reappraisal processes.

Not every coping strategy applies to each stressor (e.g., an agent cannot be problem directed if it is unaware of any actions that may change the situation), but multiple strategies can apply to the same stressor. EMA proposes strategies in parallel but adopts them sequentially. A set of preferences resolves ties. For example, EMA prefers problem-directed strategies if control is appraised as high (take action, plan, seek information), procrastination if changeability is high, and emotion-focused strategies if control and changeability are low.

To summarize, an agent's causal interpretation is equated with the output and intermediate results of processes that relate the agent to its physical and social environment. This configuration of beliefs, desires, plans, and intentions represents the agent's current view of the agent–environment relation, which may change with further observation or inference. We treat appraisal as a mapping from domain-independent features of causal interpretation to individual appraisal variables. By allowing observation and inference to maintain the domain-independent features of the causal interpretation on which appraisal is based, their mapping into (values of) appraisal variables can be fast, based on pattern matching. Multiple appraisals are aggregated into an overall emotional state (mood) that influences behavior indirectly, by biasing subsequent appraisals. Coping directs control signals to auxiliary reasoning modules (i.e., planning, action selection, belief updates, etc.) to overturn or maintain features of the causal interpretation that lead to individual appraisals.

Figure 4.1 depicts how the causal interpretation, appraisal, focus, and coping interact with each other and the agent's perceptual and inferential processes. Note that the design has several sources of dynamics. Events can happen in the world, altering the causal interpretation through perception. The agent can also execute actions, the effects of which will also alter the world and causal interpretation. The agent's own inferential processes (which here is meant to include belief maintenance, action selection, and planning) can alter the causal interpretation. These changes to the causal interpretation induce changes in appraisals. Of particular importance for the emotion processes, appraisal and coping operate within a loop whereby a situation may be appraised, which leads to emotions and coping responses that influence the agent's inferential processes that will alter the person–environment relation. This, in turn, impacts subsequent reappraisals of the situation. Thus, emotional meaning can be viewed as evolving in EMA over time as the individual interacts with the physical and social environment.

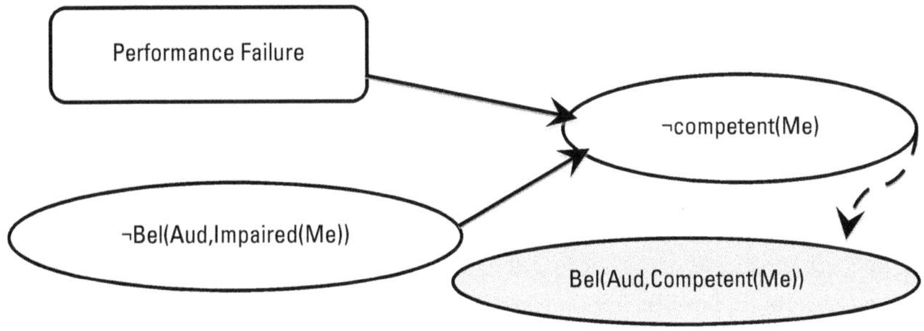

FIGURE 4.2 Model of embarrassment.

Social Emotions, Appraisal Theory, and EMA

Having provided a description of EMA, let us now return to the challenges of a social functional view that we raised in the second section of this chapter.

Social Goals and Threats. The social environment clearly plays a major role in establishing an individual's goals. We are, after all, social animals with social goals, including concerns for how others perceive us. As noted in the second section, different social emotions, such as embarrassment, shame, and guilt arise due to different social goals and patterns of threats to these goals, often depending on the individual's beliefs about the inferences formed by others.

For a computational model of appraisal, this clearly indicates a need for representing social goals such as reputation. In addition, it requires inferential processes that detect threats to those goals. In principle, this is a straightforward extension to a computational model like EMA. The key challenge is in the inferential processes that would detect threats to those goals and update the causal interpretation. Recall that those inferential processes are actually outside the appraisal process in EMA. In EMA, appraisals operate as a collection of simple, fast feature detectors on the causal interpretation.

Furthermore, it is not just representing various types of social goals. The appraisal process must treat these different types of goals and threats to them in different ways. Recall that shame and embarrassment are threats to specific kinds of goals, reputation, or self-presentation, respectively. This suggests that to distinguish these emotions from other emotions, EMA's appraisal process would have to differentially treat threats based on the types of goals threatened, so that a threat to reputation would lead to shame while a threat to self-presentation would lead to embarrassment. EMA currently does not make distinctions based on goal type.

To illustrate this, consider Figure 4.2, which lays out a simple model of embarrassment. If the person has some performance failure, for example, stumbling on stage en route to receiving the Nobel Prize and the audience ("Aud" in Figure 4.2) has no reason to believe there are extenuating circumstances ("¬Bel(Aud,Impaired(Me))"), then it reflects on the person's competence and can threaten (dotted arrow) the person's social goal (highlighted in gray) that the audience believe that the person is competent. EMA has two issues realizing this model. Foremost it doesn't distinguish the type of goal threatened. Currently EMA's appraisal process distinguishes goals only in terms of their utility and likelihood. Therefore, it would treat this threat like a threat to any goal. It would lead to fear—not embarrassment. Moreover, EMA would have difficulty representing the goal itself. The goal of having others believe that the self is competent implies some capacity to represent the beliefs of others. We will return to this point.

More subtly, to distinguish shame and embarrassment from each other would also require the model to distinguish situations in which the transgression or failure is seen, in the case of shame, as a character flaw by both self and other, versus situations where the failure is not perceived by self as a character flaw, as in the case of embarrassment.

Influence on the Appraisal Process. Another challenge raised in the second section comes from social appraisal theory. Specifically, others' emotions and appraisals may influence an individual's appraisals. This influence is not currently addressed in the EMA model.

The work of Hess on reverse-engineered appraisal (Hareli & Hess, 2009) suggests one mechanism for this, arguing that people could infer others' appraisals of a situation by reverse-engineering those appraisals from the others' emotional expressions. We will argue in the following section that in general this presupposes that an individual can model the mental constructs and processes of others, and that reverse-engineered appraisal can be viewed as a form of theory-of-mind reasoning (Premack & Woodruff, 1978). Related to this idea that a person's appraisal can be influenced by others' emotional expressions is the concept of emotional contagion (Hatfield et al., 1994), which posits a more direct connection between people's emotional states.

In terms of EMA, this influence on the appraisal process could be addressed in several ways:

- Given EMA's approach of appraisal as fast feature detectors operating over the causal interpretation, one approach to extending the model to handle this would be to extend the inferential processes that maintain the causal interpretation to use others' appraisals as information to guide that maintenance. So seeing others in the environment express fear about an event leads to inference that the others perceive that event to be threatening and therefore that the individual should also perceive it as threatening.
- Another approach would be to make the appraisal process itself penetrable by how others appraised a situation—in essence having EMA's feature detectors be biased by others' appraisals.
- A third potential approach is through EMA's mood mechanism, whereby other's emotions could be used to transform the agent's own emotions, essentially using EMA's mood mechanism to realize a form of emotional contagion, and that, in turn, would make appraisals consistent with emotion more salient.

Note that these various mechanisms would make different predictions about how others' emotions would influence the individual's appraisal. Regardless, a question arises as to how others appraisals' and which of others' appraisal influence an individual's appraisals. For example, if a member of an in-group perceives a situation as threatening, it may have a quite different emotional meaning than if a member of an out-group perceives it so.

Socioemotive Behavior. The social expression of emotion, the regulation of expression, and coping responses presume complex behavioral consequences. Social appraisal theory argues that a person will regulate his or her emotional behavior in light of how others will interpret it. This presumes the ability to infer how others will appraise one's own emotional responses as well as the desire to influence that appraisal by regulation of one's own expression of emotion. In addition, socially oriented coping strategies and actions need to be modeled, including their effects. For instance, if an agent seeks social support, how does that benefit the agent? Specifically, how does that action impact those that the agent seeks support from, how does it impact those persons' beliefs and behavior, and how do those, in turn, impact the agent? And of course, by seeking social support it is the agent's beliefs that the action will have an impact—the agent's beliefs that others will, in fact, respond in ways the agent believes is beneficial.

A key theme here is that these socially oriented regulations of behavior and coping strategies presume some modeling of the inferential processes of others that constitute the social environment and a concern for both what the resulting inferences are and how that, in turn, impacts the agent. Again consider Figure 4.2, which presumes that the audience is drawing inferences from the stumbling.

Social Interaction. This coupling of emotion and behavior has consequences for the process by which emotion arises in a social interaction. Emotions lead to behavioral responses in face, body, and voice. These behavioral responses influence others' evolving appraisal of a social exchange, their reactions, and one's consequent reaction. This leads to a bidirectional connection between emotions and behavior that can fundamentally shape social interaction. As we noted earlier, a person leans forward (with expectation that other will lean back). If the other instead leans forward as well, it may change the person's beliefs of the other party's mental beliefs/action tendencies and perceptions of control, creating an appraisal of threat that didn't exist before, perhaps evoking anger. Thus, anger "emerges" from the social interaction. The idea of emotional meaning evolving over an interaction is consistent with EMA's appraisal–emotion–coping behavior–reappraisal loop. Under the aassumption that EMA is embedded in a perceptual/inference system that can draw inferences about the other's behavior, such meaning would evolve naturally. A similar example can be found in Marsella & Gratch (2009).

Looking back at Figure 4.1, these various requirements impact the overall architecture's components in several ways:

- *Perception:* Perception must incorporate social perception. The agent must perceive the behavior of self and others and, in particular, be aware of behaviors that have significance to the individual. These may be explicit acts that are relevant to the agent or acts that reveal information about the mental states or processes of others such as verbal and nonverbal behaviors that reveal emotions.
- *Action:* Social actions and their consequences must be modeled. These acts can be explicit, such as providing instrumental and social support, or rather subtle. Consider Figure 4.2. After our Noble Prize winner stumbles, he (she) could redress the threat to competence by simply saying to the audience with some irony: "New shoes bought especially for this ceremony," or he could simply smile, laugh at himself, and shrug as if to say that this is not a fundamental statement about his competence. To realize such behaviors, they must be modeled and incorporated into the agent's behavior.
- *Inference:* Inference must incorporate social inferences, inferences related to the social environment, including what others believe, their emotions, and how they might act. Note that to maintain beliefs about what others believe implies an ability to model what others perceive and what inferences they draw from their perceptions—both of which may differ from what the agent perceives and infers. In our embarrassment example, the winner must explicitly or implicitly take into account the perceptual processes of others—what they will infer from the stumble as well as the repair attempted by the laugh and shrug—so the agent's beliefs about what others believe is updated. Furthermore, the underlying inference process that others use may itself be different in behavior, and ideally in the agent's reasoning about the perceptual processes of others, so the agent's beliefs about what others believe is updated.
- *Causal interpretation:* The causal interpretation must now incorporate the results of social perception, action, and inference. This would involve extensions to fully incorporate beliefs about others such as whether others believe one is competent.

Although these various changes may seem complex, we argue that they are all tightly coupled to beliefs about what others believe, and suggest a rather elegant way that many of them can be addressed. We turn to this next.

Addressing the Requirements: Theory of Mind

In discussing a social functionalist view of appraisal theory, a recurring theme that has been raised is that a social functionalist view often presumes that the individual possesses beliefs about the mental states and processes of others as well as some idealized model of self.

Specifically, the assumption that people have implicit or explicit beliefs about others and have goals associated with those beliefs was a common theme in the discussion of the differences between shame and embarrassment and, more generally, the concept of social appraisal. In the case of shame and embarrassment, a person has a concern that the other may assess him or her as failing some standard and, in the case of embarrassment, there is the concern that a failure is assessed as some fundamental flaw in character. Scherer (2001) argues that anger arises if another agent's transgression was deemed to be intentional and negligent, which again assumes some process that can infer the other agent's intentions and goals.

Taken as a whole, these findings and theories suggest that social emotions involve some form of distinguishing self from other as well as inferential processes that can determine the beliefs, goals, and intentions of the other. In other words, implicit in distinguishing these emotions is some form of theory of mind, the capacity of an agent to possess beliefs about another agent's beliefs, goals, and intentions, and to draw inferences from those beliefs and maintain them in the face of observations. Of course, there is no claim here about the necessary sophistication or accuracy of this capacity. Nevertheless, without this capacity it is not possible to model the distinction between shame and embarrassment, and it is not possible in the case of anger to model the transgressor's act as intentional.

Similarly, social appraisal theory argues that others' appraisals influence the individual's appraisals. However, without some form of theory-of-mind capacity, it is unclear how this could be modeled. Lacking a representation of others' beliefs and goals would limit the ability to infer others' appraisals. Even assuming some other way of inferring others' appraisal, such as directly from behavioral responses, the agent could not represent the resulting inference of the others' appraisal as beliefs about the other.

In addition to some form of theory of-mind capacity being required to model these social emotion distinctions, it is also required to model the consequences of emotion. Specifically, to model the coping processes, such as seek social support, make amends, or mitigate responsibility, all suppose that an agent at least acts as if it believes that others have beliefs that can be influenced and that such strategies may influence those beliefs. In fact, theory of mind may play a larger role in the behavioral consequences of emotion than it plays in the causes. In particular, a person's models of self and others, including that person's beliefs and goals concerning what others believe about him/her, play a critical role as we try to use rationalizations to mitigate responsibility for our behavior (see Martinovski & Marsella, 2003, 2005).

Furthermore, self and other are not the only identities that influence emotions. Individuals have social identities as member of groups and experience emotions as members of those groups. From an appraisal theory perspective, this implies that the individual can appraise events from the perspective of the group's goals and beliefs (Garcia-Prieto & Scherer, 2006). Arguably, this suggests another form of theory-of-mind capacity that allows modeling the beliefs and goals of groups.

In terms of the EMA model specifically, theory of mind largely posits a requirement on the causal interpretation representation and the inferential processes that operate on it, as opposed to the appraisal process itself. The causal interpretation currently used in EMA has the capacity to represent the goals of other agents, but largely no capacity to distinguish beliefs between agents—all agents, including others and the self, share the same beliefs. It is assumed what an agent believes is believed by others. This, in turn, implies that there are no recursive beliefs—what the self believes that another agent believes about the self, for example, cannot be represented. This also means there cannot be goals associated with such beliefs. So, in particular, there is currently no way to represent the distinction between the causes or behavioral consequences of shame and embarrassment. This can also lead to coping responses with interesting consequences—when an agent shifts blame by altering its own responsibility for a harmful event, it changes its own belief as well as the belief it presumes others have.

The work of Pynadath et al. (Chapter 5, this volume) discusses in greater detail the role of theory of mind in modeling the social aspects of appraisal. In particular, it proposes the novel view that a social agent's cognitive processes pose requirements on the agent's decision making and belief maintenance that subsume the appraisal processes. It lays out in detail how the various appraisal checks, such as desirability, unexpectedness, and blameworthiness, are required of any social agent regardless as to whether they have emotions. Finally, it argues for a uniformity of representation and processes whereby the same form of representations and mental processes that guide the agent's own perception, beliefs, and actions can guide and maintain its models of self and others.

On consequence of this assumption in modeling emotion's impact on the agent means that the agent itself may also model in others how their emotions arise and impact on behavior. Thus, phenomena like reverse-engineered appraisal or social appraisal theory do not have to be explicitly, distinctly modeled—they are simply a by-product of maintaining beliefs about others as socioemotive agents. Another's emotional responses are simply evidence that informs an observer's beliefs about the other's appraisal and goals. Similarly, concern for another's appraisal of one's own behavior is a by-product of seeing that other as being like oneself—as an agent that models others as agents that have emotions that influence their behavior.

We can characterize this theory-of-mind perspective on appraisal by reassessing the various appraisal components used in EMA that were discussed earlier:

- *Relevance and desirability:* Clearly any agent must be able to assess relevance and desirability of events in order to guide its attention and responses. For a social agent that must be concerned about relationships with others, whether competitive or cooperation, these assessments will be tied to others goals and reactions.
- *Perspective*: Clearly any social agent would benefit from a basic theory-of-mind ability to assess situations from other perspectives. How is a family member, colleague, or foe going to respond, and what responses does that elicit—pride, happiness, empathy, or schadenfreude?
- *Expectedness*: The appraisal of the predictability of a state is particularly critical from a belief maintenance perspective. Unexpected events or behaviors of others are critical signals that one's

beliefs about the social environment may be amiss. Furthermore, unexpected, relevant events may also be particularly deserving of immediate attention and response.

- *Causal attribution*: Any social agent would be wise to maintain beliefs about who deserves credit or blame that are key to maintaining productive relationships.
- *Controllability and changeability*: These appraise whether an outcome can be altered by actions of the agent whose perspective is taken or by the actions of some other causal agent. Such determination is critical for a social agent to determine whether and how to react, including whether to elicit help from others.

Discussion

Although appraisal theories often characterize appraisal as an assessment of events from the self-centered perspective of the individual's concerns, appraisal theory and the computational models that are derived from it are not incompatible with a social functional view of emotion. Although self-centered, the appraisal process occurs in a social environment that might potentially impact the individual's emotions in several ways. The individual has goals with respect to this social environment, such as maintaining one's reputation. Threats to such a goal will lead to emotions. The social environment may also impact the results of the appraisal process itself. For example, if others see a situation as motivationally incongruent, that may impact an individual's appraisal. Finally, the social environment may require special coping strategies to deal with threats, especially threats to social goals such as maintaining reputation.

EMA models appraisal as distinct from, but tightly coupled to, the perceptual, inference, and behavioral processes. Inference and perception encode the personal relevance of events in ways that make appraisal simple, fast, and general. Appraisal and coping are tightly coupled to the perception, inference, and behavior processes that inform appraisal and are, in turn, informed by coping responses. EMA also generalizes the role of emotion in the overall architecture of an agent. In contrast to the view that emotion and coping are often assumed to be responses limited to highly stressful events, appraisal and coping in EMA play a central role in mediating response for the agent generally and not just in response to highly stressful events.

In EMA, the generality of appraisal to address a wide range of phenomena, from social interactions to physical threats, is in large measure due to the separation of appraisal from other inferential and behavioral processes. However, it is also constrained by those other processes. EMA is coupled to perceptual and inferential processes that currently provide limited awareness of mental processes and nonverbal behaviors of others. As a consequence, EMA cannot leverage representations in the causal interpretation to model the influence that others' behavior has on its own appraisal processes as postulated by social appraisal theory. Conversely, nor can it model the impact its body's behavior has on others' appraisals or, more generally, the impact it has social interaction. Although this problem can be addressed by adding specific representations of others' specific mental states and behavioral expressions, a more general capacity to model the other's goals, beliefs, and mental processes, including appraisals, would be a more flexible, general solution.

Another area of improvement concerns the modeling of types of goals. EMA reasons about the relationship between events and goals but doesn't make explicit distinctions between types of goals. On the other hand, a social functional view argues that there are different classes of goals depending on the social considerations they involve. Some goals are purely individual and don't depend on other social actors for their satisfaction. Other goals are inherently social. For example, imagine an agent choosing whether to defect in a prisoner's dilemma game. This choice presumably impacts its individual goal of gaining material resources. It might threaten a social goal of acting fairly toward others. Finally, its choice might impact "second-order" goals such as "I want my partner to believe I'm fair." Social appraisal theories argue that threats to these goals lead to very different emotions: guilt or shame, respectively. Closely coupled with modeling classes of goals are the actions that impact those goals. In expanding such work, one organizing concept could be to map out how goals differ with respect to the social manipulations required to establish or repair them. For example, individual goals can be achieved by purely individual acts. Joint goals (goals in which both parties must contribute to its achievement) may require actions that impact the other party's motivational state. Second-order goals (e.g., "I want you to think I'm smart"), can ignore the other party's motivations but must influence their belief state. Social appraisal theory argues that emotional displays of guilt, shame, and embarrassment achieve these targeted social manipulations—though whether a virtual agent can implement and achieve these targeted effects is an empirical question, as yet untested.

Acknowledgments

This work was sponsored by the U.S. Army Research, Development, and Engineering Command (RDECOM) and the Air Force Office of Scientific Research under the grant #FA9550–06–1-0206. The content does not necessarily reflect the position or the policy of the government, and no official endorsement should be inferred.

References

Barrett, L. F. (2006). Emotions as natural kinds? *Perspectives on Psychological Science, 1*, 28–58.

Campos, J. J. (1983). The importance of affective communication in social referencing: A commentary on Feinman. *Merrill-Palmer Quarterly* 29, 83–87.

Campos, J. J., Thein, S., & Daniela, O. (2003). A Darwinian legacy to understanding human infancy: Emotional expressions as behavior regulators. In P. Ekman, J. J. Campos, R. J. Davidson, & F. B. M. de Waal (Eds.), *Emotions inside out: 130 years after Darwin's The Expression of the Emotions in Man and Animals* (pp. 110–134). New York: New York Academy of Sciences.

Clore, G., Schwarz, N., & Conway, M. (1994). Affect as information. In J. P. Forgas (Ed.), *Handbook of affect and social cognition* (pp. 121–144). Mahwah, NJ: Lawrence Erlbaum.

Ekman, P., & Friesen, W. V. (1982). Felt, false, and miserable smiles. *Journal of Nonverbal Behavior*, 6(4), 238–252.

Festinger, L. (1954). A theory of social comparison processes. *Human relations*, 7(2), 117–140.

Folkman, S., & Moskowitz, J. T. (2004). Coping: Pitfalls and promise. *Annual Review of Psychology, 55*, 745–774.

Garcia-Prieto, P., & Scherer, K. R. (2006). Connecting social identity theory and cognitive appraisal theory of emotions. In R. Brown & D. Capozza (Eds.), *Social identities: Motivational, emotional, cultural influences* (pp. 189–208). Hove, UK: Psychology Press.

Gratch, J., & Marsella, S. (2004). A domain independent framework for modeling emotion. *Journal of Cognitive Systems Research*, 5(4), 269–306.

Gratch, J., Marsella, S., Wang, N., & Stankovic, B. (2009, September). *Assessing the validity of appraisal-based models of emotion*. Paper presented at the International Conference on Affective Computing and Intelligent Interaction, Amsterdam, The Netherlands.

Hareli, S., and Hess, U. (2009). What emotional reactions can tell us about the nature of others: An appraisal perspective on person perception. *Cognition & Emotion, 24(1), 128–140.*

Hatfield, E., Cacioppo, J. T., & Rapson, R. L. (Eds.). (1994). *Emotional contagion*. Cambridge, UK: Cambridge University Press.

Keltner, D., and Haidt, J. (1999). Social Functions of Emotions at Four Levels of Analysis. *Cognition and Emotion, 13*(5), 505–521.

Lazarus, R. (1991). *Emotion and adaptation*. New York: Oxford University Press.

Lazarus, R. (1999). *Stress and emotion*. New York: Springer.

Leary, M. R., Landel, J. L., & Patton, K. M. (1996). The motivated expression of embarrassment following a self-presentational predicament. *Journal of Personality and Social Psychology, 64*, 619–636.

Manstead, A. S. R., & Fischer, A. H. (2001). Social appraisal: The social world as object of and influence on appraisal processes. In K. R. Scherer, A. Schorr, & T. Johnstone (Eds.), *Appraisal processes in emotion: Theory, methods, research* (pp. 221–232). New York: Oxford University Press.

Mao, W., & Gratch, J. (2005, September). *Social causality and responsibility: Modeling and evaluation*. Paper presented at the International Working Conference on Intelligent Virtual Agents, Kos, Greece.

Marsella, S., & Gratch, J. (2009). EMA: A model of emotional dynamics. *Journal of Cognitive Systems Research, 10*(1), 70–90.

Marsella, S., Gratch, J., Wang, N., & Stankovic, B. (2009, September). *Assessing the validity of a computational model of emotional coping*. Paper presented at the International Conference on Affective Computing and Intelligent Interaction, Amsterdam, The Netherlands.

Marsella, S., Gratch, J., & Petta, P. (2010). Computational models of emotion. In K. R. Scherer, T. Bänziger, & E. Roesch (Eds.), *A blueprint for affective computing: A sourcebook and manual* (pp. 21–46). New York: Oxford University Press.

Martinovski, B., and Marsella, S. (2003). Coping processes in discourse: dynamic reconstruction of selfhood. Proceeding of the 4th International Conference on Cognitive Science, Sydney, Australia.

Martinovski, B., and Marsella, S. (2005). Theory of mind and coping in discourse. *Artificial intelligence and the simulation of behavior, Paper presented at the Convention on Artificial Intelligence and the Simulation of Behavior. Hatfield, UK, April.*

Parkinson, B. (2001). Putting appraisal in context. In K. Scherer, A. Schorr, & T. Johnstone (Eds.), *Appraisal processes in emotion: Theory, methods, research* (pp. 173–186). London: Oxford University Press.

Premack, D., & Woodruff, G. (1978). Does the chimpanzee have a theory of mind? *Behavioral and Brain Sciences, 1*, 515–526.

Scherer, K. R. (2001). Appraisal considered as a process of multilevel sequential checking. In K. R. Scherer, A. Schorr, & T. Johnstone (Eds.), *Appraisal processes in emotion: Theory, methods, research* (pp. 92–120). Oxford University Press.

Snyder, C. (1989). Reality negotiation: From excuses to hope and beyond. *Journal of Social and Clinical Psychology*, 8(2), 130–157.

Snyder, C., & Higgins, R. L. (1997). Reality negotiation: Governing one's self and being governed by others. *Review of General Psychology, 1*(4), 336.

Zajonc, R. B. (1980). Feeling and thinking: Preferences need no inferences. *American Psychologist, 35*, 151–175.

5

Modeling Theory of Mind and Cognitive Appraisal With Decision-Theoretic Agents

David V. Pynadath, Mei Si, & Stacy Marsella

1. Introduction

Computational models of social interaction have become increasingly important in both basic research on human social behavior and a range of applications. For example, computational models of psychological or sociological theories promise to transform how theories of human behavior are formulated and evaluated (Marsella et al., 2010). In addition, computational models of human social interaction have also become increasingly important as a means to create simulated social environments used in a variety of training and entertainment applications (McAlinden et al., 2009). For example, many serious games have used models of social interaction as the basis for virtual (typically embodied) autonomous characters (Aylett et al., 2006; Paiva et al., 2004; Si et al., 2005a; Swartout et al., 2001; Traum et al., 2005).

We argue that such models of social interaction must address the fact that people interact within a complex social framework. A central factor in social interaction is the beliefs we have about each other, a *theory of mind* (Whiten, 1991). Our choice of action is influenced by how we believe others will feel and react. Whether we believe what we are told depends not only on the content of the communication but also on our model of the communicator. How we emotionally react to another's action is influenced by our beliefs as well, for example, whether we believe he or she intended to cause harm (Scherer, 2001). The central goal of our research is to bring such theory of mind capacities to the design of computational models of social interaction both as a basic research tool and as a framework for virtual character design.

Unfortunately, traditional artificial intelligence techniques are ill suited for modeling theory of mind. Representations using first-order logic are often insensitive to the distinctions among conflicting goals that people must balance in a social interaction. For example, psychological research has identified a range of goals that motivate classroom bullies (e.g., peer approval, sadism, tangible rewards) (Schwartz, 2000).

Different bullies may share the same goals, but the relative priorities that they place on them will lead to variations in their behavior. Resolving the ambiguity among equally possible, but unequally plausible or preferred, options requires a quantitative model of uncertainty and preference. Unfortunately, more quantitative frameworks, like decision theory and game theory, face their own difficulties in modeling human psychology. Game-theoretic frameworks typically rely on concepts of equilibria that people rarely achieve in an unstructured social setting like a classroom. Decision-theoretic frameworks typically rely on assumptions of rationality that people violate.

We have developed a social simulation framework, PsychSim (Marsella et al., 2004; Pynadath & Marsella, 2005), that operationalizes existing psychological theories as boundedly rational computations to generate more plausibly human behavior. PsychSim allows a user to quickly construct a social scenario where a diverse set of entities, groups, or individuals interact and communicate. Each entity has its own preferences, relationships (e.g., friendship, hostility, authority) with other entities, private beliefs, and mental models about other entities. The simulation tool generates the behavior for these entities and provides explanations of the result in terms of each entity's preferences and beliefs. The richness of the entity models allows one to explore the potential consequences of minor variations on the scenario.

A central aspect of the PsychSim design is that agents have fully specified decision-theoretic models of others. Such quantitative recursive models give PsychSim a powerful mechanism to model a range of factors in a principled way. For instance, we exploit this recursive modeling to allow agents to form complex attributions about others, send messages that include the beliefs and preferences of others, and use their observations of another's behavior to influence their model of that other.

In operationalizing psychological theories within PsychSim, we have taken a strong architectural stance. We assume that decision-theoretic agents that incorporate a theory of mind provide a uniform, sufficient computational core for modeling the factors relevant to human social interaction. While the sufficiency of our framework remains an open question, such a strong stance yields the benefit of uniform processes and representations that cover a range of phenomena. Our stance thus provides subsequent computational benefits, such as optimization and reuse of the core algorithms that provide the agent's decision-making and belief revision capacities.

More significantly, this uniformity begins to reveal common elements across apparently disparate psychological phenomena that typically have different methodological histories. To illustrate such common elements, we have demonstrated how a range of human psychological and social phenomena can be modeled within our framework, including wishful thinking (Ito et al., 2010), influence factors (Marsella et al., 2004), childhood aggression (Pynadath & Marsella, 2005), and emotion (Si et al., 2010b).

In this chapter, we discuss two of those models. First, we use a model of childhood aggression to motivate the discussion of the overall framework as well as to demonstrate its expressiveness. Second, in keeping with the theme of this volume, we go into considerable detail on how PsychSim's decision-theoretic agents with a theory of mind provide a particularly effective basis for a computational model of emotion.

Computational models of emotion have largely been based on appraisal theory (Dias & Paiva, 2005; Elliott, 1992; El Nasr et al., 2000; Marinier et al., 2009; Moffat & Frijda, 1995; Ortony et al., 1998; Reilly & Bates, 1992; Velasquez, 1997), a leading psychological theory of emotion. Appraisal theory argues that a person's subjective assessment of his or her relationship to the environment determines his or her emotional responses (Frijda, 1987; Lazarus, 1991; Lazzaro, 2004; Ortony et al., 1998; Roseman, 1984; Scherer, 2001; Smith & Ellsworth, 1987, Smith & Lazarus, 1990). This assessment occurs along several dimensions, such as motivational congruence, accountability, novelty, and control. For example, an event that leads to a bad outcome for a person (motivationally incongruent) and is believed to be caused by others (accountability) is likely to elicit an anger response. On the other hand, if the event is believed to be caused by the person himself/herself, he/she is more likely to feel guilt or regret (Roseman, 1984).

We approach the task of incorporating appraisal into the existing PsychSim multiagent framework as a form of thought experiment: Can we leverage the existing processes and representations in PsychSim to model appraisal? The motivations for this thought experiment are threefold. First, we seek to demonstrate overlap between the theoretical model of appraisal theory and decision-theoretic, social agents of PsychSim. Specifically, we are interested in whether appraisal offers a possible blueprint, or requirements specification, for intelligent social agents by showing that an existing framework not predesigned with emotion or appraisal in mind has, in fact, appraisal-like processes already present.

Conversely, we seek to illustrate the critical role that subjective beliefs about others plays in allowing agents to model social emotions. Because the agent's representations and decision-making processes are rooted in a theory-of-mind capacity, and incorporating and maintaining beliefs about others, the appraisal process inherits this social frame, allowing the agent to appraise events from its own perspective as well as others'. Thus, in keeping with the tenets of *social appraisal* (Manstead & Fischer, 2001), the behaviors, thoughts, and emotions of the other can also be appraised and thereby influence the agent.

Finally, we seek a design that is elegant, by reusing architectural features to realize new capabilities such as emotion. Alternative approaches for creating embodied conversational agents and virtual agents often integrate separate modules for emotion, decision-making, dialogue, and so on, which leads to sophisticated but complex architectures (Swartout et al., 2001). The work here is an alternative minimalist agenda for agent design. In particular, based on the core theory of mind reasoning processes, appraisal can be derived with few extensions.

We begin the chapter with a demonstration of PsychSim's application to a childhood aggression scenario. We then discuss how PsychSim can represent appraisal theory and present a preliminary assessment of its implementation.

2. The Agent Models

This section describes PsychSim's underlying architecture, using a school bully scenario for illustration. The agents represent different people and groups in the school setting. The user can analyze the simulated behavior of the students to explore the causes and cures for school violence. One agent represents a bully, and another represents the student who is the target of the bully's violence. A third agent represents the group of onlookers, who encourage the bully's exploits by, for example, laughing at the victim as he is beaten up. A final agent represents the class's teacher trying to maintain control of the classroom, for example, by doling out punishment in response to the violence. We embed PsychSim's agents within a decision-theoretic framework for quantitative modeling of multiple agents. Each agent maintains its independent beliefs about the world and has its own goals and own policies for achieving those goals.

2.1. Model of the World

Each agent model starts with a representation of its current state and the Markovian process by which that state evolves over time in response to the actions performed.

2.1.1. State

Each agent model includes several features representing its "true" state. This state consists of objective facts about the world, some of which may be hidden from the agent itself. For our example bully domain, we included such state features as power (agent), to represent the strength of an agent. "Trust" (truster, trustee) represents the degree of trust that the agent truster has in another agent trustee's messages. "Support" (supporter, supportee) is the strength of support that an agent supporter has for another agent supportee. We represent the state as a vector, $\vec{S}^t$, where each component corresponds to one of these state features and has a value in the range $[-1, 1]$.

2.1.2. Actions

Agents have a set of actions that they can choose to change the world. An action consists of an action type (e.g., punish), an agent performing the action (i.e., the actor), and possibly another agent who is the object of the action. For example, the action laugh (onlooker, victim) represents the laughter of the onlooker directed at the victim.

2.1.3. World Dynamics

The state of the world changes in response to the actions performed by the agents. We model these dynamics using a transition probability function, $T(\vec{S}_i, \vec{a}, \vec{S}_f)$, to capture the possibly uncertain effects of these actions on the subsequent state (Equation 1):

$$\Pr(\vec{S}^{t+1} = \vec{S}_f \mid \vec{S}^t = \vec{S}_i, \vec{a}^t = \vec{a}) = T(\vec{S}_i, \vec{a}, \vec{S}_f) \quad (1)$$

For example, the bully's attack on the victim impacts the power of the bully, the power of the victim, and so on. The distribution over the bully's and victim's changes in power is a function of the relative powers of the two—for example, the larger the power gap that the bully enjoys over the victim, the more likely the victim is to suffer a big loss in power.

2.2. Preferences

PsychSim's decision-theoretic framework represents an agent's incentives for behavior as a reward function that maps the state of the world into a real-valued evaluation of benefit for the agent. We separate components of this reward function into two types of subgoals. A goal of *Minimize/maximize* feature (agent) corresponds to a negative/positive reward proportional to the value of the given state feature. For example, an agent can have the goal of maximizing its own power. A goal of *Minimize/maximize* action (actor, object) corresponds to a negative/positive reward proportional to the number of matching actions performed. For example, the teacher may have the goal of minimizing the number of times any student teases any other.

We can represent the overall preferences of an agent, as well as the relative priority among them, as a vector of weights, $\vec{g}$, so that the product, $\vec{g} \cdot \vec{S}^t$, quantifies the degree of satisfaction that the agent receives from the world, as represented by the state vector, $\vec{S}^t$. For example, in the school violence simulation, the bully's reward function consists of goals of maximizing power (bully), minimizing power (victim), and maximizing laugh (onlookers, victim). By modifying the weights on the different goals, we can alter the motivation of the agent and, thus, its behavior in the simulation.

2.3. Beliefs About Others

As described by Sections 2.1 and 2.2, the overall decision problem facing a single agent maps easily into a partially observable Markov decision problem (POMDP) (Smallwood & Sondik, 1973). Software agents can solve such a decision problem using existing algorithms to form their beliefs and then determine the action that maximizes their reward given those beliefs. However, we do not expect people to conform to such optimality in their behavior. Thus, we have taken the POMDP algorithms as our starting point and modified them in a psychologically motivated manner to capture more human-like behavior. This "bounded rationality" better captures the reasoning of people in the real world, as well as provides the additional benefit of avoiding the computational complexity incurred by an assumption of perfect rationality.

2.3.1. Nested Beliefs

The agents have only a *subjective* view of the world, where they form beliefs, $\vec{b}^t$, about what they *think* is the state of the world, $\vec{S}^t$. Agent A's beliefs about agent *B* have the same structure as the real agent *B*. Thus, our agent belief models follow a recursive structure, similar to previous work on game-theoretic agents (Gmytrasiewicz & Durfee, 1995). Of course, the nesting of these agent models is potentially unbounded. However, although infinite nesting is required for modeling optimal behavior, people rarely use such deep models (Taylor et al., 1996). In our school violence scenario, we found that 2-level nesting was sufficiently rich to generate the desired behavior. Thus, the agents model each other as 1-level agents, who, in turn, model each other as 0-level agents, who do *not* have any beliefs. Thus, there is an inherent loss of precision (but with a gain in computational efficiency) as we move deeper into the belief structure.

For example, an agent's beliefs may include its subjective view on states of the world: "The bully believes that the teacher is weak," "The onlookers believe that the teacher supports the victim," or "The bully believes that he/she is powerful." These beliefs may also include its subjective view on beliefs of other agents: "The teacher believes that the bully believes the teacher to be weak." An agent may also have a subjective view of the *preferences* of other agents: "The teacher believes that the bully has a goal to increase his power." It is important to note that we also separate an agent's subjective view of itself from the real agent. We can thus represent errors that the agent has in its view of itself (e.g., the bully believes himself to be stronger than he actually is).

Actions affect the beliefs of agents in several ways. For example, the bully's attack may alter the beliefs that agents have about the state of the world—such as beliefs about the bully's power. Each agent updates its beliefs according to its subjective beliefs about the world dynamics. It may also alter the beliefs about the bully's preferences and policy. We discuss the procedure of belief update in Section 2.4.

2.3.2. Policies of Behavior

Each agent's policy is a function, $\pi(\vec{b})$, that represents the process by which it selects an action or message based on its beliefs. An agent's policy allows us to model critical psychological distinctions such as reactive versus deliberative behavior. We model each agent's real policy as a bounded lookahead procedure that seeks to maximize expected reward simulating the behavior of the other agents and the dynamics of the world in response to the selected action/message (Equations 2 and 3). Each agent i computes a quantitative value, $V_a(\vec{b}_i^t)$, of each possible action, a, given its beliefs, $\vec{b}_i^t$.

$$V_a^N(\vec{b}_i^t) = \vec{g}_i \cdot \vec{b}_i^t + \sum_{\vec{b}_i^{t+1}} V^{N-1}(\vec{b}_i^{t+1}) \Pr(\vec{b}_i^{t+1} \mid \vec{b}_i^{t+1}, a, \vec{\pi}_{-i}(\vec{b}_i^{t+1})) \quad (2)$$

$$V^N(\vec{b}_i^t) = \max_a V_a^N(\vec{b}_i^t) \quad (3)$$

The agent computes the posterior probability of subsequent belief states $\Pr(\vec{b}_i^{t+1})$ by using the transition function, T, to project the immediate effect of the action, a, on its beliefs. It then projects another N steps into the future, weighing each state against its goals, $\vec{\vec{g}}$. At the first step, agent i uses its model of the policies of all of the other agents, $\vec{\pi}_{-i}$, and, in subsequent steps, it uses its model of the policies of all agents, including itself, π. Thus, the agent is seeking to maximize the expected reward of its behavior as in a POMDP. However, PsychSim's agents are only boundedly rational, given that they are constrained, both by the finite horizon, N, of their lookahead and the possible error in their belief state, $\vec{b}$. By varying N for different agents, we can model entities who display different degrees of reactive versus deliberative behavior in their thinking.

2.3.3. *Stereotypical Mental Models*

If we applied this full lookahead policy within the nested models of the other agents, the computational complexity of the top-level lookahead would quickly become infeasible as the number of agents grew. To simplify the agents' reasoning, these mental models are realized as simplified stereotypes of the richer lookahead behavior models of the agents themselves. For our simulation model of a bullying scenario, we have implemented mental models corresponding to *attention-seeking*, *sadistic*, *dominance-seeking*, and so on. For example, a model of an attention-seeking bully specifies a high priority on increasing the approval (i.e., support) that the other agents have for it, a dominance-seeking bully specifies a high priority on increasing its power as paramount, and a bully agent specifies a high priority on hurting others.

These simplified mental models also include potentially erroneous beliefs about the policies of other agents. Although the real agents use lookahead exclusively when choosing their own actions (as described in Section 2.3.2), the agents *believe* that the other agents follow much more reactive policies as part of their mental models of each other. PsychSim models reactive policies as a table of "Condition ⇒ Action" rules. The left-hand side conditions may trigger on an *observation* of some action or a *belief* of some agent (e.g., the bully believing himself as powerful). The conditions may also be more complicated combinations of these basic triggers (e.g., a *conjunction* of conditions that matches when each and every individual condition matches).

The use of these more reactive policies in the mental models that agents have of each other achieves two desirable results. First, from a human modeling perspective, the agents perform a shallower reasoning that provides a more accurate model of the real-world entities they represent. Second, from a computational perspective, the direct action rules are cheap to execute, so the agents gain significant efficiency in their reasoning.

2.4. Modeling Influence and Belief Change

2.4.1. *Messages*

Messages are attempts by one agent to influence the beliefs of another. Messages have four components: source, recipients, subject, and content. For example, the teacher (source) could tell the bully (recipient) that the principal (subject of the message) will punish violence by the bully (content). Messages can refer to beliefs, preferences, policies, or any other aspect of other agents. Thus, a message may make a claim about a state feature of the subject ("the principal is powerful"), the beliefs of the subject ("the principal believes that he is powerful"), the preferences of the subject ("the bully wants to increase his power"), the policy of the subject ("if the bully thinks the victim is weak, he will pick on him"), or the stereotypical model of the subject ("the bully is selfish").

2.4.2. *Influence Factors*

A challenge in creating a social simulation is addressing how groups or individuals influence each other, and how they update their beliefs and alter behavior based on any partial observation of, as well as messages from, others. Although many psychological results and theories must inform the modeling of such influence (e.g., Abelson et al., 1968; Cialdini, 2001; Petty & Cacioppo, 1986), they often suffer from two shortcomings from a computational perspective. First, they identify factors that affect influence but do not operationalize those factors. Second, they are rarely comprehensive and do not address the details of how various factors relate to each other or can be composed. To provide a sufficient basis for our computational models, our approach has been to distill key psychological factors and map those factors into our simulation framework. Here, our decision-theoretic models are helpful in quantifying the impact of factors in such a way that they can be composed. Specifically, a survey of the social psychology literature identified the following key factors:

Consistency: People expect, prefer, and are driven to maintain consistency, and avoid cognitive dissonance, between beliefs and behaviors.

Self-interest: The inferences we draw are biased by self-interest (e.g., motivated inference), and how deeply we analyze information in general is biased by self-interest.

Speaker's self-interest: If the sender of a message benefits greatly if the recipient believes it, there is often a tendency to be more critical and for influence to fail.

Trust, likability, affinity: The relation to the source of the message, whether we trust, like, or have some group affinity for him, impacts whether we are influenced by the message.

2.4.3 Computational Model of Influence

To model such factors in the simulation, one could specify them exogenously and make them explicit, user-specified factors for a message. This tactic is often employed in social simulations in which massive numbers of simpler, often identical, agents are used to explore emergent social properties. However, providing each agent with quantitative models of itself and, more importantly, of other agents gives us a powerful mechanism to model this range of factors in a principled way. We model these factors by a few simple mechanisms in the simulation: *consistency*, *self-interest*, and *bias*. We can render each as a quantitative function of beliefs that allows an agent to compare alternate candidate belief states (e.g., an agent's original $\vec{b}$ vs. the $\vec{b}'$ implied by a message).

Consistency is an evaluation of the degree to which a potential belief agreed with prior observations. In effect, the agent asks itself, "If this belief holds, would it better explain the past than my current beliefs?" We use a Bayesian definition of consistency based on the relative likelihood of past observations given the two candidate sets of beliefs (e.g., my current beliefs with and without believing the message). An agent assesses the quality of the competing explanations by a resimulation of the past history. In other words, it starts at time 0 with the two worlds implied by the two candidate sets of beliefs, projects each world forward up to the current point of time, and computes the probability of the observation it received. The higher the value, the more likely that agent is to have chosen the observed action, and, thus, the higher the degree of consistency.

In previous work, we have investigated multiple methods of converting such action values into a degree of consistency (Ito et al., 2007). For the purposes of the current work, we use only one of those methods, defining the consistency of a sequence of observations, ω^0, ω^1, …, with a given belief state, $\vec{b}$, in Equation 4:

$$\text{consistency}(\vec{b}^t,[\omega^0,\omega^1,\cdots,\omega^{t-1}]) = \Pr([\omega^0,\omega^1,\cdots,\omega^{t-1}]|\vec{b}^t)$$
$$\alpha\sum_{\tau=0}^{t-1}\sum_{\alpha\in A} e^{\text{rank}(V_\alpha(\vec{b}^\tau)\Pr(\omega^\tau|a,\vec{b}^\tau))} \quad (4)$$

The algorithm first ranks the utilities of the actor's alternative actions in reversed order (rank(υ)). The value function, V, is computed with respect to the agent performing the action at time τ. Thus, the higher the rank of the likelihood of the observation, the more consistent it is with the candidate belief state.

Self-interest is similar to consistency, in that the agent compares two sets of beliefs, one which accepts the message and one which rejects it. However, while consistency evaluates the past, we compute self-interest by evaluating the future using Equation 3. An agent can perform an analogous computation using its beliefs about the sender's preferences to compute the sender's self-interest in sending the message.

Bias factors represent subjective views of the message sender that influence the receiver's acceptance/rejection of the message. We treat support (or affinity) and trust as such a bias on message acceptance. Agents compute their support and trust levels as a running history of their past interactions. In particular, one agent increases (decreases) its trust in another when the second sends a message that the first decides to accept (reject). Similarly, an agent increases (decreases) its support for another when the second selects an action that has a high (low) reward, with respect to the preferences of the first. In other words, if an agent selects an action *a*, then the other agents modify their support level for that agent by a value proportional to $\vec{g} \cdot \vec{b}$, where $\vec{g}$ corresponds to the goals, and $\vec{b}$ the new beliefs of the agent modifying its support.

Upon receiving any information (whether message or observation), an agent must consider all of these various factors in deciding whether to accept it and how to alter its beliefs (including its mental models of the other agents). For a message, the agent determines acceptance using a weighted sum of the five components: consistency, self-interest, speaker self-interest, trust, and support. Whenever an agent observes an action by another, it checks whether the observation is consistent with its current beliefs (including mental models). If so, no belief change is necessary. If not, the agent evaluates alternate mental models as possible new beliefs to adopt in light of this inconsistent behavior. Agents evaluate these possible belief changes using the same weighted sum as for messages.

Each agent's decision-making procedure is sensitive to these changes that its actions may trigger in the beliefs of others. Each agent accounts for the others' belief update when doing its lookahead, as Equations 2 and 3 project the future beliefs of the other agents in response to an agent's selected action. Similar to work by De Rosis et al. (2003), this mechanism provides PsychSim agents with a potential incentive to deceive, if doing so leads the other agents to perform actions that lead to a better state for the deceiving agent.

We see the computation of these factors as a toolkit for the user to explore the system's behavior under existing theories, which we can encode in PsychSim. For example, the elaboration likelihood model (ELM) (Petty & Cacioppo, 1986) argues that the way messages are processed differs according to the relevance of the message to the receiver. High relevance or importance would lead to a deeper assessment of the message, which is consistent with the self-interest calculations our model performs. PsychSim's linear combination of factors is roughly in keeping with ELM because self-interest values of high magnitude would tend to dominate.

3. Childhood Aggression Model

The research literature on childhood aggression provides interesting insight into the role that theory of mind plays in human behavior. Investigations of bullying and victimization (Schwartz, 2000) have identified four types of children; we focus here on *nonvictimized aggressors*, those who display proactive aggression due to positive outcome expectancies for aggression. Children develop expectations on the likely outcomes of aggression based on past experiences (e.g., did past acts of aggression lead to rewards or punishment?). This section describes the results of our exploration of the space of different nonvictimized aggressors and the effectiveness of possible intervention strategies in dealing with them.

3.1. Scenario Setup

The user sets up a simulation in PsychSim by selecting generic agent models that will play the roles of the various groups or individuals to be simulated and specializing those models as needed. In our bullying scenario, we constructed generic bully models that compute outcome expectancies as the expected value of actions (V_a from Equation 2). Thus, when considering possible aggression, the agents consider the immediate effect of an act of violence, as well as the possible consequences, including the change in the beliefs of the other agents. In our example scenario, a bully has three subgoals that provide incentives to perform an act of aggression: (1) to change the power dynamic in the class by making himself stronger, (2) to change the power dynamic by weakening his victim, and (3) to earn the approval of his peers (as demonstrated by their response of laughter at the victim). Our bully agent models the first incentive as a goal of maximizing power (bully) and the second as minimizing power (victim), both coupled with a belief that an act of aggression will increase the former and decrease the latter. The third incentive seeks to maximize the laugh actions directed at the victim, so it must consider the actions that the other agents may take in response.

For example, a bully motivated by the approval of his classmates would use his mental model of them to predict whether they would laugh along with him. We implemented two possible mental models of the bully's classmates: *encouraging*, in which the students will laugh at the victim, and *scared*, in which the students will laugh only if the teacher did not punish them for laughing last time. Similarly, the bully would use his mental model of the teacher to predict whether he will be punished or not. We provide the bully with three possible mental models of the teacher: *normal*, in which the teacher will punish the bully in response to an act of violence; *severe*, in which the teacher will more harshly punish the bully than in the *normal* model; and *weak*, in which the teacher never punishes the bully.

The relative priorities of these subgoals within the bully's overall reward function provide a large space of possible behavior. When creating a model of a specific bully, PsychSim uses a fitting algorithm to automatically determine the appropriate weights for these goals to match observed behavior. For example, if the user wants the bully to initially attack a victim and the teacher to threaten the bully with punishment, then the user specifies those behaviors and the model parameters are fitted accordingly (Pynadath & Marsella, 2004). This degree of automation significantly simplifies simulation setup. In this experiment, we selected three specific bully models from the overall space: (1) *dominance-seeking*, (2) *sadistic*, and (3) *attention-seeking*, each corresponding to a goal weighting that favors the corresponding subgoal.

TABLE 5.1 Outcomes of Intervention Strategies

Bully type	*Punish whom?*	*Model of students*	*Model of teacher*	*Success?*
Sadistic	Bully	*	Severe	N
			Severe	Y
	Class	Scared	*	N
		Encouraging	Severe	N
			Severe	Y
	No One	*	Severe	N
			Severe	Y
Attention seeking	Bully	*	*	N
	Class	Scared	Weak	N
			Normal	Y
			Severe	Y
		Encouraging	*	N
	No One	*	*	N
Dominance seeking	*	*	Weak	N
			Normal	Y
			Severe	Y

3.2. Experimental Results

PsychSim allows one to explore multiple tactics for dealing with a social issue and to see the potential consequences. Here, we examine a decision point for the teacher after the bully has attacked the victim, followed by laughter by the rest of the class. At this point, the teacher can punish the bully, punish the whole class (including the victim), or do nothing. We explore the impact of different types of proactive aggression by varying the type of the bully; the teacher's decision to punish the bully, the whole class, or no one; and the mental models that the bully has of the other students and the teacher.

A successful outcome is when the bully does not choose to act out violently toward the victim the next time around. By examining the outcomes under these combinations, we can see the effects of intervention over the space of possible classroom settings. Table 5.1 shows all of the outcomes, where we use the "*" wildcard symbol to collapse rows where the outcome was the same. Similarly, a row with "severe" in the "Teacher" row spans the cases where the bully's mental model of the teacher is either *normal* or *weak*.

We first see that the PsychSim bully agent meets our intuitive expectations. For example, we see from Table 5.1 that if the bully thinks that the teacher is too weak to ever punish, then no immediate action by the teacher will change the bully from picking on the victim. Thus, it is critical for the teacher to avoid behavior that leads the bully to form such mental models. Similarly, if the bully is of the *attention-seeking* variety, then punishment directed at solely himself will not dissuade him, as he will still expect to gain peer approval. In such cases, the teacher is better off punishing the whole class.

We can see more interesting cases as we delve deeper. For example, if we look at the case of a *sadistic* bully when the teacher punishes the whole class, we see that bully can be dissuaded only if he thinks that the other students will *approve* of his act of violence. This outcome may seem counterintuitive at first, but the *sadistic* bully is primarily concerned with causing suffering for the victim and thus does not mind being punished if the victim is punished as well. However, if the bully thinks that the rest of the class is *encouraging*, then the teacher's punishment of the whole class costs him peer approval. On the other hand, if the bully thinks that the rest of the class is already *scared*, so that they will not approve of his violence, then he has no peer approval to lose.

Such exploration can offer the user an understanding of the potential pitfalls in implementing an intervention strategy. Rather than provide a simple prediction of whether a strategy will succeed or not, PsychSim maps out the key conditions, in terms of the bully's preferences and beliefs, on which a strategy's success depends. PsychSim provides a rich space of possible models that we can systematically explore to understand the social behavior that arises out of different configurations of student psychologies. We are continuing to investigate more class configurations and the effects of possible interventions as we expand our models to cover all of the factors in school aggression identified in the literature.

4. A Model of Appraisal

To further illustrate the capacity of these decision-theoretic agents to model social interaction, we also used them to implement a computational model of emotion, largely based on Smith and Lazarus's theory of cognitive appraisal (Smith & Lazarus, 1990). As noted in Section 1, our implementation was driven by a thought experiment: Can we leverage the existing processes and representations in PsychSim to model appraisal? The motivations for this thought experiment are threefold. First, we seek to demonstrate an intrinsic coupling between the theoretical model of appraisal and decision-theoretic social reasoning. Specifically, we wish to show that an existing social framework with no explicit emotion or appraisal capabilities has, in fact, appraisal-like processes already present as part of its decision-making processes. Second, we also seek to illustrate the critical role that subjective beliefs about others play in modeling social emotions. Finally, we seek a minimalist design that elegantly reuses architectural features to model new social phenomena, like emotion.

This work on modeling appraisal is in the spirit of EMA (Gratch & Marsella, 2004; Marsella & Gratch, 2009) (see also Chapter 4 of this volume), which defines appraisal processes as operations over a plan-based representation (a *causal interpretation*) of the agent's goals and how events impact those goals. The agent's existing cognitive processes maintain the causal interpretation, which appraisal-specific processes leverage. Thus, in EMA, the cognitive processes for constructing the person–environment relation representation are distinct from appraisal itself, which is reduced to simple and fast pattern matching over the plan representation.

We seek to eliminate this distinction by demonstrating how the cognitive processes for decision making can also generate appraisals. While EMA uses a uniform *representation* across cognition and appraisal, we seek to additionally establish uniformity over the *algorithms* underlying both cognition and appraisal. In so doing, we can establish that appraisal itself is already an integral part of the cognitive processes that a social agent must perform to maintain its beliefs about others and to inform its decision making in a multiagent social context.

Specifically, we treat appraisal as leveraging component algorithms already present in a PsychSim agent by deriving key appraisal variables from the outputs of these algorithms. Furthermore, the appraisal process inherits the intrinsic social nature of these algorithms, allowing the agent to appraise events from another's perspective, as well as from its own. Thus, in keeping with Manstead and Fischer's concept of social appraisal, the behaviors, thoughts, and emotions of the other can also be appraised and thereby influence the agent.

We have modeled five appraisal dimensions so far: motivational relevance, motivational congruence, accountability, control, and novelty. We adapted Smith and Lazarus's (1990) definitions for modeling motivational relevance, motivational congruence, and accountability. Our model of control is roughly equivalent to Smith and Lazarus's (1990) definition of problem-focused coping potential. It is closer to Scherer's (Scherer, 2001) definition of control because it accounts for the overall changeability of the situation and not an individual agent's power to make a change. Finally, we modeled novelty based on Leventhal and Scherer's (Leventhal & Scherer, 1987; Scherer, 2001) definition of predictability-based novelty, as there is no equivalent concept in Smith and Lazarus.

The model of appraisal is built within Thespian (Si et al., 2005a, 2005b, 2006, 2007, 2009, 2010a, 2010b), which extends PsychSim for modeling and simulating computer-aided interactive narratives. This computational model of appraisal is one of Thespian's extensions. We demonstrate the application of the appraisal model in three different scenarios: a simple conversation between two people, a firing-squad scenario as modeled in (Mao & Gratch, 2005), and a fairy tale, "Little Red Riding Hood." The last scenario will be described in detail in the next section as it will be used as an example to motivate the discussion of our appraisal model. The details of the other two scenarios are given in Section 5.

4.1. Little Red Riding Hood Domain

The story contains four main characters, Little Red Riding Hood (Red), Granny, the hunter, and the wolf. The story starts as Red and the wolf meet each other on the outskirts of a forest while Red is on her way to Granny's house. The wolf wants to eat Red, but it dares not because there is a woodcutter close by. At this point, the wolf and Red can either have a conversation or go their separate ways. The wolf may have future chances to eat Red if he finds her alone at another location.

Moreover, if the wolf hears about Granny from Red, it can even go to Granny's house and eat her as well. Meanwhile, the hunter is searching for the wolf to kill it. Once the wolf is killed, all of the wolf's previous victims can escape. Our model of this story builds upon the base PsychSim representation, as described in Section 2.

4.2. Modeling Appraisal in Thespian

Appraisal is a continuous process (Smith & Lazarus, 1990). People constantly reevaluate their situations and cope with unfavorable situations, forming an "appraisal–coping–reappraisal" loop. In this section we illustrate how we can model this phenomenon and derive appraisal dimensions by leveraging algorithms and information within a PsychSim agent's belief revision and decision-making processes.

During decision making, the lookahead process generates the agent's expectations about possible future events so that it can choose the action with the most favorable outcome. Figure 5.1 is an example of one-step lookahead while assuming that the other characters will also perform a one-step lookahead. Bold shapes denote the actions with the highest expected

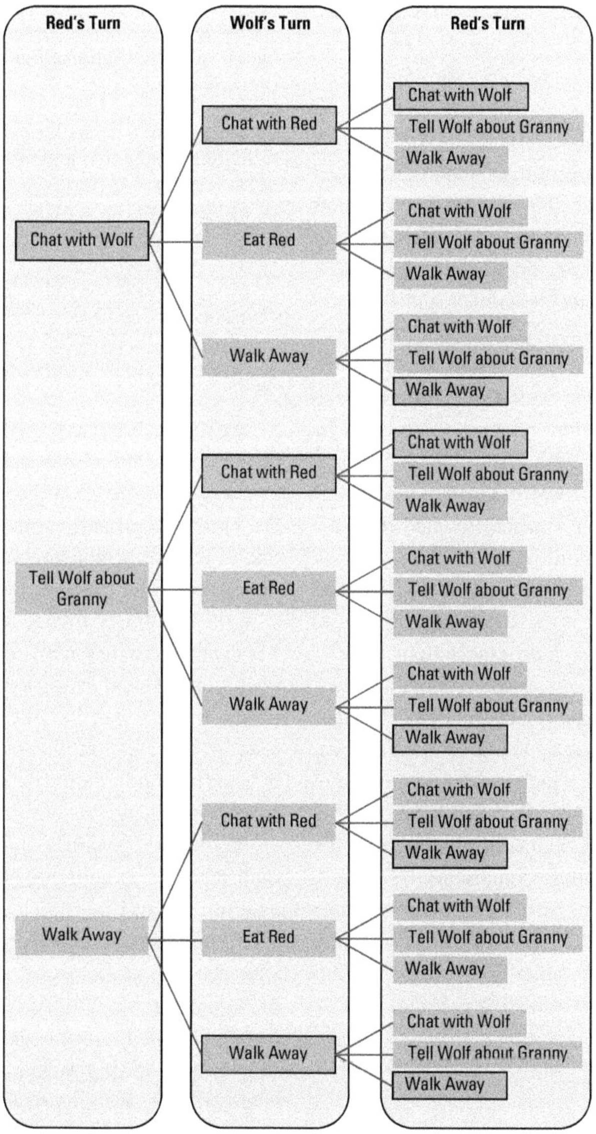

FIGURE 5.1 Red's lookahead process.

utility based on the actor's mental models. When no shapes are in bold, there are multiple actions with the same expected utility, and the actor has no specific preference over which action will be picked. Finally, this example is a simplified version of our actual implementation, in which the agents simulated more steps of lookahead and had more actions to choose from.

The agent remembers the expectations generated in its last two lookahead processes because the evaluations of some appraisal dimensions (e.g., accountability) need to trace back more than one step. Note that these expectations contain not only the agent's expectations about its own and the other agents' future actions, but also the expected states/utilities of all possible action choices of each of the agents. These state/utility traces serve as required input for the explanation algorithms that provide the user with the agent's motivations for making its observed choices.

Upon observing a new event (an action performed by an agent or the user), each agent updates its beliefs and appraises the new situation. The calculation of motivational relevance, motivational congruence, novelty, and accountability depends on only the agent's beliefs about the other agents' and its own utility values in the current and previous steps, which therefore can be derived immediately (see Section 4.3). Our calculation of control occurs only after the agent has made its own decision in response to the observed event. In fact, at this time the agent could potentially reevaluate every appraisal dimension as it computes updated information about expected states/utilities.

The mental models that Thespian agents have of each other enable them to not only have emotional responses to the environment but also form expectations of other agents' emotions. To simulate another agent's appraisal processes, the observing agent's beliefs about the other agent are used for deriving appraisal dimensions. For instance, the wolf can use its beliefs about Red to evaluate the motivational relevance and novelty of an event to her, which will most likely be totally different from the wolf's own evaluations of those dimensions. In our current implementation, if the observing agent has multiple mental models of other agents, currently it uses only the most likely mental models (rather than the entire distribution of likelihoods) to simulate their appraisals.

4.3. Appraisal Dimensions

This section illustrates how the agents can evaluate five appraisal dimensions (motivational relevance, motivation congruence or incongruence, accountability, control, and novelty) using states/utilities calculated during the agents' belief revision and decision-making processes.

4.3.1. Motivational Relevance and Motivational Congruence or Incongruence

Motivational relevance evaluates the extent to which an encounter touches upon personal goals. Motivational congruence or incongruence measures the extent to which the encounter thwarts or facilitates personal goals (Smith & Lazarus, 1990).

Algorithm 1. Motivational Relevance and Motivation Congruence

\# *preUtility*: utility before the event happens
\# *curUtility*: utility after the event happens

$$\textit{Motivational Relevance} = \left|\frac{curUtility - preUtility}{preUtility}\right|$$

$$\textit{Motivational Congruence} = \frac{curUtility - preUtility}{|preUtility|}$$

We model these appraisal dimensions as a product of the agent's utility calculations, which are integral to the agent's decision-theoretic reasoning. We use the ratio of the relative utility change and the direction of the utility change to model these two appraisal dimensions. The rationale behind this is that the same amount of utility change will result in different subjective experiences depending on the agent's current utility. For instance, if eating a person increases the wolf's utility by 10, it will be 10 times more motivationally relevant and congruent when the wolf's original utility is 1 (very hungry) than when the wolf's original utility is 10 (less hungry).

Algorithm 1 evaluates motivational relevance and motivational congruence/incongruence. *preUtility* denotes the agent's expected utility before the other agent takes an action. For agents who perform at least one step of lookahead, this value is evaluated by the agents' previous decision-making process. Taking Figure 5.1 as an example, Red's expected utility is the sum of her utility over this sequence of actions: Red chats with the wolf, the wolf chats with Red, and Red chats with the wolf again. This follows Red's expectations of the interaction. *curUtility* denotes the agent's updated expected utility, reflecting the effect of the other agent's action. Note that this value is also precomputed when the agent generated its expectations about the other agent's possible actions. For example, if the wolf chooses the action as Red has expected, then *curUtility* is the same as *preUtility* for Red. If the wolf instead chooses to walk away, then Red's expectation about future events changes. In this case, she would expect herself to walk away, too, and *curUtility* would be the sum of Red's utilities over this alternate sequence of actions: Red chats with the wolf, the wolf walks away, and Red walks away, too. If an agent does not perform any lookahead (i.e., it cares about only its immediate reward and not the responses of the other agents), the value of *curUtility* will not be calculated by the agent's previous decision-making process. It *will* be calculated when the agent updates its beliefs to compute its immediate reward in the next time step, and the evaluation of the appraisal dimensions will happen at that time.

The sign of *Motivational Congruence* indicates whether the event is motivationally congruent or incongruent to the agent. When the value is negative, the event is motivationally incongruent to the extent of *Motivational Relevance*, and otherwise the event is motivationally congruent to the agent.

Agents can also have goals to help or hinder other agents in the pursuit of their own goals. If an action helps advance a Thespian agent's self-centered goals but hurts a friend's goals (where a friend is someone whom the agent has a goal to help), then the agent's overall utility is diminished, subsequently muting the action's motivational congruence and relevance. For example, while Red will derive a self-centered satisfaction from eating the cake, that satisfaction will be offset by the negative impact on Granny, who has been deprived of the cake's benefit.

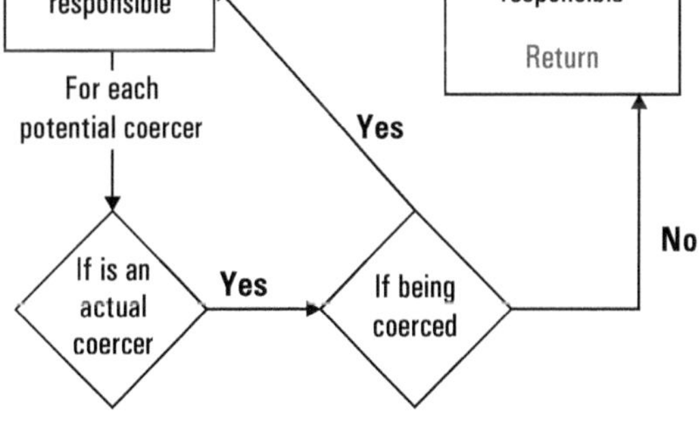

FIGURE 5.2 Accountability.

4.3.2. Accountability

Accountability determines who deserves credit or blame for a given event (Smith & Lazarus, 1990). Various theories have been proposed for assigning blame/credit (e.g., Shaver, 1985; Weiner, 1995). The reasoning usually considers factors such as who caused the event, whether the person foresaw the result, whether the person was coerced to cause the event, and so on.

Just as the appraisal of motivational relevance and motivation congruence can be performed as part of the existing Thespian/PsychSim decision-making and belief update processes, we argue here that accountability can be treated as an extension to Thespian/PsychSim's existing approach to support/affinity relationships between agents.

Figure 5.2 illustrates how an agent can determine accountability for an event's outcome. Our algorithm first looks at the agent whose action directly causes the harm/benefit and judges to what degree it should be held accountable. The algorithm uses the function *IfCoerced*() to determine whether that agent was coerced into performing the given action. If the direct actor was not coerced, it is held fully accountable for the result and the reasoning proceeds no further. Otherwise, any agents that coerced the direct actor are also held partially accountable. The algorithm judges each such coercer on whether it, too, was coerced by somebody else, with any such coercers sharing accountability as well. This process could potentially continue cascading indefinitely, but we instead limit the number of steps for which accountability extends back through the history. In the current investigation, we assume that the observing agent expects others to foresee the effects of their actions. While this assumption is not always true, people do often assume that others will project into the future to the same depth as they will themselves.

Algorithm 2 contains pseudocode for determining whether an agent was coerced, and Algorithm 3 determines who coerced the agent. Currently, we use a qualitative model to judge coercion based on the agent's utility gain/loss. If the agent's chosen action has a strictly greater utility than its other options, then we view the agent's choice as being coerced, in that its decision was driven by its circumstances. If an alternate action would not have decreased the agent's utility, then we view the agent as not being coerced, in that it was free to make a different choice without sacrificing its own utility.

We use a qualitative rather than quantitative method to decide coercion. If all other action options lead to less utility than its chosen action, then we view the agent as justified in its choice and must look back further to find the accountable agent. In the special case in which the agent's chosen action is its best choice but still results in a utility drop, the agent is regarded as not being coerced. In such cases, because the agent is going to be punished regardless of what it does, we treat it as having the freedom to pick actions that will not hurt the other agent's utility.

Algorithm 2. IfCoerced(*actor, pact*)

```
# actor: the agent being studied
# pact: the action performed by actor
# preUtility: actor's utility before doing pact
for action ∈ actor.actionOptions() do
    if action ≠ pact then
    # if there exists another action which does not hurt
    actor's own utility
    if EU (action) ≥ preUtility then
       return false
return true
```

In Algorithm 2, *preUtility* is defined as in Algorithm 1, with the important distinction that *preUtility* now refers to the beliefs of the observer (the agent who performs appraisal) about the *actor*'s expected utility. Similarly, *EU* (*action*) denotes the observer's belief about the *actor*'s utility of alternative option.

To decide who coerced an agent, we consider each agent that acted between the coerced agent's current and last actions. For each potential coercer, if the coerced agent would not have been coerced (as defined by Algorithm 2) if the potential coercer had made a different choice, then the potential coercer is judged as being a true coercer. This process is illustrated in Algorithm 3.

Algorithm 3. *Is_Coercer_For(agent, actor, agent_pact, actor_pact)*

```
# agent_pact: the action performed by agent
# actor_pact: the action performed by actor
for action ∈ agent.actionOptions() do
  if action ≠ agent_pact then
    Simulate action agent_pact
    if not IfCoerced(actor, actor_pact) then
      return true
  return false
```

4.3.3. Control

The appraisal of control evaluates the extent to which an event or its outcome can be influenced or controlled by people (Scherer, 2001). It captures not only the individual's own ability to control the situation but also the potential for seeking instrumental social support from other people. Unlike the evaluations of motivational relevance, motivational congruence, and accountability in which the most probable mental models of other agents are used for reasoning, here we factor in the probabilities of the mental models because the degree of control is affected by the estimation of how likely certain events will happen in the future.

Algorithm 4 gives the pseudocode for evaluating control. This algorithm first simulates future steps of the interaction using each possible combination of mental models of self and others and checks whether the utility drop will be recovered. The algorithm then considers the likelihood of the given mental model combination. For example, assume Granny has two mental models of the wolf. In the first mental model, the wolf will always die after being shot by the hunter. In the second mental model, the wolf will never die even after being shot. Granny believes that there is a 60% possibility that the first mental model is correct. Next, assume Granny has two mental models regarding the hunter. One mental model indicates that the hunter is close by, and this mental model has a 50% chance to be correct. The other mental model indicates that the

Algorithm 4. Control(*preUtility*)

```
# preUtility: utility before the event happens
control ← 0
for m1 ∈ mental_models_about_agent1 do
  for m2 ∈ mental_models_about_agent2 do
    for m3 ∈ mental_models_about_self do
      # project limited steps into the future using this set of
      mental models lookahead(m1,m2,m3)
      # curUtility: utility after the lookahead process
      if curUtility ≥ preUtility then
        control ← control + p(m1) * p(m2) * p(m3)
  return control
```

hunter is far away. After Granny is eaten by the wolf, the only event that can help her is the wolf being killed by the hunter. In this case, her sense of control is: 60% · 50% = 30%.

Algorithm 4 contains pseudocode for a three-agent interaction, but it is straightforward to configure the algorithm for any number of agents. In this algorithm, *preUtility* is defined as in Algorithm 1, but *curUtility* denotes the agent's utility associated with its state after the lookahead projection.

4.3.4. *Novelty*

In this work, we adapt Leventhal and Scherer's definition of "novelty at the conceptual level," that is, whether the event is expected from the agent's past beliefs[1] (Leventhal & Scherer, 1987; Scherer, 2001). In our model, novelty appraisal is treated as a by-product of an agent's belief maintenance. Specifically, in a multiagent context the novelty of an agent's behavior is viewed as the opposite of the agent's motivational consistency; in other words, the more consistent the event is with the agent's motivations, the less novel. Of course, this evaluation is performed from the observing agent's perspective and using the observing agent's beliefs, and there can be discrepancies between what the observing agent feels and what the agent who did the action feels. Computationally, we define novelty as 1 − *consistency*, where *consistency* is calculated as described in Section 2.4.3. The less consistent an action is with the observing agent's expectation about the actor, the higher the novelty if that action happens. For example, if from Red's perspective the wolf did an action that has the second highest utility among the wolf's five alternative actions, the amount of novelty Red will feel if seeing that action is calculated as:

$$1-\frac{e^{3}}{\sum_{j=0}^{4} e^{j}}=0.37$$

5. Appraisal Model in Action

All the previous examples of our new appraisal model are derived from a Thespian implementation of the Little Red Riding Hood story. In this section we provide two additional scenarios to illustrate the usage of our computational model of appraisal in modeling social interactions. In particular, in Section 5.1 we demonstrate the tight relationship between emotion and cognitive decision making by showing how appraisal is affected by the depth of reasoning in decision making. In Section 5.2 we provide a complex situation for accountability reasoning and show that the result of our model is consistent with another validated computational model of social attribution.

5.1. Small Talk

To reveal the tight relationship between cognitive processes and emotion in our model, we implemented an abstract domain of two persons (A and B) taking turns talking to each other. Both of them have these goals: to be talkative and to obey social norms. In fact, just the norm-following behavior itself is an incentive to them—they will be rewarded whenever they do an action that is consistent with social norms. Table 5.2 contains the two persons' appraisals of motivational relevance regarding each other's actions. We did not include results of other appraisal dimensions as they are less interesting in this scenario.

In PsychSim, we explicitly model the depth of reasoning in agents as the number of steps they project into the future. In this example we provide a comparison of appraisal results when the person's previous reasoning process takes a different number of steps. It can be observed in Table 5.2 that different depths of reasoning lead to different appraisals. A person appraises another person's initiatives as irrelevant when performing shallow reasoning (lookahead steps = 1). In this case, even though the person has predicted the other person's action, because the action does not bring him/her immediate reward, the person cannot see the relevance of the action. Once the person reasons one step further, he/she finds out that by opening up a topic the other person provides him/her a chance to engage in further conversation and perform a norm- following action, and the person will then appraise the other person's action as relevant.

5.2. Firing Squad

We implemented the firing-squad scenario from (Mao & Gratch, 2005) to illustrate accountability reasoning in which agents are coerced and have only partial responsibility. The scenario goes like this: *In a firing-squad, the commander orders the marksmen to shoot a prisoner. The marksmen refuse the order. The commander*

TABLE 5.2 Small Talk Between Two Persons

Step	*Action*	*Perspective*	*Lookahead steps*	*Motivational relevance*
1	A greets B	B	1	0
		B	2	100
2	B greets A	A	1	0
		A	2	0.99
3	A asks B a question	B	1	0
		B	2	0.99
4	B answers the question	A	1	0
		A	2	0.49

insists that the marksmen shoot. They shoot the prisoner and he dies.

We modeled the commander as an agent with an explicit goal of killing the prisoner, and the marksmen as having no goals related to the prisoner, but they will be punished if they do not obey the commander's order. Using our appraisal model, from the prisoner's perspective, the marksmen hold responsibility for his/her death because they are the persons who directly perform the action. Further, the prisoner can simulate the decision-making process of the marksmen, which will lead him/her to find out that the marksmen are coerced because their utilities will be hurt if they do anything else other than shoot. The commander acts right before the marksmen in the scenario and therefore is identified as a potential coercer for the marksmen. Using Algorithm 3, we can predict that the prisoner can see that if the commander chose a different action, the marksmen would not be coerced to shoot. Assuming the prisoner does not find a coercer for the commander, he/she will now believe that the commander holds full responsibility for his/her death. This prediction is consistent with the prediction from Mao's model of social attribution and the data collected from human subjects to validate that model (Mao & Gratch, 2005).

6. Discussion of Appraisal Model

In PsychSim, comparison among expected utilities plays the central role in decision making and mental model update. Comparison of expected utilities also plays a central role for deriving appraisal dimensions. Our algorithms for deriving appraisal dimensions demonstrate that no additional calculation of utilities or states other than what has already been performed in the Thespian agent's existing decision-making and belief revision processes is required for appraisal. Table 5.3 summarizes the relationship between PsychSim's existing processes and the evaluation of appraisal dimensions.

Compared with other computational models of appraisal, the main advantage of this model is that the agents explicitly model other agents' goals, states, and beliefs (theory of mind). Modeling theory of mind makes this model particularly suitable for simulating emotions in social interactions in two ways. First, appraisals are strongly embedded in the social context. For example, novelty is not simply evaluated as whether the physical stimulus is unexpected, but whether the other agents behave as expected. Second, appraisals that are explicitly relevant to social interaction and derivation of social emotion (e.g., accountability) have to leverage theory of mind.

Further, the fact that Thespian agents have a theory-of-mind capability enables them to simulate the emotions of others. This ability allows us to simulate an agent's potential misexpectations about other agents' emotional states. For example, if Granny believes that the hunter can always kill the wolf successfully and the hunter believes that he can only kill the wolf successfully 60% of the time, Granny's control when being eaten by the wolf will be evaluated differently from Granny's and the hunter's perspectives.

The appraisal model cannot only simulate egocentric emotions but also simulate emotions that take social relationships into account. Thespian agents can have goals regarding other agents' utilities and emotions (emotion can be modeled as a feature of an agent's state). Therefore, an agent's emotion can be related to other agents' utility changes and emotions. For example, we can simulate an agent having goals of facilitating another agent's goals, or even more specifically having goals of making the other agent feel happy. This agent will act deliberately to help the other agent and "feel" bad if it hurts the other agent's utility or emotional state.

Finally, the underlying PsychSim framework allows us to explicitly model the depth of reasoning in agents. As shown in Section 5.1, different depths of reasoning lead to different appraisals. Though we have only demonstrated this effect using one appraisal dimension (motivational relevance), this effect is general. Different steps of projection lead to different expectations of future events, and an agent's expectations affect its reasoning about whether an event is novel, whether the effect of the event is changeable, and who caused the event.

TABLE 5.3 Appraisal Tightly Coupled With Decision Making

Appraisal dimension	*Existing PsychSim processes*
Motivational relevance	Decision-making (exploit utility calculations based on single mental model)
Motivational congruence	Decision-making (exploit utility calculations based on single mental model)
Accountability	Belief (mental model) update (support relationship)
Control	Decision-making (exploit utility calculations based on alternative mental models)
Novelty	Belief (mental model) update

In terms of future work, one of the extensions we are considering concerns *social appraisal* (Manstead & Fischer, 2001), which argues that another's behaviors, thoughts, or feelings can influence an agent's own appraisals. In the current framework, the capacity of the agent to appraise from another's perspectives provides a way for the agent to infer another agent's appraisals. It therefore provides a framework for exploring the various ways those appraisals can influence the agent's own appraisals.

7. Conclusion

We have discussed PsychSim, an environment for multiagent simulation of human social interaction that employs a formal decision-theoretic approach using recursive models. This approach allows us to model phenomena rarely addressed in simulated worlds. We have exploited the recursive models to provide a psychologically motivated computational model of how agents influence each other's beliefs. We have also developed a range of technology to simplify the task of setting up PsychSim models, exploring the simulation and analyzing results. Discussion of this technology is beyond the scope of this chapter, but they provide users with automated algorithms for fitting simulation parameters to observed behavior, reporting sensitivities in the results, and suggesting potentially interesting perturbations to the scenario (Pynadath & Marsella, 2004). We believe PsychSim has a range of innovative applications, including computational social science and the modeling of social training environments.

As an illustration of such applications, and PsychSim's expressiveness, we provide a computational model of appraisal for POMDP-based agents, implemented in the Thespian framework for interactive narrative. The focus is on five key appraisal dimensions for virtual agents: motivational relevance, motivational congruence, accountability, control, and novelty. The approach argues that appraisal is an integral part of a social agent's cognitive processes.

All of these capabilities of the appraisal model derive from the basic PsychSim cognitive components as laid out in Section 2. We were thus able to leverage the decision-theoretic theory of mind as implemented in our agents to realize appraisal theory, even though modeling appraisal was not an original intention of the agents' design. The reuse of architectural features therefore provides, not only a novel computational model of emotion, but also a demonstration of a tight relationship between emotion and cognition, suggesting a uniform cognitive structure for emotion and cognition. In addition, by demonstrating how a theory-of-mind capacity is critical to deriving appraisals, and in particular modeling appraisals critical to social emotions like anger, this work argues for the critical role for theory of mind in modeling social interaction generally.

Acknowledgments

This work was sponsored by the U.S. Army Research, Development, and Engineering Command (RDECOM), and the content does not necessarily reflect the position or the policy of the Government, and no official endorsement should be inferred.

Notes

1. Leventhal and Scherer have also defined novelty at the sensory-motor level and schematic level. We did not model them because they are mainly related to people's low-level perceptual processes rather than cognitive processes.

References

Abelson, R. P., Aronson E., McGuire ,W. J., Newcomb, T., Rosenberg M., & Tannenbaum, P. H. (Eds.). (1968). *Theories of cognitive consistency: A sourcebook*. Chicago: Rand McNally.

Aylett, R., Dias, J., & Paiva, A. (2006). An affectively-driven planner for synthetic characters. In *Proceedings of the International Conference on Automated Planning and Scheduling* (pp. 2–100. Menlo Park, CA: The AAAI Press.

Cialdini, R. *Influence: Science and practice*. (2001). Boston: Allyn and Bacon.

de Rosis, F., Castelfranchi, C., Carofiglio, V., & Grassano, G. (2003). Can computers deliberately deceive? A simulation tool and its application to Turing's imitation game. *Computational Intelligence, 19*(3), 253–263.

Dias, J., & Paiva, A. (2005). Feeling and reasoning: A computational model for emotional characters. In *Proceedings of the Portuguese Conference on Artificial Intelligence* (pp. 127–140). Springer Berlin Heidelberg.

El Nasr, M. S., Yen, J., & Ioerger, T. (2000). Flame: Fuzzy logic adaptive model of emotions. *Autonomous Agents and Multi-Agent Systems*, 3(3), 219–257.

Elliott, C. (1992). *The affective reasoner: A process model of emotions in a multi-agent system*. (Unpublished doctoral dissertation). Northwestern University Institute for the Learning Sciences, Evanston, IL.

Frijda, N. (1987). *The emotions*. Cambridge, UK: University Press.

Gmytrasiewicz, P. J., & Durfee, E. H. (1995). A rigorous, operational formalization of recursive modeling. In *Proceedings of the International Conference on Multi-Agent Systems* (pp. 125–132). AAAI Press: Menlo Park, CA.

Gratch, J., & Marsella, S. (2004). A domain-independent framework for modeling emotion. *Cognitive Systems Research*, 5(4), 269–306.

Ito, J. Y., Pynadath, D. V., & Marsella, S. C. (2007). A decision-theoretic approach to evaluating posterior probabilities of mental models. In *AAAI Workshop on Plan, Activity, and Intent Recognition* (pp. 60–65). Menlo Park, CA: The AAAI Press.

Ito, J. Y., Pynadath, D. V., Sonenberg, L., & Marsella, S. C. (2010). Wishful thinking in effective decision making. In *Proceedings of the International Conference on Autonomous Agents and Multiagent Systems* (pp. 1527–1528). Richland, SC: International Foundation for Autonomous Agents and Multiagent Systems.

Lazarus, R. S. *Emotion & adaptation*. (1991). New York: Oxford University Press.

Lazzaro, N. (March, 2004). Why we play games: Four keys to more emotion in player experiences. In *Game Developers Conference*. San Jose, CA

Leventhal, H., & Scherer, K. R. (1987). The relationship of emotion and cognition: A functional approach to a semantic controversy. *Cognition and Emotion, 1*, 3–28.

Manstead, A., & Fischer, A. (2001). Social appraisal: The social world as object of and influence on appraisal processes. In T. J. K. R. Scherer & A. Schorr (Eds.), *Appraisal processes in emotion: Theory, research, application* (pp. 221–232). New York: Oxford University Press.

Mao, W., & Gratch, J. (2005). Social causality and responsibility: Modeling and evaluation. In *Proceedings of the International Conference on Virtual Agents, Kos, Greece* (pp. 191–204). Springer: Berlin Heidelberg.

Marinier, R., Laird, J., & Lewis, R. (2009). A computational unification of cognitive behavior and emotion. *Journal of Cognitive Systems Research, 10*(1), 48–69.

Marsella, S. C., & Gratch, J. (2009). EMA: A process model of appraisal dynamics. *Journal of Cognitive Systems Research, 10*(1), 70–90.

Marsella, S., Gratch, J., & Petta, P. (2010). Computational models of emotion. In K. Scherer, T. Bänziger, & E. Roesch (Eds.), *A blueprint for an affectively competent agent: Cross-fertilization between Emotion Psychology, Affective Neuroscience, and Affective Computing* (pp. 21–46). Oxford, UK: Oxford University Press.

Marsella, S. C., Pynadath, D. V., & Read, S. J. (2004). PsychSim: Agent-based modeling of social interactions and influence. In *Proceedings of the International Conference on Cognitive Modeling* (pp. 243–248). Pitttsburgh: Psychology Press.

McAlinden, R., Gordon, A., Lane, H. C., & Pynadath D. (2009). UrbanSim: A game-based simulation for counterinsurgency and stability-focused operations. In *Proceedings of the AIED Workshop on Intelligent Educational Games* (pp. 41–50).

Moffat, D., & Frijda, N. (1995). Where there's a Will there's an agent. In *Proceedings of the ECAI Workshop on Agent Theories, Architectures, and Languages, Amsterdam* (pp. 245–260). Springer: Berlin Heidelberg.

Ortony, A., Clore, G. L., & Collins A. (1998). *The cognitive structure of emotions*. Cambridge, UK: Cambridge University Press.

Paiva, A., Dias, J., Sobral, D., Aylett, R., Sobreperez, P., Woods, S., & Zoll, C. (2004). Caring for agents and agents that care: Building empathic relations with synthetic agents. In *Proceedings of the International Conference on Autonomous Agents and Multi-Agent Systems* (pp. 194–201). International Foundation for Autonomous Agents and Multiagent Systems.

Petty, R., & Cacioppo, J. (1986). *Communication and persuasion: Central and peripheral routes to attitude change*. New York: Springer.

Pynadath, D. V., & Marsella, S. C. (2004). Fitting and compilation of multiagent models through piecewise linear functions. In *Proceedings of the International*

Conference on Autonomous Agents and Multi Agent Systems (pp. 1197–1204). International Foundation for Autonomous Agents and Multiagent Systems.

Pynadath, D. V., & Marsella, S. C. (2005). PsychSim: Modeling theory of mind with decision-theoretic agents. In *Proceedings of the International Joint Conference on Artificial Intelligence* (pp. 1181–1186). International Joint Conferences on Artificial Intelligence.

Reilly, W. S., & Bates J. (1992). *Building emotional agents.* (Technical Report CMU-CS-92-143). Pittsburgh, PA: Carnegie Mellon University.

Roseman, I. (1984). Cognitive determinants of emotion: A structural theory. *Review of Personality and Social Psychology*, 2, 11–36.

Scherer, K. (2001). Appraisal considered as a process of multilevel sequential checking. In K. Scherer, A. Schorr, & T. Johnstone (Eds.), *Appraisal processes in emotion: Theory, methods* (pp. 92–120). Oxford, UK: Oxford University Press.

Schwartz, D. (2000). Subtypes of victims and aggressors in children's peer groups. *Journal of Abnormal Child Psychology*, 28, 181–192.

Shaver, K. G. (1985). *The attribution theory of blame: Causality, responsibility and blameworthiness.* Springer-Verlag: New York, NY.

Si, M., Marsella, S. C., & Pynadath, D. V. (2005a). Thespian: An architecture for interactive pedagogical drama. In *Proceedings of the Conference on Artificial Intelligence in Education.* IOS Press: Amsterdam, Netherlands.

Si, M., Marsella, S. C., & Pynadath, D. V. (2005b). Thespian: Using multi-agent fitting to craft interactive drama. In *Proceedings of the International Conference on Autonomous Agents and Multi-Agent Systems* (pp. 21–28). International Foundation for Autonomous Agents and Multiagent Systems.

Si, M., Marsella, S. C., & Pynadath, D. V. (2006). Thespian: Modeling socially normative behavior in a decision-theoretic framework. In *Proceedings of the Conference on Intelligent Virtual Agents* (pp. 369–382). Springer: Berlin Heidelberg.

Si, M., Marsella, S. C., & Pynadath, D. V. (2007). Proactive authoring for interactive drama: An author's assistant. In *Proceedings of the Conference on Intelligent Virtual Agents, Paris, France.* (pp. 225–237). Springer.

Si, M., Marsella, S. C., & Pynadath, D. V. (2009). Directorial control in a decision-theoretic framework for interactive narrative. In *Proceedings of the International Conference on Interactive Digital Storytelling* (pp. 221–233). Springer: Berlin Heidelberg.

Si, M., Marsella, S. C., & Pynadath, D. V. (2010a). Evaluating directorial control in a character-centric interactive narrative framework. In *Proceedings of the International Conference on Autonomous Agents and Multi-Agent Systems* (pp. 1289–1296). International Foundation for Autonomous Agents and Multiagent Systems, Richland, SC.

Si, M., Marsella, S. C., & Pynadath, D. V. (2010b). Modeling appraisal in theory of mind reasoning. *Journal of Autonomous Agents and Multi-Agent Systems*, *20*(1), 14–31.

Smallwood, R. D., & Sondik, E. J. (1973). The optimal control of partially observable Markov processes over a finite horizon. *Operations Research*, *21*, 1071–1088.

Smith, C. A., & Ellsworth, P. C. (1987). Patterns of appraisal and emotion related to taking an exam. *Personality and Social Psychology*, 52, 475–488.

Smith, C. A., & Lazarus, R. S. (1990). Emotion and adaptation. In L. A. Pervin (Ed.), *Handbook of personality: Theory and research* (pp. 609–637). New York: Guilford.

Swartout, W., Hill, R., Gratch, J., Johnson, W., Kyriakakis, C., LaBore, C., Lindheim, R., Marsella, S. C., Miraglia, D., Moore, B., et al. (2001). Toward the holodeck: Integrating graphics, sound, character and story. In *Proceedings of the International Conference on Autonomous Agents* (pp. 409–416) . International Foundation for Autonomous Agents and Multiagent Systems. ACM: New York, NY.

Taylor, J., Carletta, J., & Mellish, C. (1996). Requirements for belief models in cooperative dialogue. *User Modelling and User-Adapted Interaction*, 6(1), 23–68.

Traum, D. R., Swartout, W., Marsella, S. C., & Gratch, J. (2005). Fight, flight, or negotiate: Believable strategies for conversing under crisis. In *Proceedings of the Conference on Intelligent Virtual Agents* (pp. 52–64). Springer: Berlin Heidelberg.

Velasquez, J. Modeling emotions and other motivations in synthetic agents. (1997). In *Proceedings of the National Conference on Artificial Intelligence* (pp. 10–15). Menlo Park, CA:AAAI Press.

Weiner, B. (1995). *The judgment of responsibility: A foundation for a theory of social conduct.* New York, NY: The Guilford Press.

Whiten, A. (Ed.). (1991). *Natural theories of mind.* Oxford, UK: Basil Blackwell.

6

Automatic Facial Expression Recognition

Jacob Whitehill, Marian Stewart Bartlett, & Javier R. Movellan

Imago animi vultus est, indices oculi.

—Cicero

1. Introduction

The face is innervated by two different brain systems that compete for control of its muscles: a cortical brain system related to voluntary and controllable behavior, and a subcortical system responsible for involuntary expressions. The interplay between these two systems generates a wealth of information that humans constantly use to read the emotions, intentions, and interests (Keltner & Ekman, 2000) of others.

Given the critical role that facial expressions play in our daily life, technologies that can interpret and respond to facial expressions automatically are likely to find a wide range of applications. For example, in pharmacology, the effect of new antidepression drugs could be assessed more accurately based on daily records of the patients' facial expressions than by asking the patients to fill out a questionnaire, as it is currently done (Cohn et al., 2009). Facial expression recognition may enable a new generation of teaching systems to adapt to the expression of their students in the way good teachers do (Whitehill et al., 2008). Expression recognition could be used to assess the fatigue of drivers and airplane pilots (Vural et al., 2007, 2010). Daily-life robots with automatic expression recognition will be able to assess the states and intentions of humans and respond accordingly (Movellan et al., 2007). Smart phones with expression analysis may help people to prepare for important meetings and job interviews.

Thanks to the introduction of machine learning methods, recent years have seen great progress in the field of automatic facial expression recognition. Commercial real-time expression recognition systems are starting to be used in consumer applications, for example, smile detectors embedded in digital cameras (Whitehill et al., 2009). Nonetheless, considerable progress has yet to be made: Methods for face detection and tracking (the first step of automated face analysis) work well for frontal views of adult Caucasian and Asian faces (Rose, 2010), but their performance needs to be improved for a wider range of conditions. Expression classification works reasonably well for posed expressions, such as posed smiles, but its performance drops quite dramatically on spontaneous expressions elicited during natural conversations. Part of the reason for this difficulty may stem from differing *temporal dynamics* between posed and spontaneous expressions: Much of the existing work on automatic expression recognition focuses on static image analysis. While static images are sufficient for recognizing intense, posed expressions, facial coding experts rely heavily on expression dynamics when analyzing subtle, spontaneous expressions. Thus, the development of methods to capture spatiotemporal information has become a very important endeavor as we try to develop automatic systems that approximate the performance levels of human experts.

In this chapter we review the state of the art in expression recognition technologies. We focus on approaches that rely on supervised machine learning methods, in other words, that learn to recognize expressions from example images and videos of faces labeled with the observed expressions. These approaches are currently the most successful and popular by a wide margin. In Section 2 we explore some critical dimensions of the facial expression problem space. Section 3 describes the most prominent databases of facial expression that are suitable for training automatic classifiers, as well as different performance metrics, that are used to evaluate supervised learning-based systems. In Section 4 we explain the typical processing pipeline of current facial expression recognition systems. We then focus of the different stages of this pipeline: Registration (Section 5), Feature Extraction (Section 6), Classification (8), and Temporal Integration (Section 9). Finally, we provide a brief overview of current research challenges and an outlook for the near future (Section 11).

2. Problem Space

Automatic expression recognition systems differ widely in their goals and target application conditions. There are three important axes along which systems can vary: the level of description of expression, the type of lighting conditions under which expressions are permitted to occur, and the elicitation—posed or spontaneous—of the facial movements.

2.1 Level of Description

An important axis of variability is the *level of description*. On one end of the spectrum, there are systems that focus on recognition of a small set of facial displays, such as smiles, the six basic emotional expressions (Ekman & Friesen, 1978), or expressions of states such as "thinking," "bored," "confused," and so on (Kaliouby & Robinson, 2005). On the other end, there are systems that decompose facial expression into individual components. This distinction between special purpose and comprehensive systems has an analogue in automatic speech recognition, where some systems focus on recognizing a few words, for example, "Yes" and "No," and others decompose sounds into components (e.g., phonemes), thus allowing recognition of vocabularies of arbitrary size.

In the behavioral sciences, the Facial Action Coding System (FACS) (Ekman & Friesen, 1978) is one of the most popular and best known methods to decompose facial expressions into elementary components. The FACS describes facial expressions in terms of 46 component movements, named Action Units, which roughly correspond to the individual facial muscle movements. FACS has proved useful in the behavioral sciences for discovering facial movements that are indicative of cognitive and affective states (see Ekman & Rosenberg, 2005, for a review of facial expression studies using FACS).

Automating comprehensive coding systems such as FACS can have important advantages. If successful, such systems can relieve higherlevel special-purpose applications (e.g., emotion recognition, deception detection, psychiatric drug monitoring, detection of fatigue) from the burden of dealing with raw images. The hope is that the intermediate representation provided by the automatic FACS coding systems will make possible the development of higher level expression recognition systems at very low cost.

Efforts to automate the Facial Actions Coding System started at the end of the 20th century (Donato et al., 1999) and have now become the focus of academic teams (Bartlett et al., 2006; D'Mello et al., 2007; Koelstra et al., 2010; Littlewort et al., 2006; Picard, 2000; Ryan et al., 2009) and commercial ventures.

2.2 Structured Versus Free Rendering Conditions

The type of rendering conditions—laboratory versus real life—is a second important axis of variability. Focusing too much on the former, that is, controlled laboratory conditions, is a potential pitfall for the facial expression recognition community. In other words, whether expression recognition systems target

TABLE 6.1 Action Unit Recognition Performance (2AFC score) for Posed (Cohn-Kanade and Ekman-Hager Dataset) and Spontaneous (RU-FACS Dataset) Facial Actions

AU	1	2	4	5	6	7	9	10	11	12
Posed	95	92	91	96	96	95	100	90	74	98
Spontaneous	78	62	74	71	90	64	88	62	73	86
AU	**14**	**15**	**16**	**17**	**20**	**23**	**24**	**25**	**26**	
Posed	85	91	92	93	84	70	88	93	85	
Spontaneous	70	69	63	74	66	69	64	70	63	

Note. Performance as reported in Bartlett et al. (2006).

structured or free rendering conditions can make a large difference in terms of accuracy of commercial systems. In general, recognizing expressions in free rendering conditions is much more challenging: It was reported in Whitehill, Littlewort et al. (2009), for example, that a smile detector based on linear regression performed at 97% accuracy (2AFC score) on a widely used dataset (Cohn-Kanade) collected in structured conditions. The same smile detector, when applied to natural conditions, dropped in accuracy to 72%, rendering it unusable for most practical applications.

2.3 Posed Versus Spontaneous Facial Displays

The third dimension of the expression recognition problem space we consider is whether the target expressions are posed by subjects on command (e.g., "smile," "look sad," "look surprised") or whether they are spontaneous expressions displayed in natural interactions. The importance of making a clear distinction between spontaneous and deliberately displayed facial behavior for developing and testing computer vision systems becomes apparent when one considers the different neurological substrates that mediate these two types of expressions. Volitional facial movements originate in the cortical motor strip, whereas the involuntary expressions originate in the subcortical areas of the brain (e.g., Miehlke, 1973). The facial expressions mediated by these two pathways have differences both in their morphology (which facial muscles move) and in their dynamics (how they move) (Ekman, 2001; Ekman & Rosenberg, 2005). Subcortically initiated facial expressions tend to be more symmetrical, consistent, and reflex-like, whereas cortically initiated facial expressions tend to be less smooth and have more variable dynamics (Ekman & Rosenberg, 2005; Rinn, 1984).

Expressions often exhibit dynamic interactions between the cortical and subcortical systems. For example, controlled expressions may be replaced for short periods of time (1/4 of a second) by full displays of emotions. These are known as *microexpressions* (Ekman, 2001). Blended expressions in which a felt emotion (e.g., sadness) is combined with a controlled expression (e.g., smile), are also common.

Spontaneous expressions are typically much more difficult to recognize in automatic systems. As an example, Bartlett et al. (2006) trained an expression recognizer of FACS action units on two datasets (Cohn-Kanade and Ekman-Hager) of posed facial expression. When they then applied this system to a database of spontaneous facial behavior (the RU-FACS database), performance fell by over 20% (see Table 6.1). Some factors contributing to this difference in performance include the generally lower intensity of spontaneous expressions, their subtle dynamics, the blending with movements such as speech articulations, and the changes in head pose that occurs when people communicate with each other.

3. Databases of Facial Expression

Machine learning has revolutionized both computer vision in general and automatic facial expression recognition in particular. However, machine learning methods for expression recognition pose the considerable challenge of obtaining a large and rich set of training data consisting of thousands or even millions of face images and videos. Supervised learning-based methods additionally require the annotation of associated *labels* describing the expression of each image or video. Such databases are important both for training expression recognizers and for evaluating trained systems. The existence of publicly available, high-quality databases is especially important when one wishes to compare competing approaches.

Unfortunately, collecting facial expression datasets is laborious and expensive, and the number of publicly available datasets is relatively small (see below). This fact exacerbates the tension that exists between the desire to maximize the amount of data used for training, and the need to set aside data (not used for training) in order to accurately estimate system performance. In general, there is no comprehensive dataset of face images that could provide a basis for all different efforts in the research on machine analysis of facial expressions; only isolated pieces of such a facial database exist. We will discuss the most widely used datasets. For a more comprehensive view through 2005, see Pantic et al. (2005).

3.1 Commonly Used Databases

The Cohn-Kanade facial expression database (Kanade et al., 2000) is the most widely used database in research on automated facial expression analysis. This database contains image sequences of approximately 100 subjects posing a set of 23 facial displays, and it contains FACS codes in addition to basic emotion labels. The release of this database to the research community enabled a large amount of research on facial expression recognition and feature tracking. Two main limitations of this dataset are as follows: First, each recording ends at the apex of the shown expression, which limits research of facial expression temporal activation patterns (onset—apex—offset). Second, many recordings contain the date/time stamp recorded over the chin of the subject. This makes changes in the appearance of the chin less visible and motions of the chin difficult to track. In 2010, the same research group released the Extended Cohn-Kanade Dataset (CK+) (Lucey et al., 2010), which contains more sequences and subjects, higher quality labels of the emotions, and some spontaneous expressions.

In an attempt to address some of the problems with the Cohn-Kanade dataset, the Man–Machine Interaction (MMI) facial expression database was developed by Pantic et al. (2005). It has two parts, containing deliberately and spontaneously displayed facial expressions, respectively. The first part contains over 4,000 videos as well as over 600 static images depicting facial expressions of single AU activation, multiple AU activations, and six basic emotions. It has profile as well as frontal views and was FACS coded by two certified coders. The second part contains 65 videos of spontaneous facial displays that were coded in terms of displayed AUs and emotions by two certified coders. Subjects were 18 adults between 21 and 45 years old, and 11 children between 9 and 13 years old. They were 48% female, and 66% Caucasian, 30% Asian, and 4% African. Expressions were recorded while the subjects watched television programs or movies, or when listening to jokes told by a professional comedian. The recordings contain mostly facial expressions of different kinds of laughter, surprise, and disgust expressions, which were accompanied by (often large) head motions, and were made under variable lighting conditions.

The MMI facial expression database is to date the most comprehensive publicly available database containing recordings of spontaneous facial behavior. However, presently the database lacks potentially important metadata regarding the context in which the recordings were made, for example, stimuli, environment, presence of other people, and so on.

Mark Frank, in collaboration with Javier Movellan and Marian Bartlett, collected a FACS coded dataset of spontaneous facial behavior in an interview setting (Bartlett et al., 2006). This dataset, called the RU-FACS Spontaneous Expression Dataset, consists of 100 subjects participating in a "false opinion" paradigm. In this paradigm, subjects first fill out a questionnaire regarding their opinions about a social or political issue. Subjects are then asked to either tell the truth or take the opposite opinion on an issue on which they rated strong feelings, and convince an interviewer they are telling the truth. Interviewers were retired police and FBI agents. The stakes of the interview were raised by giving the subjects $50 if they succeeded in fooling the interviewer. The participants were also told that if the interviewer finds out that they are lying they would receive no cash and would have to fill out a long and boring questionnaire. In practice, everyone received a minimum of $10 for participating, and no one had to fill out the questionnaire. This paradigm has been shown to elicit a wide range of emotional expressions, including microexpressions and blended expressions that indicate engagement of the cortical and subcortical brain systems. This dataset is particularly challenging both because of the presence of speech-related mouth movements, and because of out-of-plane head rotations, which tend to be present during discourse. Subjects' faces were digitized by four synchronized Dragonfly cameras from Point Grey (frontal, two partial profiles at 30 degrees, and one view from below). Two minutes of each subject's behavior were FACS coded by two certified FACS coders. FACS codes include the apex frame as well as the onset and offset frame for each action unit. To date, 33 subjects have been FACS coded. This dataset will be made available to the research community once the FACS coding is completed.

3.2 Performance Metrics

The use of standard datasets is a key requirement for making meaningful comparisons between different automated systems. In addition to analyzing the same data, the same *performance metric* must also be used. Commonly used metrics are the recognition rate (percent of correctly classified images), area under the Receiver Operating Characteristics curve (AROC), Precision-Recall curve, 2AFC score, and hit rates for given false alarm rates. Due to the varying performance metric used in the literature, comparisons of accuracy statistics between publications is regrettably often meaningless.

The AROC is a popular statistic that describes the sensitivity of a binary classifier independent of its bias. It requires computing the false alarm rate and hit rate of the system for a wide range of thresholds. The hit rates are then plotted as a function of the false alarm rates. The obtained points are interpolated to form a curve, namely the Receiver Operating Characteristics curve, and then this curve is integrated to find the AROC. In practice we have found that the AROC value can change significantly depending on the number of thresholds being used, the interpolation scheme, and the numerical integration algorithm.

We favor the 2AFC score, for it has an intuitive interpretation, there is a unique algorithm for computing it that does not depend on interpolation methods, and it is directly related to the AROC statistic. The 2AFC score represents the performance of the system on a 2 Alternative Forced Choice task. For a given dataset, we present the system with all possible pairs of positive and negative examples. If the output of the system is larger for the positive example than for the negative example, the pair is scored as 1. If the output is equal, it is scored as 0.5; otherwise, it is scored as 0. The 2AFC score is the average score across all possible pairs. It thus can be interpreted as the expected performance of the system in a 2AFC task. A 2AFC score of 0.5 means that the system is at chance. A 2AFC score of 1 means that the system can perfectly discriminate positive from negative examples. A well-known theorem from signal detection theory states that under some reasonable conditions the 2AFC statistic equals the area under the AROC. Thus, the 2AFC statistic can also be interpreted as a particular method for computing the AROC. In the Appendix we present Matlab code for computing the 2AFC score.

4. Typical Architecture of an Expression Recognition System

Nearly all current expression recognition systems follow the same processing "pipeline" (see Figure 6.1). The input to the system is a sequence of 2D video frames. These may be consecutive frames from a video

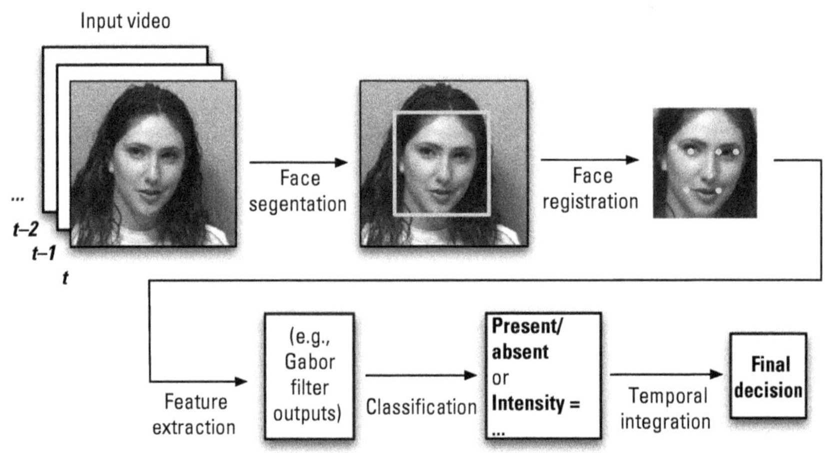

FIGURE 6.1 Common architecture of most automatic facial expression recognition systems.

or independent images. For each frame the system executes the following stages:

1. *Face segmentation:* The location of a face on the image plane is found and the corresponding patch is segmented out. This stage makes the overall system shift invariant, in other words, insensitive to the location of the face on the image plane.
2. *Face registration:* The appearance of the segmented face patch is normalized to compensate for changes in scale, face geometry, and variations due to pose (in plane and out-of-image plane rotation).
3. *Feature extraction:* Either geometric information about the relative positions of facial features, such as the eyes, nose, and mouth, are tracked, or appearance-based information on the pixel values are extracted. For appearance-based features, the pixels obtained from the face patches are converted into a new representation consisting of the real-valued outputs of a set of functions of the pixel values. This set of functions is typically referred to as a "filter bank."

   The goal of the filter bank representation is to reduce sensitivity to changes in illumination and to errors in the face registration process. If the output of the filters is a function of the pixels in a single video frame, it is known as a spatial filter. If it is a function of several frames, it is known as a spatiotemporal filter.
4. *Expression classification:* The extracted features are fed into a decision engine, which outputs an estimate of different expression categories. The output may be one of a finite set of values (e.g., {Smile, NotSmile}) or a real-valued estimate of expression intensity (e.g., Smile 1.31).
5. *Temporal integration* (optional): The output of the classifier may be integrated over time to produce estimates of internal states, such as alertness level, confusion, deceit, and so on.

To a significant extent, these pipeline stages are independent of each other. For example, in many cases the face detection and registration algorithm could be replaced by a more accurate method without adversely affecting the later stages in the pipeline. It is due to this modularity that we address each stage independently. Care must be taken, however: In practice it is often beneficial to retrain later processing stages when changes are made to earlier processing stages due to subtle differences in the performance of an upstream pipeline stage. For example, if the registration system is inaccurate, it is important to use filters that are insensitive to registration errors. However, if a more accurate registration is used, the expression classifier could benefit from using filters that are less invariant to bad registration but, in turn, are highly discriminative of changes in the facial expression. Finally, some recent research is examining how to combine the feature extraction and classification stages by formulating them as a joint optimization problem (Ashraf & Lucey, 2010).

5. Face Detectors

Thanks to the use of machine learning methods, real-time face detection has become a reality, and the research has percolated into some high-quality commercial products such as the Omron face detector (Omron, 2008). There is still considerable room for improvement, however. In particular, current systems tend to work better with Asian and Caucasian faces than with dark-skinned faces. They are also significantly less accurate in difficult lighting conditions, including backlighting and outdoor conditions with strong shadows. Face detection algorithms can be divided into two categories: absolute and differential.

5.1 Absolute Face Detectors

Absolute detectors, aka frame-by-frame detectors, determine the location of the face independently for each video frame. The name "absolute detector" is in analogy with the absolute encoders used in servomotors. An absolute detector has many advantages: it can be easily parallelized across multiple video frames in time, it is very responsive to sudden changes in the number of faces on the image plane, and it does not drift over time. The disadvantage is that it does not use temporal constraints that could be used to improve the speed and accuracy of the system.

Most absolute face detection algorithms are based on the Viola–Jones object detection architecture (Viola & Jones, 2004), which is a particularly efficient implementation of the Rowley-Kanade sliding window architecture (Rowley et al., 1998). First, a classifier is trained to discriminate patches of faces from patches of nonfaces. Depending on the system, these patches can be from 16×16 to 48×48 pixels in size. In the

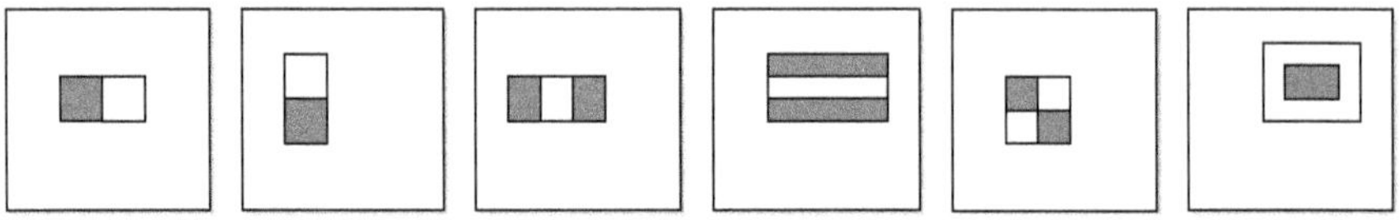

FIGURE 6.2 Six kinds of box filter features commonly used in computer vision applications.

Viola–Jones approach, the face detectors are based on 2D box filters (see Figure 6.2). The advantage of these filters is that their output can be computed in a few CPU instructions. Multiple filters are combined to create complex classifiers using the Adaboost learning algorithm (Freund & Shapire, 1995; Viola & Jones, 2004) or variations such as Gentleboost (Fasel et al., 2005; Friedman et al., 2000). Typically it takes on the order of 30, 000 example patches of faces and on the order of 1 billion example patches of nonfaces to train a reliable classifier to be capable of discriminating patches rendered by an upright face from all other naturally occurring patches. A standard detector can recognize faces accurately for deviations of about 10 to 20 degrees from frontal. Face detectors that work on a wider range of poses are typically based on a collection of detectors, each one specialized in a different pose.

Given a new image, faces are found by scanning the image over a large number of locations and scales. For each location and scale, a patch is extracted, scaled to a common size (e.g., 16 × 16 pixels), and passed to the patch classifier. The classifier decides whether this particular patch renders a face or not. This approach allows for detection of an arbitrary number of faces in the image. In addition, the search operation can be parallelized across locations and/or scales for better performance.

Critical to being able to perform the scanning operation in real time is the use of sequential decision-making procedures (Fasel et al., 2005; Movellan et al., 2005; Viola & Jones, 2004). The key is that most of the image patches can be recognized as nonfaces very quickly using simple detectors. More complex and computationally intensive detectors are applied only to a handful of patches on which the simple detectors are unsure.

5.2 Differential Face Detectors

At the other end of the spectrum are differential detectors, aka face trackers, that can accurately estimate the likely location of the face at time $t + \Delta t$ provided the location of the face at time t is known. These differential detectors typically use optic-flow algorithms or dynamically update features such as color histograms to compute the probable movement of the face. Arguably the most popular differential detectors approaches use active appearance models (AAMs) (Cootes et al., 2001; Lucey et al., 2010). AAMs provide an integrated approach to face segmentation, registration, and feature extraction, and hence, we will discuss them in each of the corresponding sections of this chapter.

In AAMs, the face is represented as a triangulated mesh shape model consisting of about 70 finely spaced feature points. Before tracking, a model must be constructed from example faces exhibiting a variety of expressions, in which the feature point positions are marked. Principal components analysis is employed to compute a space of rigid and nonrigid motion parameters that captures the majority of variance in the feature point positions. Both person-dependent models and person-independent models are possible. The former offers higher tracking accuracy if the target person is known, whereas the latter can generalize better to novel individuals. At run-time, the locations of all feature points in the first video frame must be initialized, either manually or using an absolute tracker. For subsequent video frames, feature point locations are tracked automatically by searching over both rigid and nonrigid deformation parameters. The objective is to minimize the difference between the face model and the given video frame by varying the parameter values. This amounts to an optic flow computation, typically using the Lucas–Kanade algorithm. More recently, Constrained Local Models (CLMs) have been proposed, which take advantage of discriminative feature detection models (Wang et al., 2008). The intuition in using AAMs for facial expression recognition is that once the rigid face deformation has been subtracted out, the nonrigid deformation parameters will reveal the facial expression.

The disadvantage of differential trackers such as AAMs is that small errors in the temporal derivative quickly accumulate, resulting in significant drift from which it may be difficult to recover. After a few seconds, these trackers, if not corrected periodically, can drift off the face and track spurious image locations. Recent research has investigated how to combine absolute tracking with differential tracking. The differential tracking algorithms provide speed and accuracy over short timescales, and the absolute tracking algorithms help with error recovery and rapid adaptation to faces moving in and out of the image plane (Morency et al., 2009).

6. Face Registration

Once the faces are detected, image patches containing faces are extracted for further processing. These patches are first scaled to a common size, typically anything between 16 × 16 to 96 × 96 pixels, depending on the application. The next stage is to *register* the face, that is, to morph the face onto a canonical view. Face registration is designed to reduce variations due to face geometry, and face pose. Typically this is done by identifying a number of facial features, such as the eyes, nose, and mouth, and warping the image so as to approximate a common geometry. The number and types of features being used varies between systems.

6.1 Facial Feature Detection

Some of the most successful systems use detectors that find features within a face in a manner similar to the way faces are found within an image (Fasel et al., 2005). These feature detectors are trained to discriminate between two categories: (1) image patches in which the target feature is located in the center of the patch and (2) image patches in which the target feature is off center. Some systems rely on a few feature detectors (eye corners, nose, mouth) that are trained on a very large number of images from different people and illumination conditions (Eckhardt et al., 2009; Fasel et al., 2005; Whitehill et al., 2009). This approach works quite well as long as the head does not rotate more than 45 degrees from a target view, typically the frontal view. Other systems use a larger number of less reliable but faster feature detectors datasets. Finally, some systems track a large number of very simple features that are trained on a specific person (Brand, 2001; Marks et al., 2010; Torresani et al., 2001).

After the face is found, a search is performed around probable feature locations given the detected face. For each pixel the feature detector outputs the likelihood that the feature is centered at that pixel location. This pixel-by-pixel likelihood is multiplied by a prior probability score to obtain a posterior probability value for each pixel location. Some systems search for peaks of the posterior distribution using algorithms such as mean-shift (Cheng, 1995). Other systems fit quadratic functions over the posterior distribution and find the peak of the quadratic function analytically (Wang et al., 2008). Another possibility is to use Monte-Carlo methods to find the peak of the posterior distribution for an entire set of features that are coupled via a deformable 3D model of the face (Marks et al., 2010). Finally, Active Appearance Models use a differential tracking approach: assuming the locations of about 70 feature points are known from the first video frame, their locations in subsequent frames can be tracked using optic flow.

Given the location of the tracked facial feature points, the expression recognition system will either use these locations directly for classification (this is the case for *geometry-based approaches*), or instead use them to map the facial appearance onto a canonical view. Depending on the approach, the morphing may use planar models of the face (Littlewort et al., 2006; Marks et al., 2010), cylindrical models of the face (la Cascia et al., 2000), ellipsoid models (Morency et al., 2009), 2D active appearance models based on a triangulated mesh (Lucey et al., 2010), or 3D deformable models (Brand, 2001; Marks et al., 2010; Torresani et al., 2001).

7. Feature Extraction

Feature extraction procedures can be divided into *geometric approaches* and *appearance-based approaches*. Geometric approaches typically extract the location of a large number of facial features and directly recognize facial expressions from the locations of those features alone. Thus, after the features of interest are located, these systems do not use an image morphing process; instead, the features are obtained directly from the face registration stage. It appears intuitive, for example, that by tracking the location of the brows one can discriminate whether the brows are up or down without the need to further examine the appearance of the brows. Based on this intuition, location-based systems were initially quite popular and thought to be more promising than appearance-based systems. While the issue is not yet definitively resolved, the empirical evidence suggests that, in fact, appearance-based approaches are more robust and provide superior performance. In essence, the problem with location-based approaches is that it is very difficult to reliably track the location of face features. Thus, location-based approaches may be attempting to recognize facial expressions by solving a problem (feature tracking) that may be more difficult than the expression recognition problem itself. This is a recurrent theme in the history of computer vision.

In the sections that follow, we review popular feature types used in facial expression recognition system along with the corresponding citations:

1. *Gabor filters:* 2D spatial and 3D spatiotemporal energy filters (Bartlett et al., 2006; Littlewort et al., 2006; Wu et al., 2010).
2. *Box/Haar-like filters:* 2D spatial and 3D spatiotemporal box filter features (Whitehill et al., 2009; Yang et al., 2009).
3. *Local binary pattern (LBP) features:* 2D spatial and 3D spatiotemporal box filter features (Zhao & Pietikäinen, 2007).
4. *Optic flow features* (Koelstra et al., 2010; Pantic & Patras, 2005).
5. *Geometric features:* based on relative positions of facial features (eyes, nose, mouth, etc.) (Ryan et al., 2009).

The first four categories can all be considered appearance-based features. When dealing with the appearance-based features, we subdivide our review of feature types into two categories: *spatial* and *spatiotemporal* features.

7.1 Spatial Features

7.1.1. Gabor Energy Filters

Gabor filters are frequency-tuned band-pass filters. They consist of a sinusoid carrier signal modulated by a Gaussian. The sinusoid determines the frequency the filter is tuned to, and the width of the Gaussian envelope determines the filter bandwidth. Gabor filters can be formulated for an arbitary number of dimension but are most commonly implemented in 1D (temporal Gabors), 2D (spatial Gabors), and 3D (spatiotemporal Gabors).

Gabor filters are complex valued. In pattern recognition applications, the complex filter response is typically separated either into real and imaginary components, or alternatively, into a magnitude and phase. Although the real and imaginary components are linear functions of the input pixels, the magnitude is a nonlinear function and represents the energy of the response, hence the name *Gabor energy filters*. Out of all the feature types used in expression recognition, the Gabor energy filter enjoys probably the strongest motivation from neurobiology: It is now well known that Gabor energy filters approximate the responses of complex cells in primary visual cortex. Examples of spatial Gabor filters are shown in Figure 6.3; for a mathematical derivation of Gabor filters, see (Movellan, 2005). Some of the most successful facial

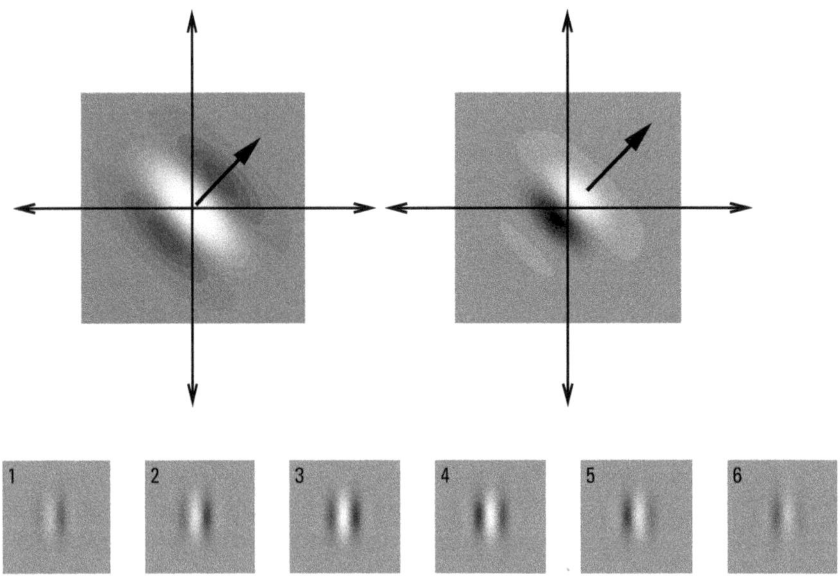

FIGURE 6.3 (Above): The even (left) and odd (right) components of a spatial 2D Gabor filter. (Below): A spatiotemporal Gabor, that is, a spatial 2D Gabor modulated by a 1D temporal Gabor.

expression recognition systems to date utilize Gabor energy filters. One reason for their success may stem from the fact that they are invariant to contrast polarity and that they provide some invariance to slight errors in face registration. Using spatial Gabor energy filters as the feature type, Littlewort et al. (2006) achieved the highest accuracy reported (over 93%) to date on the Cohn-Kanade dataset when classifying the seven basic emotions (including neutral). Gabor filters are also the filter extraction method used in the same research group's real-time Facial Action Detector (Bartlett et al., 2006).

7.1.2. Box Filters

Originally used by the computer graphics community (McDonnell, 1981), box filter features (also known as Haar-like filters) gained renown in the computer vision literature through the Viola–Jones face detector (Viola & Jones, 2004). Similar to Gabor filters, box filters features capture local image properties, such as edges. Their advantage over Gabor filters is that they can be computed more efficiently than Gabor filters on current digital computers. The fast processing speed is facilitated by the "integral image" method (Shen & Castan, 1985; Viola & Jones, 2004). This low processing overhead makes box filter features very attractive for facial expression recognition, especially compared with more intensive approaches such as Gabor filters. Examples of box filter features are shown in Figure 6.2. Box filters have been shown to be highly discriminative for detecting smiles in natural image settings (Whitehill et al., 2009). For the recognition of facial action units, the success is mixed: In a preliminary comparison (Whitehill & Omlin, 2006) between box filters and Gabor filters on a subset of the Cohn-Kanade dataset, it was found that box filters yielded accuracies that were equally good as for the 2D Gabors on just a few action units. On other action units, accuracy was significantly less.

While box filter–based expression classifiers are extremely efficient to compute at test time, such classifiers can be very costly to train. The problem is that, in a typical implementation, the number of box filters scales very poorly (i.e., is very large) for an image of a given size, even compared to a bank of Gabor filters. This results in a large feature space that must be searched through and thus long training times. In order to keep the computational complexity in check, the resolution of the scaled face image is usually kept fairly small ($< 48 \times 48$). However, this in turn means that the classifier may be missing valuable information about the face's high-frequency components.

7.1.3. Local Binary Patterns

Local binary pattern (LBP) (Ojala et al., 1996) features have garnered considerable attention in computer vision applications in recent years. They are simple to implement, fast to compute, and have led to high accuracy on texture recognition tasks. In their simplest, 2D form, the LBP around a center image pixel consists of a binary vector such that the ith component corresponds to the pixel's ith neighbor. Each component is 1 if the neighbor's pixel value exceeds the value of the center pixel, and 0 otherwise. The LBP feature value at that point in the image is then represented as the magnitude of that binary vector. The values of the LBP vectors are often histogrammed before being passed to the classifier.

The reasons for the success of LBP in face analysis are not entirely clear. In contrast to Gabor filters, for instance, there is not an immediately apparent biological or signal processing basis for their effectiveness. A partial explanation may have to do with the nonlinearity that LBPs induce on top of the raw pixel values: It was reported in (Whitehill et al., 2009) that the use of LBP features yielded a significantly (2%) higher smile detection accuracy compared with raw pixels when using a linear SVM as the classifier. However, our recent experience is that their performance deteriorates, when compared with Gabor filters, when using more challenging datasets, like the RU-FACS dataset (Wu et al., 2012).

7.1.4. Geometric Features

The three feature types described above are all appearance based, that is, they describe some local properties of the image. An alternative approach is to encode the geometry of the face, typically of the location of a set of feature points. One of the long-standing debates in the expression recognition community is whether geometric features or appearance-based features are superior. One of the most prominent real-time systems employing geometric features has been that of the Jeff Cohn group at CMU/Pitt. Their systems during the last decade have utilized active appearance models for face registration, thus allowing them to estimate the locations of 68 different feature points, which are then classified into an expression. It is noteworthy, however, that their group has recently augmented the feature vector of their expression recognizer with appearance-based features: Given an AAM fitted to the face, the feature vector then consists of the nonrigid shape parameters (geometric features), concatenated with the pixel values of the face after removing the nonrigid shape variation by warping it back onto a canonical face model (Ashraf et al., 2009; Ryan et al., 2009). The combined feature vector is then classified by a support vector machine.

The same group performed a comparative study (Lucey et al., 2010) assessing the relative importance of the geometric versus appearance-based features: On a set of 17 facial action units, using the area under the ROC curve as the performance metric, the nonrigid shape parameters yielded an accuracy of 90.0%, and the appearance-based features after warping yielded an accuracy of 91.4%. By concatenating the two feature vectors, an accuracy of 94.5% was achieved. Thus, according to this experiment, neither feature type clearly performs better than the other, and they contain complementary information. It should be noted that the appearance-based features in their system were extracted *after* removing the nonrigid deformation of the face, and that this was enabled by using an AAM.

7.2 Spatiotemporal Features

Up to now we have described only spatial feature types, that is, features extracted from a single video frame. While spatial features work well for recognizing certain expressions such as smile, many other expressions can be discerned only through their temporal dynamics. The closure of the eyes, for example, could be caused either by a blink or due to a conscious, slow movement of the eyelids, depending on the speed of the event.

Incorporating the dynamics into the expression recognition engine raises the issue of which stage in the processing should analyze the dynamics. When time is considered at the feature extraction stage, we call this *early temporal integration*. When the dynamics are considered after the classification stage, we call it *late temporal integration*. Early temporal integration is implemented using spatiotemporal features and is the subject of the following subsections.

7.2.1. Local Binary Patterns

Zhao and Pietikäinen (2007) proposed two techniques for extending LBP across time—volume LBP (VLBP), and LBP-Three Orthogonal Planes (LBP-TOP)—for the task of recognizing the six basic human emotions, using the Cohn-Kanade dataset for experimentation. In VLBP, the 2D LBP vectors from three video frames consecutive in time are concatenated. This can result in a large dimensionality for the combined binary vector, and hence a large number of histogram bins, which in turn can lead to overfitting during training. LBP-TOP was proposed to address this issue: instead of forming a volume 3 units wide across time, three orthogonal planes across the x, y, x, t, and y, t axes are formed, and 2D LBP features are computed across these planes. In empirical evaluation on the Cohn-Kanade dataset for recognizing six basic emotions, they showed that the LBP-TOP performed slightly better than VLBP. However, our experience is that the current version of the LBP-TOP is very sensitive to errors in the registration process, and its performance rapidly deteriorates when using more challenging datasets (Wu et al., 2012).

7.2.2. Gabor Filters

Wu et al. (2010) compared the spatial Gabor energy filters to spatiotemporal Gabors. They used frequency-tuned Gabors, which means that the spatiotemporal filter can be separated into a temporal Gabor on top of a spatial Gabor, thus speeding up the computation. While expression recognition accuracies were very similar between the two approaches when classifying the six basic emotions at their *apex*, a substantial performance gain was observed for the spatiotemporal Gabors when examining expressions at their *onset*. This suggests that spatiotemporal features may be better suited for capturing subtle expression dynamics than are spatial filters.

The spatiotemporal Gabor filters used in Wu et al. used separable spatial and temporal dimensions. In practice they can be seen as temporal Gabor filters applied to the outputs of the spatial Gabor filters, thus requiring little computational effort once the outputs of the spatial Gabor filters have been obtained.

In recent, not yet published data we have found that for challenging datasets, like RU-FACS, spatiotemporal Gabors provided the best performance when compared with spatial Gabors, spatial LBPs and spatiotemporal LBPs (Wu et al., 2012).

7.2.3. Optic Flow

Optic flow is a popular computer vision algorithm that formed the basis for some of the first expression recognition systems (Mase, 1991) and yet still inspires systems created today. Optic flow analysis assigns a vector to each pixel in a frame of video indicating the estimated magnitude and direction of motion of the object rendered by that pixel. In this way, optic flow-based methods naturally capture facial motion that can be correlated with expression.

Pantic and Patras (2006), as well as Koelstra et al. (2010) compared novel adaptations of two alternative methods—motion history images (Davis & Bobick, 1997), and free-form deformations (Rueckert et al., 1999)—for the task of recognizing facial action units of the MMI dataset. Motion history images are computed using a pixel-wise sum of thresholded difference images between consecutive frames of video. Free-form deformations are based on interpolated b-splines among a set of facial control points. For both techniques, they employed a temporal history parameter θ, which implicitly controls the velocity and maximum history length at which flow is measured. Given a field of optic flow vectors at each pixel location in the face, their system extracts histograms of oriented flow (in the manner of Lowe, 1999), as well as vector-geometric properties such as divergence and curl of these vector fields. The authors used a single point along a precision-recall curve as the accuracy metric, and hence, it is difficult to compare accuracy with other methods. However, they found that the free-form deformation delivered superior accuracy to the motion history image method.

It is interesting to note that this optic flow approach has some similarities to the spatiotemporal Gabor method of (Wu et al., 2010): The temporal history parameter θ used by Koelstra et al. (2010) is similar to the width of the Gaussian envelope of the 1D temporal filter used by Wu et al. (2010). Furthermore, the histograms of oriented gradient for the optic flow approach capture similar information to the variously oriented spatial Gabor filters.

7.2.4. Box Filters

Yang et al. (2009) recently explored the extension of box filter features into the third dimension (time). In their implementation, a 3D "dynamic Haar-like feature" consisted of the same spatial 2D box filter extracted from a temporal window consisting of multiple video frames consecutive in time. From each frame in the window, the 2D filter value was computed and then thresholded using an expression-dependent threshold. This results in a binary number representation for each 3D box filter feature, in which the length of the binary number equals the length of the temporal window. These binary numbers were then classified by weak learners that were combined using Adaboost. Accuracy of this proposed method was assessed on the Cohn-Kanade dataset. On the task of recognizing basic emotions, the authors found that the dynamic box filter representation yielded accuracies (area under the ROC curve), at 96.6%, significantly (6%) higher than a 2D box filter approach. On FACS (Action Units 1, 2, 4, 5, 10, 12, 14, and 20), the 3D box filters achieved a mean accuracy of 76.7% compared with only 69.2% for the 2D box filters.

8. Classification

After features are extracted from the face, they must be analyzed and converted into a decision value for the target expression. In case of a binary classification problem (e.g., Smile versus Non-smile), the value can be either discrete valued (e.g., from $\{+1, -1\}$) or real valued. Real-valued classifier outputs can express either the confidence in the classification, or the intensity of the expression.

There are two main kinds of approaches for converting extracted features into a facial expression class. These are rule-based expert systems (e.g., Pantic & Patras, 2005), and machine learning classifiers. The latter type has become dominant over the last decade. However, machine learning approaches require collecting and labeling large diverse datasets, which is always a challenge.

The most popular machine learning classifiers for facial expression recognition are currently support vector machines (Vapnik, 1998) (SVMs), and boosting methods such as AdaBoost (Freund & Shapire, 1995) or Gentleboost (Friedman et al., 2000). These are both inherently binary classifiers that decide between two classes. Popular multiclass classifiers include *k*-nearest neighbors, multivariate logistic regression (MLR), and multilayer neural networks. Multilayer neural networks have become less popular perhaps because of the fact that training time tends to be slower and the analyst needs to make architectural decisions on parameters such as the number of hidden units or number of units per layer. However, there is also a growing renaissance of neural networks with the recent research attention paid to Deep Belief Nets (Hinton et al., 2006).

In general, the choice of machine learning classifier is not considered as important for performance as the choice of feature types. However, in some cases strong interactions have been reported between classifier type and feature type. For example Whitehill et al. (2009) developed a state-of-the-art smile detection system. They reported that Gabor filters worked well with SVM classifiers and box filters worked well with Gentleboost classifiers. However, Gabor filters did not work as well when combined with Gentleboost classifiers, and Box filters did not work well with SVMs.

There is strong evidence that facial expression cannot be classified accurately using a linear function on top of the grayscale values of the face (Donato et al., 1999). Hence, if the features are linear in the pixel values, then the classifier must be able to handle nonlinearly separable problems in order to perform well. However, it is our experience that with many of the popular nonlinear filter representations, such as Gabor energy filters, or the thresholded pixel difference in LBP features, the linear classifiers (e.g., linear SVMs or logistic regression) often deliver good performance. The advantage of a linear classifier is that it typically results in faster training and run time classification than nonlinear classification methods.

9. Temporal Integration

Two approaches exist to integrate information received from video over time in order to make a decision regarding the facial expression. These are *early temporal integration* and *late temporal integration*. Early temporal integration takes place during the feature extraction stage and captures spatiotemporal information stored in the current frame as well as frames in a window in time near the current frame. An example of early temporal integration is the used of Gabor spatiotemporal filters or optic flow features. Late temporal integration is performed after classification and combines the expression estimates for multiple frames as a postprocessing step. The two approaches are not mutually exclusive; both early and late temporal integration can be performed in one system, as in (Koelstra et al., 2010). Examples of late temporal integration methods include the use of hidden Markov models, Kalman filters, or temporal histograms. This can be particularly useful when modeling high-level states, such "fatigued," "deceitful," "focused," and so on (Kaliouby & Robinson, 2005). In such an approach, the outputs of the facial expression recognizer can serve as observations to the HMM, and the estimated latent cognitive state are the system's final output.

10. Applications

The advances in machine learning and computer vision have given rise to a first generation of commercially available face detectors and expression recognizers. Perhaps the most widely used of such systems are the face detectors embedded in most modern digital cameras and many smartphones. Sony additionally offers a "Smile Shutter" feature, which uses a smile detector to take a picture when all persons in the viewscreen are smiling.

With the introduction of commercially available real-time systems to recognize facial expressions, higher level applications utilizing the recognized expressions, both academic and commercial, are also starting to emerge. Automated facial expression recognition is, for instance, a boon to psychological research: Instead of tediously coding videos of human subjects' faces by hand, an automated classifier can label each video frame in a fraction of a second. The fine grain of temporal locality enabled by automated coding also facilitates the study of facial expression dynamics.

In the sections that follow, we describe a few recent applications using automatic facial expression recognition as the first tier.

10.1. Automated Discrimination of Real From Faked Expressions of Pain

Given the two different neural pathways for facial expressions, one may expect to find differences between genuine and posed expressions of states such as pain. An automated discriminator of faked versus genuine pain could, in effect, serve to differentiate the two forms of neural control. This would hold out the prospect of illuminating basic questions pertaining to the behavioral fingerprint of neural control systems and open many future lines of inquiry.

Littlewort and colleagues (2009) used automatic facial expression recognition software to recognize the Action Units that occurred in spontaneous versus posed facial expressions of pain (see Figure 6.4).

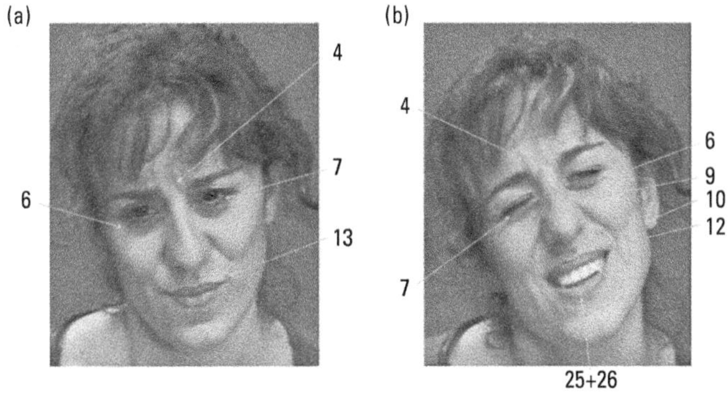

FIGURE 6.4 Facial expression of faked pain (a) and real pain (b), with corresponding FACS codes.

In this study, 26 participants were videotaped under three experimental conditions: baseline, posed pain, and real pain. The real-pain condition consisted of cold pressor pain induced by submerging the arm in ice water. The study assessed whether the automated measurements were consistent with expression measurements obtained by human experts, and also how well a machine learning classifier could distinguish the faked- and real-pain conditions. The classifier was constructed in a two-stage fashion: First, recognize the individual AUs and compute measures of AU dynamics. Second, pass these AU measurements to a nonlinear support vector machine designed to discriminate faked from real pain.

As a comparison with the automated pain classifier, naïve human subjects were tested on the same set of videos. They were at chance for differentiating faked from real pain expressions, obtaining only 49% accuracy, where chance is 50%. The automated system was successfully able to differentiate faked from real pain, with an accuracy (2 alternative forced choice) of 88% for subject-independent classification over the 26 subjects. Moreover, the most discriminative facial actions in the automated system were consistent with findings using human expert FACS codes. In particular, in the faked-pain condition the automated system output showed exaggerated activity of the brow-lowering action (corrugator, as well as inner brow raise [central frontalis]), and eyelid tightening, which were consistent with a previous study on faked versus real cold-pressor pain that employed manual FACS coding (Larochette et al., 2006). The temporal event analysis performed significantly better than an SVM trained just on individual frames, suggesting that the real-versus-faked expression discrimination depends not only on which subset of AUs are present at which intensity, but also on the duration and number of AU events.

10.2. Automated Detection of Driver Fatigue

It is estimated that driver drowsiness causes more fatal crashes in the United States than drunk driving (U.S. Dept. of Transportation, 2001). Hence, an automated system that could detect drowsiness and alert the driver or truck dispatcher could potentially save many lives. Previous approaches to drowsiness detection by computer make assumptions about the relevant behavior, focusing on blink rate, eye closure, yawning, and head nods (Gu & Ji, 2004). While there is considerable empirical evidence that blink rate can predict falling asleep, it was unknown whether there were other facial behaviors that could predict sleep episodes. Vural et al. (2007) employed a machine learning architecture to recogne drowsiness in real human behavior. In this study, facial motion was analyzed automatically using the Computer Expression Recognition Toolbox (CERT) (Bartlett et al., 2006), and head acceleration was measured using an accelerometer placed on the subject's head. Steering inputs were recorded from a digital steering wheel. Four subjects participated in a driving simulation task over a 3-hour period between midnight and 3:00 AM. Videos of the subjects' faces and time-locked crash events were recorded (Figure 6.5). The subjects' data were partitioned into drowsy and alert states as follows: The one minute preceding a crash was labeled as a drowsy state. A set of "alert" video segments was identified from the first 20 minutes of the task in which there were no crashes by any subject. This resulted in a mean of 14 alert segments and 24 crash

FIGURE 6.5 Driving simulation task. (Reprinted from Vural et al., 2007.)

segments per subject. In order to understand how each Action Unit is associated with drowsiness across different subjects, a multinomial logistic ridge regressor (MLR) was trained on each facial action individually. The five most predictive facial actions whose intensities increased in drowsy states were blink, outer brow raise, frown, chin raise, and nose wrinkle. The five most predictive actions that decreased in intensity in drowsy states were smile, lid tighten, nostril compress, brow lower, and jaw drop. The high predictive ability of the blink/eye closure measure was expected. However, the predictability of the outer brow raise was previously unknown. It was observed during this study that many subjects raised their eyebrows in an attempt to keep their eyes open. Also of note is that action 26, jaw drop, which occurs during yawning, actually occurred less often in the critical 60 seconds prior to a crash.

A fatigue detector that combines multiple AUs was then developed. An MLR classifier was trained using contingent feature selection, starting with the most discriminative feature (blink), and then iteratively adding the next most discriminative feature given the features already selected. MLR outputs were then temporally integrated over a 12-second window. Best performance of .98 area under the ROC was obtained with five features.

Changes were also observed in the coupling of behaviors with drowsiness. For some of the subjects, coupling between brow raise and eye openness increased in the drowsy state (Figures 6.6a & 6.6b). Subjects appear to have pulled up their eyebrows in an attempt to keep their eyes open. Head motion was next examined. Head motion increased as the driver became drowsy, with large roll motion coupled with the steering motion as the driver became drowsy. Just before falling asleep, the head would become still; see Figures 6.6c and 6.6d. This is the first work to our knowledge to reveal significant associations between facial expression and fatigue beyond eyeblinks. The project also revealed a potential association between head roll and driver drowsiness, and the coupling of head roll with steering motion during drowsiness. Of note is that a behavior that is often assumed to be predictive of drowsiness, yawn, was, in fact, a negative predictor of the 60-second window prior to a crash. It appears that in the moments just before falling asleep, drivers may yawn less, not more, often. This highlights the importance of designing a system around real, not posed, examples of fatigue and drowsiness.

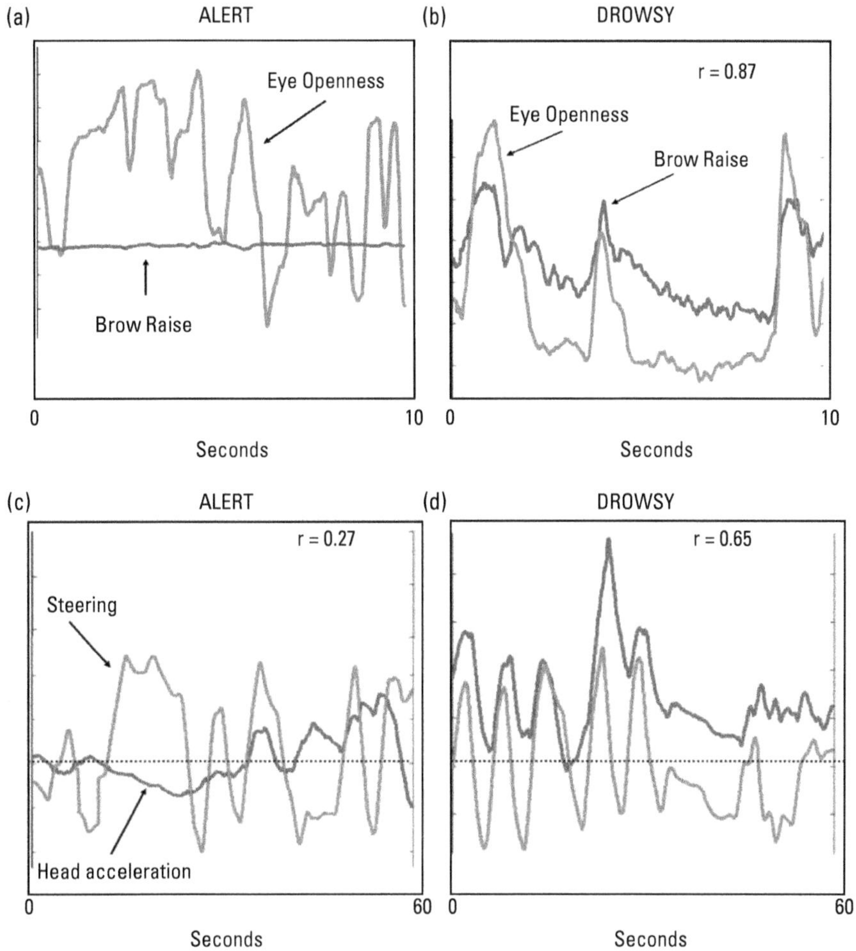

FIGURE 6.6 Changes in movement coupling with drowsiniess. (a, b) : Eye Openness (red) and Eye Brow Raise (AU2) (blue) for 10 seconds in an alert state (a) and 10 seconds prior to a crash (b), for one subject. (c, d): Head motion (blue) and steering position (red) for 60 seconds in an alert state (c) and 60 seconds prior to a crash (d) for one subject. Head motion is the output of the roll dimension of the accelerometer. (In grayscale, gray = blue, red = black.) (Reprinted from Bartlett et al., 2010.)

10.3. Automated Teaching Systems

There has been a growing thrust to develop tutoring systems and agents that respond to students' emotional and cognitive state and interact with them in a social manner (e.g., D'Mello et al., 2007; Kapoor et al., 2007). Whitehill et al. (2008) conducted a pilot experiment in which expression was used to estimate the student's preferred viewing speed of the videos, and the level of difficulty, as perceived by the individual student, of the lecture at each moment of time. This study took first steps toward developing methods for closed-loop teaching policies, that is, systems that have access to real-time estimates of cognitive and emotional states of the students and act accordingly.

In this study, 8 subjects separately watched a video lecture composed of several short clips on mathematics, physics, psychology, and other topics. The playback speed of the video was controlled by the subject using a keypress. The subjects were instructed to watch the video as quickly as possible (so as to be efficient with their time) while still retaining accurate knowledge of the video's content, since they would be quizzed afterward.

While watching the lecture, the student's facial expressions were measured in real time by the CERT system (Bartlett et al., 2006). After watching the video

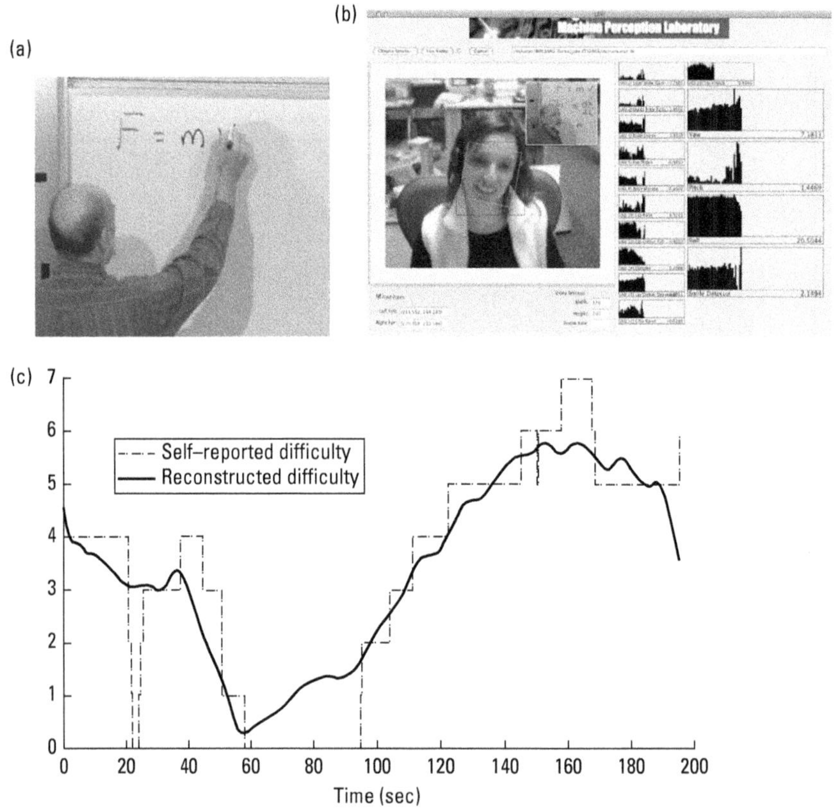

FIGURE 6.7 (a) Sample video lecture. (b) Automated facial expression recognition is performed on subject's face as she watches the lecture. (c) Self-reported difficulty values (dashed), and the reconstructed difficulty values (solid) computed using linear regression over facial expression movements for one subject. (Reprinted from Whitehill et al., 2008.)

and taking the quiz, each subject then watched the lecture video again at a fixed speed of 1.0. During this second viewing, subjects specified how easy or difficult they found the lecture to be at each moment in time using the keyboard.

For each subject, a regression analysis was performed to predict perceived difficulty and preferred viewing speed from the facial expression measures. The expression intensities, as well as their first temporal derivatives (measuring the instantaneous change in intensity), were the independent variables in a standard linear regression. An example of such predictions is shown in Figure 6.7c for one subject. The facial expression measures were significantly predictive of both perceived difficulty ($r = .75$) and preferred viewing speed ($r = .51$). The correlations on validation data were 0.42 and 0.29, respectively. The specific facial expressions that were correlated with difficulty and speed varied highly from subject to subject. The most consistently correlated expression was AU 45 ("blink"), in which subjects blinked less during the more difficult sections of video. This is consistent with previous work associating decreases in blink rate with increases in cognitive load (Holland and Tarlow, 1975).

Overall, this study provided proof of principle, that fully automated facial expression recognition at the present state of the art can be used to provide real-time feedback in automated tutoring systems. The recognition system was able to extract a signal from the face video in real time that provided information about internal states relevant to teaching and learning.

A related project that attempts to approximate the benefits of face-to-face tutoring interaction is a collaboration between the MIT media lab and the developers of AutoTutor (D'Mello et al., 2008). AutoTutor is an intelligent tutoring system that interacts with students using natural language to teach physics, computer literacy, and critical thinking skills. The current system adapts to the cognitive states of the learner as inferred from dialogue and performance. A new affect-sensitive version is presently under development (D'Mello et al., 2007), which detects four emotions (boredom, flow/engagement, confusion, frustration) by monitoring conversational cues, gross body language, and facial expressions. Toward this end, they have developed a database of spontaneous expressions while interacting with the automated tutor, which will significantly advance the field.

11. Future Challenges

We identify six key challenges for progress in the near future: (1) generalization to multiple poses, (2) generalization to a wide range of ethnicities, (3) development of realistic datasets, (4) development of algorithms for learning from unlabeled or weakly labeled databases, (5) development of a realistic evaluation infrastructure, and (6) commercialization.

Generalization to Multiple Poses. The recognition of facial expressions in a manner that is relatively invariant to the orientation of the head is arguably the single most important challenge for practical applications. Current expression recognizers typically work accurately for head orientations that deviate no more than 15 degrees from frontal. This range is still too limiting for most applications. Currently there are three main approaches to recognizing facial expression in multiple poses. The first approach is to place multiple cameras at different viewing angles. Each camera yields an independent expression estimate, and these estimates are then integrated. The most straightforward integration scheme is to accept the opinion of the camera in which the face is captured closest to frontal.

The second approach is to use 3D models to rotate and morph the appearance of the face into a frontal view. The third approach is to employ a different expression classifier depending on the pose of the face as estimated by an automated pose detector (Murphy-Chutorian & Trivedi, 2009). This, in turn, necessitates the collection of a dataset of expressions recorded from different camera angles. The CMU Multi-PIE dataset (Gross et al., 2009) is an example of such an approach, although they recorded only a very small number of different facial expressions.

Generalization to Multiple Ethnicities. It is now well known that current face detectors and expression analyzers work better for light-skinned faces than for dark-skinned faces. The exact cause is not yet clear—it is possible that the computer vision problem is simply more challenging for dark-skinned faces. It is also possible that the type of features currently popular are not well suited for dark-skinned images, and that individuals of some ethnicities are not represented well enough in current training datasets.

If the problem does stem from a lack of training examples, then collecting more examples of dark-skinned faces would ameliorate the problem. If not, then the issue could be tackled similarly to the multipose issue problem: First discern the face's ethnicity, and then apply an ethnicity-specific face detector and/or expression recognizer.

Learning Algorithms. One of the difficulties of creating new FACS datasets is the cost in both time and money of labeling video. A possible strategy for mitigating this issue is to use algorithms that do not require as much human labeling. A promising approach is the use of active learning strategies, such as information maximization control, whereby only the video frames whose labels would carry the most information, conditional on the faces' appearance, are actually labeled.

Another approach to reduce the cost of dataset labeling is the use of crowdsourcing: Recent work on crowdsourcing analysis (Whitehill et al., 2009) has shown that, on a Duchenne versus non-Duchenne smile– labeling task, the accuracy of expert FACS coders can be closely approximated by optimally integrating the opinions of many amateur FACS labelers from the Amazon Mechanical Turk.

Datasets. Whenever one is developing machine learning–based pattern recognizers, it is crucial to understand which methods are performing best, under what conditions, and why they are superior. The facial expression recognition literature addresses these questions only partially, as often varying performance metrics and test datasets are used across papers. The collection—and public dissemination—of high-quality datasets of spontaneous facial actions in natural imaging conditions (lighting, geography, occlusions, etc.) is crucial. These datasets are important both for training of the classifier and for evaluation thereof.

Evaluation Infrastructure. A popular approach for evaluating algorithms is the use of cross-validation methods. These methods proceed as follows: a dataset is divided into a randomly selected training set and a test set. A system is trained on the training set, and its performance is evaluated on the test set. Cross-validation methods are important to get unbiased estimates of the performance of the algorithm in cases that were not used for training. Our experience is that this approach often results in inflated estimates of performance in the current literature. The reason is that researchers often perform a wide range of experiments but only report those techniques that worked best on the test set. Thus, they are implicitly using the test set for training. Standard culprits are the number of features used for training, the point at which training is stopped, and the regularization constant. One way of preventing this problem is to use double cross-validation methods; in other words, parameters such as regularization are chosen on the first cross-validation round, and the final performance is evaluated on a second cross-validation round. We believe, however, that it is critical for future datasets to include blind sets that are not made publicly available. Researchers can submit their system's predictions and receive performance measures without having direct access to the stimulus images and their labels.

Commercialization. Companies like Sony have commercialized simple applications, such as the Smile Shutter, which has been embedded in their line of digital cameras.

Small companies, like Machine Perception Technologies Inc., Affective Interfaces, and Afectiva, are attempting to commercialize the current expression recognition systems for niche applications such as academic research, marketing research, and automatic analysis of interviews.

Expression recognition is still an emerging technology whose potential we are only starting to understand. At this point it is not yet clear whether it will follow the path of technologies such as speech recognition that slowly lingered into niche applications used by a small proportion of the population, or whether it will follow the explosive growth of technologies such as Web Search Engines. As computers become more powerful and less energy demanding, this technology has the potential to become part of our daily life and to revolutionize the way we interact with machines.

12. Appendix

```
% function s=Calc2AFC(x,y)
%
% Computes the 2AFC score.
% x is a real valued vector
% y is a binary vector of labels.
It should be of the same size as x
%
% Example
% x = [ 1 2 3 4 3 4 5 6]'
% y = [ 0 0 0 0 1 1 1 1]'
%
% s = Calc2AFC(x,y)
% s in this case should be 0.875
%
function s=Calc2AFC(x,y)
c = unique(y);
x0 = x(y== c(1));
x1 = x(y== c(2));
n0 = length(x0);
n1 = length(x1);
s=0;
for k=1: n0
    n = sum(x1> x0(k)) +
        0.5*sum(x1 == x0(k));
    s =s + n/(n1*n0);
end
```

References

Ashraf, A., & Lucey, S. (2010). Re-interpreting the application of gabor filters as a manipulation of the margin in linear support vector machines. *Pattern Analysis and Machine Intelligence*, 32(7), 1335–1341.

Ashraf, A. B., Lucey, S., Cohn, J. F., Chen, T., Ambadar, Z., Prkachin, K. M., & Solomon, P. E. (2009). The painful face—Pain expression recognition using active appearance models. *Image and Vision Computing*, 27(12), 1788–1796. Visual and multimodal analysis of human spontaneous behaviour.

Bartlett, M., Littlewort, G., Frank, M., Lainscsek, C., Fasel, I., & Movellan, J. (2006). Automatic recognition of facial actions in spontaneous expressions. *Journal of Multimedia*, *1*(6), 22–35.

Bartlett, M., Littlewort, G., Whitehill, J., Vural, E., Wu, T., Lee, K., Ercil, A., Cetin, M., & Movellan, J. (2010). Insights on spontaneous facial expressions from automatic expression measurement. In M. Giese, C. Curio, & H. Bulthoff (Eds.), *Dynamic faces: Insights from experiments and computation*. Cambridge, MA: MIT Press (pp. 211–238).

Brand, M. (2001). Flexible flow for 3D nonrigid tracking and shape recovery. In *Proceedings of the IEEE Conference on Computer Vision and Pattern Recognition*, *1*, 315–322.

Cheng, Y. (1995). Mean shift, mode seeking, and clustering. *Pattern Analysis and Machine Intelligence*, 17(8), 790–799.

Cohn, J., Kreuz, T., Matthews, I., Yang, Y., Nguyen, M. H., Padilla, M., Zhou, F., & de la Torre, F. (2009). Detecting depression from facial actions and vocal prosody. In *Affective Computing and Intelligent Interaction* (pp. 1–7).

Cootes, T., Edwards, G., & Taylor, C. (2001). Active appearance models. *Pattern Analysis and Machine Intelligence, 23*(6), 681–684.

Davis, J., & Bobick, A. (1997). The representation and recognition of human movement using temporal templates. In *Proceedings of the IEEE Computer Vision and Pattern Recognition* (pp. 928–934).

D'Mello, S., Picard, R., & Graesser, A. (2007). Towards an affect-sensitive autotutor [Special Issue on Intelligent Educational Systems]. *IEEE Intelligent Systems,* 22(4), 53–61.

Donato, G., Bartlett, M., Hager, J., Ekman, P., & Sejnowski, T. (1999). Classifying facial actions. *IEEE Transactions on Pattern Analysis and Machine Intelligence, 21*(10), 974–989.

Eckhardt, M., Fasel, I., & Movellan, J. R. (2009). Towards practical facial feature detection. *International Journal of Pattern Recognition and Artificial Intelligence (IJPRAI), 23*(3), 379–400.

Ekman, P. (2001). *Telling lies: Clues to deceit in the marketplace, politics, and marriage.* New York: W.W. Norton and Company.

Ekman, P., & Friesen, W. (1978). *The Facial Action Coding System: A technique for the measurement of facial movement.* San Francisco: Consulting Psychologists Press, Inc.

Ekman, P., & Rosenberg, E. (Eds.). (2005). *What the face reveals: Basic and applied studies of spontaneous expression using the FACS.* Oxford, UK: Oxford University Press.

Fasel, I., Fortenberry, B., & Movellan, J. R. (2005). A generative framework for real-time object detection and classification. *Computer Vision and Image Understanding,* 98(1), 182–210.

Freund, Y., & Schapire, R. E. (1995). A decision-theoretic generalization of on-line learning and an application to boosting. In *Proceedings of the European Conference on Computational Learning Theory* (pp. 23–37). London: Springer-Verlag.

Friedman, J., Hastie, T., & Tibshirani, R. (2000). Additive logistic regression: A statistical view of boosting. *Annals of Statistics,* 28(2), 337–407.

Gross, R., Matthews, I., Cohn, J., Kanade, T., & Baker, S. Multi-PIE. (2009). *Image and Vision Computing.*

Gu, H., & Ji, Q. (2004). An automated face reader for fatigue detection. In *Proceedings of the International Conference on Automated Face and Gesture Recognition, IEEE: city is Seoul, South Korea,* (pp. 111–116).

Hinton, G., Osindero, S., & Teh, Y. (2006). A fast learning algorithm for deep belief nets. *Neural Computation, 18,* 1527–1554.

Holland, Morris, K., & Tarlow, G. (1975). Blinking and thinking. *Perceptual and motor skills, 41*(2), 403–406.

Kaliouby, R. E., & Robinson, P. (2005). Generalization of a vision-based computational model of mind-reading. In *Proceedings of the 1st International Conference on Affective Computing and Intelligent Interaction, LNCS 3784* (pp. 582–589). Springer.

Kanade, T., Cohn, J., & Tian, Y.-L. (2000). Comprehensive database for facial expression analysis. In *Proceedings of the 4th IEEE International Conference on Automatic Face and Gesture Recognition (FG'00)* (pp. 46–53). IEEE: France.

Kapoor, A., Burleson, W., & Picard, R. (2007). Automatic prediction of frustration. *International Journal of Human-Computer Studies, 65*(8), 724–736.

Keltner, D., & Ekman, P. (2000). Facial expression of emotion. In M. Lewis & J. Haviland-Jones (Eds.), *Handbook of emotions* (pp. 236–249). New York: Guilford Publications, Inc.

Koelstra, S., Pantic, M., & Patras, I. (2010). A dynamic texture based approach to recognition of facial actions and their temporal models. *Pattern Analysis and Machine Intelligence,* 32(11), 1940–1954.

la Cascia, M., Schlaroff, S., & Athitsos, V. (2000). Fast, reliable head tracking under varying illumination: An approach based on registration of texture-mapped 3d models. *Pattern Analysis and Machine Intelligence,* 22(4), 322–336.

Larochette, A., Chambers, C., & Craig, K. (2006). Genuine, suppressed and faked facial expressions of pain in children. *Pain, 126*(1–3), 64–71.

Littlewort, G., Bartlett, M., Fasel, I., Susskind, J., & Movellan, J. (2006). Dynamics of facial expression extracted automatically from video. *Image and Vision Computing, 24*(6), 615–625.

Littlewort, G., Bartlett, M., & Lee, K. (2009). Automatic coding of facial expressions displayed during posed and genuine pain. *Image and Vision Computing,* 27(12), 1797–1803.

Lowe, D. (1999). Object recognition from local scale-invariant features. In *Proceedings of the International Conference on Computer Vision* (pp. 1150–1157). IEEE: Greece.

Lucey, P., Cohn, J., Kanade, T., Saragih, J., & Ambadar, Z. (2010). The extended cohn-kanade dataset (CK+): A complete dataset for action unit and emotion-specified expression. In *CVPR Workshop on Human Communicative Behavior Analysis* (pp. 94–101). IEEE: San Francisco.

Marks, T., Hershey, J. R., & Movellan, J. R. (2010). Tracking motion, deformation, and texture using conditionally gaussian processes. *Pattern Analysis and Machine Intelligence*, 32(2), 348–363.

Mase, K. (1991). Recognition of facial expression from optical flow. *IEICE Transactions*, *E74*(10), 3474–3483.

McDonnell, M. (1981). Box-filtering techniques. *Computer Graphics and Image Processing*, *17*(1), 65–70.

Miehlke, A. *Surgery of the facial nerve*. (1973). Philadelphia: Saunders.

Morency, L., Whitehill, J., & Movellan, J. (2010). Monocular head pose estimation using generalized adaptive view-based appearance model. *Image and Vision Computing*, 28(5), 754–761.

Movellan, J. (2005). Tutorial on gabor filters. (Technical Report). San Diego, CA: MPLab Tutorials, UCSD MPLab.

Movellan, J. R., Bartlett, M. S., & Littlewort, G. C. (2005). Weak hypothesis generation apparatus and method, learning apparatus and method, detection apparatus and method, facial expression learning apparatus and method, facial expression recognition apparatus and method, and robot apparatus. *U.S. Patent: US20080247598 A1*. Washington, DC: U.S. Patent and Trademark Office.

Movellan, J. R., Tanaka, F., Fasel, I. R., Taylor, C., Ruvolo, P., & Eckhardt, M. (2007). The RUBI project: A progress report. In *Proceedings of the 2nd ACM/IEEE International Conference on Human-Robot Interaction* (pp. 333–339). ACM: New York, NY.

Murphy-Chutorian, E., & Trivedi, M. (2009). Head pose estimation in computer vision: A survey. *Pattern Analysis and Machine Intelligence*, *31*(4), 607–626.

Ojala, T., Pietikainen, M., & Harwood, D. (1996). A comparative study of texture measures with classification based on feature distributions. *Pattern Recognition*, 29(1), 51–59.

Omron. (2008). OKAO vision brochure (p. 1).

Pantic, M., & Patras, I. (2006). Dynamics of facial expression: Recognition of facial actions and their temporal segments from face profile image sequences. *Systems, Man, and Cybernetics—Part B: Cybernetics*, 36(2), 433–449.

Pantic, M., & Patras, P. (2005). Detecting facial actions and their temporal segments in nearly frontal-view face image sequences. In *Proceedings of the International Conference on Systems, Man and Cybernetics* (pp. 3358–3363). IEEE: Waikoloa, Hawaii.

Pantic, M., Valstar, M., Rademaker, R., & Maat, L. (2005). Web-based database for facial expression analysis. In *Proceedings of the International Conference on Multimedia and Expo* (pp. 317–321). IEEE: Amsterdam, Netherlands.

Picard, R. (2000). *Affective computing*. Cambridge, MA: MIT Press.

Rinn, W. (1984). The neuropsychology of facial expression: A review of the neurological and psychological mechanisms for producing facial expressions. *Psychological Bulletin*, 95(1), 52–77.

Rose, A. (2010). Are face-detection cameras racist? *Time*, Friday, January 22, 2010.

Rowley, H. A., Baluja, S., & Kanade, T. (1998). Neural network-based face detection. *Pattern Analysis and Machine Intelligence*, *20*(1), 23–38.

Rueckert, D., Sonoda, L., Hayes, C., Hill, D., Leach, M., & Hakes, D. (1999). Nonrigid registration using free-form deformations: Applications to breast MR images. *Transactions on Medical Imaging*, *18*(8), 712–721.

Ryan, A., Cohn, J., Lucey, S., Saragih, J., Lucey, P., la Torre, F., & Rossi, A. (2009). Automated facial expression recognition system. In *Proceedings of the International Carnahan Conference on Security Technology* (pp. 172–177). IEEE: Zurich, Switzerland.

Shen, J., & Castan, S. (1985). Fast approximate realization of linear filters by translating cascading sum-box technique. In *Proceedings of CVPR* (pp. 678–680). IEEE: San Francisco.

Torresani, L., Yang, D., Alexander, G., & Bregler, C. (2001). Tracking and modeling non-rigid objects with rank constraints. In *Proceedings of CVPR* (pp. 493–500).

Vapnik, V. N. *Statistical learning theory*. (1998). Wiley Series on Adaptive and Learning Systems for Signal Processing, Communications, and Control. New York: John Wiley & Sons, Inc.

Viola, P., & Jones, M. (2004). Robust real-time face detection. *International Journal of Computer Vision*, 57(2), 137–154.

Vural, E., Bartlett, M., Littlewort, G., Cetin, M., Ercil, A., & Movellan, J. R. (2010). Discrimination of moderate and acute drowsiness based on spontaneous facial expressions. In *Proceedings of the International Conference on Pattern Recognition* (pp. 3874–3877).

Vural, E., Cetin, M., Ercil, A., Littlewort, G., Bartlett, M., & Movellan, J. R. (2007). Drowsy driver detection through facial movement analysis. In *Proceedings of the IEEE international conference on human-compute interaction* (pp. 6–18). IEEE: Rio de Janeiro.

U.S. Dept. of Transportation. (2001). Saving lives through advanced vehicle safety technology.

Wang, Y., Lucey, S., & Cohn, J. (2008). Enforcing convexity for improved alignment with constrained local models. In *Computer Vision and Pattern Recognition* (pp. 1–8). IEEE: Anchorage, Alaska.

Whitehill, J., Bartlett, M., & Movellan, J. (2008). Automatic facial expression recognition for intelligent tutoring systems. *Computer Vision and Pattern Recognition Workshop on Human-Communicative Behavior* (pp. 1–6). IEEE: Anchorage, Alaska.

Whitehill, J., Littlewort, G., Fasel, I., Bartlett, M., & Movellan, J. R. (2009). Towards practical smile detection. *Pattern Analysis and Machine Intelligence, 31*(11), 2106–2111.

Whitehill, J., & Omlin, C. (2006). Haar features for FACS AU recognition. In *Proceedings of the IEEE Conference on Automatic Facial and Gesture Recognition* (pp. 97–101). IEEE: Southampton.

Whitehill, J., Ruvolo, P., Wu, T., Bergsma, J., & Movellan, J. (2009). Whose vote should count more? Optimal integration of labels from labelers of unknown expertise. In Y. Bengio, D. Schuurmans, J. Lafferty, C. K. I. Williams, & A. Culotta (Eds.), *Advances in Neural Information Processing Systems* (pp. 2035–2043).

Wu, T., Bartlett, M., & Movellan, J. R. (2010). Facial expression recognition using gabor motion energy filters. In *CVPR Workshop on Human Communicative Behavior*. IEEE: San Francisco.

Wu, T., Butko, N., Ruvolo, P., Whitehill, J., Bartlett, M., & Movellan, J. (2012). Multi-layer architectures for facial expression recognition. *IEEE Transactions on Systems, Man, and Cybernetics, 42*(4), 1027–1038.

Yang, P., Liu, Q., & Metaxas, D. N. (2009). Boosting encoded dynamic features for facial expression recognition. *Pattern Recognition Letters, 30*, 132–139.

Zhao, G., & Pietikäinen, M. (2007). Dynamic texture recognition using local binary patterns with an application to facial expressions. *Pattern Analysis and Machine Intelligence*, 29(6), 915–928.

7

Toward Effective Automatic Recognition Systems of Emotion in Speech

Carlos Busso, Murtaza Bulut, & Shrikanth Narayanan

1. Introduction

Humans are emotional beings, and emotions are one of the main drivers of human thoughts and actions. Therefore, for all environments designed for humans, it is essential that emotion processing capabilities such as analysis, recognition, and synthesis be incorporated. Naturally, any type of information, such as audio, visual, written, mental, or physiological, can be used for these tasks.

In this chapter, our concentration will be on emotion recognition from speech. Specifically, this chapter discusses the collection and organization of databases and emotional descriptors; the calculation, selection, and normalization of relevant speech features; and the models used to recognize emotions. We outline achievements, open questions, and future challenges in building Effective Automatic Speech Emotion Recognition (EASER) systems.

It is known that emotions cause mental and physiological changes that also reflect in uttered speech. When processing the generated speech, one can calculate different features, which can be utilized to learn the relationship between features and emotions. Once such a relationship is learned, theoretically, one can calculate the features and then automatically recognize the emotions present in speech.

From a scientific perspective, recognition of emotions is nothing more than a mapping from a feature space to emotion descriptors or labels space. For the mapping between the two spaces, different machine learning algorithms have been used (Duda et al., 2000). In general, theories to perform the mapping have solid analytical foundations and are well defined and validated. Hardly, however, is the same true for feature and emotion spaces. In other words, it is a challenging issue to determine which features to use and how to describe emotions. The problem of emotion recognition from speech critically depends on these two factors, meaning that high and robust emotion recognition performance can be achieved only with the accurate selection of features and emotional labels.

In this chapter, selection of correct features and emotional labels will be discussed in the view of building EASER systems.

For emotion recognition from speech, time, frequency, and lexical features have been popularly used (Cowie et al., 2001; Lee & Narayanan, 2005). Examples of time domain features are fundamental frequency, duration, and energy statistics. Frequency domain features are found by applying a transform to the time domain signal. Examples of such features are Mel frequency cepstral coefficients (MFCCs), Mel filter bank (MFB) (Busso et al., 2007) coefficients, or other perceptually motivated features (Kalini & Narayanan, 2007). Lexical features, although not as popularly used as time and frequency domain features, can also be very effective as shown in (Lee et al., 2005).

There have been many studies of how to classify and describe emotions. Two of the most popular approaches are to use categorical labels or dimensional labels. Examples of categorical labels are anger, sadness, disgust, and happiness. Considering the large number of possible categorical labels—for robust and effective user- and application-specific emotion recognition applications—it is critical to select the most appropriate emotional labels and to train the emotion recognizer accordingly. When dimensional labels, such as activation, valence, and dominance, are used, emotions are described with continuous values. Later, the dimensional labels can be mapped to categorical emotional labels, if needed (Grimm et al., 2007). Each technique has its own advantages and disadvantages. As discussed in the following sections, for robust EASER systems—which can adapt to different users, environments, and applications—it is important to use the correct emotional labels.

Although it is not popularly used in any real-life applications today, we expect that recognizing emotions from speech will be very important and popular in future applications and products. Examples of possible application areas are automated call centers where a caller can be forwarded to a human agent when particular emotions are detected. In ambient intelligent (AmI) environments, atmosphere and devices can be adapted according to users' emotions. In future classrooms, students' emotional states can be used as feedback for teachers. In automated meeting summary generation and speaker diarization systems, emotional information can be added. In short, we can expect that having information about users' emotional states will improve the human–machine interactions (HMI) and therefore increase the productivity and satisfaction of the users.

The rest of the chapter is organized as follows. Section 2 gives a brief overview on the state of the art in emotion recognition from speech. Section 3 discusses in detail some aspects that need to be carefully considered for EASER systems; it also describes our contribution in the field. Section 4 presents our perspective on the directions that this area needs to take. Finally, Section 5 summarizes the chapter.

2. Overview

The idea of recognizing emotions in speech has been of interest for many years. A quick search will produce many scientific publications on the topic. It is out of the scope of this chapter to present a detailed review of the existing literature. Instead, our focus is on selected aspects that are crucial for a robust speech emotion recognition system. The reader can refer to (Cowie et al., 2001) and (Zeng et al., 2009) for reviews.

As in any pattern recognition problem, the performance of emotion recognition from speech depends on type, organization, and representation of training data. It is obvious, but nevertheless useful to recall, that a good training dataset is the one that performs well for a targeted test set or application. This statement has the following implication: *There is no training dataset that will perform well in all conditions.* Therefore, it is important that data collection, organization, and labeling are performed by taking into account the target application and users. The reverse approach of first gathering data and then defining specifications of application and target users is not suggested, as it will hardly reach the optimal performance. At least, not for a task as challenging as recognizing emotions from speech.

A popular approach to recognizing emotions is based on using acoustical information (Schuller, Seppi et al., 2007), such as prosody and spectral features. The number of features used varies depending on the application. Having a large number of features increases the complexity of the system and normally results in longer system training times. Therefore, a popular approach is to start with a larger set of features and then eliminate the less significant features to generate a more compact and robust feature set. As expected, the final compact feature sets can vary based on the database. This means that for different speakers' emotions and conditions, different feature sets can perform better. See Section 3.3 for a detailed discussion on features.

In addition to the acoustic features, lexical, semantic, and discourse information can also be used. In (Lee & Narayanan, 2005), it is shown that using language information in addition to acoustic information improves emotion recognition rates significantly.

Various recognition methods have been used in the literature. Popularly used machine learning techniques (Duda et al., 2000) are linear discriminators, Gaussian mixture models (GMMs), hidden Markov models (HMMs), neural networks (NNs), Bayes classifiers, and fuzzy classifiers. In general, any of these techniques can be employed and be advantageous to others in certain conditions, depending on signal-to-noise (SNR) ratio, recorded emotions, recording conditions, and type and size of training databases. For example, in (Pao et al., 2007, k-nearest neighbors (KNN), GMM, HMM, weighted categorical average patterns (WCAP), and weighted discrete-KNN (W-DKNN) pattern recognition methods are compared for recognizing anger, happiness, sadness, neural state, and boredom from noisy Mandarin emotional speech, and it was found that W-DKNN performs the best.

Humans take into account all of the factors, including visual, vocal, cultural, environmental, and personal clues, to classify emotions (Scherer, 2003; Scherer et al., 2001). Although it can vary significantly, in general, human performance for recognizing emotions from vocal cues is around 80%. This value can be considered as a reasonable upper limit performance that should be expected from speech emotion recognizers. As expected, some emotions are easier to recognize than others. For example, humans are much better at recognizing anger than recognizing happiness; so are the machines.

3. Analysis of Effective Automatic Speech Emotion Recognition Systems' Components

This section discusses essential aspects in the design and implementation of EASER systems. The section also presents some of our own contributions to the field.

3.1. Databases

The machine learning algorithms and statistical models used in emotion recognition systems are trained and tested with data that describes the problem at hand (data-driven approach). Therefore, the quality of emotional databases is extremely important.

Actors have played an important role in studying emotions (Douglas-Cowie et al., 2003). The main advantage of recording acted databases is that many aspects of the recording can be carefully and systematically controlled (e.g., location of the microphones/cameras, emotional and lexical content, and noise-free environment). Unfortunately, the elicitation techniques used for this task were not in accord with the well-established theories and methods used in the field of theater. In fact, most of the emotional databases in early work were recorded from actors or naïve subjects without acting experience who were asked to read sentences expressing given emotions (e.g., "read this sentence with this emotion"). As a result, the actors needed to cope with settings that were not natural for expressing emotions. The samples collected with this approach were characterized by highly prototyped emotions, which usually differed from the emotions displayed by regular people in real-life situations in which mixtures of emotions are found (Devillers et al., 2005; Douglas-Cowie et al., 2005). In real-life situations, emotions may or may not be exaggerated, and usually they consist of mixtures of several emotions. As a result, the models trained with data collected in laboratory settings are not easy to apply in real-life applications (Batliner, Fischer et al., 2000). We have argued that the main problem of acted databases is not the use of actors but the methodology used to elicit the emotions (Busso et al., 2008; Busso & Narayanan, 2008b). As suggested by the appraisal theory, emotions are expressed as a reaction to events (appraisal theory; Gratch et al., 2009; Marsella & Gratch, 2009). Therefore, instead of giving a specific emotion to the actors, the researchers should give specific scenarios that will trigger the target emotions. For example, we collected the *interactive emotional dyadic motion capture* (IEMOCAP) database, in which we used emotionally rich scripts and improvisations of fictitious situations, which were carefully designed to elicit specific emotions (Busso et al., 2008). These two elicitation techniques are rooted in the theatrical performance and are familiar to trained actors (Busso & Narayanan, 2008c; Enos & Hirschberg, 2006).

Recent efforts on recording emotional databases have been focused on natural databases (i.e., nonacted emotions). Broadcast television programs have been extensively used for this purpose (VAM [Grimm et al.,

2008], EmoTV1 [Abrilian et al., 2005], Belfast naturalistic database [Douglas-Cowie et al., 2003]). Other interesting approaches were based on recording in situ (Genova Airport Lost Luggage database [Scherer & Ceschi, 1997]), Wizard of Oz interfaces (SmartKom [Schiel et al., 2002], FAU AIBO [Steidl, 2009]), interviews (AVIC [Schuller, Muller et al., 2007)], SAL [Cowie et al., 2005]), and call center customer care (CCD [Lee & Narayanan, 2005], CEMO [Vidrascu & Devillers, 2006]). Despite limitations such as copyright issues and lack of control, these databases are an important step forward in the area of automatic emotion recognition. Given the multiple variables considered in the study of emotions, it is clear that a collection of different databases rather than a single corpus will be needed to address many of the open questions in this multidisciplinary area. The HUMAINE project portal (2009) presents further descriptions of some of the existing emotional databases.

Research areas such as music retrieval (Music Information Retrieval Evaluation eXchange (MIREX) [2012]) and different spoken language technologies (NIST [National Institute of Standards and Technology, 2009]) have greatly benefited from having open evaluations in which different approaches are compared under similar conditions. In this direction, similarly for emotion recognition, seven research centers participated in the *combining efforts for improving automatic classification of emotional user state* (CEICES) initiative (Batliner et al., 2006). The task was later extended to the research community in the InterSpeech 2009 Emotion Challenge (Schuller et al., 2009). In these competitions, the FAU AIBO corpus (Steidl, 2009) was used. This database was recorded from German children (10–13 years) who verbally interacted with a robot controlled by a human. Building upon these initiatives, it will be beneficial to add new databases for benchmark tests to include other sources of variability such as age, recording conditions, modalities, and languages. Fortunately, the recent trend for the new emotional databases is to make them available (e.g., VAM, Belfast naturalistic database, SAL) (Douglas-Cowie et al., 2007).

3.2. Emotional Descriptors

Scherer proposed using an adapted version of the Brunswik's lens model to study vocal communication of the emotions (Scherer, 2003). This model makes an explicit distinction between the encoding (speaker), the transmission, and the representation (listener) of the emotion. The speaker encodes his/her emotional state in the speech (and other modalities), producing *distal indicators* that are transmitted. The listener perceives the information, referred to as *proximal cues* in the models, and makes inferences about their attributes. All these distinctions in the models are made because expression and perception are two distinct and complex problems. The intended emotion encoded by the speaker may not necessarily match with the perceived emotion (Busso & Narayanan, 2008a). The distal indicators may be different from the proximal indicators (e.g., distortion in the transmission, structural characteristic of the perceptual organ) (Scherer, 2003). The process that transforms proximal cues into emotional attributes is intrinsically speaker dependent. As a result, it is not surprising that representing emotions is one of the most challenging tasks in emotion recognition.

Two of the most common strategies to characterize emotions are discrete categorical labels and continuous primitives attributes (Cowie & Cornelius, 2003; Picard, 1995). With discrete labels, the emotional databases are evaluated in terms of words such as *anger*, *happiness*, and *sadness*. With continuous attributes, the emotional content of the databases is projected into different dimensions with emotional connotation. The most used attributes/dimensions are valence (measuring how positive or negative the subject is) and activation or arousal (how active or passive the subject is). A third dimension, such as dominance or control, is sometimes included to make a distinction between certain emotions that share similar activation–valence properties (e.g., fear and anger). Both representations have advantages and disadvantages. For example, inter-speaker agreement is usually higher with continuous attributes. However, categorical descriptors simplify the design of interfaces (Picard, 1995). We believe that both approaches provide useful complementary information to describe the emotional content of the speaker. For instance, continuous attributes are useful to differentiate intensity levels within samples labeled with the same emotional class.

Regardless of the approach used to represent emotions, the real emotional labels or values of the attributes are unknown. As an approximation, subjective perceptive evaluations have been commonly used. These assessments are expensive and time consuming. Therefore, a limited number of labelers assess the emotional content of each sample in the corpus

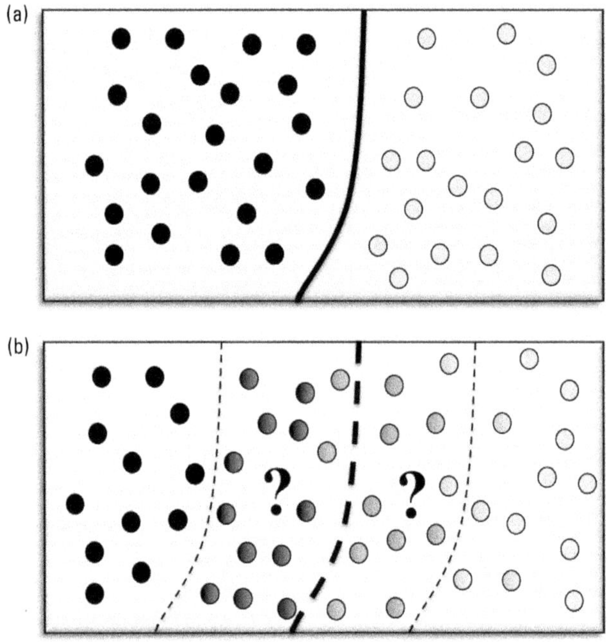

FIGURE 7.1 The main challenge in emotion recognition is the lack of clear emotional labels. Given the important differences in perception, the boundaries in emotional categories are blurred, and the models have to cope with this variability.

(e.g., [database—number of evaluators] IEMOCAP-3, VAM-17, AVIC-4, FAU AIBO-5, CCD-4). Since these evaluations are usually characterized by low interspeaker agreement, the final tags assigned to the samples are inherently noisy. This is clearly observed with nonpure emotions frequently observed in real-life interactions (Devillers et al. 2005). We have studied the mismatch between the expression and perception of the emotions (Busso & Narayanan, 2008a). Our results suggested that tags assigned by labelers might not accurately describe the true emotions conveyed by speakers. These results agree with the work of Biersack and Kempe (2005). They conducted a study with 200 speakers and four groups of 20 listeners on speech of 1-minute average duration. The study showed that the happiness mood rating reported by the speakers (i.e., self-rating) was not correlated to the happiness rating perceived by listeners (i.e, observers). This was viewed as an indication that other factors besides vocal cues play an important role in emotion perception. Another study that investigated observer and self-annotation differences and similarities was done by recording vocal and facial expressions during a multiplayer video game (Truong et al., 2008). The emotion ratings were done in arousal (i.e., how active or passive) and valence (i.e., how positive or negative) dimensions on a scale from 0 to 100 for audio only, video only, audio and visual, and audio and visual plus content data. It was found that self-rating can significantly differ from observer ratings. As expected, agreements on valence and arousal dimension were also different from each other. Since the ultimate goal of an emotion recognition system is not to recognize what others perceive, but what the user expresses or feels, subjective experiments should be viewed as an approximation.

The confusion in the emotional labels is one of the main differences between emotion recognition and conventional machine learning problems (Figure 7.1). The underlying classes in a recognition problem are perfectly defined, even when no hyperplane perfectly separates the groups. If we are interested in recognizing emotion, this property is far from true, and the models have to cope with this variability. It is for this reason that some researchers have stated that emotion recognition is an ill-defined problem.

If discrete categorical labels are used, the emotional classes need to be defined. In general, there is a trade-off between interevaluator agreement and description accuracy. If the number of emotion categories is too extensive, the agreement between evaluators will be low. If the list of emotional classes is limited, the emotional description of the utterances will be poor and likely less accurate. One popular approach is to use large numbers of classes, which are later clustered in broad emotional classes. For example, the FAU AIBO database was originally evaluated with the labels joyful, surprised, emphatic, helpless, touchy, angry, motherese, bored, reprimanding, neutral, and others (Schuller et al., 2009). These classes were grouped into five general categories (anger, emphatic, neutral, positive, and other). Another example is the SAFE corpus, in which over 20 emotional labels were grouped into four broad categories (fear, other negative emotions, and neutral and positive emotions) (Clavel et al., 2008). The main problem of this approach is identifying how to define the emotional partition without increasing the noise in the labeling. Instead of using ad hoc methods, we have proposed the use of an interval type-2 fuzzy logic system to map and cluster emotional terms (Kazemzadeh et al., 2008). In this approach, the emotional words are evaluated in terms of valence, activation, and dominance (VAD) (e.g., how do you perceive the concept "happiness" in the VAD space?). Instead of selecting a single value, double sliders are used to enclose the range in which the emotional labels are believed to be. Therefore, intersubject uncertainty is directly included in the model. This information is used to create interval type-2 fuzzy sets, which are used to map one vocabulary to another. Likewise, if databases are labeled with different emotional categories, this approach can be used to translate the labels into a common vocabulary set.

It is also unclear what is the best timescale to evaluate emotions. The conventional approach is to tag sentences or turns. However, the emotional content may not be constant within the sentences, especially for long samples (Batliner et al., 2003). The FAU AIBO database was labeled at word level to address this problem (Steidl, 2009). A heuristic approach was later used to map the labels to longer units (sentences or chunks). However, with short time units labelers may not have enough evidence to make the assessment, decreasing the interevaluator agreement. Also, it has been shown that the performance of emotion recognition is lower for short speech segments (Küstner et al., 2004). An alternative approach was presented by Cowie et al. (2000) to continuously evaluate the emotional content of data using the tool FEELTRACE. As labelers watch the clips, they are asked to continuously move a cursor controlled by a mouse in a valence–activation space. The 2D space is enriched with strategically located categorical labels. The samples do not need to be segmented for evaluation.

While evaluating a database, many variables need to be defined. As an example, consider a multimodal database in which both vocal and visual cues were recorded from actors performing short scripts (as in Busso et al., 2008). For such datasets, one can use vocal cues only, visual cues only, or vocal and visual cues together to label the perceived emotions. In addition, the emotional classification by listeners can be done on randomly distributed, isolated (i.e., out of context) samples. Listeners may receive a list of emotions from which to select one or more categories to describe the emotional content. Or, as an alternative, the evaluation can be completely open choice by asking the listeners to enter the emotion or emotions that they perceive. All these variations present advantages and disadvantages that need to be balanced in design.

We believe that the emotional labels need to be driven by the application at hand. In our previous work with the call center customer care database, the annotation was simplified to either negative or nonnegative (Lee & Narayanan, 2005). We have also argued that for many applications it may be enough to detect emotional speech (neutral versus emotional speech) (Busso, Lee, & Narayanan, 2009). By making the problem more concrete and specific, automatic emotion recognition system can become feasible tools.

Characteristics of human evaluators can also be very important, as one can expect differences in emotion perception due to differences in age, sex, culture, education, experience, and other personal factors. For a complete description of an emotional database, detailed profiles of evaluators should also be included. Such descriptions will help in defining the user profiles for the automatic emotion recognition systems. Having the systems combined with user profiles will help to improve the usage and performance of the systems.

3.3. Features

As in any machine learning problem, features with discriminative power are important for emotion recognition. A summary with the features most used to recognize emotions is presented in Table 7.1. The list includes prosodic, spectral, and voice quality features. In addition to acoustic features, lexical and discourse features have also been proposed (Batliner et al., 2003; Devillers et al., 2005; Lee & Narayanan, 2005). In fact, we have shown that these features are useful in the context of call center applications (Lee & Narayanan, 2005). This section discusses only acoustic features.

Different combinations of speech features have been proposed for emotion recognition. In machine-learning problems, the underlying conditional probability distributions are commonly unknown. Therefore, they have to be approximated from the test data. For a fixed number of training samples, the quality in the distribution approximation decreases as the dimensionality of the problem increases (Foley, 1972). Therefore, nonrelevant features will decrease the performance of the classifier. This problem, also known as the curse of dimensionality, is especially observed when nonparametrical distributions are assumed, in which more information is required from the data.

The standard approach in current emotion recognition systems is to compute a big feature vector containing all relevant acoustic information (in some cases higher than 4000; Schuller, Batliner et al., 2007). Then, the feature vector is reduced to a subset that provides better discrimination for the given task using feature selection techniques, such as forward or backward features selection, sequential forward floating search, genetic algorithms, evolutionary algorithms, linear discriminant analysis, principal component analysis, and information gain ratio (Alvarez et al., 2006; Schuller et al., 2006; Sedaaghi et al., 2007; Ververidis & Kotropoulos, 2006). Clavel et al. (2008) proposed an interesting modification based on a two-step approach. The acoustic features are separated in broad categories (spectral, prosodic, and voice quality features). In the first step, the best features within each group are selected. In the second step, the final feature set is selected from the candidate features. This approach is appealing since it enforces to some extent the contribution of features describing different aspects of speech. Even with this approach, the selected features are sensitive to the training and testing conditions (database, emotional descriptors, recording environment). Figure 7.2 shows the most emotionally salient statistics from the fundamental frequency for two databases (EMA [Lee et al., 2005] and EMO-DB, [Burkhardt et al., 2005]). As expected, the figure shows that the ranking of the best features depends on the database and the emotional labels. These examples indicate that a robust emotion recognition system should use features that are found to convey emotional information across corpora.

As an alternative approach, we have proposed to study in detail the emotional modulation observed in acoustic features (Busso, Lee, & Narayanan, 2009). In the analysis, we compared different statistics derived from the fundamental frequency in terms of their emotional modulation. The distributions of pitch-related features extracted from emotional and neutral speech were compared using symmetric Kullback–Leibler divergence. Then, the emotionally discriminative power of the pitch features was quantified by comparing nested logistic regression models. For generalization purposes, we considered cross-corpora tests with different emotional classes, speakers, recording settings, and languages. The results of this analysis suggested that gross pitch contour statistics such as mean, maximum, minimum, and range are more emotionally prominent than features describing the pitch shape, which may be dependent on the lexical content. In the final set of features used to detect emotional speech, the features were not necessarily the ones that maximize the performance for these databases, but the ones that in the analysis were found more emotionally prominent, according to the proposed experiments.

3.4. Data Normalization

Data normalization is an important aspect that needs to be considered for a robust automatic emotion recognition system (Küstner et al., 2004). Ideally, the normalization step should remove or reduce all variability in sources, while preserving the emotional differences conveyed in the speech. Two of the most important sources of variability are recording conditions and interspeaker variability.

The quality of the signal highly depends on the sensors used to capture the speech. Close-talking microphones (e.g., headphones) provide the best speech quality. However, they are not suitable for certain applications in which nonintrusive sensors are required (smart room or ambient intelligent environments). In those cases, the system may receive far-field reverberant speech with low signal-to-noise ratio. Likewise, if the speech is recorded using a phone or mobile speech system, the frequency bandwidth will be affected. The features derived from the speech signals will be directly affected by these distortions. In these cases, a robust emotion recognition system should be designed to attenuate possible mismatches between the speech set

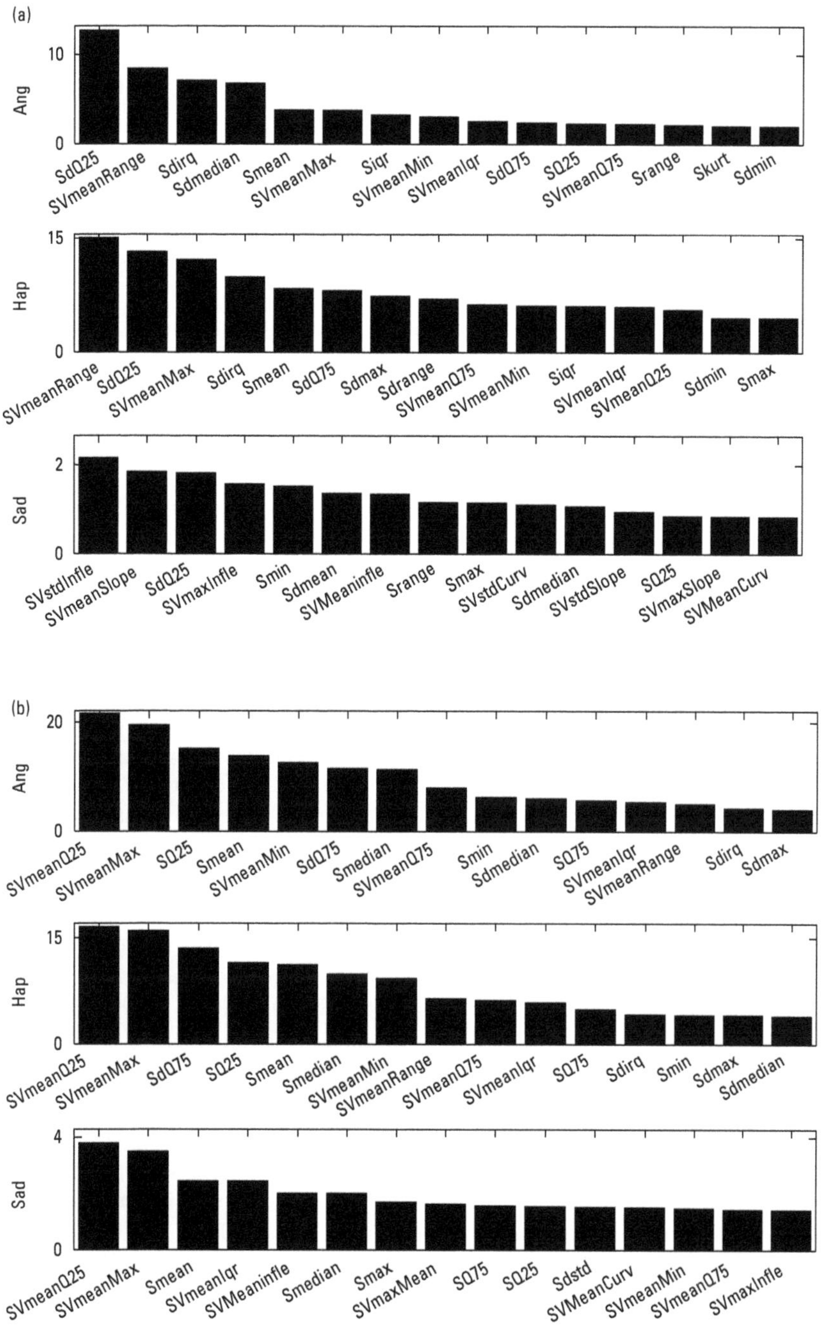

FIGURE 7.2 The most emotionally prominent features from fundamental frequency. The figures were created by estimating the symmetric Kullback–Leibler divergence between the distribution of the features derived from neutral and emotional speech. The details are given in (Busso, Lee, & Narayanan, 2009).

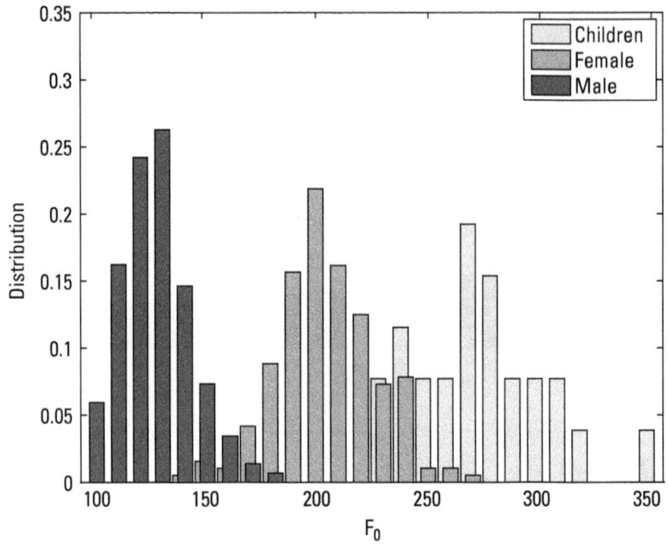

FIGURE 7.3 Interspeaker variability in pitch mean (neutral speech).

that was used to train the models and the speech set that is collected in the real-life applications. For instance, it is well known that energy tends to increase with angry or happy speech (Banse & Scherer, 1996; Cowie & Cornelius, 2003; Murray & Arnott, 1993). However, if the energy of the speech signal is not properly normalized, any difference in the microphone gain will affect the performance (i.e., loud speech may be confused with emotional speech).

Speech production is the result of controlled anatomical movements of the lungs, trachea, larynx, pharyngeal cavity, oral cavity, and nasal cavity. As a result, the properties of the speech are intrinsically speaker dependent. In fact, speech has been widely used for speaker identification (Campbell, 1997). Interestingly, some of the same features used for speaker recognition have also been proposed for emotion recognition. A robust emotion recognition system should compensate for speaker variability.

Let us consider, for example, the fundamental frequency mean, which has been extensively used as a feature to recognize emotion. In fact, our previous analysis indicated that the F0 mean is one of the most emotionally prominent aspects of the F0 contour, when properly normalized (Busso, Lee, & Narayanan, 2009). The fundamental frequency is directly constrained by the structure and size of the larynx (Deller et al., 2000). While the F0 contour for men is bounded in the range 50Hz to 250 Hz, women can reach much higher F0 values (120–500 Hz) (Deller et al., 2000). Figure 7.3 shows the distribution of the F0 mean in terms of gender, using the popular read-speech TIMIT database (Garofolo et al., 1993). The F0 mean for each of the 630 subjects was estimated (one value for each subject). In addition, the figure shows data from 26 children (10–13 years) recorded in the training set of the FAU AIBO corpus (Schuller et al., 2009; Steidl, 2009). Three separate distributions for men, women, and children are clearly seen. As a result, any emotional difference will be blurred by interspeaker differences. This point is clearly observed in Figure 7.4a. In this figure, the F0 mean is computed at sentence level to estimate the distribution of anger and neutral speech across 10 speakers recorded in the IEMOCAP database (Busso et al., 2007). Although, in general, angry speech has higher F0 values than neutral speech, mixing emotional and speaker variations will result in noisy measures in the system.

Most of the current approaches to normalize speech or speech features are based on gross manipulation of the speech at sentence level. In many cases, the normalization approach is not clearly defined. Some of the approaches that have been widely used are Z-normalization (subtract the mean and divide by the standard deviation) (Lee & Narayanan, 2005), min-max normalization (scaling features between −1 and 1) (Clavel et al., 2008), and subtraction of mean values (Küstner et al., 2004). For a given lexical unit

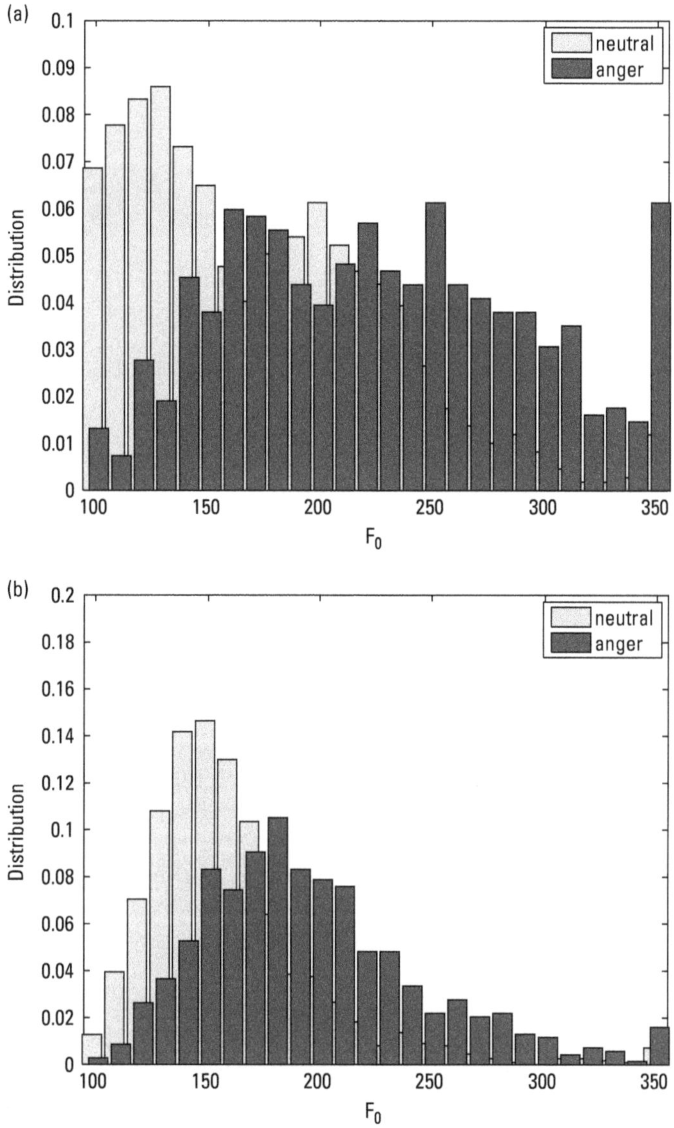

FIGURE 7.4 F_0 mean computed at sentence level for angry and neutral speech (a) before normalization, and (b) after normalization. The figure shows that mixing emotional and speaker variations will result in noisy measures in the system.

(i.e., word or phoneme), Batliner, Buckow et al. (2000) proposed to normalize speech features by estimating reference values for "average speakers" learned from a training database. These reference values were used to scale the duration and energy of the speech.

We have proposed a two-step, speaker-dependent approach to normalize the energy and the fundamental frequency (Busso, Lee, & Narayanan, 2009). The main idea is to estimate the scaling parameter using only the neutral set of the emotional database. Assuming that the speaker's identity is known, the energy and pitch are linearly modified so that their mean values are equal to predefined reference values, estimated from *The Wall Street Journal*-based Continuous Speech Recognition Corpus Phase II (Paul & Baker, 1992) corpora. Then, the normalization parameters are applied to all speech samples from that speaker, including the emotional speech set. The scaling factors will not affect

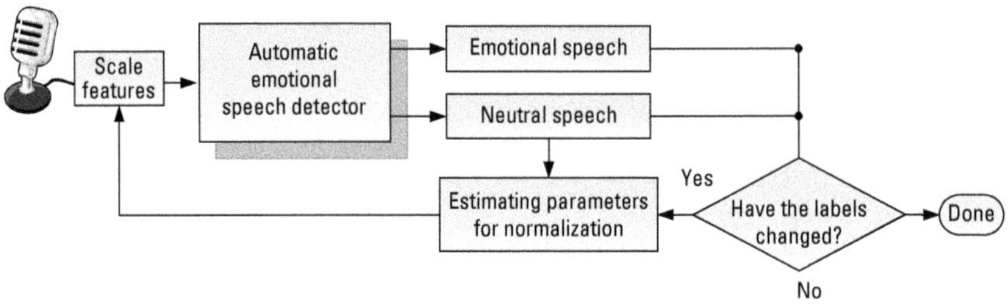

FIGURE 7.5 Approach for speaker-independent normalization. After the data is clustered using unsupervised speaker identification, an automatic emotional speech detector is used to identify neutral samples for a given speaker. The scaling factors are estimated from this neutral speech set. The process is repeated until the labels are no longer modified.

emotional discrimination in the speech, since the differences in the energy and the fundamental frequency contour across emotional categories will be preserved. Figure 7.4b shows the distribution of neutral and angry speech in the IEMOCAP database after pitch normalization. Now, the shift in the distributions can be directly associated to emotional variations.

One assumption made in this two-step approach is that neutral speech will be available for each speaker. The implications of this assumption are that speaker identities are known and that emotional labels for a portion of the data are known. For real-life applications, this assumption is reasonable when either the speakers are known or a few seconds of their neutral speech can be prerecorded. We are currently working on extending the proposed approach by using speaker-independent normalization. The first implication can be addressed with unsupervised speaker identification. The second implication can be addressed with a reinforcement framework as displayed in Figure 7.5.

3.5. Models

In daily life, people express their emotions in an exaggerated manner only in certain conditions. Most of the time, subtle emotions are expressed. Obviously, models trained on "highly emotional" data will perform well only in certain instances but poorly in general. It is still a challenging and open research area of how to process real-life emotions, especially when only vocal data ispresent. Selection of database, emotional descriptors, normalization, and feature will have an effect on the performance and, therefore, on the architecture and models selected to build an emotional speech recognizer.

In previous works, variations of machine learning approaches have been proposed for emotion recognition. Some examples are support vector machines (SVMs) (Küstner et al., 2004; Lee et al., 2004; Schuller et al., 2009), Gaussian mixture models (Busso, Lee, & Narayanan, 2009; Clavel et al., 2008), hidden Markov models (Busso et al., 2007; Lee et al., 2005; Schuller et al., 2009), fuzzy logic estimators (Grimm et al., 2007; Lee & Narayanan, 2003), neural networks (Batliner, Buckow et al., 2000; Batliner et al., 2003; Küstner et al., 2004), and linear discriminant classifiers (LDCs) (Batliner et al., 2003; Küstner et al., 2004; Lee & Narayanan, 2005). These classifiers are usually divided into two categories: static and dynamic modeling. On the one hand, static classifiers use global features derived over the entire speech segment. They usually include statistics from suprasegmental acoustic features such as F_0 range and mean duration (see Table 7.1). On the other hand, dynamic classifiers receive acoustic features at the frame level (i.e., 10–100 milliseconds). They capture the dynamic behavior of segmental acoustic features.

Instead of recognizing emotional classes, the system can be designed to estimate continuous values of the emotional primitives. We have used the rule-based fuzzy logic estimator to infer the valence, activation, and dominance of the speech (Grimm et al., 2007). Using acted and spontaneous corpora, the estimations were found to be moderately to highly correlated with human evaluations ($0.42 < r < 0.85$). In addition, this representation can be used as a midlevel representation for categorical emotion recognition. Using k-nearest neighbor classifier, these attributes were mapped into emotional categories showing an overall recognition rate up to 83.5%.

TABLE 7.1 Common Acoustic Features Used in Emotion Recognition

Description	*Features*
Suprasegmental acoustic features (prosody)	– Pitch: mean, median, standard deviation, maximum, minimum, range (max–min), linear regression coefficient, lower and upper quartile, kurtosis, skewness, slope, curvature, inflection
	– Energy: mean, median, standard deviation, maximum, minimum, range, linear regression coefficient
	– Duration: speech rate, ration of duration of voiced and unvoiced region, duration of longest voiced region
	– Zero crossing rate
Segmental acoustic features (short-term spectrum of speech)	– Mel-frequency cepstral coefficients (MFCC)
	– Mel filter bank (MFB)
	– Spectral centroid
	– Formant: F1, F2, and their bandwidth BW1, BW2
Voice quality features (intrasegmental level)	– Jitter (pitch modulation)
	– Shimmer (amplitude modulation)
	– Harmonics- to-noise ratio (HNR)
	– Noise-to-harmonics ratio (NHR)
	– Normalized amplitude quotient (NAQ)

Note. Based on the following studies: Busso, Lee, & Narayanan (2009); Clavel et al. (2008); Lee & Narayanan (2005); Schuller, Batliner et al., (2007); Seppi et al. (2008).

In our previous work, we have addressed the simplified problem of detecting emotional speech (Busso et al., 2007; Busso, Lee, & Narayanan, 2009). For this binary problem (which included neutral and emotional classes), we proposed the use of generic models trained with emotionally neutral reference speech (see Figure 7.6). The models are used to contrast the input speech. The underlying assumption is that expressive speech will differ from neutral speech in the feature space. Therefore, speech samples that differ in any aspect from neutral speech will not accurately fit the models. A fitness measure such as the likelihood scores can be used as a feature to detect emotional speech. One advantage of this approach is that there are many neutral corpora available to train robust neutral models. These models do not depend on the emotional databases, speakers, or the emotional labels used to evaluate the speech. For the neutral models, we have proposed HMM for spectral features (Busso et al., 2007; and GMM for prosodic features [Busso, Lee, &

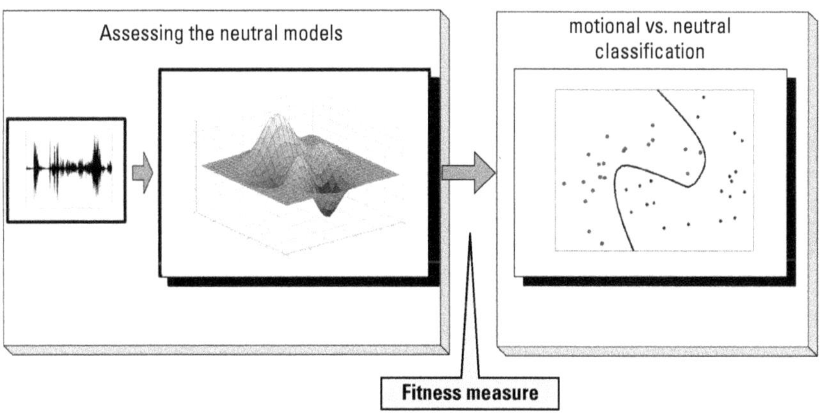

FIGURE 7.6 General framework of the proposed two step approach to discriminate neutral versus emotional speech. In the first step, the input speech is contrasted with robust neutral reference models. In the second step, the *fitness measures* are used for binary emotional classification (details are given in Busso et al., 2007; Busso, Lee, & Naryanan, 2009).

Narayanan, 2009]). In both cases, we used simple linear classifiers to discriminate between emotional and neutral speech using the likelihood scores as features. This framework not only performs better than a conventional emotion recognition system trained with the speech features but also generalizes better when there is a mismatch between the training and testing conditions (Busso, Lee, & Narayanan, 2009).

In many applications, neutral speech is more common than expressive speech. For example, 60% of the FAU AIBO data is neutral speech in spite of the explicit elicitation techniques used to induce emotion in the children. Therefore, it will be useful to have a hierarchical approach in which a robust classifier is first used to detect emotional speech. Note that this step is independent of the application. Later, the emotional speech can be further processed using emotion-specific models driven by the application at hand.

Using different machine learning frameworks, previous studies on automatic categorization of emotional speech have shown accuracy between 50% and 85% depending on the task (e.g., number of emotion labels, number of speakers, size of database) (Pantic & Rothkrantz, 2003). As expected, having a well-defined training set with high agreement (i.e., "high prototypical") on emotional content among different listeners will perform better than a database with less agreement (i.e., "less prototypical") (Seppi et al., 2008). It is important to highlight that it is unfeasible and unrealistic to target performance near perfection. As mentioned in Section 3.2, the perception of emotion is dependent on the listener. Therefore, emotional labels are noisy. In fact, Steidl et al. proposed to include the inherent inter-emotion confusion in the evaluation of emotion recognition performance (Steidl et al., 2005). If the system made errors similar to the human labelers, the performance was not considered completely wrong. Likewise, it is important to remember that speech is only one of the modalities that we use to express emotion. Even for humans, it is challenging to distinguish between certain emotions based only on speech. For example, we have shown that the fundamental frequency is a more informative measure for arousal of speech than valence of speech (Busso, Bulut et al., 2009; Busso, Lee, & Narayanan, 2009). Figure 7.7 shows the emotional classes in which the Nagelkerke r-square of logistic regression models between neutral and emotional speech (e.g., neutral versus anger) was higher (black)

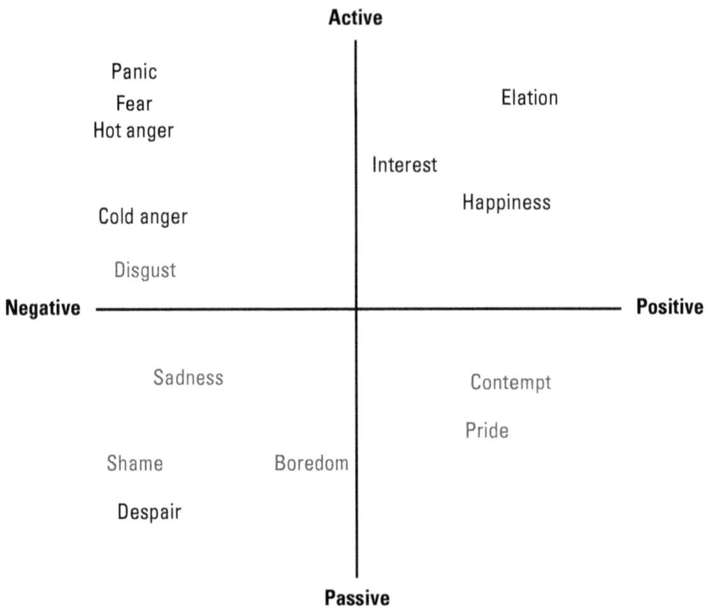

FIGURE 7.7 Location of the emotional categories in the activation–valence space. For the emotional categories in gray, the power of the logistic regression model was inadequate to accurately recognize emotional from neutral speech ($r^2 < 0.5$). The figure was adapted from (Cowie & Cornelius, 2003; Cowie et al., 2001).

or lower (gray) than 0.5 (the location of the emotion in the activation–valence space was approximated from the FEELTRACE snapshots [Cowie & Cornelius, 2003; Cowie et al., 2001]). This figure suggests that only emotion with high activation can be discriminated from neutral speech using fundamental frequency. Therefore, emotions like happiness and anger, which differ in the valence dimension, are usually confused (Yildirim et al., 2004). This confusion is observed even when other acoustic features are used.

4. Future Direction

The research in emotion recognition has progressed significantly in the past years. We expect further accelerated growth, especially when emotion recognition systems become popularly used in everyday applications. For future growth, there are many questions that need to be addressed. This section briefly describes some of the challenges ahead in emotion recognition systems.

Data are of utmost importance. Having an appropriate database that is collected with a particular application and target user profile in mind can be expected to minimize the uncertainties and confusions that occur while organizing and labeling the database. Having high prototypical data clustered in well-defined emotional spaces based on how they are perceived by target users will help to achieve optimal emotion recognition performance. The target-user-defined emotional spaces when combined with user profiles and data from other modalities (i.e., a multimodal emotional database consisting of many different sensor readings) will help to more effectively process real-life conditions and emotions.

As a first step, in view of the effort and cost required for data collection, existing general-purpose spontaneous corpora can be better utilized. For example, huge corpora such as the Fisher English Training Speech corpus (Cieri et al., 2004) and the Switchboard-I Telephone Speech Corpus (Godfrey & Holliman, 1997) are likely to contain emotional content. With the help of automatic recognition systems, this content can be detected and studied to better understand spontaneous expression of emotions.

To assist and improve emotional evaluations, data and algorithms from different sources can be used to facilitate the process (human-in-the-loop). For example, Martin et al. proposed the use of image processing to annotate and validate emotional behaviors by quantizing the movement (Martin et al., 2009).

One area that should be further studied is the development, expression, perception, and progression of emotions in longer human–human or human–machine dialogs. The proposed framework should include explicit models of the context (i.e., emotions in previous turns, discourse information). Instead of modeling emotional category, the system could be designed to detect shifts in the emotional states of the users. If the application includes multiperson interaction, the framework should model the effect of the emotion of one user on the emotion states of the others.

Another area that should be studied is the design of adaptive emotion recognition systems. With the rapid development of mobile devices, it is expected that the demand for applications with emotional capabilities will increase. In this context, the system should adapt to the specific emotional manifestations expressed by the user. Can we let the users or the applications choose the emotional labels? How can we easily modify and alter the labels to tailor them to specific applications and tools? How can we compensate for intercultural and interenvironment issues and differences? The answers to these questions are needed steps toward effective automatic speech emotion recognition systems.

There are many challenges and unknowns in research of recognizing emotions from speech. As in any research, it is essential to remember that even the smallest steps, which may seem unimportant, can be very important. For emotion recognition applications to flourish and become popular, we should design prototype systems to recognize emotions, even if they are only for constrained scenarios driven by concrete applications. In this direction, we proposed a real-time system with simple algorithms to extract and process spectral and prosodic acoustic features to detect negative speech (Kim et al., 2007). Küstner et al. (2004) proposed a demo emotional speech recognition system working in push-to-work mode. There is also commercially available software for emotion identification named Layered Voice Analysis (LVA), which is being developed by Nemesysco Ltd. of Netanya. Only if this trend continues will we be able to explore the potential of human machine interfaces with emotional capabilities.

5. Summary

Emotions are the basic characteristics of humans, and therefore, incorporating them in applications, through recognition and synthesis, can improve the quality of life. In this chapter, we have described the characteristics of effective automatic speech emotion recognition systems. Specifically, database collection and organization; emotional descriptors; selection, calculation, and normalization of features; and training models were discussed to provide a summary of the current achievements, open questions, and future challenges.

Acknowledgments

This research was supported in part by funds from the NSF (through the Integrated Media Systems Center, a National Science Foundation Engineering Research Center, Cooperative Agreement No. EEC-9529152 and a CAREER award), the Department of the Army and a MURI award from ONR. Any opinions, findings and conclusions, or recommendations expressed in this book chapter are those of the authors and do not necessarily reflect the views of the funding agencies.

References

Abrilian, S., Devillers, L., Buisine, S., & Martin, J. C. (2005). EmoTV1: Annotation of real-life emotions for the specification of multimodal affective interfaces. In *Proceedings of the 11th International Conference on Human-Computer Interaction (HCI 2005), Las Vegas, NV* (pp. 195–200) .

Alvarez, A., Cearreta, I., López, J. M., Arruti, A., Lazkano, E., Sierra, B., & Garay, N. (2006). Feature subset selection based on evolutionary algorithms for automatic emotion recognition in spoken Spanish and standard Basque language. In *Proceedings of the Ninth International Conference on Text, Speech and Dialogue (TSD 2006), Brno, Czech Republic* (pp. 565–572).

Banse, R., & Scherer, K. R. (1996). Acoustic profiles in vocal emotion expression. *Journal of Personality and Social Psychology*, 70(3), 614–636.

Batliner, A., Buckow, A., Niemann, H., Nöth, E., & Warnke, V. (2000). The prosody module. In M. T. Maybury, O. Stock, & W. Wahlster (Eds.), *VERBMOBIL: Foundations of speech-to-speech translations*, pp. 106–121. Berlin: Springer Verlag.

Batliner, A., Fischer, K., Huber, R., Spilker, J., & Nöth, E. (2000). Desperately seeking emotions or: Actors, wizards and human beings. In *ISCA Tutorial and Research Workshop (ITRW) on Speech and Emotion, Newcastle, Northern Ireland, UK* (pp. 195–200).

Batliner, A., Fischer, K., Huber, R., Spilker, J., & Nöth, E. (2003). How to find trouble in communication. *Speech Communication, 40*(1–2), 117–143.

Batliner, A., Steidl, S., Schuller, B., Seppi, D., Laskowski, K., Vogt, T., Devillers, L., Vidrascu, L., Amir, N., Kessous, L., et al. (2006). Combining efforts for improving automatic classification of emotional user states. In *Proceedings of the Fifth Slovenian and First International Language Technologies Conference (IS-LTC 2006), Ljubljana, Slovenia* (pp. 240–245).

Biersack, S., & Kempe, V. (2005). Tracing vocal emotion expression through the speech chain: Do listeners perceive what speakers feel? In *ISCA Workshop on Plasticity in Speech Perception, London* (pp. 211–214).

Burkhardt, F., Paeschke, A., Rolfes, M., Sendlmeier, W. F., & Weiss, B. (2005). A database of German emotional speech. In *Proceedings of 9th European Conference on Speech Communication and Technology (Interspeech '2005—Eurospeech), Lisbon, Portugal* (pp. 1517–1520).

Busso, C., Bulut, M., Lee, C. C., Kazemzadeh, A., Mower, E., Kim, S., Chang, J. N., Lee, S., & Narayanan, S. S. (2008). IEMOCAP: Interactive emotional dyadic motion capture database. *Journal of Language Resources and Evaluation*, 42(4), 335–359.

Busso, C., Bulut, M., Lee, S., & Narayanan, S. S. (2009). Fundamental frequency analysis for speech emotion processing. In Sylvie Hancil (Ed.), *The role of prosody in affective speech* (pp. 309–337). Berlin: Peter Lang Publishing Group.

Busso, C., Lee, S., & Narayanan, S. S. (2007). Using neutral speech models for emotional speech analysis. In *Proceedings of Interspeech 2007—Eurospeech, Antwerp, Belgium* (pp. 2225–2228).

Busso, C., Lee, S., & Narayanan, S. S. (2009). Analysis of emotionally salient aspects of fundamental frequency for emotion detection. *IEEE Transactions on Audio, Speech and Language Processing*, 17(4), 582–596.

Busso, C., & Narayanan, S. S. (2008a). The expression and perception of emotions: Comparing assessments of self versus others. In *Interspeech 2008—Eurospeech, Brisbane, Australia* (pp. 257–260).

Busso, C., & Narayanan, S. S. (2008b). Recording audio-visual emotional databases from actors: A closer look. In *Second International Workshop on Emotion: Corpora for Research on Emotion and Affect, International Conference on Language Resources and Evaluation (LREC 2008), Marrakech, Morocco* (pp. 17–22).

Busso, C., & Narayanan, S. S. (2008c). Scripted dialogs versus improvisation: Lessons learned about emotional elicitation techniques from the IEMOCAP database. In *Interspeech 2008—Eurospeech, Brisbane, Australia* (pp. 1670–1673).

Campbell, J. P. (1997). Speaker recognition: A tutorial. *Proceedings of the IEEE, 85*(9), 1437–1462.

Cieri, C., Miller, D., & Walker, K. (2004, May). *The Fisher corpus: A resource for the next generations of speech-to-text.* In International Conference on Language Resources and Evaluation (LREC 2004), Lisbon, Portugal.

Clavel, C., Vasilescu, I., Devillers, L., Richard, G., & Ehrette, T. (2008). Fear-type emotion recognition for future audio-based surveillance systems. *Speech Communication, 50*(6), 487–503.

Cowie, R., & Cornelius, R. R. (2003). Describing the emotional states that are expressed in speech. *Speech Communication, 40*(1–2), 5–32.

Cowie, R., Douglas-Cowie, E., & Cox, C. (2005). Beyond emotion archetypes: Databases for emotion modelling using neural networks. *Neural Networks, 18*(4), 371–388.

Cowie, R., Douglas-Cowie, E., Savvidou, S., McMahon, E., Sawey, M., & Schröder, M. (2000). "FEELTRACE": An instrument for recording perceived emotion in real time. In *ISCA Tutorial and Research Workshop (ITRW) on Speech and Emotion, ISCA, Newcastle, Northern Ireland, UK* (pp. 19–24).

Cowie, R., Douglas-Cowie, E., Tsapatsoulis, N., Votsis, G., Kollias, S., Fellenz, W., & Taylor, J. G. (2001). Emotion recognition in human-computer interaction. *IEEE Signal Processing Magazine, 18*(1), 32–80.

Deller, J. R., Hansen, J. H. L., & Proakis, J. G. (2000). *Discrete-time processing of speech signals.* Piscataway, NJ: IEEE Press.

Devillers, L., & Vidrascu, L. (2006). Real-life emotions detection with lexical and paralinguistic cues on human-human call center dialogs. In *Proceedings of Interspeech—International Conference on Spoken Language (ICSLP), Pittsburgh, PA* (pp. 801–804).

Devillers, L., Vidrascu, L., & Lamel, L. (2005). Challenges in real-life emotion annotation and machine learning based detection. *Neural Networks, 18*(4), 407–422.

Douglas-Cowie, E., Campbell, N., Cowie, R., & Roach, P. (2003). Emotional speech: Towards a new generation of databases. *Speech Communication, 40*(1–2), 33–60.

Douglas-Cowie, E., Cowie, R., Sneddon, I., Cox, C., Lowry, O., McRorie, M., Martin, J.-C., Devillers, L., Abrilian, S., Batliner, A., et al. (2007). The HUMAINE database: Addressing the collection and annotation of naturalistic and induced emotional data. In A. Paiva, R. Prada, & R. W. Picard (Eds.), *Affective computing and intelligent interaction* (pp. 488–500). Berlin: Springer-Verlag Press.

Douglas-Cowie, E., Devillers, L., Martin, J. C., Cowie, R., Savvidou, S., Abrilian, S., & Cox, C. (2005). Multimodal databases of everyday emotion: Facing up to complexity. In *Proceedings of the 9th European Conference on Speech Communication and Technology (Interspeech '2005), Lisbon, Portugal* (pp. 813–816).

Duda, R. O., Hart, P. E., & Stork, D. G. (2000). *Pattern classification.* New York: Wiley-Interscience.

Enos, F., & Hirschberg, J. (2006). A framework for eliciting emotional speech: Capitalizing on the actors process. In *First International Workshop on Emotion: Corpora for Research on Emotion and Affect (International Conference on Language Resources and Evaluation (LREC 2006), Genoa, Italy* (pp. 6–10).

Foley, D. (1972). Considerations of sample and feature size. *IEEE Transactions on Information Theory, 18*(5), 618–626.

Garofolo, J., Lamel, L., Fisher, W., Fiscus, J., Pallett, D., & Dahlgren, N. (1993). Timit acoustic-phonetic continuous speech corpus .

Godfrey, J. J., & Holliman, E. (1997). Switchboard-1 release 2. Linguistic Data Consortium.

Gratch J., Marsella S., & Petta P. (2009). Modeling the cognitive antecedents and consequences of emotion. *Journal of Cognitive Systems Research, 10*(1), 1–5.

Grimm, M., Kroschel, K., Mower, E., & Narayanan, S. (2007). Primitives-based evaluation and estimation of emotions in speech. *Speech Communication, 49*(10–11), 787–800.

Grimm, M., Kroschel, K., & Narayanan, S. (2008). The Vera AM Mittag German audio-visual emotional speech database. In *Proceedings of the IEEE International Conference on Multimedia and Expo (ICME 2008), Hannover, Germany* (pp. 865–868).

HUMAINE project portal. (2009). http://emotion-research.net/. Retrieved March 31st, 2009.

Kalinli, O., & Narayanan, S. (2007). Early auditory processing inspired features for robust automatic speech recognition. In *Proceedings of the XV European Signal Processing Conference (EUSIPCO 2007), Poznan, Poland* (pp. 2385–2389).

Kazemzadeh, A., Lee, S., & Narayanan, S. (2008). An interval type-2 fuzzy logic system to translate between emotion-related vocabularies. In *Inter-speech 2008—Eurospeech, Brisbane, Australia* (pp. 2747–2750).

Kim, S., Georgiou, P. G., Lee, S., & Narayanan, S. S. (2007). Real-time emotion detection system using speech: Multi-modal fusion of different timescale features. In *International Workshop on Multimedia Signal Processing (MMSP 2007), Chania, Crete, Greece* (pp. 48–51).

Küstner, O., Tato, R., Kemp, T., & Meffert, B. (2004). Towards real life applications in emotion recognition. In E. André, L. Dybkaer, W. Minker, & P. Heisterkamp (Eds.), *Affective Dialogue Systems(ADS 2005), Lecture notes in artificial intelligence 3068* (pp. 25–35). Berlin: Springer-Verlag Press.

Lee, C. M., & Narayanan, S. (2003). Emotion recognition using a data-driven fuzzy inference system. In *Proceedings of the 8th European Conference on Speech Communication and Technology (Eurospeech 2003), Geneva, Switzerland* (pp. 157–160).

Lee, C. M., & Narayanan, S. S. (2005). Toward detecting emotions in spoken dialogs. *IEEE Transactions on Speech and Audio Processing, 13*(2), 293–303.

Lee, C. M., Yildirim, S., Bulut, M., Kazemzadeh, A., Busso, C., Deng, Z., Lee, S., & Narayanan, S. S. (2004). Emotion recognition based on phoneme classes. In *Proceedings of the 8th International Conference on Spoken Language Processing (ICSLP 04), Jeju Island, Korea* (pp. 889–892) .

Lee, S., Yildirim, S., Kazemzadeh, A., & Narayanan, S. (2005). An articulatory study of emotional speech production. In *Proceedings of the 9th European Conference on Speech Communication and Technology (Interspeech '2005—Eurospeech), Lisbon, Portugal* (pp. 497–500) .

Marsella, S. C., & Gratch, J. (2009). EMA: A process model of appraisal dynamics. *Journal of Cognitive Systems Research, 10*(1), 70–90.

Martin, J.-C., Caridakis, G., Devillers, L., Karpouzis, K., & Abrilian, S. (2009). Manual annotation and automatic image processing of multimodal emotional behaviors: Validating the annotation of TV interviews. *Personal and Ubiquitous Computing, 13*(1), 69–76.

Mirex. (2012). http://www.music-ir.org/mirex/wiki/MIREX_HOME. Retrieved April 24, 2013.

Murray, I. R., & Arnott, J. L. (1993). Toward the simulation of emotion in synthetic speech: A review of the literature on human vocal emotion. *Journal of the Acoustical Society of America, 93*(2), 1097–1108.

National Institute of Standards and Technology. (2009). Spoken language technology evaluations. www.nist.gov/speech/tests/. Retrieved March 31, 2009.

Pantic, M., & Rothkrantz, L. J. M. (2003). Toward an affect-sensitive multimodal human-computer interaction. *Proceedings of the IEEE, 91*(9), 1370–1390.

Pao, T. L., Liao, W. Y., Chen, Y. T., Yeh, J. H., Cheng, Y. M., & Chien, C. S. (2007). Comparison of several classifiers for emotion recognition from noisy Mandarin speech. In *Proceedings of the Third International Conference on Intelligent Information Hiding and Multimedia Signal Processing (IIHMSP 2007), Kaohsiung, Taiwan* (Vol. 1, pp. 23–26) .

Paul, D. B., & Baker, J. M. (1992). The design for the Wall Street Journal-based CSR corpus. In *Proceedings of the 2th International Conference on Spoken Language Processing (ICSLP 1992), Banff, Alberta, Canada* (pp. 899–902) .

Picard, R. W. (1995). Affective computing. (Technical Report 321). Cambridge, MA: MIT Media Laboratory Perceptual Computing Section.

Scherer, K. R. (2003). Vocal communication of emotion: A review of research paradigms. *Speech Communication, 40*(1–2), 227–256.

Scherer, K. R., Banse, R., & Wallbott, H. G. (2001). Emotion inferences from vocal expression correlate across languages and cultures. *Journal of Cross-Cultural Psychology, 32*(1), 76.

Scherer, K. R., & Ceschi, G. (1997). Lost luggage: A field study of emotion antecedent appraisal. *Motivation and Emotion, 21*(3), 211–235.

Schiel, F., Steininger, S., & Türk, U. (2002, May). *The SmartKom multimodal corpus at BAS*. Language Resources and Evaluation (LREC 2002), Las Palmas, Spain.

Schuller, B., Arsic, D., Wallhoff, F., & Rigoll, G. (2006, May). *Emotion recognition in the noise applying large acoustic feature sets*. ISCA Speech Prosody, Dresden, Germany, ISCA.

Schuller, B., Batliner, A., Seppi, D., Steidl, S., Vogt, T., Wagner, J., Devillers, L., Vidrascu, L., Amir, N., Kessous, L., et al. (2007). The relevance of feature type for the automatic classification of emotional user states: Low level descriptors and functionals. In *Interspeech 2007—Eurospeech, Antwerp, Belgium* (pp. 2253–2256) .

Schuller, B., Mueller, R., Höernler, B., Höethker, A., Konosu, H., & Rigoll, G. (2007). Audiovisual recognition of spontaneous interest within conversations. In *Proceedings of the 9th International Conference on Multimodal interfaces (ICMI 2007)*, Nagoya, Aichi, Japan (pp. 30–37).

Schuller, B., Seppi, D., Batliner, A., Maier, A., & Steidl, S. (2007). Towards more reality in the recognition of emotional speech. In *International Conference on Acoustics, Speech, and Signal Processing (ICASSP 2007), Honolulu, HI* (Vol. 4, pp. 941–944).

Schuller, B., Steidl, S., & Batliner, A. (2009, September). *The INTERSPEECH 2009 emotion challenge.* In Interspeech 2009—Eurospeech Conference, Brighton, UK.

Sedaaghi, M. H., Kotropoulos, C., & Ververidis, D. (2007). Using adaptive genetic algorithms to improve speech emotion recognition. In *International Workshop on Multimedia Signal Processing (MMSP 2007), Chania, Crete, Greece* (pp. 461–464).

Seppi, D., Batliner, A., Schuller, B., Steidl, S., Vogt, T., Wagner, J., Devillers, L., Vidrascu, L., Amir, N., & Aharonson, V. (2008). Patterns, prototypes, performance: Classifying emotional user states. In *Interspeech 2008—Eurospeech, Brisbane, Australia* (pp. 601–604).

Steidl, S. (2009). *Automatic classification of emotion-related user states in spontaneous children's speech.* Unpublished doctoral dissertation. Universität Erlangen-Nürnberg, Erlangen, Germany.

Steidl, S., Levit, M., Batliner, A., Nöth, E., & Niemann, H. (2005). "Of all things the measure is man" automatic classification of emotions and inter-labeler consistency. In *Proceedings of the International Conference on Acoustics, Speech, and Signal Processing (ICASSP 2005), Philadelphia* (Vol. 1, pp. 317–320).

Truong, K. P., Neerincx, M. A., & van Leeuwen, D. A. (2008). Assessing agreement of observer- and self-annotations in spontaneous multimodal emotion data. In *Interspeech 2008—Eurospeech, Brisbane, Australia* (pp. 318–321).

Ververidis, D., & Kotropoulos, C. (2006). Fast sequential floating forward selection applied to emotional speech features estimated on DES and SUSAS data collections. In *XIV European Signal Processing Conference (EUSIPCO 2006), Florence, Italy* (pp. 929–932).

Vidrascu, L., & Devillers, L. (2006). Real-life emotions in naturalistic data recorded in a medical call center. In *First International Workshop on Emotion: Corpora for Research on Emotion and Affect (International Conference on Language Resources and Evaluation) (LREC 2006), Genoa, Italy* (pp. 20–24).

Yildirim, S., Bulut, M., Lee, C. M., Kazemzadeh, A., Busso, C., Deng, Z., Lee, S., & Narayanan, S. S. (2004). An acoustic study of emotions expressed in speech. In *Proceedings of the 8th International Conference on Spoken Language Processing (ICSLP 04), Jeju Island, Korea* (pp. 2193–2196).

Zeng, Z., Pantic, M., Roisman, G. I., & Huang, T. S. (2009). A survey of affect recognition methods: Audio, visual, and spontaneous expressions. *IEEE Transactions on Pattern Analysis and Machine Intelligence, 31*(1), 39–58.

8

The Role of Context in Affective Behavior Understanding

Louis-Philippe Morency

1. Introduction

Face-to-face communication is highly interactive. Even when only one person speaks at a time, other participants exchange information continuously among themselves and with the speaker through gesture, gaze, posture, and facial expressions. Such affective feedback is an essential and predictable aspect of natural conversation, and its absence can significantly disrupt participants' ability to communicate (Bavelas et al., 2000; Yngve, 1970). During multiparty interactions such as in meetings, information is exchanged between participants using both audio and visual channels. Visual feedback can range from a simple eye glance to a large arm gesture or posture change. One important visual cue is head nod during conversation. Head nods are used for displaying agreement, grounding information, or during turn taking (Dittman & Llewellyn, 1968; Duncan, 1972). Recognizing these affective gestures is important for understanding all the information exchanged during a meeting or conversation, and can be particularly crucial for identifying more subtle factors such as the effectiveness of communication (Tickle-Degnen & Rosenthal, 1990), points of confusion, status relationships between participants (Tiedens & Fragale, 2003), or the diagnosis social disorders (Rizzo et al., 2006).

This chapter argues that it is possible to significantly improve state-of-the art recognition techniques by exploiting regularities in how people communicate. People do not provide affective feedback at random. Rather, they react to the current topic, previous utterances, and the speaker's current verbal and nonverbal behavior (Allwood et al. 1992). For example, listeners are far more likely to nod or shake if the speaker has just asked them a question, and incorporating such dialogue context can improve recognition performance during human–robot interaction (Morency et al., 2007). More generally, speakers and listeners coproduce a range of lexical, prosodic, and nonverbal patterns. Our goal is to automatically discover these patterns using only easily

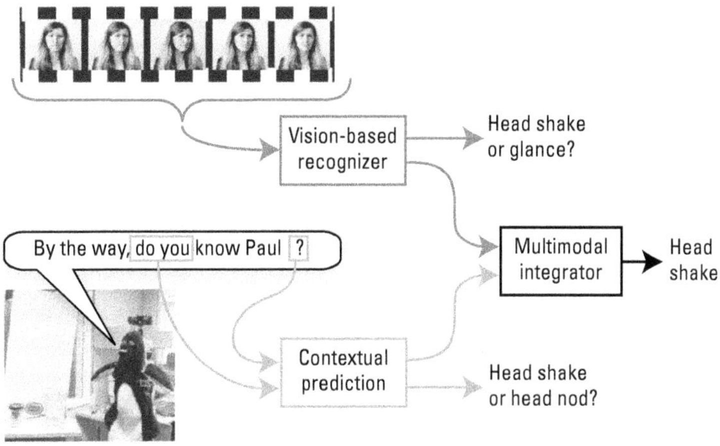

FIGURE 8.1 Contextual recognition of head gestures during face-to-face interaction with a conversational robot. In this scenario, contextual information from the robot's spoken utterance helps disambiguate the listener's visual gesture.

observable features of human face-to-face interaction (e.g., prosodic features and eye gaze), and exploit them to improve recognition accuracy.

This chapter shows that the recognition of affective gestures can be improved by considering the behaviors of other participants in the conversation. Specifically, it shows that the multimodal context from the current speaker can improve the visual recognition of listener gestures. We introduce the idea of encoding dictionary, a technique for contextual feature representation inspired by the influence speaker context has on the listener feedback. Automatic selection of relevant contextual features is performed by looking at individual and joint influences of context. The final contextual integration is done using a discriminative sequential model. We show the importance of context in affective behavior understanding on two different domains: interaction with a robot and human dyadic interaction. An important contribution of this chapter is the introduction of co-occurrence graphs, which models co-occurrence between contextual cues such as spoken words and pauses, and affective gestures. By analyzing these co-occurrence patterns, we show how to automatically select relevant contextual features and predict when visual gestures are most likely. Our context-based recognition framework allows us to predict, for example, that in certain contexts a glance is not likely whereas a head shake or nod is (as in Figure 8.1), or that a head nod is not likely and a head nod misperceived by the vision system can be ignored.

2. Context Definition

In this section we present how context can be defined during interactions with an embodied conversational agent such as a robot or virtual human, or during interactions between two or more human participants.

2.1 Robot and Agent Interactions

Figure 8.2 is a general view of the architecture for an embodied conversational agent[1]. In this architecture, the dialogue manager contains two main subcomponents, an agenda and a history. The agenda keeps a list of all the possible actions the agent and the user (i.e., human participant) can do next. This list is updated by the dialogue manager based on its discourse model (prior knowledge) and on the history. Some useful contextual cues can be estimated from the agenda:

- What will be the next spoken sentence of our embodied agent?
- Are we expecting some specific answers from the user?
- Is the user expected to look at some common space?

The history keeps a log of all the previous events that happened during the conversation. This information can be used to learn some interesting contextual cues:

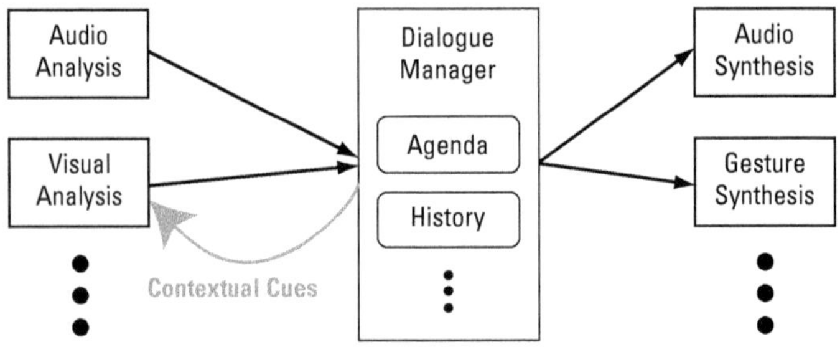

FIGURE 8.2 Simplified architecture for embodied conversational agent. Our method integrates contextual information from the dialogue manager inside the visual analysis module.

- How did the user answer previous questions (speech or gesture)?
- Does the user seem to understand the last explanation?

Based on the history, we can build a prior model about the type of visual feedback shown by the user. Based on the agenda, we can predict the type of visual feedback that will be shown by the user.

The simplified architecture depicted in Figure 8.2 highlights the fact that the dialogue manager already processes contextual information in order to produce output for the speech and gesture synthesizer. The main idea is to use this existing information to predict when visual feedback gestures from the user are likely. Since the dialogue manager is already merging information from the input devices with the history and the discourse model, the output of the dialogue manager will contain useful contextual information.

The contextual features should be seen as events or actions that can modify the interpretation of ambiguous affective behaviors. If a person is clearly smiling and laughing, then context should not change its interpretation. The same way, if a person is clearly not moving, a head nod should not be recognized just because it would be the appropriate time for head nods. Context does not dictate the interpretation of affective behaviors but gives us a tool to better interpret the ambiguous cases.

We highlight four types of contextual features easily available in the dialogue manager:

Lexical features: Lexical features are computed from the words said by the embodied agent. By analyzing the word content of the current or next utterance, one should be able to anticipate certain visual feedback. For example, if the current spoken utterance started with "Do you," the interlocutor will most likely answer using affirmation or negation. In this case, it is also likely to see visual feedback like a head nod or a head shake. On the other hand, if the current spoken utterance started with "What," then it's unlikely to see the listener head shake or head nod—other visual feedback gestures (e.g., pointing) are more likely in this case.

Punctuation: We use punctuation features output by the dialogue system as a proxy for prosody cues. Punctuation features modify how the text-to-speech engine will pronounce an utterance. Punctuation features can be seen as a substitute for more complex prosodic processing that are not yet available from most speech synthesizers. A comma in the middle of a sentence will produce a short pause, which will most likely trigger some feedback from the listener. A question mark at the end of the sentence represents a question that should be answered by the listener. When merged with lexical features, the punctuation features can help recognize situations (e.g., yes/no questions) where the listener will most likely use head gestures to answer.

Timing. Timing is an important part of spoken language, and information about when a specific word is spoken or when a sentence ends is critical. This information can aid the embodied conversation agent to anticipate visual grounding feedback. People naturally give visual feedback (e.g., head nods) during pauses of the speaker as well as just before the pause occurs. In natural language processing (NLP), lexical and syntactic features are predominant, but for face-to-face interaction with an ECA, timing is also an important feature.

Gesture display. Gesture synthesis is a key capability of ECAs, and it can also be leveraged as a context cue for gesture interpretation. As described in (Cassell & Thorisson, 1999), visual feedback synthesis can improve the engagement of the user with the ECA. The gestures expressed by the ECA influence the type of visual feedback from the human participant. For example, if the agent makes a deictic gesture, the user is more likely to look at the location that the ECA is pointing to.

2.2. Human Interactions

Communication is a joint activity, and social scientists have long argued that it cannot be properly recognized and understood by focusing on participants in isolation, but rather, one must see individual behaviors within the context of the group or dyad (Burgoon et al., 1995; Clark, 1996). Translating this proscription to the domain of gesture recognition, this argues that features outside of the person of interest should correlate with his or her behavior, and representing and exploiting these contextual features should improve recognition accuracy. Here, we explore this idea within the domain of dyadic and multiparty conversations; specifically, we consider whether adding contextual information about a speaker's behavior improves the ability to detect feedback gestures produced by listeners.

Our goal is to quantify the relationship between contextual information and visual gestures by looking at the time distribution of visual gestures given a contextual event. In our case, a contextual event can be a spoken word, a pause, or the end of a sentence. If a relationship exists between a contextual event and a specific visual gesture (e.g., head nod), then we will expect to see a structure in the relative distribution. If no relationship exists, the relative distribution should be random.

As our interest is in producing online (real-time) recognition systems, we focus on contextual features that would be readily available to a real-time system (i.e., surface behaviors rather than the privileged mental state of individual participants). We define context as the set of events happening from other sources than the person of interest. For example, in a multiparty conversation between four people, we define context for one participant as the set of events coming from the three other participants. Since our goal in this chapter is to recognize affective gestures, we focus on context events related to spoken utterances:

Prosody: Prosody refers to the rhythm, pitch, and intonation of speech. Several studies have demonstrated that listener feedback is correlated with a speaker's prosody (Nishimura et al., 2007). For example, Ward and Tsukahara (2000) show that short listener backchannels (listener utterances like "OK" or "uh-huh" given during a speaker's utterance) are associated with a lowering of pitch over some interval. We encode the following prosodic features, including standard linguistic annotations and the prosodic features suggested by Ward and Tsukahara (2000):

- Downslopes in pitch continuing for at least 40 ms
- Regions of pitch lower than the 26th percentile continuing for at least 110 ms (i.e., lowness)
- Utterances longer than 700 ms
- Drop or rise in energy of speech (i.e., energy edge)
- Fast drop or rise in energy of speech (i.e., energy fast edge)
- Vowel volume (i.e., vowels are usually spoken more softly)
- Lengthened words (e.g., "I li::ke it")
- Emphasized or slowly uttered words (e.g., "ex_a_c_tly")
- Words spoken with continuing intonation
- Words spoken with falling intonation (e.g., end of an utterance)
- Words spoken with rising intonation (i.e., question mark)

Pauses: Listener feedback often follows speaker pauses or filled pauses such as "um" (see Cathcart et al., 2003). To capture these possible associations, we use the following contextual features:

- Pause in speech (i.e., no speech)
- Filled pause (e.g. "um")

Gaze and gestures: Gestures performed by the speaker are often correlated with listener feedback (Burgoon et al., 1995). Eye gaze, in particular, has often been implicated as eliciting listener feedback. Thus, we encode the following contextual feature:

- Speaker looking at the listener

3. Context and Affective Behaviors

To study the relationship between context and affective gestures, we look at the annotations from the augmented multi-party interaction (AMI) meeting corpus

(AMI Consortium, 2007). This corpus contains 46 meetings with annotated head gestures and spoken words of all four participants[2]. Each meeting varies between 20 and 40 minutes. The corpus contains follow-up meetings with the same participants. These series usually contain three or four meetings.

Participants were video recorded using a frontal camera and a close-talking microphone. The video sequences were manually annotated with spoken words, punctuation, and head gestures (head nods and head shakes). The dataset contains 9,745 head nods and 1,279 head shakes. In our analysis, we used a total of 184 sequences (some meetings had only 3 participants annotated with head gestures).

3.1. Co-Occurrence Graphs

Our goal is to analyze the relationship between contextual events and affective gestures. Our approach is to create a co-occurrence graph for each contextual event and each possible type of affective gesture. The co-occurrence graph, centered at the contextual event, represents how many visual gesture instances happened around that event. The co-occurrence graphs can be seen as temporal generalization of the co-occurrence matrices introduced by Haralick et al. (1973).

For each instance of a contextual event, we slide a window of 0.1 second from −30 seconds before the event to 30 seconds after the event. If a visual gesture happens during a specific time window, the corresponding bin in the co-occurrence graph is incremented. By doing this for each instance of a specific contextual event, we get a time distribution of visual gesture given the contextual event. Figures 8.3 shows examples of co-occurrence graphs for different contextual events.

Figures 8.4 show cumulative co-occurrence graphs for head nods. The cumulative co-occurrence graph for head nods shows an interesting point: Most of the relationship between head nods and contextual event seems to happen between −5 and 5 seconds. Past this time, the relationship seems mostly random.

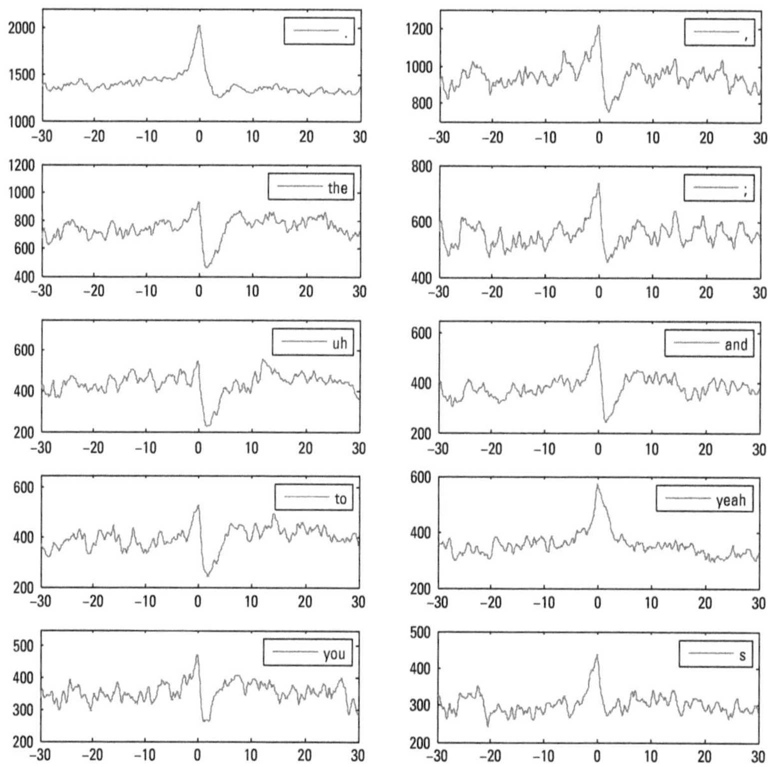

FIGURE 8.3 Examples of co-occurrence graphs. When analyzing this relationship between head nods and contextual events, three temporal patterns appear: ignition, transition, and negation.

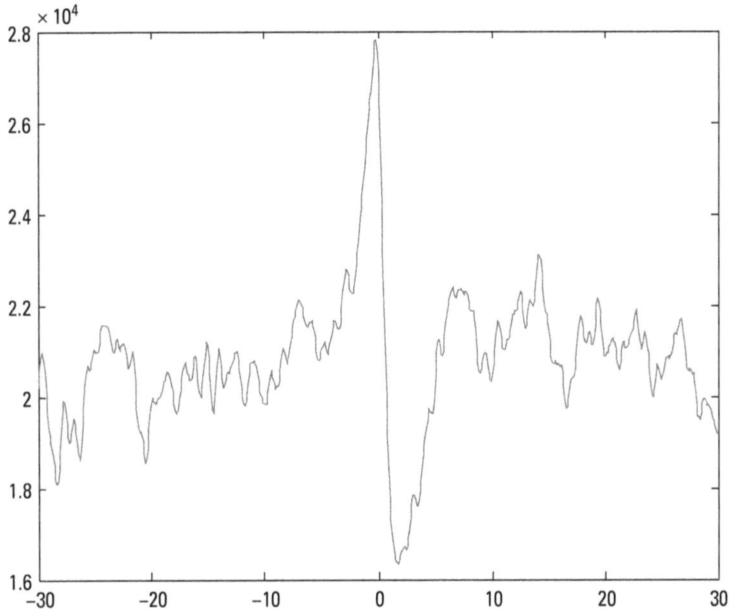

FIGURE 8.4 Cumulative number of head nods (y-axis) in function of the time alignment with all contextual events (x-axis): spoken words, prosody, and timing. We can observe a relationship between contextual events and head nods between −5 and 5 seconds.

3.2. Patterns in Co-Occurrence Graphs

By observing the co-occurrence graphs of Figure 8.3, three patterns appear: ignition, transition, and negation. These patterns are illustrated in Figure 8.5.

- *Ignition pattern*. The first pattern is the ignition pattern (left) where a contextual event positively influences visual gesture. This type of relationship means that a visual gesture is more likely to happen around the contextual event. This is true for the period, which represents the end of a sentence. This is also true for positive feed such as the word "yeah".
- *Transition pattern*. The second pattern is the transition pattern (middle) where a contextual event represents a midpoint between two phrases. This type of relation will bring a high likelihood around or before the event, but right after the event this likelihood will be lower. Two good examples of this type of events are the comma and the word "and." These events will usually occur in the middle of a sentence, between two constituents.
- *Negative pattern*. The last pattern is the "negative" pattern (right) where a contextual event negatively influences a visual gesture. This type of relation means that a visual gesture is unlikely

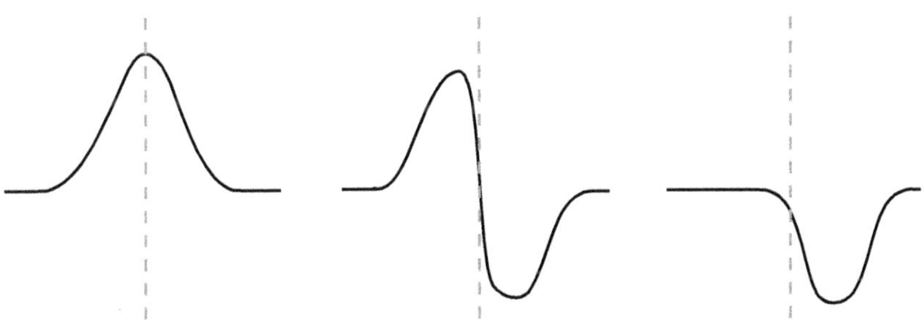

FIGURE 8.5 Schematic representation of the three patterns observed when analyzing co-occurrence of head nods and contextual events: (left) ignition pattern, (middle) transition pattern, and (right) negative pattern.

to happen after this event. The words "the" and "to" are two good examples of this type of pattern. These words do not bring visual feedback, and usually following one of these words will be a large number of other spoken words.

The analysis of the co-occurrence graphs shown in Figure 8.3 confirms our intuition that the context is related to visual feedback (e.g., head nods). Also, these co-occurrence graphs contain patterns that can potentially help to recognize when a specific gesture is more likely.

3.3. Co-Occurrence Ranking of Contextual Features

A good contextual feature is an event (1) that happens on a regular basis so that there is a good chance to see this same event in a new meeting, and (2) that is related to visual feedback. One criterion that includes both advantages is the maximum number of co-occurrences between the contextual event and the visual gesture. This criterion is equal to the maximum peak of each co-occurrence graph.

Figure 8.6 shows the top 25 contextual features. The top feature is the period, which usually represent the end of a sentence. This goes with our intuition that people usually do a grounding gesture at the end of a sentence. Also, the second feature is the comma, which represents a pause in a sentence. Pauses are also good timing for grounding gestures. The other top contextual features are more interesting since they are lexical features and bring interesting questions as why they are related with visual gestures.

4. Leaning Relevant Context

4.1. Sequential Probabilistic Model

A sequential probabilistic model takes as input a sequence of observation features (e.g., the speaker features) and returns a sequence of probabilities (i.e., probability of listener backchannel). Two of the most popular sequential models are the hidden Markov model (HMM) (Rabiner, 1989) and the conditional random field (CRF) (Lafferty et al., 2001). One of the main differences between these two models is that CRF is discriminative (i.e., tries to find the best way to differentiate cases where the listener gives backchannel to cases where it does not) while HMM is generative (i.e., tries to find the best way to generalize the samples from the cases where the listener gives backchannel without looking at the cases where the listener did not give backchannel). Our prediction model is designed to work with both types of sequential probabilistic models.

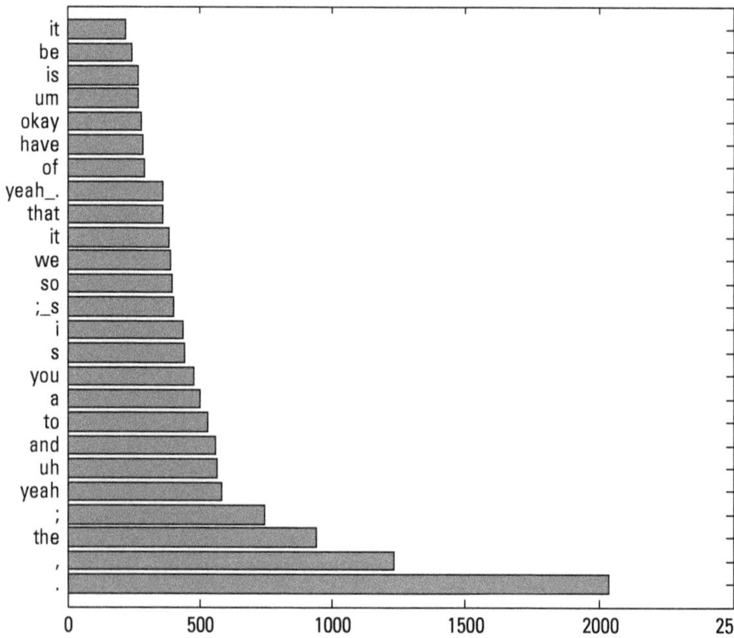

FIGURE 8.6 Top 25 contextual features. Horizontal axis: maximum number of times a head nod happened in a window of 5 seconds around the contextual feature.

Sequential probabilistic models such as HMM and CRF have some constraints that need to be understood and addressed before using them:

- *Limited learning:* The more informative your features are, the better your sequential model will perform. If the input features are too noisy (e.g., direct signal from microphone), it will make it harder for the HMM or CRF to learn the important part of the signal. Also, because of the preprocessing your input features to highlight their influences on your label (e.g., listener backchannel), you improve your chance of success.
- *Overfitting:* The more complex your model is, the more training data it needs. Every input feature that you add increases its complexity and at the same time its need for a larger training set. Since we usually have a limited set of training sequences, it is important to keep the number of input features low.

In our prediction model, we directly addressed these issues by focusing on the feature representation and feature selection problems:

- *Encoding dictionary:* To address the limited learning constraint of sequential models, we suggest using more than binary encoding to represent input features. Our encoding dictionary contains a series of encoding templates that were designed to model different relationships between a speaker feature (e.g., a speaker is not currently speaking) and listener backchannel. The encoding dictionary and its usage are described in Section 4.2.
- *Automatic feature and encoding selection:* Because of the overfitting problem happening when too many uncorrelated features (i.e., features that do not influence listener backchannel) are used, we suggest two techniques for automatic feature and encoding selection based on co-occurence statistics and performance evaluation on a validation dataset. Our feature selection algorithms are described in Section 4.3.

The following two sections describe our encoding dictionary and feature selection algorithm.

4.2. Encoding Dictionary

The goal of the encoding dictionary is to propose a series of encoding templates that capture the coarse relationship between speaker features and listener backchannel. These encoding templates will help to represent long-range dependencies (when the influence of an input feature decays slowly, possibly with a delay) that are otherwise hard to learn using a sequential probabilistic model. An example of long-range dependency is the effect of low-pitch regions on backchannel feedback with an average delay of 0.7 seconds (observed by Ward and Tsukahara, 2000). In our framework, the prediction model will pick an encoding template with a 0.5-second delay, and the exact alignment will be learned by the sequential probabilistic model, which will also take into account the influence of other input features.

The Figure 8.7 shows the 13 encoding templates used in our experiments. These encoding templates were selected to represent a wide range of ways that a speaker feature can influence the listener backchannel. These encoding templates were also selected because they can easily be implemented in real time since the only needed information is the start time of the speaker feature. Only the binary feature also uses the end time. In all cases, no knowledge of the future is needed.

The three main types of encoding templates are:

- *Binary encoding:* This encoding is designed for speaker features whose influence on listener backchannel is constraint to the duration of the speaker feature.
- *Step function:* This encoding is a generalization of binary encoding by adding two parameters: width of the encoded feature and delay between the start of the feature and its encoded version. This encoding is useful if the feature influence on backchannel is constant but with a certain delay and duration.
- *Ramp function:* This encoding linearly decreases for a set period of time (i.e., width parameter). This encoding is useful if the feature influence on backchannel is changing over time.

It is important to note that a feature can have an *individual* influence on backchannel and/or a *joint* influence. An *individual* influence means the input feature directly influences listener backchannel. For example, a long pause can by itself trigger backchannel feedback from the listener. A *joint* influence means that more than one feature is involved in triggering the feedback. For example, saying the word "and" followed by a look

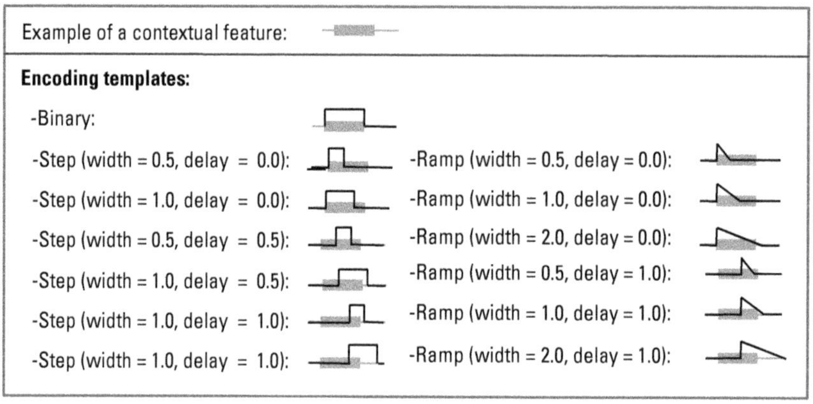

FIGURE 8.7 Encoding dictionary. This figure shows the different encoding templates used by our context-based approach. Each encoding template was selected to express a different relationship between contextual features and visual feedback. This encoding dictionary gives a more powerful set of input features to the sequential probabilistic model and improves the performance of our context-based recognizer.

back at the listener can trigger listener feedback. This also means that a feature may need to be encoded more than one way since it may have a *individual* influence as well as one or more *joint* influences.

One way to use the encoding dictionary with a small set of features is to encode each input feature with each encoding template. We tested this approach in our experiment with a set of 12 features (see Section 5), but because of the problem of overfitting, a better approach is to select the optimal subset of input features and encoding templates. The following section describes our feature selection algorithm.

4.3. Joint Feature Selection

Given the subset of features that performed best when trained individually, we now build the complete set of feature hypotheses to be used by the joint feature selection process. This set represents each feature encoded with all possible encoding templates from our dictionary. The goal of joint selection is to find a subset of features that best complement each other for prediction of backchannel. Figure 8.8 shows the first two iterations of our algorithm.

The algorithm starts with the complete set of feature hypotheses and an empty set of *best* features. At each iteration, the best feature hypothesis is selected and added to the best feature set. For each feature hypothesis, a sequential model is trained and evaluated using the feature hypothesis and all features previously selected in the best feature set. While the first iteration of this process is really similar to the individual selection, every iteration afterward will select a feature that best complements the current best features set. Note that during the joint selection process, the same feature can be selected more than once with different encodings. The procedure stops when the performance starts decreasing.

5. Examples of Affective Behavior Understanding

In this section, we show the importance of context in affective behavior understanding on two different domains: interaction with a robot and human dyadic interactions. Our hypothesis is that the inclusion of contextual information within the affective gesture recognizer will increase the number of recognized gestures while reducing the number of false detections. In both domains we compare two different configurations: (1) using the vision-only approach, and (2) combining the contextual information with the results of the visual approach (multimodal integration).

5.1. Robot Demonstration

The following experiment demonstrates how contextual features inferred from an agent's spoken dialogue can improve head nod and head shake recognition. The experiment compares the performance of the vision-only recognizer with the context-only prediction and with multimodal integration.

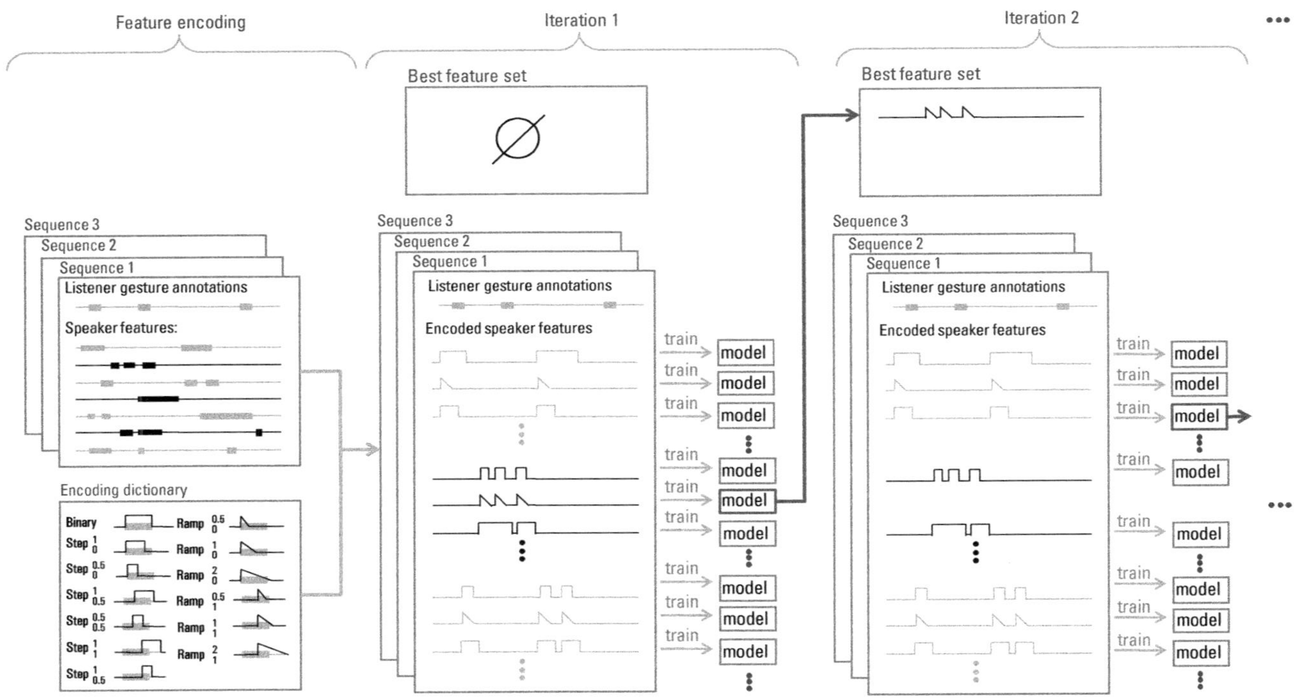

FIGURE 8.8 Joint feature selection. This figure illustrates the feature-encoding process using our encoding dictionary as well as two iterations of our joint feature selection algorithm. The goal of joint selection is to find a subset of features that best complement each other for recognition of listener visual feedback.

FIGURE 8.9 Mel, the interactive robot, can present the iGlassware demo (table and copper cup on its right) or talk about its own dialog and sensorimotor abilities.

Human participants were video recorded while interacting with the robot (see Figure 8.9). The vision-based head tracking and head gesture recognition was run online (~18 Hz). The robot's conversational model, based on COLLAGEN (Rich et al., 2001), determines the next activity on the agenda using a predefined set of engagement rules, originally based on human–human interaction (Sidner et al., 2005). Each interaction lasted between 2 and 5 minutes. During each interaction, we also recorded the results of the vision-based head gesture recognizer as well as the contextual cues (spoken utterances with start time and duration) from the dialogue manager. These contextual cues were later automatically processed to create the contextual features (see Section 2.1) necessary for the contextual predictor. For ground truth, we hand-labeled each video sequence to determine exactly when the participant nodded or shook his/her head. A total of 274 head nods and 14 head shakes were naturally performed by the participants while interacting with the robot.

Figure 8.10 shows head nod detection results for all 9 subjects used during testing. The receiver operating characteristic (ROC) curves represent the detection performance of each recognition algorithm when varying the detection threshold. The area under the curve for each technique is 0.9482 for the vision only, 0.7691 for the predictor, and 0.9678 for the integrator. For head shakes, the areas under the curve for each technique, are 0.9780 for the vision only, 0.4961 for the predictor, and 0.9872 for the integrator.

Table 8.1 summarizes the results for head nods and head shake understanding by computing the true positive rates for the fixed negative rate of 0.1. Using a standard analysis of variance (ANOVA) on all the subjects, results on the head nod detection task showed a significant difference among the means of the three methods of detection: $F(1, 8) = 62.40$, $p < 0.001$, $d = 0.97$. Pairwise comparisons show a significant difference between all pairs, with $p < 0.001$, $p = 0.0015$, and $p < 0.001$ for vision-predictor, vision-integrator, and predictor-integrator respectively. A larger number of samples would be necessary to see the same significance in head shakes.

5.2. Human Dyadic Storytelling

Data is drawn from a study of face-to-face narrative discourse ("quasi-monologic" storytelling). Seventy-six subjects from the general Los Angeles area participated in this study. Participants in groups of two entered the laboratory and were told they were participating in a study to evaluate a communicative technology. Subjects were randomly assigned the role of speaker and listener. The speaker viewed a short segment of a video clip taken from the Edge Training Systems, Inc., *Sexual Harassment Awareness* video. After the speaker finished viewing the video, the listener was led back into the computer room, where the speaker was instructed to retell the stories portrayed in the clips to the listener. The listener was asked to not talk during the story retelling. Elicited stories were approximately 2 minutes in length on average. Participants were debriefed individually and dismissed.

We collected synchronized multimodal data from each participant, including voice and upper-body

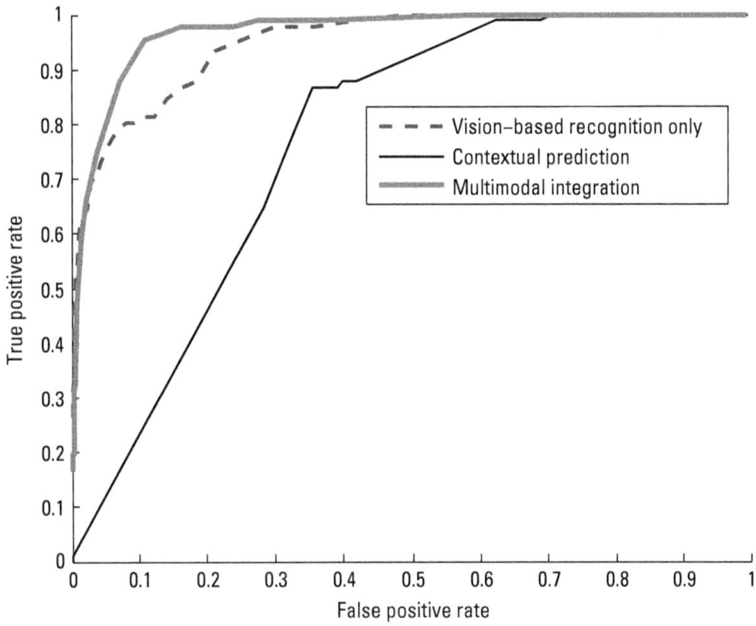

FIGURE 8.10 Results for robot demonstration: head nod recognition curves when varying the detection threshold. For a fixed false-positive rate of 0.0409 (operating point), the context-based approach improves head nod recognition from 72.5% (vision only) to 90.4%.

TABLE 8.1 True Detection Rates for a Fixed False Positive Rate of 0.1

	Vision	*Predictor*	*Integrator*
Head nods	81%	23%	93%
Head shakes	83%	10%	98%

movements (see Figure 8.11). Both the speaker and listener wore a lightweight headset with a microphone. Three Panasonic PV-GS180 camcorders were used to videotape the experiment: one was placed in front the speaker, one in front of the listener, and one attached to the ceiling to record both speaker and listener.

Our first experiment compared the performance of our context-based recognition framework with a vision-only recognizer. Figure 8.12 shows the ROC curve for both approaches. The ROC curves represent the detection performance for both recognition algorithms when varying the detection threshold. The two quantitative methods used to evaluate ROC curves are area under the curve and equal error rate. Table 8.2 shows the quantitative evaluation using both error criteria. The use of context improves recognition from 74.9% to 83.2%. Pairwise two-tailed t-test comparison show a significant difference for both error criteria, with $p = 0.021$ and $p = 0.012$ for the area under the curve and the equal error rate, respectively.

As described in Section 4, our context-based recognition framework uses two types of feature selections: individual feature selection and joint feature selection (see Section 4.3 for details). It is very interesting to look at the features and encoding selected after both processes:

- Vowel volume using ramp encoding with a width of 0.5 seconds and a delay of 0.5 seconds
- Speaker looking at the listener using a binary
- Pause using step encoding with a width of 2.0 seconds and no delay
- Low pitch using ramp encoding with a width of 0.5 seconds and no delay

These are the four feature-encoding pairs selected after the joint feature selection process, which stopped when validation performance started decreasing. We can see that only one feature was selected with binary encoding, suggesting that the use of the encoding dictionary was important. The first selected feature, vowel volume, used an encoding with a ramp and a delay of

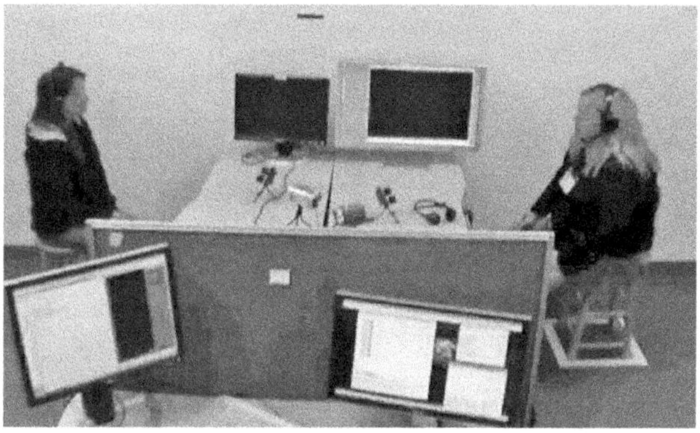

FIGURE 8.11 Setup for human dyadic storytelling. This study of face-to-face narrative discourse (i.e., quasi-monologic storytelling) included 76 subjects. The speaker was instructed to retell the stories portrayed in two video clips to the listener.

TABLE 8.2 Quantitative Comparison Between Our Context-Based Approach and a Vision-Only Approach (See Figure 8.12)

Recognizer	*Area*	*EER*
Context-based	83.2%	76.5%
Vision-only	74.9%	69.4%

Note. The table shows both the area under the curve and the equal error rate (EER).

0.5 seconds, meaning that its influence on head nods is asynchronous and decreases over time. The second selected feature is related to the eye gaze of the speaker, confirming the importance of our multimodal context. The third and fourth features have also been reported by Ward and Tsukahara (2000) as good predictive features for backchannel feedback. No lexical feature was selected by the joint selection algorithm. This result means that visual gesture recognition can be improved

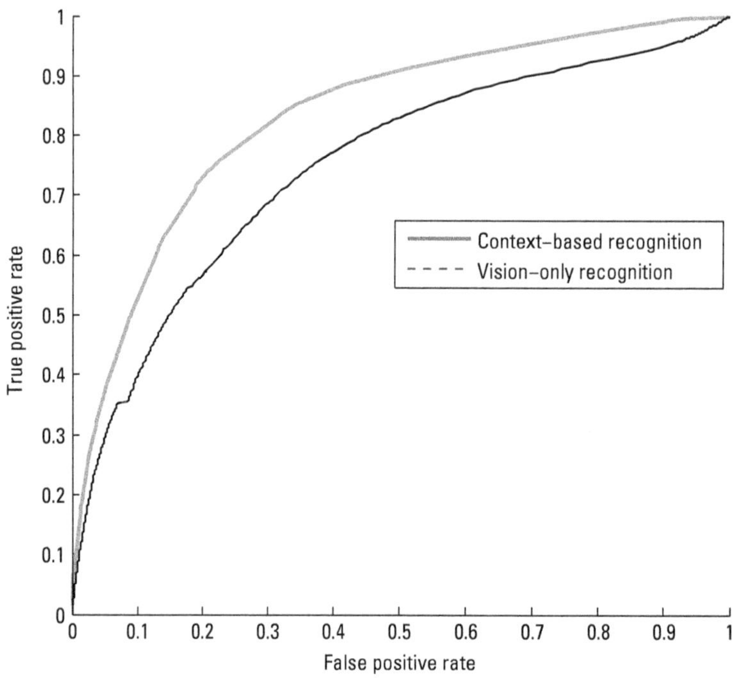

FIGURE 8.12 Results for human dyadic storytelling: ROC curves of head nod recognition comparing our context-based approach with a vision-only approach.

TABLE 8.3 Quantitative Evaluation Showing the Gain in Performance When Using Both Individual and Joint Feature Selection

Feature selection	*Area*	*EER*
Joint + Individual	83.2%	76.5%
Individual only	79.1%	72.0%

TABLE 8.4 Quantitative Evaluation Showing the Gain in Performance When Using the Encoding Dictionary for Feature Representation

Feature encoding	*Area*	*EER*
Dictionary	79.1%	72.0%
Binary	76.1%	69.9%

using only prosodic cues, pauses, and speaker visual display.

The second and third experiments were designed to understand the influence of feature selection and encoding dictionary on the context-based recognition framework. Table 8.3 compares the recognition performance when using or not using the joint feature selection after the individual feature selection. Table 8.4 compares the recognition performance when using the complete encoding dictionary to using only binary encoding. This last comparison was done after the individual feature selection.

We can see from both Table 8.3 and 8.4 that the gain in performance of our context-based recognition algorithm is directly related to the joint feature selection and the encoding dictionary. By using the encoding dictionary instead of the usual binary encoding, the performance improves from 76.1% to 79.1%. And by using the joint feature selection, the performance improves again from 79.1% to 83.2%.

Our experiments show that by using joint feature selection and an encoding dictionary, contextual information from other participants significantly improves the performance of vision-based gesture recognition.

6. Conclusion

Our results show that contextual information from other human participants can improve visual gesture recognition. We presented a context-based recognition framework that represents contextual features based on an encoding dictionary and automatically selects the optimal features based on *individual* and *joint* influence. By using simple prosodic, pauses, and visual display contextual features available in real time, we were able to improve the performance of the vision-only head gesture recognizer from 74.9% to 83.4%. An important contribution of this chapter is our contextual representation based on co-occurrence graphs, which models co-occurrence between contextual cues such as spoken words and pauses, and visual head gestures. By analyzing these co-occurrence patterns, we automatically selected relevant contextual features and predicted when visual gestures were most likely to occur. Recognizing these visual gestures is important for understanding the full meaning of a meeting or conversation, and can be particularly crucial for identifying more subtle factors such as the effectiveness of communication or diagnosis of social disorders. Another important direction for future research is the use of context in emotion encoding, as was shown by Barrett and Kensinger (2010).

Notes

1. In our work we use the COLLAGEN conversation manager (Rich et al., 2001), but other dialogue managers provide these components as well.
2. The corpus contains a larger number of meetings, but we used only the meetings that had both head gestures and spoken words annotated.

References

Allwood, J., Nivre, J., & Ahlsn, E. (1992). On the semantics and pragmatics of linguistic feedback. *Journal of Semantics*, 9(1), 1–26.

Barrett, L., & Kensinger, E. A. (2010). Context is routinely encoded during emotion perception. *Psychological Science*, *21*(4), 595–599.

Bavelas, J. B., Coates, L., & Johnson, T. (2000). Listeners as conarrators. *Journal of Personality and Social Psychology*, 79(6), 941–952.

Burgoon, J. K., Stern, L. A., & Dillman L.. (1995). *Interpersonal adaptation: Dyadic interaction patterns*. Cambridge, UK: Cambridge University Press.

Cassell J., & Thorisson, K. R. (1999). The power of a nod and a glance: Envelope vs. emotional feedback in animated conversational agents. *Applied Artificial Intelligence*, *13*, 519–538.

Cathcart, N., Carletta, J., & Klein, E. (2003). A shallow model of backchannel continuers in spoken dialogue. *European* ACL, 51–58.

Clark, H. H. *Using language.* (1996). Cambridge. Cambridge University Press.

AMI Consortium. *AMI meeting corpus.* http://corpus.amiproject.org/

Dittmann, A., & Llewellyn, L. (1968). Relationship between vocalizations and head nods as listener responses. *Journal of Personality and Social Psychology*, 9, 79–84.

Duncan, S. (1972). Some signals and rules for taking speaking turns in conversations. *Journal of Personality and Social Psychology*, 23, 283–292.

Haralick, R., Shanmugam, K., & Dinstein, I. (1973). Textural features for image classification. *IEEE Transactions on Systems, Man, and Cybernetics*, 3(6), 610–621.

Lafferty, J., McCallum, A., & Pereira, F. (2001). Conditional random fields: Probabilistic models for segmenting and labelling sequence data. *ICML*. 282–289.

Morency, L.-P., Sidner, C., Lee, C., & Darrell, T. (2007). Head gestures for perceptual interfaces: The role of context in improving recognition. *Artificial Intelligence*, *171*(8–9), 568–585.

Nishimura, R., Kitaoka, N., & Nakagawa, S. (2007). A spoken dialog system for chat-like conversations considering response timing. *LNCS*, *4629*, 599–606.

Rabiner, L. R. (1989). A tutorial on hidden Markov models and selected applications in speech recognition. *Proceedings of the IEEE*, 77(2), 257–286.

Rich, C., Sidner, C. L., & Lesh, N. (2001). Collagen: Applying collaborative discourse theory to human–computer interaction [Special Issue on Intelligent User Interfaces]. *AI Magazine*, 22(4), 15–25.

Rizzo, A. A., Klimchuk, D., Mitura, R., Bowerly, T., Buckwalter, J. G., & Parsons, T. (2006). A virtual reality scenario for all seasons: The virtual classroom. *CNS Spectrums*, *11*(1), 35–44.

Sidner, C., Lee, C., Kidd, C. D., Lesh, N., & Rich, C. (2005). Explorations in engagement for humans and robots. *Artificial Intelligence*, *166*(1–2), 140–164.

Tickle-Degnen, L., & Rosenthal, R.. (1990). The nature of rapport and its nonverbal correlates. *Psychological Inquiry*, *1*(4), 285–293.

Tiedens, L. Z., & Fragale, A. R. (2003). Power moves: Complementarity in dominant and submissive nonverbal behavior. *Journal of Personality and Social Psychology*, *84*(3), 558–568.

Ward, N., & Tsukahara, W. (2000). Prosodic features which cue back-channel responses in English and Japanese. *Journal of Pragmatics*, 32(8), 1177–1207.

Yngve, V. H. On getting a word in edgewise. (1970). In *Sixth Regional Meeting of the Chicago Linguistic Society*, 567–577.

9

Computational Models of Expressive Behaviors for a Virtual Agent

Radosław Niewiadomski, Sylwia Julia Hyniewska, & Catherine Pelachaud

1. Introduction

Embodied conversational agents, ECAs, are virtual entities with human-like communicative capabilities. They are used as a new form of human–machine interface. They often have a human-like appearance (see Figure 9.1) and are able to sustain a conversation with users or virtual agents (Cassell et al., 2000; Kopp et al., 2003; Granström et al., 2002; Gratch et al., 2007; Marsella & Gratch, 2009). ECAs communicate through verbal and nonverbal means such as facial expressions, hand and arm movements, body posture, and prosody. They can indicate a point in space (Martin et al., 2009), describe with their hands the shape of an object (Bergmann & Kopp, 2009), punctuate their speech with beats and eyebrow movements (Cassell, 2001; Granström et al., 2002), and display emotional expressions (Niewiadomski et al., 2009a, 2009b) or social signals (Bickmore & Picard, 2005). They are able to manage speaking turn exchange (Thórisson, 2002) and even show some ecologically valid listening behavior (Bevacqua et al., 2010).

ECAs have basically dual functions. On one hand they can serve various functions in a human–machine interface, and on the other they are tools to study human communication. Examples of the first application are Web agents that serve provided information, or pedagogical agents that provide support to students in their learning process (Graesser et al., 2007; Johnson et al., 2000; Moreno & Flowerday, 2006). Lately research has been undertaken to create ECAs as companions for young kids or for the elderly (Bickmore et al., 2008; Tartaro & Cassell, 2008). ECAs are fully parameterized entities. By controlling each of their parameters, one by one or in combination, one can study their role and impact. Visual prosody has been investigated by looking at the tight temporal synchrony of voice intonation and eyebrow movement (Cavé et al., 1996; Krahmer & Swerts, 2004). The role of body posture in turn taking (Cassell et al., 1999), eye movements in deictic function (Raidt et al., 2007), and importance

FIGURE 9.1 Examples of ECAs. (Left) Sam and Alex (source J. Cassell); (center) Social cognition (source J. Gratch and S. Marsella); (right) Max agent (source S. Kopp).

of multimodal behavior in communicating emotional state (Martin et al., 2006) have also been examined.

Expressivity of ECAs is crucial. It gives liveliness to the virtual humanoid and allows it to communicate with others. Expressivity embeds two factors: the set of multimodal signals that is conveyed and their coherency in the communicative and emotional context. When building an ECA, one has not only to create a large repertoire of multimodal signals but also to elaborate control mechanisms to determine when an expression should be displayed and which one it should be. Studies have shown that humans tend to interact with virtual humanoids in a similar way as they do with humans (Brave et al., 2005; Schilbach et al., 2006), and they have similar expectations in terms of politeness (Reeves & Nass, 1996; Rehm & André, 2005) and cultural rules (Endrass et al., 2009). Agents portraying emotional behaviors and following different emotion strategies such as empathy are perceived as more trustworthy and friendly; users enjoy interacting with them more (Brave et al., 2005; Ochs et al., 2008; Partala & Surakka, 2004; Prendinger et al., 2005). When communicating, the full body is at work. Gaze, hand gesture, facial expression, intonation, and body posture are used in a coordinated manner to convey semantic, syntactic, attitudinal, and emotional information (Argyle & Cook, 1976; Ekman, 1979; Heylen, 2006; Kendon, 2004; McNeill, 1992).

Regarding decoding and encoding of emotions, faces are a great vehicle of communication (Ekman, 2003b; Kaiser & Wehrle, 2001). They are able to display very subtle expressions in which a slight difference in timing or muscular activity can convey different meanings. In this chapter we will pay particular attention to the modeling of expressions of emotions. We will mainly present computational models of expressions of emotions, the aim of which is to capture this palette of possibilities.

In the next section we present how the different psychology theories explain emotional expressive behaviors. The third section describes various computational models of static and dynamic facial expressions as well as multimodal displays of emotions. The representation of behavior expressivity is presented in the following section. The fifth section deals with the regulation of emotional expressions. We end this chapter with some concluding remarks.

2. Background—Expressions of Emotion

Emotional expressions are one of the most important forms of human nonverbal communication. Human expressions, even if they are usually spontaneous displays of emotional states, can also be posed, for example, by actors (Gosselin et al., 1995). In this section we present different theoretical approaches to emotional expressions. In more detail, in the next subsection we present main theories of facial expressions of emotions while in Section 2.2 we focus on multimodal expressions of emotions. Section 2.3 is dedicated to the models of full-body expressive emotional behaviors. Finally, in Section 2.4, we discuss the socially adequate emotional displays in ECAs. We pay special attention to facial behavior regulation.

2.1 Theoretical Background for Emotional Facial Behavior

In this section we present the theoretical basis of several models of expressive behaviors. In order to preserve the credibility of virtual agents' behaviors, most of the existing computational models are based on one or more theories of emotions. Even if these theories often offer only partial explanation of the humans' emotional expressive behaviors, they may assure the validity of the mathematical models used in virtual agents. In this section we concentrate on theories that have been used so far in computational models of emotions.

2.1.1 Discrete Representations

Discrete emotion theorists claim that there are a limited number of fundamental emotions, which often are called "primary" or "basic" emotions (e.g., Izard, 1977; Plutchik, 1980). Each of these prototypical emotions is characterized by a specific adaptive function, expression (e.g., specific facial behavior), physiological pattern, distinctive conscious experience (a feeling), and instrumental action (Keltner & Buswell, 1997; Manstead et al., 2005). Emotions are common to different cultures and their manifestations are universally understood (Ekman, 1999), while an expression is a characteristic and prototypical signal of one of these emotions. Therefore, establishing the list of distinct facial expressions is equivalent to establishing a list of candidates for basic emotions. The most often used list of basic emotions was proposed by Ekman, and it contains six emotional states: anger, disgust, fear, joy, sadness, and surprise (Ekman & Friesen, 1975).

The small number of basic emotions is not sufficient to explain all human facial displays. In this tradition, a variety of emotional expressions commonly observed are often explained by introducing some "derivative" facial expressions. According to some theorists (e.g., Ekman & Friesen, 1975; Izard, 1992; Tomkins & McCarter, 1964), expressions can be mixed or blended in order to obtain expressions of compound emotional states like: "sadness and happiness at the same time." The different types of blends can appear in the form of superposition of emotions or masking of one emotion by another. Devillers et al. (2005) observe that these expressions occur often in everyday life situations. The resulting expression has some elements of facial expressions of both emotions. According to Ekman these facial expressions are obtained by the composition of expressions over different face areas. For instance, in the case of a superposition of two emotions, the display is composed of one emotional expression for the upper face area and a different one for the lower face (Ekman & Friesen, 1975). Moreover, according to some discrete emotion theorists (e.g., Ekman & Friesen, 1975), emotional expressions are affected by combinations of biological and learned factors. In particular, an expression serves to communicate an internal state, but it can be regulated according to the sociocultural factors. These factors can affect to some extent the pattern and timing of any expression. Thus, any facial expression can be, for example, concealed or simulated. The displays of "derivative" expressions mentioned above differ from the spontaneous expressions of basic emotions.

2.1.2 Dimensional Representations

According to the dimensional emotion theorists, emotions are defined as variations on a continuum of some dimensions. Several dimensional models have been proposed. Russell's circumplex model of emotions is one of the most well known, with the dimensions of valence (pleasure–displeasure) and arousal (Russell, 1980). Regarding emotional expressions it predicts the link between each facial muscle action and its position on the activation and valence level. The information from the face is not considered sufficient, however, to enable the attribution of a concrete emotional label: the emotional expression would be more easily classified in terms of valence and arousal. The emotional labels are only attributed when the context is known.

Another bidimensional theory has been proposed by Schlosberg (1952), who organized facial expressions in the pleasure–displeasure and the attention–rejection dimensions. Then he ordered six expressions in this circle: happiness, surprise, fear, anger, disgust, and contempt, according to the observed confusions between them.

Three independent dimensions are used in the PAD model (pleasure–arousal–dominance) (Mehrabian, 1980, 1995), while the model proposed by Fontaine et al. (2007) uses four dimensions for the representation of emotions: evaluation–pleasantness, potency–control, activation–arousal, and unpredictability. The latter model enables prediction of emotions in terms of dimensions and their behavior characteristics: for example, a state with high unpredictability would be characterized by raised eyebrows.

2.1.3 Componential Process Model Representations

According to appraisal theorists, an emotional state is created by the significance given to different elements of an event (Arnold, 1960; Lazarus, 1991; Scherer, 1999). This evaluation is subjective, with respect to the well being of the individual. Thus, the mental state is a function of the subjective appraisal and is not driven by a preprogrammed reaction. Furthermore, appraisal theorists see emotions as dynamic episodes that lead to changes on different levels, from cognitive and motivational processes to motor and physiological responses, or action preparation (e.g., Frijda, 1986; Roseman & Smith, 2001; Scherer, 1999).

Among these theories, the Componential Process Model (CPM; see Scherer, 1999) is often used because of its concrete predictions on the level of emotional behaviors that are linked theoretically to eliciting mechanisms. In the CPM each step of the subjective appraisal is linked to a facial response. Those facial movements are defined by Scherer and Ellgring (2007), researchers from the componential approach, in terms of action units (AU), which represent the position of particular muscles during an expression. The CPM states that it is the accumulation of the AU resulting from the step-by-step evaluation that creates the final emotional expression. Some neurophysiological studies have been realized already to confirm part of the predicted sequence of cognitive evaluations (e.g., Grandjean & Scherer, 2008).

On the level of the facial responses, the number of emotional expressions is very large, as the various elements of the facial expressions (AU) can co-occur in different patterns.

There are a great number of very differentiated emotional states, and they are captured by labels only through a process of grouping of different states, through some kind of averaging and central tendencies. Scherer names these "averaged" states "modal emotions" (Scherer, 2001). The modal emotions result from cognitive evaluation outcomes that are predominant in our daily lives. What is more, these modal states are labeled in a large number of languages through short verbal expressions, mostly single words.

2.1.4 Behavioral Ecology Representation

The *behavioral ecology view* (Fridlund, 1994) dispenses with the central role of emotions in creating facial expressions. Instead, there exist only facial displays that depend on intentions of the displayer and that are specific to the context. According to Alan Fridlund, facial displays are means of social communication rather than manifestations of internal emotional states. People may show a huge variety of facial displays that are not restricted to the expressions of their emotions. On the other hand, facial expressions like a *smile* or an *angry face* can be associated with a variety of internal states. The behavioral ecology supporters give also an alternative explanation of the concept of facial regulation of emotional displays. An expression described elsewhere as a fake one (e.g., a voluntary smile) is not an imperfect simulation of a spontaneous expression, but it is a distinct social communicative act.

2.2 Multimodal Expression of Emotions

In the previous section, we presented main theories and predictions on emotional facial displays. Recently the research on emotional displays starts being concerned with modalities different from the face. Indeed, some studies show that emotions can be also related to body movements (Pollick, 2004; Wallbott, 1998). Among others, the component process model proposed by Scherer (1999) claims that an emotion is a dynamic episode that produces a sequence of response patterns on the level of gestures, voice, and face (Scherer and Ellgring, 2007; Wallbott & Scherer, 1986). Moreover, some observational studies have explored the complexity of emotional expressions in terms of their dynamics and/or multimodality. Keltner (1995) studied the sequence of facial and gestural movement in embarrassment. He relied on the analysis of their appearance frequencies in audiovisual data. Shiota and colleagues studied three positive emotions: awe, amusement, and pride (Shiota et al., 2003). They showed that the three have expressions that are more than prototypical static facial expressions as described in Ekman and Friesen's work (1975). Rather, they are expressed by a set of possible signals, sometimes with asynchronous onsets, offsets, and apices. Consequently, the emotional expression is not to be seen as categorical, and not all elements have to be present in an expression at the same time, to be recognized as a display of a particular emotional state.

2.3 Emotional Expression Regulation

Although a direct link between an expression and an underlying emotion is often looked for, there is much evidence that the expressed emotion is not always the felt one (Ekman & Friesen, 1969; Fernandez-Dols & Ruiz-Belda, 1995). Indeed, the expressions of felt emotions are often suppressed, amplified, or feigned according to the social context (La France & Hecht, 2005) or personal goals (Saarni & Weber, 2005). Among others, obeying rules and social conventions often inclines people not to show their emotions in certain situations. For example, even if someone is angry with his boss, he will probably avoid expressing his emotions in front of his superior. Obeying these social rules gives a person a set of advantages of being socially acceptable.

In the Componential Process Model (Scherer, 1999), an emotion expression is driven by what Scherer calls "push and pull effects." The first one is the drive of internal changes on the exterior, motor changes, such as facial expression. The second one is the drive by social expectations and communicative codes (Scherer & Ellgring, 2007). In contrast, in behavioral ecology any expression (either felt or fake) is viewed as an important signal communicating different meaning. The management of facial behavior has also been discussed in the *discrete emotions theory* (e.g., Ekman & Friesen, 1969). According to the discrete emotion theorists, humans have a set of distinct expressions related to basic emotions at their disposal; however, these can be altered through a secondary process that acts on the normal, spontaneous, facial displays. The management of facial behavior has been studied by Ekman and Friesen, two authors who introduced the concept of *display rules*. Display rules are a set of procedures for the management of emotional displays. They reflect knowledge about how to act appropriately. There are three necessary conditions for applying display rules: knowledge, motivation, and behavior. People must *know* which facial expression is appropriate in a specific context. They must *want* to control the spontaneous facial reactions. Finally, they must *be able* to show an adequate facial display. Thus, the application of display rules implies more or less conscious control of facial behavior.

Application of a specific display rule was studied by many researchers. They individuated a set of variables that influence facial behavior management. Some of them are used to distinguish between cultures with different types of facial behavior (Americans vs. Japanese) (Kupperbusch et al., 2005; Matsumoto, 1990). A second group of variables explains the facial behavior of individuals in one culture. The use of some rules of facial behavior management may depend on the interlocutor (e.g., superior, child; Ekman & Friesen, 1975). We behave in a different way with our superior at work than with a friend. Others—so-called situational display rules, depend more on the situation than particular people involved. Thus, a certain type of behavior is expected during a funeral or wedding, irrespective of who is dead or married (Saarni & Weber, 2005). Finally, personal display rules contain particular habits and effects of past experiences as well as personality traits (Ekman & Friesen, 1975).

2.4 Expressivity

Some researchers contribute to the study of emotional expressions by focusing on their *expressivity*, that is, on the external, visible qualities of a movement, like its speed, amplitude, fluidity, and so on. Expressivity is an integral part of the communication process as it can provide information on the emotional state, mood, and personality of a person (Wallbott, 1998).

Several works on behavior expressivity of virtual agents are based on Laban Movement Analysis (LMA, Laban & Lawrence, 1974), an annotation scheme for describing human movement. In his theory, Laban proposed four main categories to describe a movement: body, effort, shape, and space. The first one describes structural and physical characteristics of the human body while moving. The *effort* component refers to the dynamics of the movement while the *shape* category to the way the body interacts with itself and its environment. The last category concerns movement in connection with the environment (e.g., spatial intention).

Many researchers like Wallbott and Scherer (1986), Gallaher (1992), and Pollick (2004) have investigated human motion characteristics and encoded them into categories. Some authors refer to body motion using dual qualifiers such as slow/fast, small/large, weak/energetic, unpleasant/pleasant. Behavior expressivity has been correlated with the energy in the communication, with the relation between temporal/spatial characteristics of gestures, and/or between personality/emotion.

For Wallbott (1998) the expressivity is related to the notion of quality of the mental, emotional, and/or physical state and to its quantity, somehow linked to the intensity factor of the mental/emotional/physical state. Behaviors encode not only the content information, that is, "What is communicated" through a gesture shape, but also the expressive information, that is, "How it is communicated" through the manner of execution of the gesture. Gallaher (1992) conducted a set of experiments to find the characteristics of the movement that capture the expressive style of the displayer. She gathers them into four dimensions: expressiveness, animation, expansiveness, and coordination. Moreover, Wallbott and Scherer (1986) and Pollick (2004) showed that the expressive qualities of nonverbal behaviors can be used to recognize emotional state in discrete and/or dimensional approaches.

3. Computational Models of Emotional Expressions

Computational models of emotional expressions have received growing interest. The models of expressive behaviors are crucial for virtual agents' believability (Aylett, 2004). The existing models of emotional behavior are based on one or more theories presented in the previous section. In this section we present a short survey of existing computational models of emotional expressions for virtual agents. First, we present models that rely on theory of discrete emotions. They combine elements of different facial expressions to obtain new ones. Then we will show various models that are based on the dimensional theories. In Section 3.3 we show first implementations of Scherer's componential theory. Finally, we show recent trials to generate multimodal expressions of emotions.

3.1 Models Based on Discrete Facial Expressions

The discrete emotion approaches provide concrete predictions on several emotional expressions. The idea of universality of the most common expressions of emotions was particularly sought to enable the generation of "well-recognizable" facial displays. What is more, the unitary nature of the expressions was particularly attractive for its simplicity for early computational models: the different elements (e.g., action units) of each expression are predicted to have a common development, with only one starting (onset) and one ending (offset) point and a common apex. However easy to categorize in terms of evoked emotions, the expressions based on discrete theory are still oversimplified. One method to enrich the emotional behavior of a virtual agent, while relying on discrete facial expressions, is to introduce blends (see Section 2.1.1). In works of Bui (2004), Niewiadomski and Pelachaud (2007, 2010), and Mao et al. (2008), these expressions are modeled using fuzzy methods.

Bui (Bui, 2004) uses a set of fuzzy rules to determine the blending expressions of six basic emotions based on works of Ekman and Friesen (1975). A subset of rules is attributed to each pair of emotions. The fuzzy inference determines the degrees of muscle contractions of the final expression as a function of the input emotion intensities. Expressions are obtained by combining expressions from the lower and upper face of both emotions. The rules are derived from Ekman and Friesen's work (1975) in which expressions of blend of emotions are detailed. For example, in the blend expression of surprise and fear, the upper face will display fear, and the lower face surprise.

Niewiadomski and Pelachaud (2010) have proposed another computational model of facial expressions based on fuzzy methods and discrete emotions theory. They use a face partition approach for the generation of various types of expressions like superposed, masked, fake, and inhibited expressions. In this approach each facial expression is defined over eight areas (brows, upper eyelids, eyes direction, lower eyelids, cheeks, nose, lips, and lips' tension). Each part of the face displays an emotion. In complex expressions, different emotions can be expressed on different areas of the face. The algorithm uses fuzzy rules to assign which signals of which simple expression go on the eight different facial areas. For example, in the expression of "sadness masked by happiness," sadness is shown on the eyebrows and upper eyelids area while happiness is displayed on the lips' areas. The method is extended to any simple facial expression of emotion by the application of fuzzy similarity (Niewiadomski & Pelachaud, 2007).

In Mao et al.'s (2008) model, the generation of the facial expression is realized in three layers, the first one being the physiological, the second emotional, and the third social layer. The authors consider: 14 physiological variables on the physiological level (e.g., adrenaline, blood pressure, or sneezing), 36 predefined emotional expressions (e.g., fear, reproach, or satisfaction), and six social expressions on the social level (e.g., disagreement or winking), and the resulting facial behavior is composed of the output of each layer processed separately, while taking in count the priorities given to each layer. In particular, the emotional layer outputs displays of complex emotional states. In more detail, the complex expression results from the processing of a fuzzy relation matrix between 36 predefined facial expressions and a number of emotions (i.e., the emotional state of the agent). This matrix contains many-to-many mappings between the fuzzy emotion vector and the fuzzy facial expression vector. Each value (e, f) in this matrix is a degree of membership expressing the probability that an emotion e is mapped to the expression f. Given an emotional states vector as input, the output is the fuzzy facial vector that is defuzzified to obtain a concrete (complex) expression. In the algorithm, the first and last layers work in parallel. The first layer may influence the way facial behavior is realized while the last layer may facilitate or inhibit emotional expressions and/or use some social signals instead of the direct expression of an internal state. These layers define a hierarchical system. The output of each layer may be modified by the output of the layer that has a higher priority.

3.2 Dimensional-Based Models

Models based on the dimensional approach are most often used because they allow the creation of a variety of expressions with subtle differences for related emotional states. In the models presented in this section, while the dimensional approach is crucial, they often propose a fusion with the discrete approach. For the purpose of this chapter, we divided the dimensional-based models into two sets: one group uses the linear interpolation between several discrete emotions, and the other uses the experimental empirical data and tries to associate some elements of facial expressions with certain areas of multidimensional space.

3.2.1 Linear Interpolation

Several models combine the dimensional and the discrete approaches. They use the expressions of simple emotional states, and they apply on them some arithmetical operations according to the position they occupy in some multidimensional spaces. The model called *Emotion Disc* (Ruttkay et al., 2003) uses a bilinear interpolation between two basic expressions and the neutral one. In the Emotion Disc, six expressions are spread evenly around the disc according to the Schlosberg's model (1952; see Section 2.1.2), while the neutral expression is represented by the center of it. The distance from the center of the circle represents the intensity of expression. The spatial relations are used to establish the expression corresponding to any point of the Emotion Disc.

Two models by Tsapatsoulis and colleagues (2002) and by Albrecht and colleagues (2005) use a similar approach to compute new emotional displays. Both models use the expressions of two "neighboring" emotions to compute the facial expressions for nonbasic emotions. For this purpose they use different multidimensional spaces, in which emotional labels are placed. In both approaches new expressions are constructed starting from the six Ekmanian expressions: anger, disgust, fear, happiness, sadness, and surprise. In more detail, in Tsapatsoulis et al.'s (2002) model two different approaches are used. First of all, a new expression can be derived from a basic one by "scaling" it. In the second approach, a new expression is generated by looking for the spatially closest two basic emotions as defined within the dimensional spaces proposed by Whissell (1989) and Plutchik (1980). Then the parameters of these expressions are weighted with their coordinates. Albrecht et al. (2005) proposed an extended approach. The authors use a three-dimensional space of emotional states defined by activation, evaluation, and power and anatomical model of the face based on FACS (Ekman et al., 2002).

The PAD model (see Section 2.2) was used in a study in which participants navigated in a 3D space with corresponding facial animations using a 3D control device (Courgeon et al., 2008). In this work eight expressions (fear, admiration, anger, joy, reproach, relief, distress, and satisfaction) were attributed to the extreme points of the three dimensions (valence, arousal, and dominance) while an interpolation of facial parameters defining an expression allowed for the generation of intermediate expressions (Courgeon et al., 2008).

3.2.2 Empirically Grounded Dimensional Models of Facial Behavior

Several models of emotional behavior link separate facial actions with some emotional dimensions like valence. Interestingly, most of them use the PAD model, which is a three-dimensional model defining emotions in terms of pleasure, arousal, and dominance (Mehrabian, 1980; see Section 2.2). Among others, Zhang and colleagues proposed an approach for the synthesis of facial expressions from PAD values (Zhang et al., 2007). First, the authors proposed a new parameterization of facial expressions: Partial Expression Parameters (PEPs). Each PEP defines a facial movement in a specific area of the face. A perceptive study evaluated how their set of PEPs is linked to participants' attributions of P, A, and D values. The validity of the expressions generated from PAD values was confirmed in an evaluation study, where participants had to attribute the PAD and emotional labels to the animations (Zhang et al., 2007).

Another facial expression model based on the three-dimensional model was proposed by Boukricha et al. (2009). An empirical study enabled the authors to map a correspondence between randomly generated facial expressions composed of several action units as defined with FACS (Ekman et al., 2002) and ratings in term of PAD values. These PAD ratings resulted from naive participants' evaluation of bipolar adjectives using a Likert scale (Semantic Differential Measures of Emotional State or Characteristic [Trait] Emotions), as proposed by Mehrabian and Russell (1974). The evaluated expressions were placed in the dimensional space, where Dominance takes one of two discrete values (high or low dominance) while Pleasure and Arousal values are mapped into a continuous space. A facial expressions control space is constructed with multivariate regressions, which enables the authors to associate a facial expression to each point in the space.

A similar method was applied previously by Grammer and Oberzaucher (2006), whose work relies only on the two dimensions of pleasure and arousal. Their model can be used for the creation of facial expressions relying on the action units defined in the FACS (Ekman et al., 2002) and situated in the two-dimensional space. The authors also run a perceptive study to place randomly generated facial expressions in the dimensional space and performed a multiple-multivariate regression, enabling a mapping between AUs and the two dimensions. This model was validated by checking the position of the six basic emotions in their 2D space.

Arya and colleagues (2009) propose a perceptually valid model for emotion blends. In a perceptive study, human participants had to create facial expressions associated to mixed emotions on a 3D face model. For this purpose they were asked to illustrate short stories with blending expressions. A PCA analysis was performed to find the association between facial actions and emotions. Fuzzy rules are generated from the statistical analysis of the facial expressions created in the experiment by the participants. These rules associate specific facial actions with the three-dimensional space of valence, arousal, and agency. Contrary to Bui, whose fuzzy rules were activated depending on the intensity of emotions, in Arya et al.'s (2009) model the fuzzy values in 3D space are used to activate the agent's face.

Recently, Stoiber et al. (2009) proposed an interface for the generation of facial expressions of a virtual agent. The interface allows one to generate facial expressions of the agent using 2D custom control space. The underlying graphics model is based on the analysis of the deformation of a real human face. For this purpose an image database has been elaborated. It contains sequences of unlabeled images of an actor performing various facial expressions of different intensities. Facial expressions are created through the deformation of both the geometry and the texture of a facial model. The approach is based on the principal component analysis of the facial expressions database. The geometrical and textural variation of the human face is detected and automatically described in a low-dimensional space. The authors do not rely on a predefined emotional dimensional space (see models presented in Section 3.2.1), but they build a custom 2D control space. With such an approach, it is assured that each point of the space corresponds to a realistic facial expression. Using this interface the user can create a large variety of emotional expressions of different intensities, including various mixed expressions, as well as the fluent sequences of expressions.

3.3 Beyond Static Expressions of Emotions

As we have seen in an earlier section, most research on models of emotional displays focus on facial expressions. Recent results in psychology (e.g., Keltner, 1995; Shiota et al., 2003) show, however, that several emotions are expressed by a set or a sequence of different nonverbal behaviors, which are arranged in a certain interval of time rather than by a static facial expression. The expressions of emotional states are dynamic, and they can be displayed over different modalities like the face, gaze, and head movement (Keltner, 1995); gestures (Keltner, 1995); or even posture (Pollick, 2004; Wallbott, 1998). The multimodal expression of emotions in ECA recently gained interest. Among others, Clavel et al. (2009) studied the role of the face and posture in the recognition of ECAs' emotional expressions through two studies. One study showed that the integration of the facial and postural changes into the ECAs' emotional behavior affects users' overall perception of basic emotions and has an impact on the attribution of the valence and activation values to the animations. A second study shows an improvement of emotion recognition when facial and postural changes are congruent. The authors observed that the judgments were mainly based on the information sent by the face, although adding congruent postures improves the interpretation of the facial expression (Clavel et al., 2009).

In the sections that follow, we present some recent models of emotional displays that introduce the multimodality and sequentiality into nonverbal emotional ECA behavior. First, we focus on the works that model the dynamics of emotional display. Then we present models that enable the generation of dynamically changing multimodal expressions of emotions. Often they combine several theories, like the discrete with the componential (Niewiadomski et al., 2009a, 2009b) or the discrete with the dimensional one (Lance & Marsella, 2007).

3.3.1 Dynamic Expressions of Emotions Based on Observational Studies

The dynamics of emotional expressions is modeled by Pan et al. (2007). First of all, certain sequences of signals (facial expressions and head movements) were extracted from a videocorpus. From this real data, Pan et al. built a motion graph in which the arcs are the observed sequences of signals and nodes are possible transitions between them. The different paths in the graph correspond to different expressions of emotions. Thus, new animations can be generated by reordering the observed displays. Mana and Pianesi (2006) use Hidden Markov Models to model the dynamics of emotional expressions during speech acts. The system was trained on the acted samples that contain nonsense utterances and acted emotional facial expressions with different intensities. Then it was used to animate the Xface toolkit (Balci et al., 2007).

3.3.2 Models Based on the Componential Appraisal Theory

Some researchers were inspired by the Componential Process Model (Scherer, 2001), which states that different cognitive evaluations of the environment lead to specific facial behaviors. Paleari and Lisetti (2006) and Malatesta et al. (2009) focus on the temporal relations between different facial actions predicted by the sequential evaluation checks (SECs) of the CPM model. Some of these (novelty, intrinsic pleasantness, conduciveness, and coping potential; see Scherer, 2001) are linked to expectations in terms of particular subexpressions that are defined in terms of facial action units (Ekman, Friesen, & Hager, 2002). In Paleari et al.'s (2007) work, the different facial parameters are activated at different moments. The final animation that is generated on the virtual agent's face is a sequence of several subexpressions linked to the SECs's cognitive evaluations.

Also in Malatesta et al.'s (2009) work, the emotional expressions are created manually from sequences predicted in Scherer's theory (2001). Differently from Paleari and Lisetti's work, each expression is derived from the addition of a new AU to the former ones. What is more, Malatesta et al. (2009) compared an additive approach (where each predicted AU contributes to a facial expression by being activated along the former AUs) with a sequential one (where each predicted AU is activated after the offset of former AUs and not along). Results show an above-chance-level recognition in the case of the additive approach, whereas the sequential approach gives recognition results marginally above random choice (Malatesta et al., 2009).

3.3.3 Multimodal Sequential Expressions of Emotions Based on Observational Studies

In this section we present recent models that generate both sequential and multimodal expressions of emotions. Lance and Marsella (2007, 2008) propose a model of emotional gaze shifts toward an arbitrary target. In their approach they combine two animation methods: motion capture based and procedural animation. First of all, Lance and Marsella (2007) focus on the head and body movements in gaze shifts. They map these movements into the PAD dimensional model. For this purpose, a set of parameters called Gaze Warping Transformation (GWT), describing how the emotional multimodal displays differ from the neutral ones, has been extracted from the recordings of acted emotional displays. The head and body movement data were captured through three motion sensors. The Gaze Warping Transformations are a combination of temporal scaling and spatial transformation parameters that are obtained from the difference between two gaze shifts directed from the same point to the same target, one being emotionally expressive and the other emotionally neutral. Finally, any emotionally expressive gaze shifts toward an arbitrarily placed target can be produced by applying GWTs to any captured neutral gaze shift.

In a second stage, a procedural model of eye movement has been added to the gaze shifts model (Lance and Marsella, 2008). This model uses several classes of gaze movements that are composed of saccade and vestibulo-ocular reflex movements. Finally, the procedural eye movement is automatically added to head and torso movement generated with GWT. Consequently, an emotional state of the agent is expressed using the GWT, while the procedural model of eye movement ensures realistic motion. The model is able to generate sequences of gaze shifts expressing the same or different emotional states.

The model presented by Niewiadomski et al. (2009a, 2009b) generates emotional expressions composed of nonverbal behaviors displayed over different modalities, of a sequence of behaviors or of expressions within one modality that change dynamically. The model is based on both video annotations and

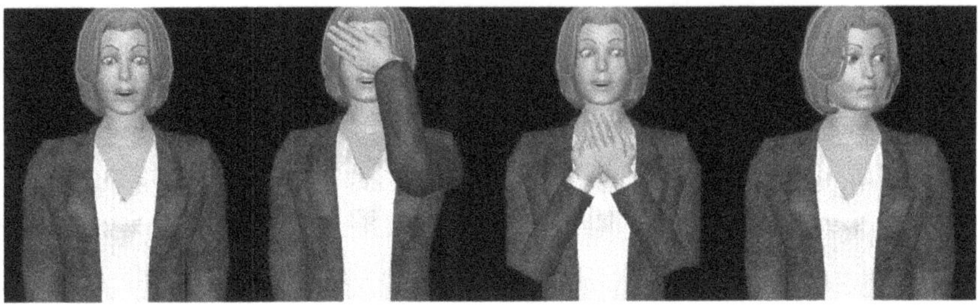

FIGURE 9.2 An example of a multimodal expression, based on the annotation of panic fear (source: Niewiadomski et al., 2009a).

on the data reported from the literature (see Section 2.2). Videos are annotated with FACS (Ekman et al., 2002) for the face and with free labels for the other parts of the body (e.g., head nod, raising of an arm). From the analysis of the multimodal annotation emerge that these signals are not arranged freely and that some relational patterns can be established. Signal description is gathered into two sets: behavior set and constraint set. Each emotional state has its own behavior set, which contains signals that might be used by the virtual agent to display that emotion. Then, relations between the signals of one behavior set are described in a constraint set with an XML-based language. Two types of constraints are considered. *Temporal* constraints specified by arithmetic operators define the relations between the starting and ending time of a signal while *appearance* constraints describe more general relations between the signals (e.g., if two signals cannot appear together, or that the appearance of one signal always coincides with the appearance of another one).

The algorithm takes as input a given emotion and generates a sequence of signals, in other words, the animation of a given duration *t* composed of a sequence of signals on different modalities. It does so by choosing an appropriate subset of signals from the behavior set, their durations, and order of display. Each generated sequence has to satisfy all temporal and appearance constraints. The model was integrated within the Greta agent (Niewiadomski et al., 2009c). Figure 9.2 illustrates a sequence of signals related to the panic fear emotion. This algorithm can generate different animations, each satisfying the temporal and appearance constraints, for a given emotion. Figure 9.3 shows two sequences for a same emotion, embarrassment.

4. Behavior Expressivity

The qualitative execution of a gesture and of an expression is very representative for an emotional state (Wallbott & Scherer, 1986). Behavior expressivity has been studied through perceptual tests (Wallbott, 1998), analysis models (Caridakis et al., 2006), and also in the context of dance (Laban & Lawrence, 1974).

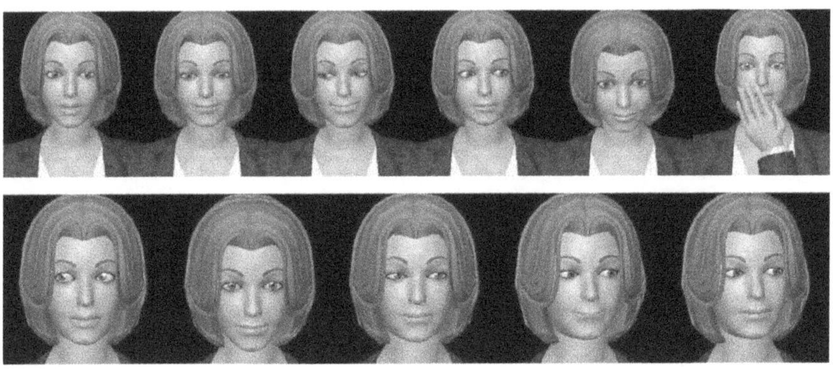

FIGURE 9.3 Two examples of a multimodal expression of embarrassment (source: Niewiadomski et al., 2009b).

In ECAs' domain, Ruttkay and colleagues have proposed a representation language that encompasses behavior styles (Ruttkay & Noot, 2005). An agent is described along a large number of dimensions ranging from its cultural, professional, emotional, and physical states. All these dimensions act on the way the agent behaves.

Several agent systems are able to modulate the execution of nonverbal behaviors. In Allbeck and Badler (2003), the choice of nonverbal behavior and the movement quality depends on the agent's personality and its emotional state. The way in which the agent performs its movements is influenced by a set of high-level parameters derived from the Laban Movement Analysis (Laban & Lawrence, 1974; see also Section 2.4), and implemented in the Expressive Motion Engine (EMOTE; Chi et al., 2000). The authors use two of the four categories of the Laban's annotation schema: *Effort* and *Shape*. The Effort corresponds to the dynamics of the movement, and it is defined in this model by four parameters: space: (relation with the surrounding space: direct/indirect), weight (impact of movement: strong/light), time (urgency of movement: sudden/sustained), and flow (control of movement: bound/free). The Shape component describes the body movement in relation to the environment. In Allbeck and Badler's model, this component is described using three dimensions: horizontal (spreading/enclosing), vertical (rising/sinking), and sagittal (advancing/retreating). Once it has been computed, EMOTE acts on the animation as a filter. The model adds expressivity to the final animation. It can also be used to express some properties of the agent or its emotional state. For this purpose the EMOTE parameters were mapped to the emotional states (OCC model; Ortony et al., 1988) and personality traits (OCEAN model; Goldberg, 1993).

Neff and Fiume (2002, 2003) proposed a pose control model that takes into account several features of the nonverbal behavior such as the timing of movement, the fluent transition between different poses, and its expressive qualities. In particular, for each defined body posture different properties can be defined like its tension, amplitude, or extent. The model allows an animator to vary, for example, how much space an agent occupies during a movement or to define whether the posture should be relaxed or tensed.

Hartmann et al. (2006) proposed a nonverbal behavior expressivity model based on perceptual studies conducted by Gallaher (1992), Wallbott and Scherer (1986), and Wallbott (1998). These works define a large number of dimensions that characterize expressivity. Hartmann et al. have implemented six of them (see Figure 9.4). Three of them, spatial extent, temporal extent, and power, act on the parameters defining the gestures and the facial expressions. They modify, respectively, the amplitude of a signal that corresponds to the physical displacement of a facial feature or the wrist position, movement duration (linked to the execution velocity of the movement), and the dynamic properties of movement (namely, the acceleration). Another dimension, fluidity, works over several behaviors of a given modality. It specifies the degree of fluidity between consecutive behaviors. The last two dimensions, global activity and repetitivity, refer to the quantity of signals and to their repetition. This model has been used to create distinctive agents, that is, agents whose communicative behaviors can be distinguished one from the others (Mancini & Pelachaud, 2008) (see Figure 9.5). In their model Mancini and Pelachaud use these six parameters to define both overall and dynamic qualities of the agent's nonverbal behaviors. They introduce two structures: the *Baseline* is a set of fixed parameters that represent the overall agent behavior through time, while the *Dynamicline* corresponds to the expressive qualities of the nonverbal behaviors influenced by the current communicative goals and emotional state of

FIGURE 9.4 Variation of the spatial extent parameter (Hartmann et al., 2006).

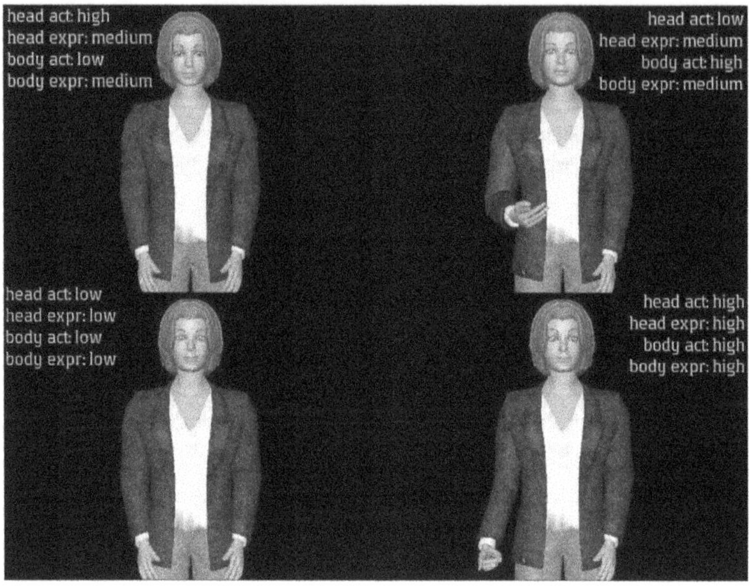

FIGURE 9.5 Examples of distinctive agents (Mancini & Pelachaud, 2008). The four agents displayed different communicative behaviors depending on their behavior expressivity.

the agent. This approach allows one to generate animations that differ in the quality of movement for different agents as well as to modify the expressive qualities of nonverbal behavior for a particular emotional state. Thus, for example, if an agent has a general tendency (Baseline) to perform few movements with a slow speed and low amplitude, then in a sad state it could simply stop moving, as sadness tends to reduce the activation parameter; on the other hand, an agent with a general tendency of moving a lot with fast and large movements will continue to make movements even when being sad, although with a lower frequency, speed, and amplitude.

5. Emotional Expression Regulation Models

When we interact we take into account several factors to decide in a more or less conscious way which intentions and emotional states to communicate. These factors encompass the social and affective relations we have with our interlocutor, our respective roles, the power one has on the interlocutor, and so on. Growing up and living in a given society, we learn not to be impulsive and to control our behavior. We are aware of the expressions that can be displayed in different circumstances and to whom. Ekman and Friesen (1969) use the term *display rules* to describe the rules that are prescribed in our social, cultural, professional, and affective environments. ECAs are viewed as social entities, and as such it is important to consider social context when determining which emotional display the ECA should show.

Several research teams studied the role of appropriate emotional displays on the perception of virtual agents. An inattentive application of facial expressions to virtual agents may influence negatively the user's evaluation of the agent. In Walker et al.'s study (Walker et al., 1994), people liked less the facial interface that displayed a negative expression compared with the one that showed a neutral expression. It does not mean that the negative expressions are not desirable at all. In a card game scenario, the negative expressions expressed by an agent (if situated in the context) were evaluated positively. The agent that expressed only positive expressions, irrespective of the situation, was evaluated to be worse that the other one that expressed also negative emotions (Becker et al., 2005). Thus, even in ECAs the emotional displays should be adequate to the context. Niewiadomski et al. (2010) evaluated the believability, warmth, and competence of virtual agents showing various nonverbal emotional displays. In their evaluation study, the authors used three different versions of the agent showing (non)appropriate and/or (non)plausible emotional displays. Interestingly, human subjects evaluated as more warm the agent showing nonplausible expressions than the one showing nonappropriate (i.e., not adapted to the context) but plausible emotional displays.

There exist several models that adapt the verbal context to the situation (e.g., André et al., 2004; Walker et al., 1996). Surprisingly, only few models of facial behavior regulation of an ECA have been proposed so far. Prendinger and Ishizuka modeled "social role awareness" in animated agents (Prendinger & Ishizuka, 2001). They introduced a set of procedures called "social filter programs." These procedures are like rules for facial expression management. Defining social filter programs, the authors considered both social conventions (politeness) and personalities of interlocutors. The social filter program defines the intensity of an expression as the function of a social threat (power and distance), user personality (agreeableness, extroversion), and the intensity of emotion. As a result, it can either increase or decrease the intensity of facial expression, or even totally inhibit it. The evaluation study shows the influence of "social role awareness" on the perception of "naturalness" of the agent.

The agent called *Reflexive Agent* (de Carolis et al., 2001) is also able to adapt its expressions of emotions according to the situational context. This agent analyzes various factors in order to decide about either displaying or not its emotional state: emotional nature factors (i.e. valence, social acceptance, emotion of the addressee) and scenario factors (i.e., personality, goals, type of relationship, type of interaction). In particular, the Reflexive Agent uses regulation rules that define for which values of these factors a concrete emotion can (or cannot) be displayed (de Carolis et al., 2001).

In Niewiadomski and Pelachaud (2010), a virtual agent can inhibit an expression, mask it by another one, or show a fake expression depending on the social context. The facial expression management model is based on two out of the three variables defined in Brown and Levinson's (1987) theory of politeness, namely, social and power distances. The output of the management module is a complex expression (see Section 3.1) defined as the modulation of the agent's default emotional displays depending on the valence of the agent's displayed emotion and the social distance and power between interlocutors.

Niewiadomski et al. (2008) studied the appropriate emotional displays of a virtual agent in empathic situations. They distinguish between four types of expressions: the egocentric expression of a felt emotional state, the expression of empathic emotion, and two different blends of both of them (superposition and masking). According to the evaluation results, people find more adequate facial expressions that contain elements of emotion of empathy. Thus, the agents should, rather, hide their real emotional states and show the empathic emotions.

6. Conclusion

In this chapter we have presented various computational models of expressive behaviors for virtual agents. These models are based on different theories of emotions. Some models, in particular, the early models, consider mainly the expressions of the six basic emotions as predicted by the discrete emotion theory, in particular by Ekman (2003b). Models based on the dimensional approach compute facial expressions of an emotion specified by its coordinates in 2D or 3D space using a combinatorial approach. These approaches ensure the creation of a large variety of facial expressions.

Both of these types of models view the expressions of emotions as conveyed mainly by static facial expressions. Other works, based on the appraisal theory, have developed dynamic models of behaviors; that is, the emotional behavior of an agent is obtained by a rapid succession of subexpressions. The subexpressions can be defined either from theory, and more particularly on Scherer's work (2001), or from videocorpus annotation.

Few models encompass multimodality. Emotions are not conveyed solely through the face but also with the whole body. The modalities are not independent from one another. They are coordinated to convey a coherent message. Last but not least, behavior expressivity is an important factor of emotion communication and has been implemented within virtual agents.

The latest works are looking into subtle and complex research areas such as multimodality or social context. Some interesting results have been obtained. However, more research needs to be undertaken, especially in modeling a large variety of emotional expressions and how social and cultural context modulate their communication. When conversing with a human user, in a particular context, for a given role and application, agents need to follow the corresponding sociocultural rules and display emotional expressions accordingly. Agents should be endowed with the capacity to mask their emotional states, to exaggerate one, and so on. Another direction of research regards the modeling of individual differences in expressions. Agents have generic behaviors. They can hardly be distinguished one from the others. It is a necessary step to develop agents differing not only by their geometry but also by their expressive behaviors.

Acknowledgments

The authors of this chapter have been partially supported by the EU-funded Social Signals Processing Network of Excellence (SSPNET) and by the French projects ANR-IMMEMO and ANR-CECIL.

7. References

Allbeck, J., & Badler, N. (2003). Representing and parameterizing agent behaviors. In, H. Prendinger & M. Ishizuka (Eds.), Life-like Characters: Tools, affective functions and applications (pp. 19–38). Germany: Springer.

Albrecht, I., Schröder, M., Haber, J., & Seidel, H. P. (2005). Mixed feelings: Expression of non-basic emotions in a muscle-based talking head. Special issue of *Journal of Virtual Reality* on "Language, Speech and Gesture," 8(4), 201–212.

André, E., Rehm, M., Minker, W., & Buhler, D. (2004). Endowing spoken language dialogue systems with emotional intelligence. In E. André, L. Dybkjær, W. Minker, & P. Heisterkamp (Eds.), *Affective dialogue systems,* Lecture Notes in Computer Science Volume 3068 (pp. 178–187), Springer Berlin Heidelberg.

Argyle, M., & Cook, M. (1976). *Gaze and mutual gaze.* Cambridge University Press.

Arnold, M. B. (1960). *Emotion and personality.* New York: Columbia University Press.

Arya, A., Di Paola, S., & Parush, A. (2009). Perceptually valid facial expressions for character-based applications. *International Journal of Computer Games Technology, 2009,* 1–13.

Aylett, R. S. (2004, May). Agents and affect: Why embodied agents need affective systems. Invited paper, 3rd Hellenic Conference on AI, Samos. *Springer Verlag LNAI, 3025,* 496–504.

Balci, K., Not, E., Zancanaro, M., & Pianesi, F. (2007). Xface open source project and SMIL-agent scripting language for creating and animating embodied conversational agents. ACM Multimedia, 1013–1016.

Becker, C., Wachsmuth, I., Prendinger, H., & Ishizuka, M. (2005). Evaluating affective feed-back of the 3D agent Max in a competitive cards game. In J. Tao, T. Tan, & R.W. Picard (Eds.), *Proceedings of the International Conference on Affective Computing and Intelligent Interaction (ACII), Beijing, China,* Lecture Notes in Computer Science Volume 3784 (pp. 466–473). Springer Berlin Heidelberg .

Bergmann, K., & Kopp, S. (2009). Increasing expressiveness for virtual agents – Autonomous generation of speech and gesture for spatial description tasks. In K. Decker, J. Sichman, C. Sierra, & C. Castelfranchi (Eds.), *Proceedings of the 8th International Conference on Autonomous Agents and Multiagent Systems (AAMAS 2009),* Budapest, Hungary (pp. 361–368), International Foundation for Autonomous Agents and Multiagent Systems.

Bevacqua, E., Prepin, K., Niewiadomski, R., de Sevin, E., & Pelachaud, C. (2010). Greta: Towards an interactive conversational virtual companion. In Y. Wilks (Ed.), *Close engagements with artificial companions: Key social, psychological, ethical and design issues* (pp. 143–156). John Benjamins Publishing Company.

Bickmore, T., & Picard, R.W. (2005). Establishing and maintaining long-term human-computer relationships. *ACM Transactions on Computer Human Interaction* (ToCHI), 59(1), 21–30.

Bickmore, T., Pfeifer, L., & Yin, L. (2008). The role of gesture in document explanation by embodied conversational agents. *International Journal of Semantic Computing,* 2(1), 47–70.

Boukricha, H., Wachsmuth, I., Hofstaetter, A., & Grammer, K. (2009). Pleasure-arousal-dominance driven facial expression simulation. In *Proceedings of Third International Conference on Affective Computing and Intelligent Interaction (ACII 2009)* (pp. 119–125). Amsterdam, IEEE Computer Society.

Brave, S., Nass, C., & Hutchinson, K. (2005). Computers that care: Investigating the effects of orientation of emotion exhibited by an embodied computer agent. *International Journal of Human-Computer Studies,* 62, 161–178.

Brown, P., & Levinson, S. C. (1987). *Politeness: Some universals on language usage.* Cambridge University Press.

Bui, T. D. (2004). *Creating emotions and facial expressions for embodied agents.* (Unpublished doctoral dissertation). Center for Telematics and Information Technology, University of Twente. The Netherlands.

Caridakis, G., Raouzaiou, A., Karpouzis, K., & Kollias, S. (2006, May). Synthesizing gesture expressivity based on real sequences. In workshop "Multimodal corpora. From multimodal behaviour theories to usable models" (pp. 19–23), 5th international Conference on Language Resources and Evaluation (LREC'2006), Genova, Italy.

Cassell, J. (2001). Embodied conversational agents: Representation and intelligence in user interface. *AI Magazine*, *22*(3), 67–83.

Cassell, J., Bickmore, T. W., Billinghurst, M., Campbell, L., Chang, K., Vilhjalmsson, H. H., & Yan, H. (1999). Embodiment in conversational interfaces: Rea. In *Proceedings of the SIGCHI Conference on Human Factors in Computing Systems (CHI'99)* (pp. 520–527), ACM New York, NY.

Cassell, J., Bickmore, T., Campbell, L., Vilhjálmsson, H., & Yan, H. (2000). Human conversation as a system framework: Designing embodied conversational agents. In J. Cassell, J. Sullivan, S. Prevost, & E. Churchill (Eds.), *Embodied conversational agents* (pp. 29–63). Cambridge, MA: MIT Press.

Cavé, C., Guaïtella, I., Bertrand, R., Santi, S., Harlay, F., & Espesser, R. (1996). About the relationship between eyebrow movements and F0 variations. In *Proceedings of the 4th International Conference on Spoken Language Processing (ICSLP-1996)* (pp. 2175–2178).

Chi, D., Costa, M., Zhao, L., & Badler, N. (2000). The EMOTE model for effort and shape. In *Proceedings of SIGGRAPH'2000* (pp. 173–182).

Clavel, C., Plessier, J., Martin, J.-C., Ach, L., & Morel, B. (2009). Combining facial and postural expressions of emotions in a virtual character. In *Proceedings of the 9th International Conference on Intelligent Virtual Agents (IVA 2009), Amsterdam*, Lecture Notes in Computer Science Volume 5773 (pp. 287–300), Springer Berlin Heidelberg.

Courgeon, M., Martin, J. C., & Jacquemin, C. (2008). User's gestural exploration of different virtual agents' expressive profiles. In *Proceedings of the 7th International Joint Conference on Autonomous Agents and Multiagent Systems (AAMAS 2008), Estoril, Portugal* (pp. 1237–1240), International Foundation for Autonomous Agents and Multiagent Systems.

De Carolis, B., Pelachaud, C., Poggi, I., & De Rosis, F. (2001). Behavior planning for a reflexive agent. *Proceedings of the 17th International Joint Conference on Artificial Intelligence (IJCAI 2001), Seattle, WA* (pp. 1059–1064), Morgan Kaufmann Publishers Inc., San Francisco, CA

Devillers, L., Abrilian, S., & Martin, J.-C. (October, 2005). *Representing real life emotions in audiovisual data with non basic emotional patterns and context features.* First International Conference on Affective Computing and Intelligent Interaction (ACII'2005), Beijing, China, Lecture Notes in Computer Science Volume 3784 (pp. 519–526), Springer Berlin Heidelberg.

Ekman, P. (1979). About brows: Emotional and conversational signals. In M. von Cranach, K. Foppa, W. D. Lepenies, & D Ploog (Eds.), *Human ethology* (pp. 169–248). Cambridge, UK: Cambridge University Press.

Ekman, P. (1999). Facial expressions. In T. Dalgleish & T. Power (Eds.), *The handbook of cognition and emotion* (pp. 301–320). Sussex, UK: John Wiley and Sons, Ltd.

Ekman, P. (2003a). Darwin, masking, and facial expression. *Annals of the New York Academy of Sciences, 1000*, 205–221.

Ekman, P. (2003b). *The face revealed.* London: Weidenfeld and Nicolson.

Ekman, P., & Friesen, W. V. (1969). The repertoire of nonverbal behavior: Categories, origins, usage, and coding. *Semiotica, 1*, 49–98.

Ekman, P., & Friesen, W. (1975). *Unmasking the face. A guide to recognizing emotions from facial clues.* Englewood Cliffs, NJ: Prentice-Hall, Inc.

Ekman, P., Friesen, W. V., & Hager, J. C. (2002). Facial Action Coding System: The Manual on CD ROM. A Human Face, Salt Lake City.

Endrass, B., Rehm, M., & André, E. (2009). Culture-specific communication management for virtual agents. In *Proceedings of 8th International Conference on Autonomous Agents and Multiagent Systems (AAMAS 09), Budapest, Hungary* (pp. 281–288), International Foundation for Autonomous Agents and Multiagent Systems, Richland, SC.

Fernandez-Dols, J. M., & Ruiz-Belda, J. A. (1995). Are smiles a sign of happiness? Gold medal winners at the Olympic Games. *Journal of Personality and Social Psychology*, *69*(6), 1113–1119.

Fontaine, J. R., Scherer, K. R., Roesch, E. B., & Ellsworth, P. (2007). The world of emotion is not two-dimensional. *Psychological Science, 13*, 1050–1057.

Fridlund, A. (1994). *Human facial expression: An evolutionary view.* San Diego, CA: Academic Press.

Frijda, N. H. (1986). *The emotions.* Cambridge, UK; New York: Cambridge University Press.

Gallaher, P. (1992). Individual differences in nonverbal behavior: Dimensions of style. *Journal of Personality and Social Psychology*, *63*, 133–145.

Goldberg, L. R. (1993). The structure of phenotypic personality traits. *American Psychologist, 48*, 26–34.

Gosselin, P., Kirouac, G., & Dore, F. Y. (1995). Components and recognition of facial expression in the communication of emotion by actors. In P. Ekman & E. L. Rosenberg (Eds.), *What the face reveals: Basic and applied studies of spontaneous expression using the Facial Action Coding System (FACS)* (pp. 243–267). New York: Oxford University Press.

Graesser, A., Chipman, P., King, B., McDaniel, B., & D'Mello, S. (2007). Emotions and learning with AutoTutor. In *Proceedings of the 2007 Conference on Artificial Intelligence in Education* (pp. 569–571), IOS Press Amsterdam, The Netherlands.

Grammer, K., & Oberzaucher, E. (2006). The reconstruction of facial expressions in embodied systems: New approaches to an old problem. *ZIF Mitteilungen, 2*, 14–31.

Grandjean, D., & Scherer, K. R. (2008). Unpacking the cognitive architecture of emotion processes. *Emotion*, 8(3), 341–351.

Granström, B., House, D., & Beskow, J. (2002). Speech and gestures for talking faces in conversational dialogue systems. In B. Granström, D. House, & I. Karlsson (Eds.), *Multimodality in language and speech systems* (pp. 209–241). Dordrecht, The Netherlands: Kluwer.

Gratch, J., Wang, N., Gerten, J., Fast, E., & Duffy, R. (September, 2007). *Creating rapport with virtual agents*. 7th International Conference on Intelligent Virtual Agents, Paris, Lecture Notes in Computer Science Volume 4722 (pp. 125–138). Springer Berlin Heidelberg.

Hartmann, B., Mancini, M., & Pelachaud, C. (2006). Implementing expressive gesture synthesis for embodied conversational agents. In *Proceedings of International Gesture Workshop, Lecture Notes in Computer Science* (Vol. 3881, pp. 188–199). Springer Berlin Heidelberg .

Heylen, D. K. J. (2006). Head gestures, gaze and the principles of conversational structure. *International Journal of Humanoid Robotics*, 3(3), 241–267.

Izard, C. E. (1977). *Human emotions*. New York: Plenum.

Izard, C. E. (1992). Basic emotions, relations among emotions, and emotion-cognitive relations. *Psychological Review*, 99, 561–565.

Johnson, W. L., Rickel, J. W., & Lester, J. (2000). Animated pedagogical agents: Face-to-face interaction in interactive learning environment. *International Journal of Artificial Intelligence in Education, 11*, 47–78.

Kaiser, S., & Wehrle, T. (2001). Facial expressions as indicators of appraisal processes. In K. R. Scherer, A. Schorr, & T. Johnstone (Eds.), *Appraisal processes in emotions: Theory, methods, research* (pp. 285–300). New York: Oxford University Press.

Keltner, D. (1995). Signs of appeasement: Evidence for the distinct displays of embarrassment, amusement, and shame. *Journal of Personality and Social Psychology*, 68, 441–454.

Keltner, D., & Buswell, B. N. (1997). Embarrassment: Its distinct form and appeasement functions. *Psychological Bulletin, 122*, 250–270.

Kendon, A. (2004). *Gesture: Visible action as utterance.* Cambridge University Press.

Kopp, S., Jung, B., Leßmann, N., & Wachsmuth, I. (2003). Max—A multimodal assistant in virtual reality construction. *KI-Künstliche Intelligenz, 4*, 17–23.

Krahmer, E., & Swerts, M. (2004). Signaling and detecting uncertainty in audiovisual speech by children and adults. In Proceedings of Interspeech 2004: 8th International Conference on Spoken Language Processing, Jeju Island (Korea) 1141–1144, Sunjin Printing Company.

Kupperbusch, C., Matsumoto, D., Kooken, K., Loewinger, S., Uchida, H., Wilson-Cohn, C., & Yrizarry, N. (2005). Cultural influences on nonverbal expressions of emotion. In P. Philippot, R. S. Feldman, & E. J. Coats (Eds.), *The social context of nonverbal behavior (studies in emotion and social interaction)* (pp. 17–44). Cambridge University Press.

Laban, R., & Lawrence, F. (1974). *Effort: Economy in body movement.* Boston: Plays Inc.

La France, M., & Hecht M. A. (2005). *Option or obligation to smile: The effects of power and gender and facial expression.* In P. Philippot, R. S. Feldman, & E. J. Coats (Eds.), The social context of nonverbal behavior (studies in emotion and social interaction) (pp. 45–70). Cambridge University Press.

Lance, B. J., & Marsella, S. C. (2007). Emotionally expressive head and body movements during gaze shifts. In *Proceedings of the 7th International Conference on Intelligent Virtual Agents (IVA), Paris.* Springer. Lecture Notes in Computer Science Volume 4722 (pp. 72–85), Springer Berlin Heidelberg.

Lance, B. J., & Marsella, S. C. (2008). A model of gaze for the purpose of emotional expression in virtual embodied agents. In *Proceedings of the 7th International Joint Conference on Autonomous Agents and Multiagent Systems, Estoril, Portugal* (pp. 199–206). International Foundation for Autonomous Agents and Multiagent Systems, Richland, SC.

Lazarus, R. (1991). *Emotion and adaptation.* New York: Oxford University Press

Malatesta, L., Raouzaiou, A., Karpouzis, K., & Kollias, S. D. (2009). Towards modeling embodied conversational agent character profiles using appraisal theory predictions in expression synthesis. *Applied Intelligence*, 30(1), 58–64.

Mana, N., & Pianesi, F. (2006). HMM-based synthesis of emotional facial expressions during speech in synthetic talking heads. In *Proceedings of the 8th International Conference on Multimodal interfaces (ICMI 2006)* (pp. 380–387), ACM New York, NY

Mancini, M., & Pelachaud, C. (2008). Distinctiveness in multimodal behaviors. In *Proceedings of the Seventh International Joint Conference on Autonomous Agents and Multi-Agent Systems*, AAMAS'08, Estoril Portugal (pp. 159–166), International Foundation for Autonomous Agents and Multiagent Systems, Richland, SC.

Manstead, A. S. R., Fischer, A. H., & Jakobs, E. B. (2005). The social and emotional functions of facial displays. In P. Philippot, R. S. Feldman, & E. J. Coats (Eds.), *The social context of nonverbal behavior (studies in emotion and social interaction)* (pp. 287–316). Cambridge University Press.

Mao, X., Xue, Y., Li, Z., & Bao, H. (2008). Layered fuzzy facial expression generation: Social, emotional and physiological. In Or, J. (Ed.), *Affective computing, focus on emotion expression, synthesis and recognition* (pp. 185–218). Vienna, Austria: I-Tech Education and Publishing.

Marsella, S., & Gratch, J. (2009). EMA: A process model of appraisal dynamics. *Cognitive Systems Research, 10*(1), 70–90.

Martin, J.-C., Buisine, S., Pitel, G., & Bernsen, N. O. (2006). Fusion of children's speech and 2D gestures when conversing with 3D characters. *Journal Signal Processing. Special Issue on Multimodal Human-Computer Interfaces*, 86(12), 3596–3624.

Martin, J.-C., Sansonnet, J.-P., Braffort, A., & Verrecchia, C. (2009, February). *Informing the design of deictic behaviors of a web agent with spoken and sign language video data.* 8th International Gesture Workshop (GW 2009), Bielefeld University, Bielefeld, Germany.

Matsumoto, D. (1990). Cultural similarities and differences in display rules. *Motivation and Emotion, 14*(3), 195–214.

McNeill, D. (1992). *Hand and mind—What gestures reveal about thoughts.* Chicago: University of Chicago Press.

Mehrabian, A. (1995). Framework for a comprehensive description and measurement of emotional states. *Genetic, Social, and General Psychology Monographs, 121*(3), 339–361.

Mehrabian, A. (1980). *Basic dimensions for a general psychological theory: Implications for personality, social, environmental, and developmental studies.* Cambridge, MA: Oelgeschlager, Gunn & Hain.

Mehrabian, A., & Russell, J. A. (1974). *An approach to environmental psychology*. Cambridge, MA: MIT Press.

Moreno, R., & Flowerday, T. (2006). Students' choice of animated pedagogical agents in science learning: A test of the similarity attraction hypothesis on gender and ethnicity. *Contemporary Educational Psychology, 31*, 186–207.

Neff, M., & Fiume, E. (July, 2002). *Modeling tension and relaxation for computer animation.* ACM SIGGRAPH Symposium on Computer Animation, San Antonio, Texas (pp. 81–88), ACM New York, NY.

Neff, M., & Fiume, E. (July, 2003). *Aesthetic edits for character animation.* ACM SIGGRAPH/Eurographics Symposium on Computer Animation, San Diego, California (pp. 239–244), Eurographics Association Aire-la-Ville, Switzerland.

Niewiadomski, R., Bevacqua, E., Mancini, M., & Pelachaud, C. (2009c). Greta: An interactive expressive ECA system. In *Proceedings of the Eighth International Conference on Autonomous Agents and Multiagent Systems, Budapest* (pp. 1399–1400). International Foundation for Autonomous Agents and Multiagent Systems, Richland, SC.

Niewiadomski, R., Demeure, V., & Pelachaud, C. (2010). Warmth, competence, believability and virtual agents. *Proceedings of the 10th International Conference on Intelligent Virtual Agents*, Philadelphia (pp. 272–285), Springer-Verlag Berlin, Heidelberg.

Niewiadomski, R., Hyniewska, S., & Pelachaud, C. (2009a). Evaluation of multimodal sequential expressions of emotions in ECA. In *Proceedings of Third International Conference on Affective Computing and Intelligent Interaction (ACII 2009), Amsterdam* (pp. 635–641), IEEE Computer Society.

Niewiadomski, R., Hyniewska, S., & Pelachaud, C. (2009b). Modeling emotional expressions as sequences of behaviors. In *Proceedings of the 9th International Conference on Intelligent Virtual Agents*, Amsterdam, Lecture Notes in Computer Science Volume 5773 (pp. 316–322). Springer Berlin Heidelberg.

Niewiadomski, R., Ochs, S., & Pelachaud, C. (2008). Expressions of empathy in ECAs. In *Proceedings of the 8th International Conference on Intelligent Virtual Agents, Tokyo*, Lecture Notes in Computer Science Volume 5208 (pp. 37–44). Springer Berlin Heidelberg.

Niewiadomski, R., & Pelachaud, C. (2007). Fuzzy similarity of facial expressions of embodied agents. In *Proceedings of the 7th International Conference on Intelligent Virtual Agents, Paris.* Lecture Notes in Computer Science Volume 4722 (pp. 86–98). Springer Berlin Heidelberg.

Niewiadomski, R., & Pelachaud, C. (2010). Affect expression in ECAs: Application to politeness displays, *International Journal Human-Computer Studies, 68*, 851–871.

Ochs, M., Pelachaud, C., & Sadek, D. (2008). An empathic virtual dialog agent to improve human-machine interaction. In *Proceedings of the Seventh International Joint Conference on Autonomous Agents and Multi-Agent Systems, AAMAS'08, Estoril, Portugal* (pp. 89–96),

International Foundation for Autonomous Agents and Multiagent Systems, Richland, SC.

Ortony, A., Clore, G. L., & Collins, A. (1988). *The cognitive structure of emotions*. Cambridge, UK: Cambridge University Press.

Paleari, M., Grizard, A., & Lisetti, C. L. (2007, May). *Adapting psychologically grounded facial emotional expressions to different anthropomorphic embodiment platforms*. 20th International Florida Artificial Intelligence Research Society Conference (FLAIRS 2007), Key West, FL.

Paleari, M., & Lisetti, C. (June, 2006). Psychologically grounded avatars expressions. First Workshop on Emotion and Computing at KI 2006, 29th Annual Conference on Artificial Intelligence, Bremen, Germany.

Pan, X., Gillies, M., Sezgin, T. M., & Loscos, C. (2007). Expressing complex mental states through facial expressions. In *Proceedings of the Second International Conference on Affective Computing and Intelligent Interaction (ACII)* (pp. 745–746). Springer-Verlag Berlin, Heidelberg.

Partala, T., & Surakka, V. (2004). The effects of affective interventions in human-computer interaction. *Interacting with Computers, 16*, 295–309.

Plutchik, R. (1980). *Emotions: A psychoevolutionary Synthesis*. New York: Harper and Row.

Pollick, F. E. (2004). The features people use to recognize human movement style. In A. Camurri & G. Volpe (Eds.) *Gesture-based communication in human-computer interaction—GW 2003, ser. Lecture notes in artificial intelligence* (no. 2915, pp. 10–19). NewYork: Springer-Verlag.

Prendinger, H., & Ishizuka, M. (2001). Social role awareness in animated agents. In *Proceedings of the Fifth International Conference on Autonomous Agents* (pp. 270–277). ACM New York, NY.

Prendinger, H., Yingzi, J., Kazutaka, K., & Ma, C. (2005). Evaluating the interaction with synthetic agents using attention and affect tracking. In *Proceedings of the Fourth International Joint Conference on Autonomous Agents and Multiagent Systems (AAMAS 2005)* (pp. 1099–1100). ACM New York, NY

Raidt, S., Bailly, G., & Elisei, F. (2007). Analyzing and modeling gaze during face-to-face interaction. In *Proceedings of 7th International Conference on Intelligent Virtual Agents, IVA'2007*, Paris, Lecture Notes in Computer Science Volume 4722 (pp. 403–404). Springer Berlin Heidelberg.

Reeves, B., & Nass, C. (1996). *The media equation: How people treat computers, television, and new media like real people and places*. Cambridge University Press.

Rehm, M., & André, E. (2005). Catch me if you can—Exploring lying agents in social settings. In F. Dignum, V. Dignum, S. Koenig, S. Kraus, M. P. Singh, & M. Woolridge (Eds.), *Proceedings of International Joint Conference on Autonomous Agents and Multi-Agent Systems (AAMAS), Utrecht, The Netherlands* (pp. 937–944). ACM New York, NY.

Roseman I. J., & Smith, C. A. (2001). Appraisal theory: Overview, assumptions, varieties, controversies. In K. R. Scherer, A. Schorr, & T. Johnstone (Eds.), *Appraisal processes in emotion: Theory, methods, research* (pp. 3–34). New York: Oxford University Press.

Russell, J. A., A circumplex model of affect. *Journal of Personality and Social Psychology*, 39(6), 1161–1178, 1980.

Ruttkay, Z., & Noot, H. (2005). Variations in gesturing and speech by GESTYLE. *International Journal of Human Computer Studies*, Special Issue on "Subtle Expressivity for Characters and Robots," 62(2), 211–229.

Ruttkay, Z., Noot, H., & ten Hagen, P. (2003). Emotion disc and emotion squares: Tools to explore the facial expression face. *Computer Graphics Forum*, 22(1), 49–53.

Saarni, C., & Weber, H. (2005). Emotional displays and dissemblance in childhood: Implications for self-presentation. In P. Philippot, R. S. Feldman, & E. J. Coats (Eds.), *The social context of nonverbal behavior (studies in emotion and social interaction)* (pp. 71–108). Cambridge University Press.

Scherer, K. R. (1999). Appraisal theories. In T. Dalgleish & M. Power (Eds.), *Handbook of cognition and emotion* (pp. 637–663). Chichester, UK: Wiley.

Scherer, K. R. (2001). Appraisal considered as a process of multilevel sequential checking. In K. Scherer, A. Schorr, & T. Johnstone (Eds), *Appraisal processes in emotion: Theory, methods, Research* (pp. 92–119). New York: Oxford University Press.

Scherer, K. R., & Ellgring, H. (2007). Multimodal expression of emotion: Affect programs or componential appraisal patterns? *Emotion*, 7, 158–171.

Schilbach, L., Wohlschläger, A., Krämer, N., Newen, A., Shah, N., Fink, G., & Vogeley, K. (2006). Being with virtual others: Neural correlates of social interaction. *Neuropsycholgia, 44*, 718–730.

Schlosberg, H. (1952). The description of facial expression in terms of two dimensions. *Journal of Experimental Psychology*, 44(4), 229–237.

Shiota, M. N., Campos, B., & Keltner, D. (2003). The faces of positive emotion: Prototype displays of awe, amusement, and pride. *Annals of the New York Academy of Sciences,. 1000*, 296–299.

Stoiber, N., Séguier, R., & Breton, G. (2009). Automatic design of a control interface for a synthetic face. In *Proceedings of the 13th International Conference on Intelligent User Interfaces* (pp. 207–216). ACM New York, NY.

Tartaro, A., & Cassell, J. (2008). Playing with virtual peers: Bootstrapping contingent discourse in children with autism. *Proceedings of International Conference of the Learning Sciences (ICLS), June 24–28, Utrecht, Netherlands* (pp. 382–389). International Society of the Learning Sciences.

Thórisson, K. R. (2002). Machine perception of multimodal natural dialogue. In P. S. McKevitt, Ó. Nulláin, & C. Mulvihill (Eds.), *Language, vision and music* (pp. 97–115). Amsterdam: John Benjamins.

Tomkins, S. S., & McCarter, R. (1964). What and where are the primary affects? Some evidence for a theory. *Perceptual Motor Skill, 18*, 119–158.

Tsapatsoulis, N., Raouzaiou, A., Kollias, S., Crowie, R., & Douglas-Cowie, E. (2002). Emotion recognition and synthesis based on MPEG-4 FAPs. In I. Pandzic & R. Forchheimer (Eds.), MPEG-4 facial animation. *The standard, implementations, applications* (pp. 141–167). UK: John Wiley and Sons.

Walker, J., Sproull, L., & Subramani, R. (1994). Using a human face in an interface. In *Proceedings of the SIGCHI Conference on Human Factors in Computing Systems: Celebrating Interdependence, Boston* (pp. 85–91). ACM New York, NY.

Walker, M., Cahn, J., & Whittaker, S. (1996). Linguistic style improvisation for lifelike computer characters. *Proceedings of the AAAI Workshop on AI, Alife and Entertainment* (pp. 61–68), The AAAI Press, Menlo Park, California.

Wallbott, H. (1998). Bodily expression of emotion. *European Journal of Social Psychology*, 28, 879–896.

Wallbott, H. G., & Scherer, K. R. (1986). Cues and channels in emotion recognition. *Journal of Personality and Social Psychology, 51*, 690–699.

Whissell, C. (1989). The dictionary of affect in language, In R. Plutchik & H. Kellerman (Eds.), *Emotion: Theory, research, and experience, volume 4: The measurement of emotions* (pp. 113–131). San Diego: Academic Press, Inc.

Zhang, S., Wu, Z., Meng, H. M., & Cai, L. (2007). Facial expression synthesis using PAD emotional parameters for a Chinese expressive avatar. In *Proceedings of Second Affective Computing and Intelligent Interaction Conference (ACII 2007)*, Lecture Notes in Computer Science Volume 4738 (pp. 24–35). Springer Berlin Heidelberg.

10

Early Emotional Communication: Novel Approaches to Interaction

Daniel S. Messinger, Mohammad H. Mahoor, Sy-Miin Chow, John D. Haltigan, Steven Cadavid, & Jeffrey F. Cohn

This chapter is concerned with the emergence of emotional communication—transactional emotions—early in life. We review methodological and conceptual issues in research on early interaction and then present two studies of emotional communication. The first study uses computer vision to describe infant–mother interaction from a microanalytic perspective. It reveals evidence of changing infant–mother emotional dynamics during the course of interaction. The second study formally models these changing dynamics utilizing continuous ratings of affective valence. Each study utilizes a different approach for continuously measuring emotion during interaction that may resolve methodological impasses and shed new light on emotional transactions.

Early Emotional Interaction

In this chapter, we describe a class of dyadic interactions characterized by intense emotional communication. These interactions regularly involve peals of laughter and, at times, tears of desperation. While one partner in the interaction often appears entirely devoted to the other, the second partner may appear relatively unconcerned with the expectations of the first. These patterns of behavior are not rare events that are coincident with infrequent happenings such as homecomings or relationship dissolution. They characterize the day-to-day interactions between infants and their parents.

Emotional Interaction and Development

The infant–parent relationship is a prototype for social relationships throughout life. During interaction, infants and parents seem to respond to one another, and enter into and out of shared joyous states. Parent–infant interactions are characterized by nonverbal emotional communication. These are the infant's first experiences of feeling with another, a potential basis of emotional contagion and rapport. We study these interactions as a tractable model system for understanding communicative development.

The patterning of infant–parent interaction has a central role in early development. Synchronous interaction between infant and parent—high correlations between emotional engagement states—is predicted by the rhythmicity of infants' early physiological (e.g., sleep–wake) cycles (Feldman, 2006). The patterning of infant–parent interaction, likewise, predicts later developmental achievements. The predilection of parents to shift affective states to match those of their infants is related to increases in infants' self-control and cognitive performance at 2 years (Feldman & Greenbaum, 1997; Feldman, Greenbaum, & Yirmiya, 1999; Feldman, Greenbaum, Yirmiya, & Mayes, 1996). More generally, interaction patterns characterized by maternal responsivity and positive affect predict later toddler internalization of social norms (Feldman et al., 1999; Kochanska, 2002; Kochanska, Forman, & Coy, 1999; Kochanska & Murray, 2000).

Why is it the case that early parental positive affect and responsivity predict self-control and normative behavior? Normative behavior is implicitly interactive in two senses. First, it involves acting with respect to the expectations of a generalized other; second, it involves the expectation that one's actions affect others (Kochanska, 2002). We posit that young infants who act with the developing expectation of eliciting positive affect in the parent develop to be young children who regulate themselves to please their parents. It may also be the case that infants who are developing responsivity to their parents become increasingly responsive to the expectations of others.

As suggested by these explanations of the longitudinal predictions found by developmental psychologists, a fundamental question in infant–parent interaction concerns communicative influence. Do infant behaviors influence the parent? Do parent behaviors influence the infant? The converse of one partner's influence is the other partner's responsivity. Only if partners influence each other can we meaningfully refer to their interaction. Substantively, there is little attention in the infant–parent interaction literature to the possibility that interactive influence varies in time. Yet it appears possible that there are temporal variations in the responsivity of each partner to the other. Both empirical studies in this chapter tackle this issue. To place those studies in context, we begin by reviewing two conventional approaches to measuring influence during interactions—contingency analyses of discrete behaviors and time series analyses of ordinal rating scales.

Contingency Analyses of Discrete Behaviors

One approach to the question of influence involves manually measuring discrete infant and parent behaviors (Kaye & Fogel, 1980; Van Egeren, Barratt, & Roach, 2001) such as facial expressions (Elias & Broerse, 1995; Jaffe, Beebe, Feldstein, Crown, & Jasnow, 2001), and gazes and vocalizations (Crown, Feldstein, Jasnow, Beebe, & Jaffe, 2002). Interaction is conceptualized with respect to the sequencing of dyadic states. Contingency analyses are typically employed to examine the likelihood of one partner's discrete behavior (e.g., a smile or vocalization) predicting the onset of the partner's behavior (Fogel, 1988; Kaye & Fogel, 1980; Malatesta, Culver, Tesman, & Shepard, 1989; Symons & Moran, 1994; Van Egeren et al., 2001).

In general, infant positive expressions such as smiles tend to elicit parent positive expressions. Parent positive expressions typically precede but are not sufficient for eliciting infant positive expressions (Cohn & Tronick, 1987; Kaye & Fogel, 1980; Symons & Moran, 1994). Our analyses of dyadic smiling (Cohn & Tronick, 1987; Messinger, Fogel, & Dickson, 1999, 2001) reveal that parents respond both to the onset and to the offset of their infants' smiles. These patterns might be phrased as a set of dyadic "rules," although the rules are more obligatory for parents than for infants. Parents tend to smile before infants, although infants, particularly by 6 months of age and beyond, may initiate smiling. Parents must smile in response to an infant smile. Infants are free to smile or not in response to a parent smile. Once both partners are smiling, the infant may stop smiling; parents, however, must not stop smiling until the infant has stopped smiling.

Time Series Analyses of Ordinal Behavior Scales

Another approach to the question of influence involves measuring infant and parent behavior with ordinal scales composed of affective engagement states (Beebe & Gerstman, 1984; Cohn & Tronick, 1988b; Weinberg, Tronick, Cohn, & Olson, 1999). These engagement states index aggregates of behaviors reflecting a continuum from negative to neutral to positive affective engagement (Cohn & Tronick, 1988b; Weinberg et al., 1999). Interaction is conceptualized with respect to associations between ordinal gradations in infant and parent engagement. These associations are typically examined with time series analyses.

In time series analyses, the influence of each partner on the other is examined with regression methods after having removed variance associated with autocorrelation (Cohn & Tronick, 1988b). Early work using time series analyses established that parent and infants display nonperiodic (variable) cyclicity (Cohn & Tronick, 1988b). That is, parents do not merely insert their behaviors in the midst of ongoing periodic (regular) infant behavioral cycles. Instead, infants and parents interact stochastically by influencing the likelihood of a change in the other partner's behavior (Cohn & Tronick, 1988a, 1988b).

Like contingency analyses, time series analyses typically indicate strong infant-to-parent interactive influence. They also reveal a developmental increase in parent-to-infant influence. Between 3 and 9 months, infants become increasingly responsive to their interactive partners. In some dyads, the joint presence of infant-to-parent and parent-to-infant influence yields bidirectional influence (Cohn & Tronick, 1987, 1988b; Feldman, Greenbaum, Mayes, & Erlich, 1997; Feldman et al., 1996; Weinberg et al., 1999; Yirmiya et al., 2006). Bidirectional influence occurs when each partner's behavior impacts that of the other.

The Need for New Approaches

Discrete and ordinal measurement approaches both offer insights into infant–parent interaction, but both have limitations. A discrete behavior approach characterizes the temporal association of expressive behaviors exactly but does not provide a description of the rhythmicity of interaction. Ordinal scaling approaches capture the rhythmicity—the pseudoperidicity—of interactions, but each step of the scale lacks behavioral specificity. This lack of specificity means it is not entirely clear which behaviors of an infant or parent might be impacting the other partner.

In addition to this analytic impasse, both discrete and ordinal measurement approaches involve practical difficulties. Each typically relies on labor-intensive, manual coding of behavior (Cohn & Kanade, 2007). The laborious quality of manual coding represents a challenge for detailed measurement of human expressivity. Efficient measurement of human expressivity is essential for understanding real-time interaction and development. Conceptually and practically, then, alternative measurement approaches are necessary.

In this chapter, we describe two alternatives to the conceptual and practical problems with current measurement approaches. First, we employ automated measurement of behavior using computer vision and machine learning. Second, we ask nonexpert observers to make continuous ratings of affective valence using a joystick interface. On the face of it, these approaches appear to be quite different. Automated measurement is objective while the continuous ratings are subjective. Yet both approaches are oriented toward meaningful continuous measurement of ongoing interactions. Moreover, both promise efficiencies of measurement when compared with traditional manual measurement by human experts. Finally, each approach has the potential to uncover changes in infant–parent interactive dynamics over time. We begin by reviewing what is known about positive emotional expression as a medium for communication in infant–parent interaction.

Positive Emotion Expression

Early infant–parent interaction has no topic external to the displays of the partners themselves and frequently involves the communication of positive emotion. Parents attempt to elicit smiles from infants during interaction, and episodes of joint smiling appear to represent high points of the dyadic transaction. The smile is the prototypic expression of positive emotion (joy) in infants and mothers. In smiling, the zygomatic major pulls the lip corners obliquely upward. There are, however, similarities and differences in *how* parents and infants smile.

Among both infants and adults, stronger smiles involving greater lip corner movement tend to occur during conditions likely to elicit positive emotion (Bolzani-Dinehart et al., 2005; Ekman & Friesen, 1982; Fogel, Hsu, Shapiro, Nelson-Goens, & Secrist, 2006; Schneider & Uzner, 1992). By the same token, infant and adult smiles with eye constriction—Duchenne smiles—tend to occur in situations likely to elicit positive affect (Fogel, Nelson-Goens, Hsu, & Shapiro, 2000; Fox & Davidson, 1988; Lavelli & Fogel, 2002; Messinger et al., 2001). We refer to these smiles—in which the orbicularis oculi (pars lateralis) raises the cheek under the eye and compresses the eyelid—as smiles with eye constriction. Stronger smiles and smiles with eye constriction are perceived to be more emotionally positive than smiles without these characteristics (Bolzani-Dinehart et al., 2005; Ekman, Davidson, & Friesen, 1990; Fogel, Hsu, et al., 2006; Fox & Davidson, 1988; Frank, Ekman, & Friesen, 1993; Messinger, 2002; Messinger et al., 2001).

Among infants, smiling involving mouth opening also tends to involve eye constriction, and smiles with these characteristics tend to be stronger smiles (Fogel, Hsu et al., 2006; Messinger et al., 2001). In infants, combined open-mouth, cheek-raise smiling tends to occur during unambiguously positive periods of interaction (Dickson, Walker, & Fogel, 1997; Fogel et al., 2000; Messinger et al., 2001). More generally, degree of lip corner movement, mouth opening, and eye constriction all appear to index the positive emotional intensity of infant smiles (Bolzani-Dinehart et al., 2005; Carvajal & Iglesias, 2002; Fogel, Hsu et al., 2006; Fogel et al., 2000; Harker & Keltner, 2001; Keltner & Ekman, 2000; Keltner, Kring, & Bonanno, 1999; Messinger, 2002; Messinger, Cassel, Acosta, Ambadar, & Cohn, 2008; Messinger, Mahoor, Chow, Cadavid, & Cohn, 2008; Oster, 2006).

Smile intensity and eye constriction also appear to index the positive emotional intensity of smiles in adults. The role of mouth opening in adult smiles is less clear, although adult open-mouth, cheek-raise smiles tend to occur in response to humorous stimuli (Ruch, 1995). In fact, surprisingly little is known about the facial expressions of parents engaged in interacting with their infants (Chong, Werker, Russell, & Carroll, 2003).

A paucity of descriptive information also impedes our understanding of infant emotional dynamics during face-to-face interactions. Infant facial expressions are typically described generally, for example, as negative cry faces, neutral, and different types of positive smiles, but rarely in fine-grained fashion. Nevertheless, infants engage in a variety of nonsmiling actions that may communicate subtle negative affect or an attenuation of positive affect (e.g., dimpling of the lips and lip tightening). Automated measurement is a promising approach to measuring such expressions (Cohn & Kanade, 2007; Messinger, Mahoor, Chow, Cadavid et al., 2008; Oster, 2006; Tronick et al., 2005; Weinberg & Tronick, 1998). Ultimately, our application of automated measurement to early interaction was aimed at a better understanding of early emotional communication. As long-time investigators of infant–parent interaction, two things have become clear to us. On the one hand, detailed measurement is necessary to understand how communication is occurring. On the other hand, manual coding of that communication is not tenable for large-scale studies.

Automated Measurement of Early Interaction

Automated measurement has the potential to objectively document real-time behavior (Bartlett et al., 2006; Cohn & Kanade, 2007). Ultimately, automated measurement may provide a means for objectively measuring aspects of behavior that human beings notice but are not able to reliably and efficiently document. Our goal, then, is to supplement and complement, rather than replace, human observation.

Historically, computer vision systems have been limited to the recognition of deliberate (i.e., posed) facial expressions recorded under controlled conditions that did not involve significant head motion (Essa & Pentland, 1994; Padgett, Cottrell, & Adolphs, 1996; Yacoob & Davis, 1997). More recent systems (Bartlett et al., 2005, 2006; Lien, Kanade, Cohn, & Li, 2000; Tian, Kanade, & Cohn, 2001, 2002) have achieved some success in the more difficult task of recognizing facial Action Units of the Facial Action Coding System (FACS) (Ekman & Friesen, 1978; Ekman, Friesen, & Hager, 2002). FACS—and its application to infants (BabyFACS) (Oster, 2006)—is the gold-standard manual system for objectively recording anatomically based appearance changes in the form of facial Action Units.

We recently developed a system capable of FACS action unit recognition in naturalistic interaction (Lucey, Ashraf, & Cohn, 2007). We then measured the strength of specified Action Units using the FACS (A–E, minimal–maximal) intensity metric (Mahoor et al., 2008). In other words, the system produces precise measurements of behavior on a meaningful continuous metric. This approach allows for a synthesis of the discrete and ordinal measurement approaches discussed previously. We use these measurements of intensity to examine the flow of interaction between infant and parent. While it is technically possible to conduct continuous manual coding of the intensity of FACS Action Units, we know of no examples of this somewhat impractical approach. Ultimately, we are using automated measurement to turn up a virtual microscope that may reveal how early interaction itself dynamically changes in time.

Applying Automated Measurement to Early Interaction

Here we report on the exploration of dyadic expressivity in two 6-month-old infants engaged in face-to-face interaction with their mothers (Messinger, Mahoor, Chow, & Cohn, 2008). Mothers were asked to play with their infants as they normally would at home for 3 minutes. We designated the mother–infant dyads A (male infant) and B (female infant). We describe our measurement system in some depth because its focus on the intensity of emotional expressions is relatively novel.

Our automated measurement approach had two steps. First we tracked and measured information in the face using computer vision. Next we measured facial action intensity, primarily using a machine learning approach. This combined approach enabled us to document the coherence of expressions of positive emotion, changing levels of synchrony and tickling, and a class of infant facial actions that appeared to attenuate smiling. We supplemented these automated measurements with manual coding of mother tickling the infant, an activity that was central to dyadic emotional communication.

Facial Tracking

Our computer vision approach was based on active appearance and shape models (AAMs). AAMs detect, track, and measure the face in a video record using a fitting algorithm (see Figure 10.1). In the current application, AAMs were trained using 3% of the frames in the video record. In these training frames, the software provided an approximate fit of the mesh to the videotaped image of the face, and a research assistant adjusted the vertices to ensure fit. Using the training frames as data, the model overlays the mesh on the facial image using a fitting algorithm that is guided by a Principal Components Analysis. Here, the AAM independently models the entire video sequence (including training frames) based on variation in the principal components.

AAMs are anatomic models of an individual's head and face. AAMs consist of a shape component and an appearance component (Cootes, Edwards, & Taylor, 2001). The shape component is a triangulated mesh model of the face containing 66 vertices, each of which has an X and Y coordinate (Baker, Matthews, & Schneider, 2004; Cohn & Kanade, 2007) (see Figure 10.2). The mesh moves and deforms in response to changes in parameters

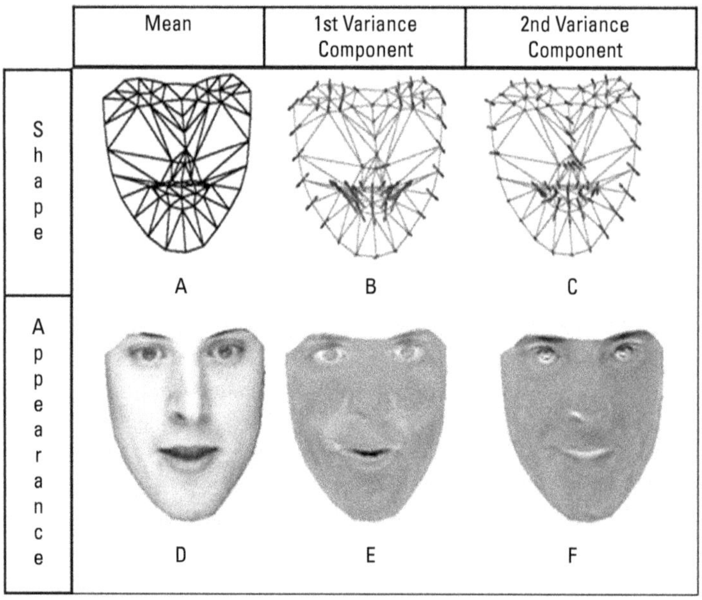

FIGURE 10.1 Active appearance and shape model. The shape model consists of a network of geometric points located on facial landmarks. The appearance model contains the grayscale values of the pixels within the shape model. For both shape and appearance, a mean model is displayed along with the first two variance components. These are principal components that parsimoniously describe changes in each of the models. They are derived from training images and used to track and measure the video sequence in its entirety.

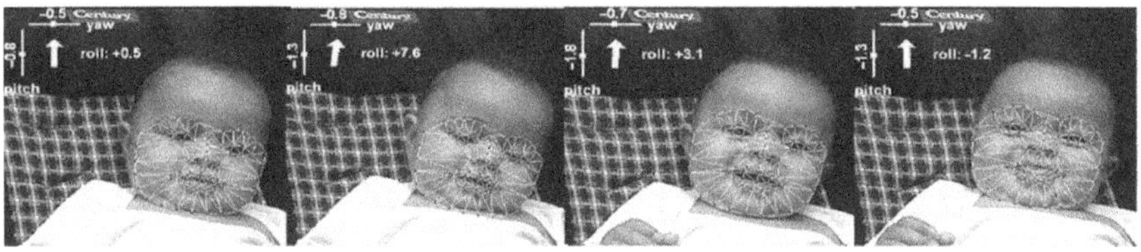

FIGURE 10.2 Display of the shape model of an AAM applied to video frames of an infant interaction. A 2D+3D AAM is shown, which yields 3D shape and rigid motion and 3D nonrigid motion of expression.

corresponding to a face undergoing both whole-head rigid motion and nonrigid motion (facial movement). In the current application, we measured mouth opening directly from the shape component of the AAM as the mean vertical distance between the upper and lower lips.

The appearance component of the AAM contains the 256 grayscale values (lightness/darkness) for each pixel contained in the modeled face. The appearance data generated by the AAM are highly complex, containing 256 possible grayscale values for each of the approximately 10,000 pixels in the AAM for each frame of video. We used manifold learning (Belkin & Niyogi, 2003)—a nonlinear technique—to reduce the dimensionality of the appearance and shape data to 12 variables per frame. This reduced data metric was used to train support vector machines (SVMs).

Support Vector Machine Classification

SVMs are machine learning algorithms frequently used in computer vision applications (Chang & Lin, 2001). Littlewort, Bartlett, & Movellan (2001), for example, used SVMs to distinguish the presence of eye constriction (AU6) in adult smiles (Littlewort, Bartlett, & Movellan, 2001). Employing the reduced shape and appearance dataset, we trained separate instances of SVMs to measure three classes of expressive action. We specifically measured smiling intensity (AU12, from absent to maximal) and eye constriction (AU6, from absent to maximal). We also measured the presence of a class of infant actions that appeared to be subtle signs of upset or, at least, reductions in positive affect expression (e.g., lip tightening, AU23). Each instance of training was carried out using a separate sample of the frames that were selected to encompass the entire range of actions being classified.

In the next section, we examine the convergent and construct validity of the automated measurements of facial actions. We then use the measurements to examine the structure of infant and mother smiling with the goal of identifying summary measures of emotional intensity with which to describe interaction. Our treatment of interaction involves a microanalytic description of how infants and mothers interact, and how this interaction changes in time.

Automated Measurement: Convergent and Construct Validity

Convergent Validity. We first established the convergent validity of automated measurement of the intensity of

FIGURE 10.3 This composite rendering illustrates the measurement of infant and mother facial expressions during an interaction. Automated tracking of the lips, eyes, brows, and portions of the facial outline are outlined in white on the infant's and mother's face.

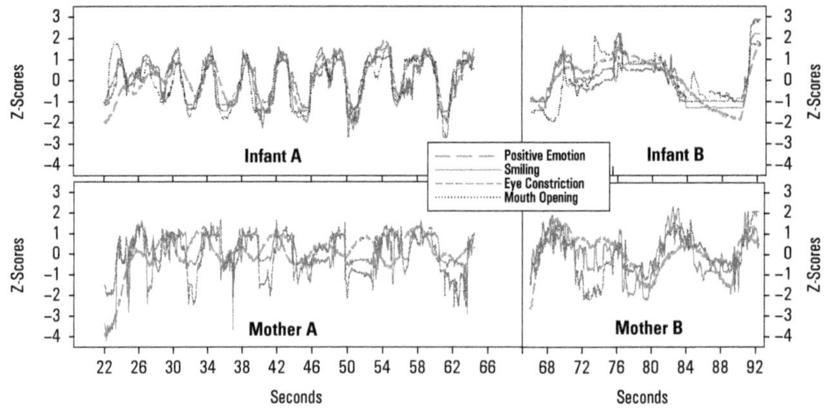

FIGURE 10.4 Smile parameters and rated positive emotion over time. Infant graphs show the association of automated measurements of smile strength, eye constriction, mouth opening, and rated positive emotion. Mother graphs show the association of automated measurements of smile strength, eye constriction, and rated positive emotion. Positive emotion is offset by three fifths of a second to account for rating lag.

infant and mother expressive actions (see Figure 10.3). Correlations between automated measurements and manual coding were high. Mean correlations for infant and mother smiling and eye constriction were above .9; the mean for mouth opening was around .8. The high associations between automated and manual measurements of smiling and eye constriction are illustrated in. Automated measurements of the presence and absence of individual infant actions that might be associated with smile attenuation (e.g., lip tightening) showed adequate agreement with manual measurements (89%, K = .54) (Bakeman & Gottman, 1986). In all cases, reliability between automated and manual measurements was comparable or better than interrater reliability assessed between two manual raters. The results suggest the concurrent validity of automated measurements of expressive actions.

Assessing Construct Validity via Ratings. We were interested in ascertaining the degree to which automated measurements of smiling-related facial actions were associated with positive emotion expression. To do this, we employed the Continuous Measurement System (CMS)[1] as a check on construct validity for one segment of interaction for partners in each dyad. Employing a joystick interface, undergraduates were asked to rate "positive emotion, joy, and happiness" using *none* and *maximum* as anchors as the video segment was shown. To offset for the lag between videotaped behavior and joystick movement, ratings were corrected for 3/5 of a second. We calculated the mean of the ratings for each second of interaction because of the well-documented reliability of aggregated measures of the estimates of independent observers (Ariely, 2000).

Construct Validity Results. Infant smile strength, eye constriction, and mouth opening were all highly associated with infant positive emotion with a mean correlation of almost .8 (see Figure 10.4). This suggests that infant positive emotion is expressed by a set of facial actions including and related to smiling. Mother smile strength exhibited moderate correlations (almost .6) with mother positive emotion, while mother eye constriction and mouth opening exhibited lower correlations (approximately .3 and .35, respectively). These more variable associations may reflect the multiple roles parents occupy when interacting with their infants (see Cohn et al., 2004). They are responsible not only for engaging positively with their infants but also for simultaneously entertaining their infants and maintaining their emotional states. Parents' multiple roles may reduce the degree to which eye constriction and mouth opening are associated with perceived maternal positive emotion.

The Structure of Infant and Mother Smiling

Infant Smiling. Measurements of intensity levels allowed us to explore the structure of infant and mother smiling. The intensities of infant smile strength and eye constriction were highly correlated (around .85), and the correlations of these actions with degree of mouth opening were moderate to high (around .6). This suggests that early infant positive emotion is a unitary construct expressed through the intensity of smiling and a set of linked facial actions (Messinger & Fogel, 2007). This interpretation is supported by research indicating that infants preferentially produced smiles with these characteristics in periods of interaction likely to elicit positive emotion (Fogel, Hsu et al., 2006; Messinger et al., 1999, 2001).

Mother Smiling. Infants and mothers showed similarities and differences in their expression of positive emotion. As with infants, the intensity of mother smile strength and eye constriction were highly associated (correlations around .8). However, the correlations of mother mouth opening with eye constriction (around .2 and .3) and with smile strength (around .2 and .5) were lower and more variable than among infants. Mothers appeared to use mouth opening in part to convey positive affective intensity, but also as an element in visual displays used to entertain infants. A common pattern, for example, involved a mother leaning back from an infant, opening her mouth wide, and then bringing her face toward the infant while closing her mouth and vocalizing.

Smiling As a Continuous Process. For both infants and mothers, then, smile strength and eye constriction (the Duchenne marker) were linked indices of the intensity of positive emotional communication. For both infants and mothers, it was not clear that there were different "types" of smiling during interactions (see Messinger, Cassel et al., 2008, for similar results with a different set of infants). This is relevant because dichotomies between different forms of smiling are prevalent in the literature. Duchenne smiles, for example, are thought to be expressions of joy while smiles without the Duchenne marker (eye constriction) are thought to be nonemotional social signals. For mothers and infants, however, the appropriate question was not "Is a Duchenne smile being displayed?" but "How much Duchenne smiling is being displayed?" In fact, given the association of smiling strength with other characteristics of smiling, the most appropriate questions appeared to be simply, "How much smiling is present?"

A Composite Index of Smiling. The association of smile strength and eye constriction within infants and within mothers led us to take the mean of these variables to create a single index of smiling activity for each partner over the course of the interactions. This smiling activity index can be understood as a measure of the intensity of each partner's Duchenne smiling. The associations of individual facial actions between infants and mothers support the construction of this index. In each dyad, degree of mouth opening exhibited weak and sometimes negative associations with the smile strength and eye constriction of the other partner. However, associations of the intensity of smile strength and eye constriction were moderately positive between partners. This suggests level of Duchenne smiling activity was a preeminent communicative signal between infants and mothers.

Mean Smiling Levels. Overall, mothers smiled for more time, and smiled more intensely, than their infants. The two mothers smiled for over three quarters of the interaction while infants smiled for approximately two thirds of the interaction. The mean intensity level of mother smiling was about three quarters of a point (on the 5-point intensity scale) than the mean intensity level of infant smiling. Moreover, when infants were smiling and mothers were not smiling, mothers often appeared to be actively trying to elicit infant smiles by, for example, pursing their lips and vocalizing.

General Interaction Patterns

The face-to-face interactions were characterized by variability in the associations between tickling, infant smiling activity, and mother smiling activity. The interactions were divided into segments, between which there was occlusion (i.e., obstruction) of the face. These were typically caused by mothers engaging in actions designed to hide her face from the infant (e.g., peek-a-boo). These occlusions divided the interactions into segments between which interactive variability could be assessed (see Figure 10.5).

Nonsmiling Actions. Overall, Dyad A's interactions appeared to be more fast paced than Dyad B's. Infant A also displayed a large set of nonsmiling actions not displayed by Infant B. At times, these actions appeared to attenuate positive affect expression (e.g., lip tightening and dimpling); at other times, they appeared subtly negative (e.g., upper lip raising and lip stretching at the trace level); and, at other times, they appeared to be clear instances of dysregulation (e.g., a brief instance of spitting up). Mother tickling almost never occurred with these infant actions, perhaps because the actions were interpreted by the mother as indices of overarousal and potential fussiness. When the infant displayed these

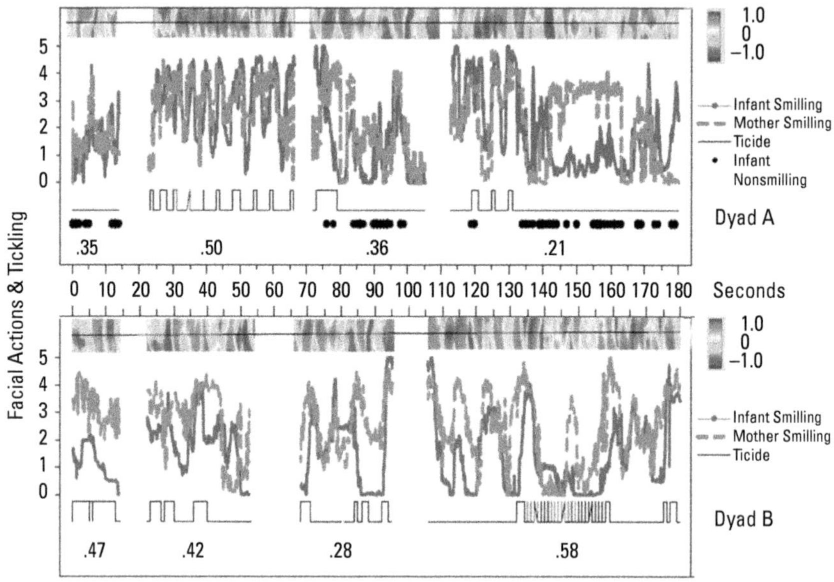

FIGURE 10.5 Tickling and smiling activity are plotted over seconds. Smiling activity is the mean of smile strength and eye constriction intensity. Correlations between infant and mother smiling activity for each segment of interaction are displayed below that segment. Above each segment of interaction is a plot of the corresponding windowed cross-correlations between infant and mother smiling activity. The horizontal midline of these plots indicates the zero-order correlation between infant and mother smiling activity. The correlations are calculated for successive 3-second segments of interaction. The plots also indicate the associations of one partner's current smiling activity with the successive activity of the other partner. Area above the midline indicates the correlation of current infant activity with successive lags of mother smiling activity. Area beneath the midline indicates the correlation of mother smiling activity with successive lags of infant smiling activity. Three lags of such activity are shown. For example, the area at the very bottom of a plot shows the correlation of a window of 3 seconds of current mother activity with a window of 3 seconds of infant activity that is to occur after three fifths of a second. A color version of this figure can be found on Oxford Scholarship Online.

nonsmiling actions, his smiling activity intensity level was reduced, and so, too, was that of his mother. Strikingly, these nonsmiling actions were associated with reductions in infant–mother synchrony, the magnitude of the correlation between infant and mother smiling activity. The potentially nonlinear role of infant negative affect expressions in transforming an interaction—e.g., by changing the parent's goal from eliciting smiles to reducing fussing—is a promising goal of future research.

Tickling. Tickling, which occurred in the interactions of both dyads, is of interest because it may elicit positive affect in the infant but is not necessarily expressive of maternal positive affect. Tickling has received surprisingly little attention in investigations of early interaction (but see Fogel, Hsu et al., 2006). When tickling, mothers engaged in more intense smiling activity. This may serve to emphasize tickling's playful intent despite its faux aggressive—"I'm gonna get ya"—quality (Harris, 1999). Although tickling often appeared to elicit increased infant smiling activity, this was not always the case, (i.e., in the last two segments of Dyad B's interaction). Tickling and other forms of touch represent a tactile mode of communication, which, like fussing, can introduce nonlinear changes in infant–mother communication.

Variability Between Segments of Interaction. Within each dyad, the association of infant and mother smiling activity showed substantial variability between segments of interaction (see Figure 10.5). The interactive meaning behind this variability can be illustrated by examining specific segments of Dyad A's interaction. Dyad A's second segment of interaction involved closely matched, regular rhythms of oscillating infant and mother smiling activity in which peaks of joint smiling coincided with mother tickling the infant. During these periods of tickling and intense smiling, the infant would look away from the mother, only to look toward the mother again, as if to elicit another round of tickling (Fogel, Hsu et al., 2006; Fogel et al., 2000). The third segment contained apparent mismatches in levels of infant and mother smiling activity, followed by a brief spit-up on the part of the infant, and expressions of concern on the part of the mother; these were followed by a brief synchronization of levels of infant and mother smiling activity, an interactive repair. The final segment began with rhythmic simultaneous peaks and valleys of smiling activity, punctuated by tickling, which then proceeded, in the face of infant fussing actions, to a long period of relatively constant levels of mother smiling and low levels of infant smiling. In sum, there appeared to be meaningful moment-to-moment changes in levels of dyadic synchronization.

Local Interaction Patterns

Local Cross-Correlations. To explore the possibility that there were moment-to-moment changes in the association of infant and mother smiling activity, we examined successive 3-second windows of the interaction (Boker, Rotondo, Xu, & King, 2002). Within these windows, we calculated the zero-order correlations between infant and mother smiling activity. We also calculated predictive cross-correlations within these windows, which indicate the degree to which the infant's current smiling activity predicted the mother's subsequent smiling activity, and vice versa. This was done with software based on Boker et al. (2002).[2]

Changing Correlations. Changing values of zero-order correlations correspond to the different colors displayed on the midline of the rectangular plots in Figure 10.5. For both dyads, local zero-order correlations alternated between highly positive (red), moderately positive (yellow), moderately negative (light blue), and highly negative (dark blue) values. The changing values index dramatic changes in the level of dyadic synchrony over time. Substantively, they point to the importance of local processes in negotiating affective communication early in life.

Mirroring. Each partner tended to mirror changes in the other partner's level of smiling activity. This mirroring can be seen in the lagged correlations that are displayed above and below the midline of the rectangular plots in Figure 10.5. Area above the midline indicates the correlation of infant smiling activity with successive lags of mother smiling activity. Area beneath the midline indicates the correlation of mother smiling activity with successive lags of infant smiling activity. Prominent throughout each dyad's interaction were symmetries between the top and the bottom halves of the cross-correlation plots. These are bands representing a relatively uniform value for a local period of infant–mother correlation that extend from the top to the bottom of the plot. Red bands, for example, indicate that each partner was mirroring the other's changes in smiling activity. Similar patterns have been described by Boker et al. (2002) in analyses of head movement during conversation. Increases and decreases in smiling activity were an essentially dyadic phenomenon. Substantively, it was not always possible to discern which partner began an episode of smiling.

Time-Varying Changes in Interaction. In this study, we utilized adopted automated measurement of moment-to-moment communication to understand the process of interaction. This represents an increase in the magnification level of a virtual microscope. Analyses of automated measurements of facial expressivity suggested that the disruption and repair of emotional engagement (Schore, 1994; Tronick & Cohn, 1989) was a common feature of infant–mother interactions. These are time-varying changes in the association of the partner's behaviors, a violation of the assumption of (soft) stationarity between the parent and infant time series (Boker, Xu, Rotondo, & King, 2002; Newtson, 1993). A subjective parallel would be finding oneself becoming more or less responsive to a conversational partner during the course an interaction, or noticing changing levels of responsivity in one's partner. We pursued this possibility with a more formal investigation of interactive influence using nonexpert ratings of affective valence.

Continuous Ratings of Early Interaction

The second study examined changes in interactive influence and self-regulation utilizing continuous ratings of early interaction. The ratings are made by nonexperts moving a joystick in correspondence with the affective valence they perceive in the infant or mother. This approach unites continuous ratings of affect (Gottman & Levenson, 1985; Levenson & Gottman, 1983; Ruef & Levenson, in press), with mean measures of multiple nonexpert evaluations (Waldinger, Schulz, Hauser, Allen, & Crowell, 2004). The resulting continuous nonexpert ratings have strong face validity. Measurements are based on a brief, layperson's description so that results reflect a precise but easily interpretable understanding of a construct.

We used the continuous ratings to examine self-regulation and interactive influence in the context of the face-to-face/still-face procedure (FFSF). The FFSF was used to examine naturalistic interaction and its perturbation (Adamson & Frick, 2003; Bendersky & Lewis, 1998; Cohn, Campbell, & Ross, 1991; Delgado, Messinger, & Yale., 2002; Matias & Cohn, 1993; Tronick, Als, Adamson, Wise, & Brazelton, 1978; Yale, Messinger, & Cobo-Lewis, 2003). The procedure involves a 3-minute naturalistic face-to-face (FF) interaction, and a 2-minute still-face (SF) in which the parent is asked not to initiate or respond to the infant, and ends with a 3-minute "reunion" in which the parent attempts to reengage with the infant.

Interactive Influence in the FFSF. Generally, there is a weak tendency for the level of matching engagement states between infant and parent to decline following the still-face (Tronick et al., 2005), suggesting an overall decrease in interactive coordination following this stressor. We have found, however, that infants' coordination of their communicative behaviors approaches chance levels during the still-face but returns to baseline levels in the reunion (Yale et al., 2003). This suggests that the parent's interactive behavior scaffolds the infant's ability to create meaningful patterns of expressive behavior but that infant coordination of communicative behaviors recovers robustly after perturbation. In this study, we examined the possibility that levels of interactive influence or self-regulation change over time. We thought these changes might be more evident in the reunion that followed the still-face perturbation and more evident among infants who were not at risk.

Autism Risk. The primary risk factor in this study was being an ASD-Sib, that is, being the younger sibling of a child with an autism spectrum disorder (ASD). ASDs involve qualitative impairments in nonverbal social interaction, verbal communication, and the presence of repetitive/stereotyped behaviors (American Psychiatric Association, 2000; Lord, Rutter, & Le Couteur, 1994). ASD-Sibs are at risk not only for developing an ASD but also for a spectrum of related difficulties including expressions of ASD-related symptomatology that are below threshold for a clinical diagnosis (Boelte & Poustka, 2003; Bolton, Pickles, Murphy, & Rutter, 1998; Constantino et al., 2006; Murphy et al., 2000; Wassink, Brzustowicz, Bartlett, & Szatmari, 2004). Autistic symptomatology is highly heritable (Szatmari et al., 2000), and we were interested in potential deficits in reciprocal social interaction (Constantino et al., 2003) in ASD-Sibs as a group.

ASD-Sib Affect. As a group, infant siblings of children with ASD and their parents show behavioral deficits that may be related to the broad spectrum of autism symptomatology. Individuals with ASDs show a propensity toward expressive neutrality (flatness) and negativity (Adrien, Perrot, Sauvage, Leddet & et al., 1992; Bryson et al., 2004; Joseph & Tager-Flusberg, 1997; Kasari, Sigman, Mundy, & Yirmiya, 1990; Mariëlle Stel, Claudia van den Heuvel, & Smeets, 2008; McIntosh, Reichmann-Decker, Winkielman, & Wilbarger, 2006; Yirmiya, Kasari, Sigman, & Mundy, 1989; Zwaigenbaum et al., 2005). Likewise, there is subtle evidence for behavioral flatness—increased neutrality and decreased smiling—in ASD-Sibs during the FFSF (Cassel et al., 2007; Yirmiya et al., 2006). There is also evidence for subtle deficits in self-regulation and interactive influence in dyads composed of a parent and an ASD-Sib, an infant sibling of a child with an ASD. Yirmiya et al. (2006) found that the parents of ASD-siblings showed lower levels of responsivity to their infants in the FFSF than comparison parents.

Sample and Ratings. To engage questions of autism risk, we collected a sample of 38 infants who were 6 months of age and their parents (Chow, Haltigan, & Messinger, 2010). Twenty infants were ASD-Sibs and 18 were younger siblings of a child with no known psychopathology (COMP-Sibs). Separate video clips of infants and of parents were created for each episode of the FFSF. The emotional valence of infants and parents was rated by undergraduates using a joystick interface (see Figure 10.6). Ratings captured a scale from positive emotion (joy, happiness, pleasure) to neutral to negative emotion (distress, sadness, anger). Ratings were made individually and a given rater rated either infants or parents. Ratings from approximately 18 undergraduates were averaged to create a mean emotional valence time series for each second of interaction.

Rating Validity. Continuous nonexpert ratings have strong face validity. Measurements are based on a brief, layperson's description; results, then, reflect a precise but easily interpretable understanding of a construct.

FIGURE 10.6 A representation of the Continuous Measurement System used for continuous rating.

Raters showed high levels of consistency with each other both at a second-to-second level and at the level of FFSF episode. Mean ratings showed reasonable associations with objective measurements of facial expression within time (Figure 10.4) and high associations when summed over the episodes of the FFSF.

Affective Valence Levels. Mean levels of infant affective valence were higher in face-to-face interactions than in the still-face or reunion episodes. Higher valence reflects ratings that are more positive and less negative. Parent affective valence also showed a dip in the still-face, essentially a manipulation check. The rating study revealed subtle differences in mean levels of affective valence related to risk. Infant siblings of children with ASDs showed lower levels of rated positive affect (ratings above neutral) in the still-face than did infant siblings of typical comparison children (Baker, Haltigan, Brewster, Jaccard, & Messinger, 2010).

Interactive Influence. Both infant-to-parent and parent-to-infant interactive influence were evident. However, infant affective valence had a greater impact on parent affective valence than vice versa. As expected, interactive influence in each direction was stronger during the interactive episodes—face-to-face and reunion—than during the still-face. These findings emerged in a set of bivariate time series models with random effects designed to explore between-dyad differences in self-regulation and interactive dynamics. This is one of the first group time series models to rigorously demonstrate this fundamental feature of early interaction (see Figure 10.7).

Self-Regulation. Group differences in level of self-regulation were also evident (Chow et al., 2010). Infant siblings of children with ASDs exhibited higher levels of self-regulation than comparison infants. This was indexed by lower values of the autoregression variance parameter among ASD-Sibs. In other words, there was less variability in temporally based self-regulatory dynamics among ASD-Sibs than COMP-Sibs. The effect was only evident during the still-face and reunion, that is, during and after the perturbation introduced by asking the parent to be nonresponsive.

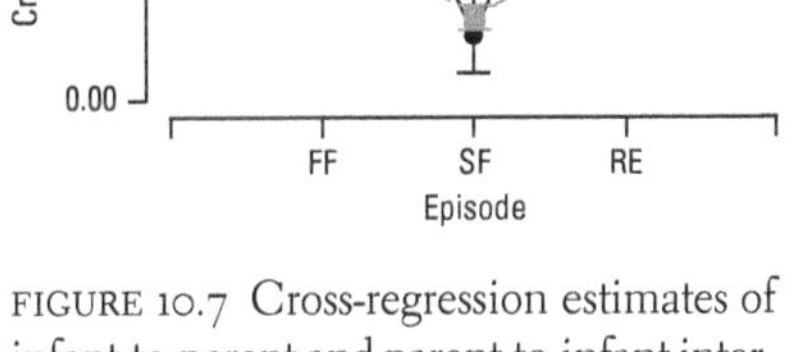

FIGURE 10.7 Cross-regression estimates of infant-to-parent and parent-to-infant interactive influence are shown for the face-to-face (FF), still-face (SF), and reunion (RE) episodes of the procedure. Infant-to-parent influence is higher than the reverse in episodes involving interaction.

On average, then, ASD-Sibs were less emotionally perturbed by the FFSF procedure than other infants.

Summary. Our microanalytic investigation using automated measurement led us to ask whether interactive influence parameters might change in time. Stochastic regression models revealed significant variance in the impact of the parent's affective valence on that of the infant over the course of an interactive episode. The strength of interactive influence varied with time during the face-to-face and reunion episodes, but not during the still-face. There also appeared to be greater interactive variance over time in the reunion than in the face-to-face interaction, suggesting subtle effects of the still-face perturbation (see Figure 10.7). These analyses confronted the problem of nonstationarity by modeling interactive influence. The time-dependent changes in interactive influence were allowed to vary randomly. In subsequent modeling we hope to ask substantive questions about time-varying influence. One might expect, for example, parent-to-infant influence in facial expressions of emotion to be attenuated during tickling but strengthened when the infant is gazing at the parent's face.

Conclusion

Obtaining efficient, replicable measurement of ongoing behavior is a chronic difficulty for students of interaction. This chapter presents new approaches to studying early emotional transactions by combining the collection of continuous measures of emotional intensity with appropriate analysis tools. These approaches helped produce meaningful measures of continuously occurring interaction, helping to overcome the dichotomy between discrete behavior and ordinal engagement scales. The results raised questions about the temporal stability of early interaction and its links to later development. We first consider methodological and then substantive implications of our work.

Methodology

We first employed an automated measurement approach that combined facial image analysis using computer vision and categorization of facial action intensity using machine learning. This microanalytic approach was supplemented with examination of local windows of correlation between infant and mother smiling to reveal changes in mother emotional interaction at a variety of timescales. We next separately collected nonexpert's continuous ratings of infant and mother emotional valence during interactions. These were modeled using stochastic regression techniques that allowed us to assess temporal changes in interactive influence and self-regulation. Despite their differences, each approach is oriented toward understanding continuous interactive processes as they occur in time.

Automated Measurement Limitations. It is worth noting limitations of our automated measurement approach, and future directions in its application. Our particular automated measurement approach emulated the intensity measurements of FACS Action Units, yielding precise assessment of emotional expression in time. This may be a limitation, however, in that the FACS intensity metric is ordinal (1–5) and designed to be readily identifiable by human beings. It is possible that other automated measurement approaches will bypass FACS to produce bottom-up measurements of facial activity that can be used to reliably index emotional communication. While it is technically possible to conduct continuous manual coding of the intensity of FACS Action Units, we know of no examples of this somewhat impractical approach. Nevertheless, despite the potential efficiency of automated measurement, we are unaware of empirical comparisons of the efficiency of automated and manual coding.

Automated Measurement: Future Directions and Recent Advances. We are currently training active appearance and shape models with frames from multiple subjects (infants and parents). This minimizes the training needed for any given subject. We have also achieved high levels of reliability employing a leave-one-out approach with support vector machines. This means the SVMs are trained and tested on different subjects. Finally, we have expanded the range of actions we measure to include indices of negative emotion and infant gaze direction. This approach is part of a broader movement toward automating the measurement of human communication (see Chapters 6 and 7 by Whitehill et al. and Busso et al., respectively, in this volume).

Limitations and Potential of Continuous Rating. The use of nonexpert continuous ratings is also evolving to realize its potential for providing efficient measurement of emotional and other types of communication. The method provides less temporal precision than automated measurement because it is dependent on rater reaction time. Ratings nevertheless revealed both infant-to-parent and parent-to-infant influence during interaction, suggesting their sensitivity to time-dependent signals. Other sets of nonexpert ratings are exhibiting high levels of association with expert ratings of maternal sensitivity and family conflict, suggesting the broad applicability of this procedure to multiple, emotionally relevant constructs.

Substantive Findings—Time-Varying Changes

Substantively, we used the automated measurement and continuous ratings to investigate time-linked changes in interactive influence. Automated measurements followed by windowed cross-correlation analyses revealed changes in interactive synchrony. We demonstrated the existence of these changes in interactive synchrony statistically using continuous ratings of emotional valence. The ubiquity of these time-varying changes is not surprising given that variable responsivity and change are hallmarks of human interaction (Fogel, Garvey, Hsu, & West-Stroming, 2006).

Prediction. In longitudinal research, summary measures of infant–parent interactive influence are used to predict outcome. While it is not clear that relevant influence and related parameters are stable over the course of an interaction, it appears that influence parameters represent a strong dyadic signal with an important place in development. It will be crucially important to determine whether real-time variance in interaction can contribute to our understanding of individual differences in development. We speak to these issues in the sections that follow.

Variability in Communicative Modality. Variability in influence over time is mirrored by variability in interactive influence in different modalities of communication. Beebe and her colleagues (Beebe et al., 2007) have related these different patterns of influence to personality characteristics. Depressed mothers, for example, who were more self-critical, showed lowered levels of responsivity to infant gaze direction and emotional expression, yet they exhibited greater responsivity of their own touch to infant touch. Thus, there may be psychologically important variability in responsivity between different modalities of communication.

Variable Patterning and Development. Different patterns of contingency in different communicative modalities occurring in different contexts may also be associated with different outcomes. In the realm of positive emotional communication, higher levels of parental responsivity appear most predictive of optimal development (Kochanska, 2002; Kochanska et al., 1999; Kochanska & Murray, 2000). By contrast, the level of influence (midrange versus high) in vocal turn taking, which is associated with infant security of attachment, may vary depending upon the context (home or laboratory) in which the original interaction was observed (Jaffe et al., 2001). These patterns point to the possibility that variability in influence patterns is more widespread—and developmentally significant—than is typically acknowledged.

Variability in Influence as Development. Finally, variability of influence parameters in time may play a role in development. Infants become more responsive to their parents between 2 and 6 months, setting the stage for the possibility of reciprocal (bidirectional) influence (Cohn & Tronick, 1987; Kaye & Fogel, 1980). Infants also become more likely to initiate smiles and positive greetings as they reach 6 months and beyond. This type of greeting or bidding is developmentally crucial. It represents an action that may be taken with the goal of eliciting a reaction. At the same time, such initiations are, somewhat by definition, not contingent on what has occurred previously. They represent, then, a breaking of synchrony, variability in time-varying influence parameters (Boker et al., 2002). This capacity to alter influence patterns may also be a precursor to the infant's use—later in the first year of life—of gaze, gesture, and smiling to intentionally refer to objects and events (Jones & Hong, 2001; Parlade et al., 2008; Venezia, Messinger, Thorp, & Mundy, 2004).

Conclusion. Finally, the dyadic or transactional nature of early interaction may be its most important feature. In the interactions explored with automated measurements, for example, both infants had their smiles reciprocated and intensified by their caregivers. These smiles are likely to unite (a) the affective facial-feedback characteristic of the smile with (b) the arousal frequently coincident with gazing at another with (c) the perception of the other's smile (Messinger & Fogel, 2007). These temporally linked experiences and actions are likely part of a process in which the perception of joy in the parent and the infants' perceptions of their own affect become the warp and woof of a single fabric. In this sense, these are transactional processes involving the dynamic emergence of coconstructed states of dyadic positivity.

Acknowledgments

The research was supported by NICHD R01 047417, R01057284, and R21 052062; NIMH R01051435; Autism Speaks; and the Marino Autism Research Institute. The authors thank the families who participated, the editor, and two anonymous reviewers, and the research team, including Ryan Brewster and Maria Kimijima.

Notes

1. Here we use the Continuous Measurement System (CMS) as a construct validity check. Later in the chapter, we employ it as a measurement instrument in its own right. The CMS can also be used to conduct continuous behavioral coding (e.g., FACS/BabyFACS) via mouse and keyboard. The CMS is available for download at http://measurement.psy.miami.edu/cms.phtml.

2. Software to calculate and view running cross-correlations is available for download at http://measurement.psy.miami.edu/wcc.phtml.

References

Adamson, L. B., & Frick, J. E. (2003). The still-face: A history of a shared experimental paradigm. *Infancy*, 4(4), 451–474.

Adrien, J. L., Perrot, A., Sauvage, D., Leddet, I., et al. (1992). Early symptoms in autism from family home movies: Evaluation and comparison between 1st and 2nd year of life using I.B.S.E. Scale. *Acta Paedopsychiatrica: International Journal of Child & Adolescent Psychiatry*, 55(2), 71–75.

American Psychiatric Association (2000). *Diagnostic and statistical manual of mental disorders DSM-IV-TR fourth edition (text revision)*. Washington, DC: American Psychiatric Association.

Ariely, D., Au, W.T., Bender, R. H., Budescu, D. V., Dietz, C., Gu, H., Wallsten, T. S., Zauberman, G. (2000). The effects of averaging subjective probability estimates between and within judges. *Journal of Experimental Psychology: Applied*, 6, 30–147.

Bakeman, R., & Gottman, J. (1986). *Observing interaction: An introduction to sequential analysis*. New York: Cambridge University Press.

Baker, J., Haltigan, J. D., Brewster, R., Jaccard, J., & Messinger, D. (2010). Non-expert ratings of infant and parent emotion: Concordance with expert coding and relevance to early autism risk. *International Journal of Behavioral Development*, 34, 88–95.

Baker, S., Matthews, I., & Schneider, J. (2004). Automatic construction of active appearance models as an image coding problem. *IEEE Transactions on Pattern Analysis and Machine Intelligence*, 26(10), 1380–1384.

Bartlett, M. S., Littlewort, G., Frank, M., Lainscsek, C., Fasel, I., & Movellan, J. (2005). Recognizing facial expression: Machine learning and application to spontaneous behavior. *Proceedings of the 2005 IEEE Computer Society Conference on Computer Vision and Pattern Recognition*, (Volume 2, pp. 568–573), IEEE Computer Society, Los Alamitos, CA .

Bartlett, M., Littlewort, G., Frank, M., Lainscsek, C., Fasel, I., & Movellan, J. (2006). Automatic recognition of facial actions in spontaneous expressions. *Journal of Multimedia*, 1(6), 22–35.

Beebe, B., & Gerstman, L. (1984). A method of defining "packages" of maternal stimulation and their functional significance for the infant with mother and stranger. *International Journal of Behavioral Development*, 7(4), 423–440.

Beebe, B., Jaffe, J., Buck, K., Chen, H., Cohen, P., Blatt, S., Kaminer, T., et al. (2007). Six-week postpartum maternal self-criticism and dependency and 4-month mother-infant self- and interactive contingencies. *Developmental Psychology*, 43(6), 1360–1376.

Belkin, M., & Niyogi, P. (2003). Laplacian Eigenmaps for dimensionality reduction and data representation. *Neural Computation Archive*, 15(6), 1373–1396.

Bendersky, M., & Lewis, M. (1998). Arousal modulation in cocaine-exposed infants. *Developmental Psychology*, 34(3), 555–564.

Boelte, S., & Poustka, F. (2003). The recognition of facial affect in autistic and schizophrenic subjects and their first-degree relatives. *Psychological Medicine*, 33(5), 907–915.

Boker, S. M., Rotondo, J. L., Xu, M., & King, K. (2002). Windowed cross-correlation and peak picking for the analysis of variability in the association between behavioral time series. *Psychological Methods*, 7(3), 338–355.

Bolton, P., Pickles, A., Murphy, M., & Rutter, M. (1998). Autism, affective and other psychiatric disorders: Patterns of familial aggregation. *Psychological Medicine*, 28(Mar), 385–395.

Bolzani-Dinehart, L., Messinger, D. S., Acosta, S., Cassel, T., Ambadar, Z., & Cohn, J. (2005). Adult perceptions of positive and negative infant emotional expressions. *Infancy*, 8(3), 279–303.

Bryson, S. E., Landry, R., Czapinski, P., McConnell, B., Rombough, V., & Wainwright, A. (2004). Autistic spectrum disorders: Causal mechanisms and recent findings on attention and emotion. *International Journal of Special Education, 19*(1), 14–22.

Carvajal, F., & Iglesias, J. (2002). The Duchenne smile with open mouth in infants with Down syndrome. *Infant Behavior & Development, 24*(3), 341–346.

Cassel, T., Messinger, D. S., Ibanez, L., Haltigan, J. D., Acosta, S., & Buchman, A. (2007). Early social and emotional communication in the infant siblings of children with autism spectrum disorders: An examination of the broad phenotype. *Journal of Autism and Developmental Disorders, 37*, 122–132.

Chang, C. C., & Lin, C. J. (2001). LIBSVM: A library for support vector machines. Retrieved 4/7/2008 from http://www.csie.ntu.edu.tw/~cjlin/libsvm

Chong, S. C. F., Werker, J. F., Russell, J. A., & Carroll, J. M. (2003). Three facial expressions mothers direct to their infants. *Infant and Child Development, 12*, 211–232.

Chow, S., Haltigan, J. D., & Messinger, D. S. (2010). Dynamic affect coupling between infants and parents during face-to-face and still-face paradigm: Inter- and intra-dyad differences. *Emotion, 10*, 101–114.

Cohn, J., Campbell, S. B., & Ross, S. (1991). Infant response in the still-face paradigm at 6 months predicts avoidant and secure attachment at 12 months. *Development and Psychopathology, 3*(4), 367–376.

Cohn, J., & Kanade, T. (2007). Automated facial image analysis for measurement of emotion expression. In J. A. Coan & J. B. Allen (Eds.), *The handbook of emotion elicitation and assessment* (pp. 222–238). New York: Oxford.

Cohn, J., & Tronick, E. (1987). Mother-infant face-to-face interaction: The sequence of dyadic states at 3, 6, and 9 months. *Developmental Psychology, 23*(1), 68–77.

Cohn, J. F., Reed, L., Moriyama, T., Xiao, J., Schmidt, K., & Ambadar, Z. (2004). Multimodal coordination of facial action, head rotation, and eye motion. *Proceedings of the Sixth IEEE International Conference on Automatic Face and Gesture Recognition* (pp. 129–135), IEEE Computer Society, Los Alamitos, CA.

Cohn, J. F., & Tronick, E. Z. (1988a). Discrete versus scaling approaches to the description of mother-infant face-to-face interaction: Convergent validity and divergent applications. *Developmental Psychology, 24*(3), 396–397.

Cohn, J. F., & Tronick, E. Z. (1988b). Mother-infant face-to-face interaction: Influence is bidirectional and unrelated to periodic cycles in either partner's behavior. *Developmental Psychology, 24*(3), 386–392.

Constantino, J. N., Davis, S. A., Todd, R. D., Schindler, M. K., Gross, M. M., Brophy, S. L., Metzger, L. M., Shoushtari, C. S., Splinter, R., & Reich, W. (2003). Validation of a brief quantitative measure of autistic traits: Comparison of the Social Responsiveness Scale with the Autism Diagnostic Interview-Revised. *Journal of Autism and Developmental Disorders, 33*(4), 427–433.

Constantino, J., Lajonchere, C., Lutz, M., Gray, T., Abbacchi, A., McKenna, K., Singh, D., et al. (2006). Autistic social impairment in the siblings of children with pervasive developmental disorders. *American Journal of Psychiatry, 163*(2), 294–296.

Cootes, T. F., Edwards, G. J., & Taylor, C. J. (2001). Active appearance models. *Pattern Analysis and Machine Intelligence, 23*, 681–685.

Crown, C. L., Feldstein, S., Jasnow, M. D., Beebe, B., & Jaffe, J. (2002). The cross-modal coordination of interpersonal timing: Six-week-olds infants' gaze with adults' vocal behavior. *Journal of Psycholinguistic Research, 31*, 1–23.

Delgado, E. F., Messinger, D. S., & Yale, M. E. (2002). Infant responses to direction of parental gaze: A comparison of two still-face conditions. *Infant Behavior and Development, 137*, 1–8.

Dickson, K. L., Walker, H., & Fogel, A. (1997). The relationship between smile-type and play-type during parent-infant play. *Developmental Psychology, 33*(6), 925–933.

Ekman, P., Davidson, R. J., & Friesen, W. (1990). The Duchenne smile: Emotional expression and brain physiology II. *Journal of Personality and Social Psychology, 58*, 342–353.

Ekman, P., & Friesen, W. (1978). *The Facial Action Coding System*: Palo Alto, CA: Consulting Psychologists Press.

Ekman, P., Friesen, W., & Hager, J. C. (2002). *The Facial Action Coding System on CD ROM*. Network Information Research Center.

Elias, G., & Broerse, J. (1995). Temporal patterning of vocal behaviour in mother–infant engagements: Infant-initiated "encounters" as units of analysis. *Australian Journal of Psychology, 47*(1), 47–53.

Essa, I. A., & Pentland, A. (1994, June). *A vision system for observing and extracting facial action parameters*. Paper presented at the IEEE CVPR, Seattle, Washington.

Feldman, R. (2006). From biological rhythms to social rhythms: Physiological precursors of mother-infant synchrony. *Developmental Psychology, 42*(1), 175–188.

Feldman, R., & Greenbaum, C. W. (1997). Affect regulation and synchrony in mother-infant play as precursors to the development of symbolic competence. *Infant Mental Health Journal, 18*(1), 4–23.

Feldman, R., Greenbaum, C. W., Mayes, L. C., & Erlich, S. H. (1997). Change in mother-infant interactive behavior: Relations to change in the mother, the infant, and the social context. *Infant Behavior and Development*, *20*(2), 151–163.

Feldman, R., Greenbaum, C. W., & Yirmiya, N. (1999). Mother-infant affect synchrony as an antecedent of the emergence of self-control. *Developmental Psychology*, *35*(1), 223–231.

Feldman, R., Greenbaum, C. W., Yirmiya, N., & Mayes, L. C. (1996). Relations between cyclicity and regulation in mother-infant interaction at 3 and 9 months and cognition at 2 years. *Journal of Applied Developmental Psychology*, *17*(3), 347–365.

Fogel, A. (1988). Cyclicity and stability in mother-infant face-to-face interaction: A comment on Cohn and Tronick. *Developmental Psychology*, *24*(3), 393–395.

Fogel, A., Garvey, A., Hsu, H.-C., & West-Stroming, D. (2006). *Change processes in relationships: A relational-historical research approach.* New York: Cambridge University Press.

Fogel, A., Hsu, H.-C., Shapiro, A. F., Nelson-Goens, G. C., & Secrist, C. (2006). Effects of normal and perturbed social play on the duration and amplitude of different types of infant smiles. *Developmental Psychology*, *42*, 459–473.

Fogel, A., Nelson-Goens, G. C., Hsu, H.-C., & Shapiro, A. F. (2000). Do different infant smiles reflect different positive emotions? *Social Development*, *9*(4), 497–520.

Fox, N., & Davidson, R. J. (1988). Patterns of brain electrical activity during facial signs of emotion in 10 month old infants. *Developmental Psychology*, *24*(2), 230–236.

Frank, M. G., Ekman, P., & Friesen, W. V. (1993). Behavioral markers and the recognizability of the smile of enjoyment. *Journal of Personality and Social Psychology*, *64*(1), 83–93.

Gottman, J., & Levenson, R. W. (1985). A valid measure for obtaining self-report of affect. *Journal of Consulting and Clinical Psychology*, *53*, 151–160.

Harker, L., & Keltner, D. (2001). Expressions of positive emotion in women's college yearbook pictures and their relationship to personality and life outcomes across adulthood. *Journal of Personality and Social Psychology*, *80*(1), 112–124.

Harris, C. R. (1999, July–August). The mystery of ticklish laughter. *American Scientist*, *87*(4), 344.

Jaffe, J., Beebe, B., Feldstein, S., Crown, C. L., & Jasnow, M. D. (2001). Rhythms of dialogue in infancy: Coordinated timing in development. *Monographs of the Society for Research in Child Development*, *66*(2), vi–131.

Jones, S. S., & Hong, H.-W. (2001). Onset of voluntary communication: Smiling looks to mother. *Infancy*, *2*(3), 353–370.

Joseph, R., & Tager-Flusberg, H. (1997). An investigation of attention and affect in children with autism and Down syndrome. *Journal of Autism and Developmental Disorders*, *27*(4), 385–396.

Kasari, C., Sigman, M., Mundy, P., & Yirmiya, N. (1990). Affective sharing in the context of joint attention interactions of normal, autistic, and mentally retarded children. *Journal of Autism and Developmental Disorders*, *20*(1), 87–100.

Kaye, K., & Fogel, A. (1980). The temporal structure of face-to-face communication between mothers and infants. *Developmental Psychology*, *16*(5), 454–464.

Keltner, D., & Ekman, P. (2000). Facial expression of emotion. In M. Lewis & J. M. Haviland-Jones (Eds.), *Handbook of emotions* (2nd ed., pp. 236–249). New York: Guilford Press.

Keltner, D., Kring, A. M., & Bonanno, G.A. (1999). Fleeting signs of the course of life: Facial expression and personal adjustment. *Current Directions in Psychological Science*, *8*(1), 18–22.

Kochanska, G. (2002). Mutually responsive orientation between mothers and their young children: A context for the early development of conscience. *Current Directions in Psychological Science*, *11*(6), 191–195.

Kochanska, G., Forman, D. R., & Coy, K. C. (1999). Implications of the mother-child relationship in infancy socialization in the second year of life. *Infant Behavior & Development*, *22*(2), 249–265.

Kochanska, G., & Murray, K. T. (2000). Mother-child mutually responsive orientation and conscience development: From toddler to early school age. *Child Development*, *71*(2), 417–431.

Lavelli, M., & Fogel, A. (2002). Developmental changes in mother-infant face-to-face communication: Birth to 3 months. *Developmental Psychology*, *38*(2), 288–305.

Levenson, R. W., & Gottman, J. M. (1983). Marital interaction: Physiological linkage and affective exchange. *Journal of Personality & Social Psychology*, *45*, 587–597.

Lien, J. J., Kanade, T., Cohn, J. F., & Li, C.-C. (2000). Detection, tracking, and classification of subtle changes in facial expression. *Journal of Robotics and Autonomous Systems*, *31*, 131–146.

Littlewort, G., Bartlett, M. S., & Movellan, J. R. (2001). Are your eyes smiling? Detecting genuine smiles with support vector machines and Gabor wavelets. *Proceedings of the 8th Annual Joint Symposium on Neural Computation*, La Jolla, CA.

Lord, C., Rutter, M., & Le Couteur, A. (1994). Autism Diagnostic Interview-Revised: A revised version of a diagnostic interview for caregivers of individuals with possible pervasive developmental disorders.

Journal of Autism Development Disorders, 24(Oct), 659–685.

Lucey, S., Ashraf, A. B., & Cohn, J. (2007). Investigating spontaneous facial action recognition through AAM representations of the face. In K. Kurihara (Ed.), *Face recognition*. Mammendorf, Germany: Pro Literatur Verlag.

Mahoor, M. H., Messinger, D. S., Ibanez, L., Kimijima M., Wang, Y., Cadavid, S., & Cohn, J. F. (2008, August). *Studying facial expressions using manifold learning and support vector machines*. Paper presented at the IEEE 7th International Conference on Development and Learning, Monterey, CA.

Malatesta, C. Z., Culver, C., Tesman, J. R., & Shepard, B. (1989). The development of emotion expression during the first two years of life. *Monographs of the Society for Research in Child Development*, 54(1–2), 1–104.

Matias, R., & Cohn, J. F. (1993). Are MAX-specified infant facial expressions during face-to-face interaction consistent with differential emotions theory? *Developmental Psychology*, 29(3), 524–531.

McIntosh, D. N., Reichmann-Decker, A., Winkielman, P., & Wilbarger, J. L. (2006). When the social mirror breaks: Deficits in automatic, but not voluntary, mimicry of emotional facial expressions in autism. *Developmental Science*, 9, 295–302.

Messinger, D. (2002). Positive and negative: Infant facial expressions and emotions. *Current Directions in Psychological Science*, *11*(1), 1–6.

Messinger, D., Cassel, T., Acosta, S., Ambadar, Z., & Cohn, J. (2008). Infant smiling dynamics and perceived positive emotion. *Journal of Nonverbal Behavior*, 32, 133–155.

Messinger, D., & Fogel, A. (2007). The interactive development of social smiling. In R. Kail (Ed.), *Advances in Child Development and Behavior* (Vol. 35, pp. 328–366). Oxford, UK: Elsevier.

Messinger, D., Fogel, A., & Dickson, K. (1999). What's in a smile? *Developmental Psychology*, 35(3), 701–708.

Messinger, D., Fogel, A., & Dickson, K. (2001). All smiles are positive, but some smiles are more positive than others. *Developmental Psychology*, 37(5), 642–653.

Messinger, D., Mahoor, M., Chow, S., Cadavid, S., & Cohn, J. F. (2008, August). *Early interactive emotional development*. Paper presented at the IEEE 7th International Conference on Development and Learning, Monterey, CA.

Messinger, D., Mahoor, M., Chow, S., & Cohn, J. F. (2009). Automated measurement of facial expression in infant-mother interaction: A pilot study. *Infancy*, *14*, 285–305. NIHMS99269.

Murphy, M., Bolton, P. F., Pickles, A., Fombonne, E., Piven, J., & Rutter, M. (2000). Personality traits of the relatives of autistic probands. *Psychological Medicine*, *30*(6) 1411–1424.

Newtson, D. (1993). The dynamics of action and interaction. In Anonymous (Ed.), *A dynamic systems approach to development: Applications* (pp. 241–264). Cambridge, MA: MIT Press.

Oster, H. (2006). *Baby FACS: Facial Action Coding System for infants and young children*. Unpublished monograph and coding manual, New York: New York University.

Padgett, C., Cottrell, G. W., & Adolphs, B. (1996, July). Categorical perception in facial emotion classification. Paper presented at the Cognitive Science Conference San Diego, CA.

Parlade, M. V., Messinger, D. S., van Hecke, A., Kaiser, M., Delgado, C., & Mundy, P. (2008). Anticipatory smiling: Linking early affective communication and social outcome. *Infant Behavior & Development*, 32(1), 33–43.

Ruch, W. (1995). Will the real relationship between facial expression and affective experience please stand up: The case of exhilaration. *Cognition and Emotion*, 9, 33–58.

Ruef, A. M., & Levenson, R. W. (2007). Continuous measurement of emotion: The affect rating dial. In J. A. C. J. J. B. Allen (Ed.), *Handbook of emotion elicitation and assessment* (pp. 286–297). New York: Oxford University Press.

Schneider, K., & Uzner, L. (1992). Preschoolers' attention and emotion in an achievement and an effect game: A longitudinal study. *Cognition and Emotion*, 6(1), 37–63.

Schore, A. N. (1994). *Affect regulation & the origin of self: The neurobiology of emotional development*. Hillsdale, NJ: Erlbaum.

Stel, M., van den Heuvel, C., & Smeets, R. (2008). Facial feedback mechanisms in autistic spectrum disorders. *Journal of Autism and Developmental Disorders*, 38(7), 1250–1258.

Symons, D., & Moran, G. (1994). Responsiveness and dependency are different aspects of social contingencies: An example from mother and infant smiles. *Infant Behavior and Development*, 17(2), 209–214.

Szatmari, P., MacLean, J. E., Jones, M. B., Bryson, S. E., Zwaigenbaum, L., Bartolucci, G., Mahoney, W. J., et al. (2000). The familial aggregation of the lesser variant in biological and nonbiological relatives of PDD probands: A family history study. *Journal of Child Psychology and Psychiatry*, *41*(5), 579–586.

Tian, Y., Kanade, T., & Cohn, J. F. (2001). Recognizing action units for facial expression analysis. *IEEE Transactions on Pattern Analysis and Machine Intelligence*, 23(2), 97–116.

Tian, Y. L., Kanade, T., & Cohn, J. F. (2002, May). Evaluation of Gabor-wavelet-based facial action unit recognition in image sequences of increasing complexity. Paper presented at the Proceedings of the Fifth IEEE International Conference on Automatic Face and Gesture Recognition, Washington, DC.

Tronick, E. Z., Als, H., Adamson, L., Wise, S., & Brazelton, B. (1978). The infant's response to entrapment between contradictory messages in face-to-face interaction. *American Academy of Child Psychiatry, 17*, 1–13.

Tronick, E. Z., & Cohn, J. F. (1989). Infant-mother face-to-face interaction: Age and gender differences in coordination and the occurrence of miscoordination. *Child Development, 60*(1), 85–92.

Tronick, E. Z., Messinger, D., Weinberg, K. M., Lester, B. M., LaGasse, L., Seifer, R., Bauer, C., et al. (2005). Cocaine exposure compromises infant and caregiver social emotional behavior and dyadic interactive features in the face-to-face still-face paradigm. *Developmental Psychology, 41*(5), 711–722.

Van Egeren, L. A., Barratt, M. S., & Roach, M. A. (2001). Mother-infant responsiveness: Timing, mutual regulation, and interactional context. *Developmental Psychology*, 37(5), 684–697.

Venezia, M., Messinger, D. S., Thorp, D., & Mundy, P. (2004). The development of anticipatory smiling. *Infancy, 6*(3), 397–406.

Waldinger, R. J., Schulz, M. S., Hauser, S. T., Allen, J. P., & Crowell, J. A. (2004). Reading others' emotions: The role of intuitive judgments in predicting marital satisfaction, quality, and stability. *Journal of Family Psychology, 18*, 58–71.

Wassink, T. H., Brzustowicz, L. M., Bartlett, C. W., & Szatmari, P. (2004). The search for autism disease genes. *Mental Retardation and Developmental Disabilities Research Reviews, 10*(4), 272–283.

Weinberg, K. M., & Tronick, E. Z. (1998). *Infant and Caregiver Engagement Phases System.* Boston: Harvard Medical School.

Weinberg, M. K., Tronick, E. Z., Cohn, J. F., & Olson, K. L. (1999). Gender differences in emotional expressivity and self-regulation during early infancy. *Developmental Psychology*, 35(1), 175–188.

Yacoob, Y., & Davis, L. (1997). Recognizing human facial expression from long image sequence using optical flow. *IEEE Transactions on Pattern Recognition and Machine Intelligence, 18*, 636–642.

Yale, M. E., Messinger, D. S., & Cobo-Lewis, A. B. (2003). The temporal coordination of early infant communication. *Developmental Psychology*, 39(5), 815–824.

Yirmiya, N., Gamliel, I., Pilowsky, T., Feldman, R., Baron-Cohen, S., & Sigman, M. (2006). The development of siblings of children with autism at 4 and 14 months: Social engagement, communication, and cognition. *Journal of Child Psychology and Psychiatry*, 47(5), 511–523.

Yirmiya, N., Kasari, C., Sigman, M., & Mundy, P. (1989). Facial expressions of affect in autistic, mentally retarded and normal children. *Journal of Child Psychology and Psychiatry*, 30(Sep), 725–735.

Zwaigenbaum, L., Bryson, S., Rogers, T., Roberts, W., Brian, J., & Szatmari, P. (2005). Behavioral manifestations of autism in the first year of life. International Journal of Developmental Neuroscience, 23, 143–152.

11

Using Social Agents to Explore Theories of Rapport and Emotional Resonance

Jonathan Gratch, Sin-Hwa Kang, & Ning Wang

Introduction

Emotions are often described as momentary, even discrete, reactions to some specific event. For example, we see a bear in the forest, and fear seems to emerge without bidding, fully formed. Writing around the same time as William James, George Herbert Mead employed a very different metaphor to emphasize how emotions can incrementally unfold and resonate between social actors. He asks us to imagine two angry dogs preparing to fight (Mead, 1934, pp. 42–43):

> The act of each dog becomes the stimulus of the other dog for his response. There is then a relationship between these two; and as the act is responded to by the other dog, it, in turn, undergoes change. The very fact that the dog is ready to attack another becomes a stimulus to the other dog to change his own position of his own attitude. He has no sooner done this than the change of attitude in the second dog in turn causes the first dog to change his attitude.... [More generally, referring to human combatants,] If the individual is successful a great deal of his attack and defense must be not considered, it must take place immediately. He must adjust himself "instinctively" to the attitude of the other individual. He may, of course, think it out. He may deliberately feint in order to open up a place of attack. But a great deal has to be without deliberation.

Of course, such "instinctive" unfolding of emotions is not limited to battles. Imagine instead two close friends engrossed in conversation. The speakers seem tightly enmeshed in something like a dance. They rapidly resonate to each other's gestures, facial expressions, gaze, and patterns of speech. Tickle-Degnen and Rosenthal (1990) referred to this seemingly automatic attunement of positive emotional displays, gaze, and gestures as *rapport* and documented a wide range of beneficial interpersonal consequences that result from its establishment.

As these two examples suggest, such unfolding and resonating patterns of emotional display can arise without conscious deliberation (Bargh, Chen, & Burrows, 1996; Lakin, Jefferis, Cheng, & Chartrand, 2003), but they are hardly fixed responses to external stimuli. The same individual that smiles reflexively to the smile of a friend may frown to the smiles of his opponent (Lanzetta & Englis, 1989). The way such interpersonal patterns unfold depends on a host of intra- and interpersonal factors including the relative power of individuals in an interaction—with weaker partners tending to mimic the more powerful but not vice versa (Tiedens & Fragale, 2003); prior expectations—with unexpectedly positive behaviors producing more favorable outcomes than expected ones (Burgoon, 1983); and conformity to social norms such as reciprocity (Roloff & Campion, 1987) or the appropriateness of expressing negative emotions (Adam, Shirako, & Maddux, 2010). More generally, as discussed by Parkinson (Chapter 2, this volume), these patterns both arise from and help to redefine an evolving affective relationship between individuals.

Building computer programs that can engage people in this unfolding emotional dance is a fascinating prospect with potentially profound practical and scientific consequences. In humans, such "emotional resonance" has been argued to play a crucial role in the establishment of social bonds (Tickle-Degnen & Rosenthal, 1990), in promoting or diffusing conflict (Lanzetta & Englis, 1989), in determining the persuasiveness of speech (Bailenson & Yee, 2005; Fuchs, 1987), and in the establishment of identity Mead (1934). Computer agents that engage people in this manner, on the one hand, could enhance our understanding of this fundamental social process by systematically manipulating nonverbal patterns in ways that are difficult or impossible for human confederates in social science experiments, allowing the possibility of studies that definitively establish whether such patterns *cause* these effects or merely reflect them (see Bailenson, Beall, Loomis, Blascovich, & Turk, 2004; Bente, Kraemer, Petersen, & de Ruiter, 2001; Forgas, 2007). Indeed, in this chapter we show that synthesized patterns of nonverbal behavior do seem to cause predicted changes in the impressions and behaviors of human subjects in laboratory studies, and give some insight into the factors that promote these effects. On the other hand, assuming theses effects can be demonstrated outside the laboratory, such emotionally resonant agents could have dramatic implications for computer-based applications to health, commerce, and entertainment.

We argue that several challenges must be overcome before realizing this vision: the computer must approach a social interaction with certain goals and expectations about the social context, it must recognize and interpret the verbal and nonverbal cues, in real-time, of its human interaction partner, it must rapidly generate responses contingent on its current goals and expectations, and it must evolve its goals and expectations of self and other, based on the unfolding interaction. More importantly, success depends not on simply overcoming these challenges, but demonstrating that establishing such interactivity has measurable and desirable consequences for human–computer interaction (see also, Gratch, 2008, 2010).

In this chapter, we describe one line of research in our laboratory that builds toward this vision of emotionally resonant agents. We describe the Rapport Agent, an interactive agent and methodological tool designed to investigate the role of nonverbal patterning in human–computer and computer-mediated interaction. The Rapport Agent recognizes and reflexively responds to certain human nonverbal cues with the aim of establishing a sense of rapport between the human and computer. In this sense, the system is solving a much simpler problem than the one outlined previously: we explore a fixed mapping between nonverbal perception and action, and ignore how these actions and reactions alter the agent's expectations and perception of the social interaction. Nevertheless, as we will outline, even this simple system yields some important insights into the social processes that govern human–agent interaction and is a stepping stone to more comprehensive models of human social behavior.

As the focus of the Rapport Agent is to establish a subjective sense of rapport in a human interaction partner, we first outline the concept of rapport. We next describe the basic mechanics of the system. We then outline a series of laboratory studies and resulting findings that give insight into how nonverbal patterns of behavior can influence both subjective perceptions (such as feelings of rapport or embarrassment) and behavioral outcomes (such as speech fluency or intimate self-disclosure). Finally we end with some speculation on the future of such human–computer systems.

Interpersonal Rapport Between People and Machine

Rapport is studied across a range of scientific disciplines for its role in fostering emotional bonds and prosocial behavior. In their seminal article, Tickle-

Degnen and Rosenthal (1990) equate rapport with behaviors indicating positive emotions (e.g., head nods or smiles), mutual attentiveness (e.g., mutual gaze), and coordination (e.g., postural mimicry or synchronized movements).[1] The role of rapport in fostering effective social interaction is well established in the field of social psychological research. Rapport is easy to assess—observers can reliably predict whether people will report feelings of rapport by watching their nonverbal behavior (Ambady, Bernieri, & Richeson, 2000)—and these judgments and feelings predict success in a surprising range of social activities (Bernieri, Gillis, Davis, & Grahe, 1996). For example, rapport is argued to underlie social engagement (Tatar, 1997), success in teacher–student interactions (Bernieri, 1988), success in negotiations (Drolet & Morris, 2000), improving worker compliance (Cogger, 1982), psychotherapeutic effectiveness (Tsui & Schultz, 1985), improved test performance in classrooms (Fuchs, 1987), and improved quality of child care (Burns, 1984).

The power of rapport in face-to-face interaction has served as an inspiration to researchers in human–computer interaction, and a number of projects have sought to endow computers with the ability to sense and respond to human nonverbal behavior. For example, Neuro Baby is a computer-generated baby that analyzes speech intonation and uses the extracted features to trigger emotional displays (Tosa, 1993). Similarly, Breazeal's Kismet robot extracts emotional qualities in the user's speech (Breazeal & Aryananda, 2002). Whenever the speech recognizer detects a pause in the speech, the previous utterance is classified (within 1 or 2 seconds) as indicating approval, an attentional bid, or a prohibition, soothing or neutral. This recognition feature is combined with Kismet's current emotional state to determine facial expression and head posture. Only a few systems can interject meaningful nonverbal feedback *during* another's speech, and these methods usually rely on simple acoustic cues. For example, REA will execute a head nod or paraverbal (e.g., "mm-hum") if the user pauses in midutterance (Cassell et al., 1999). Some work has attempted to extract extralinguistic features of a speakers' behavior, but not for the purpose of informing listening behaviors. For example, Brand's voice puppetry work attempts to learn a mapping between acoustic features and facial configurations, inciting a virtual puppet to react to the speaker's voice (Brand, 1999). Although there is considerable research showing the benefit of such feedback on human-to-human interaction, there has been almost no research on their impact on human-to-virtual human rapport (cf. Bailenson & Yee, 2005; Cassell & Thórisson, 1999; Schröder et al., 2008).

The success of such technological approaches remains an empirical question, but a more fundamental challenge lies in finding appropriate theoretical constructs to inform their design. Research by Nass and colleagues on the "Media Equation" (Reeves & Nass, 1996)—which illustrates that people will often respond to computer agents as if they are people—suggests that human–computer interactions are governed by many of the same social processes and norms that apply in human face-to-face interactions and, by inference, that social theories could be applied directly to the design of computational systems. However, agents are not people. They are far more limited in their intellectual capabilities. They can look and behave in ways that are decidedly unreal. And (currently) you can be certain you won't bump into them in the street or worry about them besmirching your reputation to your friends. Thus, a central question in designing emotionally resonant agents is whether social theories such as Rapport can be applied directly to their design, or whether we must develop unique theories to explain this new and increasingly common form of social interaction.

Rapport Agent

The Rapport Agent (see Figure 11.1) is designed to evoke subjective feelings and behavioral consequences of rapport with human participants in a restricted set of social interactions we refer to as *quasi-monologs*. In a quasi-monolog, the human does most of the talking and the agent primarily prompts human speech and provides attentive listening feedback. The Rapport Agent was originally developed to replicate findings by Duncan and colleagues on listening behaviors (Welji & Duncan, 2004). In their studies, a speaker (the narrator) retells some previously observed series of events (e.g., the events in a recently-watched video) to some listener. In our case, the listener is a computer-generated character that has been programmed to produce (or fail to produce) the type of nonverbal feedback we seen in rapportful conversations. More recently, we have explored interview settings where

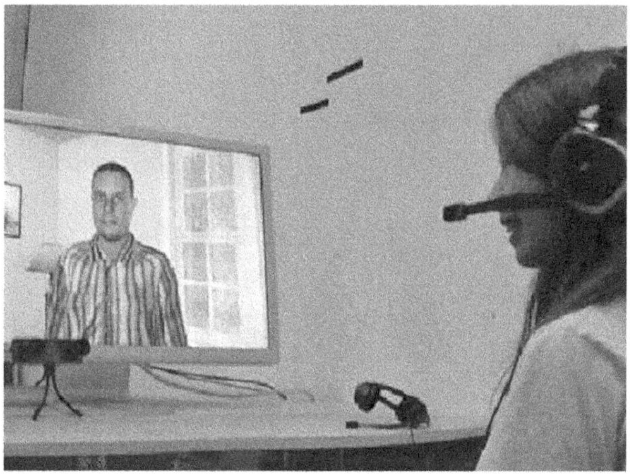

FIGURE 11.1 A speaker interacting with the Rapport Agent.

the agent asks a person a series of questions and listens attentively until it is time to ask the next question (Kang, Gratch, Wang, & Watt, 2009). By focusing on quasi monologs, rather than richer two-way conversational forms, we sidestep the current limitations in automatic natural language processing technology: the system produces what seems to be meaningful feedback without having to deeply process the meaning of the monolog. By changing these behaviors and the cover story surrounding this interaction (e.g., is the listener controlled by a computer or the behavior of an actual listener?), we hope to elicit the same correlations seen in face-to-face interaction between nonverbal behaviors, self, and other reports of rapport, and social outcomes such as liking, persuasion, and conversational fluency, as well as to unpack the factors that govern these effects.

The central challenge for the Rapport Agent is to generate the nonverbal listening feedback associated with rapportful interactions. Although our recent work has focused on how to learn to produce these behaviors automatically from examples (Huang, Morency, & Gratch, 2010; Morency, de Kok, & Gratch, 2008), the system we describe here was crafted by hand from findings in the psycholinguistic literature showing that feelings of rapport are correlated with simple contingent behaviors between speaker and listener. Such feedback includes the use of backchannel continuers (nods, elicited by speaker prosodic cues, that signify the communication is working), postural mirroring, and mimicry of certain head gestures, for example, gaze shifts and head nods (Chartrand & Bargh, 1999; Ward & Tsukahara, 2000; Yngve, 1970). The Rapport Agent generates such feedback by real-time analysis of acoustic properties of speech (detecting backchannel opportunity points, disfluencies, questions, and loudness) and speaker gestures (detecting head nods, shakes, gaze shifts, and posture shifts).

Behavior of Human Listeners

The psycholinguistic literature has identified a variety of behaviors that human listeners perform when in face-to-face conversations. Even though many listener behaviors provide feedback about the semantic content the speaker's speech, a large class of behaviors appear unrelated to specific meaning. Rather, these behaviors seem to trigger off of nonsemantic features of the speaker's presentation, may precede complete understanding of the speech content, and are often generated without the listener or speaker's conscious awareness. Nonetheless, such behaviors can significantly influence the flow of a conversation and the impressions and feelings of the participants. Here we review some of these behaviors, the circumstances that trigger their production, and their hypothesized influence on the interaction.

Backchannel Continuers

Listeners frequently nod and utter paraverbals such as "uh-huh" and "mm-hmm" as someone is speaking. Within the psycholinguistic literature, such behaviors are referred to as backchannel continuers and are considered as a signal to the speaker that the communication is working and that they should continue speaking (Yngve, 1970). Several researchers have developed models to predict when such feedback occurs. Cathcart et al. (2003) propose a model based on pause duration and trigram part-of-speech frequency. According to the model of Ward and Tsukahara (2000), backchannel continuers are associated with a lowering of pitch over some interval. Cassell (2000) argues that head nods could result from the raised voice of the speaker. The approaches of Ward and Cassell are more amenable to a real-time treatment as they are based purely on simple properties of the audio signal.

Disfluency

Spoken language often contains repetition, spurious words, pauses, and filled pauses (e.g., ehm, um, un). Such disfluency is viewed as a signal to the listener that the speaker is experiencing processing problems or experiencing high cognitive load (Clark & Wasow, 1998) and frequently elicit "take your time" feedback from the listener (Ward & Tsukahara, 2000). According to our own video analysis, rather than nod or utter sounds as in backchannel continuers, listeners tended to perform posture shifts, gaze shifts, or frowns in response to disfluency. The presumed meaning of such a posture shift is that the listener is telling the speaker to take his time (Cassell, 2000).

Mimicry

Listeners often mimic behavior of a speaker during a conversation. Although they are not necessarily aware of doing it, people in a conversation will adjust the rhythm of speech, their body posture, and even their breathing to each other (Lakin et al., 2003; McFarland, 2001; Warner, 1996). Mimicry, when not exaggerated to the point of mocking, has a variety of positive influences on the interactants. Speakers who are mimicked are more helpful and generous toward the listener (Van baaren, Holland, Kawakami, & Knippenberg, 2004). Mimicry can result in the perception of a pleasant, natural conversation (Warner, Malloy, Schneider, Kooth, & Wilder, 1987). It may also be important in synchronizing conversational flow, for example, by providing expectations on when a speaker can be interrupted. Given such influences, many of the agent's listening behaviors should mimic aspects of the speaker's behavior.

One salient speaker behavior is shifts in posture. When a speaker shifts her posture, for example, by changing her weight distribution from one leg to another, or by folding her arms, this is often mirrored by the listener. Such posture shifts, both for speakers and listeners, tend to occur at discourse segment boundaries and may function to help manage such transitions (Cassell, Nakano, Bickmore, Sidner, & Rich, 2001). When present, such mimicry has been shown to positively influence the emotional state of the speaker (Van baaren et al., 2004). Gaze is also an important aspect of a speaker's behavior. Speakers will often gaze away from the listener; for example, when mentioning a concrete object within his vicinity, he will often look at it. Listeners will frequently mimic the head gestures of a speaker also. If a speaker shakes or nods his head, listeners may repeat this gesture. Although this may simply reflect an understanding and agreement with the speaker's utterance, many of us have probably been in conversations where such gestures were produced without any real understanding. In any event, an agent can easily mimic such gestures without explicit understanding.

Other External Influences

Many factors may influence the occurrence of gestures during a conversation. For example, listeners frequently mimic the facial expression of speakers, and this apparently plays an important role in the perception of empathy (Sonnby-Borgstrom, Jonsson, & Svensson, 2003). Individuals also differ in their response to the same speech based on a variety of dispositional and situational factors. There are people who almost do not gesture at all, and there are people who gesture like it is a workout. Often, this is related to the speaker's emotions during the conversation. For example, people tend to gesture more when excited and less when sad. Also, the relation of the two people is of importance. People tend to gesture remarkably more when they talk to a friend than when they are talking to a complete stranger (Welji & Duncan, 2004).

Behavior of the Rapport Agent

From this literature we extract a small number of simple rules that the Rapport Agent could possibly utilize to drive its behavior. The mapping presented here (summarized in Table 11.1) is not a complete coverage of all gestures that at all times are accompanied by the certain speech features, but could be sufficient to increase the perceived authenticity of the conversation.

TABLE 11.1 Rapport Agent Behavior Mapping

Human speaker behavior	*Rapport Agent response*
Lowering of pitch	Head nod
Raised loudness	Head nod
Speech disfluency	Posture/gaze shift
Shift posture	Mimic
Gaze away	Mimic
Head nod/head shake	Mimic

Real-Time Classification of Speaker Behavior

To produce listening behaviors, the Rapport Agent first collects and analyzes the speaker's upper-body movements and voice to detect the features listed in Table 11.2.

We implement the behavior rules listed in the previous section by detecting the various implicated aspects of the speaker's behavior. As such listening behaviors occur within utterances, this imposes strong real-time requirements on what features can be reasonably extracted given the limits of current technology. Here we describe the implementation of feature detectors that support the behavioral rules.

Participant physical movements are recognized and tracked using computer vision techniques. The current version of the Rapport Agent is limited to tracking the motion of the speaker's head (see Huang, Morency, & Gratch, 2011, for more recent developments). Specifically, we use Watson, developed by Louis-Philippe Morency, an image-based tracking library that uses stereo images to track the participants' head position and orientation (Morency, Sidner, Lee, & Darrell, 2005). Watson also incorporates learned motion classifiers that detect head nods and shakes from a vector of head velocities. Other features are derived from the position and orientation of participant's head (filtered to reduce the impact of noise). For example, from the head position, given the participant is seated in a fixed chair, we can infer the posture of the spine.

From the speech signal, we extract a variety of "paralinguistic" features (i.e., features of the voice signal other than the meaning of the words). This includes such features as vocal pitch and then intensity of the speech signal (the Rapport Agent ignores the semantic content of the speaker's speech), using a signal processing package, Laun, developed by Mathieu Morales (Lamothe & Morales, 2006). Features include silent/normal/loud speech (derived from signal intensity) and "backchannel opportunity points" (pitch contours that are associated with listener feedback), derived using the approach of Ward and Tsukahara (2000). In addition, we approximately segment the audio signal into separate utterances based on silences and attempt to detect some features that hold across the utterance including pitch range (positive affect is often associated with wider pitch range).

Behavior Mapping

Recognized speaker features are mapped into listening behaviors through a set of authorable mapping rules. The language is based on five primitives:

- Each participant in the interaction is described by an *agent*. Agents consist of a set of actions, states, animations, and reactions. For the discussion that follows, we will assume two agents: the agent that represents the human speaker and the agent that represent the Rapport Agent listener.
- *Actions* represent discrete behavioral events that can be generated by an agent. These can consist of the detectable features of human behavior (Table 11.2) or arbitrary behavior outputs of the Rapport Agent.
- *States* describe characteristics of an agent that can persist over time. Typically, states are asserted as consequences of actions (e.g., after detecting LeanLeft, the speaker is in the state of LeaningLeft). States can be constrained logically (e.g., the speaker cannot be simultaneously speaking and silent) and temporally (e.g., to ensure an agent stays in some state for some period of time).
- *Animations* are physical behaviors described in the Behavior Markup Language (BML) (Kopp

TABLE 11.2 Rapport Agent Detected Speaker Features

Motion features		*Vocal features*	
Gestures	Nod, shake	Intensity	Silent, normal, loud
Head roll	Upright, lean left, lean right	Range	Wide, narrow
Gaze	Straight, up, down, left, right	Others	Backchannel opportunity

et al., 2006) that can be associated with agent actions. For example, a backchannel continuer might be associated with a nod animation.

- *Reactions* map from an action in one agent to an action in another agent. The mapping is conditional on the current state of one or more agents and can map, probabilistically, to one of a set of other actions.

Typically, reactions map actions of the speaker to actions by the Rapport Agent. For example, if Laun detects a backchannel opportunity point in the speaker, this could cause the Rapport Agent to react with a Nod with probability 0.6 or GazeUp with probability 0.2, assuming the Rapport Agent is in the state of GazingForward. The framework, however, can support more general settings. For example, one could define mapping rules for multiparty settings (e.g., multiple speakers or multiple listening agents). Alternatively, one could transform the behavior of a human listener into some, perhaps altered, animated behavior (Bailenson et al., 2004).

Animation

Rapport Agent animation commands are passed to the SmartBody animation system (Kallmann & Marsella, 2005; Thiebaux, Marshall, Marsella, & Kallmann, 2008). This is a virtual human animation system designed to seamlessly blend animations and procedural behaviors. These animations are rendered in the Unreal Tournament™ game engine and displayed to the Speaker.

System Architecture

The Rapport Agent has an open modular architecture that facilitates the incorporation of different feature detectors and animation systems, and has an easily authored mapping between features and behavior. The behavior mapping language incorporates contextual features, probabilistic responses, and some control over the temporal dynamics of behavior. We used a vision-based tracker and set the setting to a seated interaction with a life-sized image of a character's head displayed on a computer monitor. Figure 11.2 illustrates the basic outlines of the Rapport Agent architecture.

As we are simultaneously recognizing features from multiple channels (head, body and speech), and listening behaviors have some duration, it is possible that a listening behavior will be proposed that overlaps with a currently executing behavior. This could easily result in unnatural behavior.

We use a synchronization module to solve this problem. This module parses messages on the communication bus and determines if the message is intended for the agent and which type of gesture is contained in the command. Once this parsing has been done, the function accompanying that type of gesture can be called. This function determines whether a previous gesture is still performing, and when this is not the case, a message is created, which is to be sent to the agent. The module also incorporates a flexible behavior mapping allowing designers to easily experiment with alternative mappings between classes of listening behaviors and their physical manifestation.

Empirical Findings

The Rapport Agent exhibits some of the nonverbal resonances that occurs in natural conversation, but are people influenced by computer-generated behaviors? In a series of empirical studies (which we will discuss below), we have used the Rapport Agent as methodological tool to explore such questions about the role of nonverbal behaviors in human and human–computer

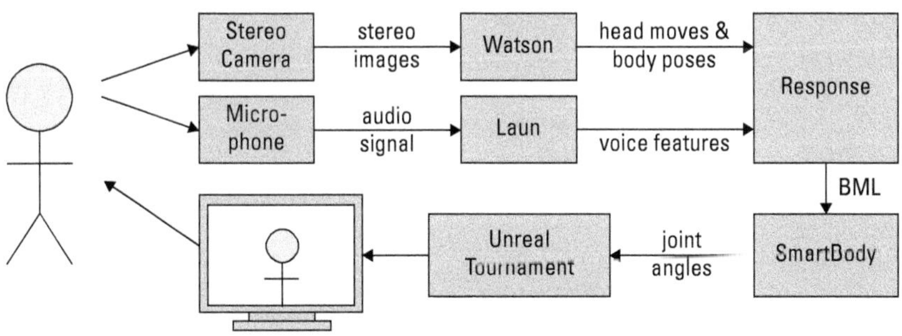

FIGURE 11.2 Rapport Agent architecture.

interaction. For example, we can demonstrate that such synthetic resonant behaviors alter participant feelings, impressions, and behavior, and that the strength of such effects are mediated by the same factors of positivity, contingency, and mutual attention that Tickle-Degnen and Rosenthal have posited for face-to-face interactions between people. Further, as posed by Nass and Reeves in their *media equation* (Reeves & Nass, 1996), such effects seem to occur even when participants know that such behaviors are "merely" produced by a computer.

In the remainder of this chapter, we outline the basic experimental paradigm by which we explore such questions and then summarize the findings of several studies. We highlight different aspects of these findings. First, we describe the consequences, subjective and behavioral, that such contingent nonverbal behaviors have on human participants. Next, we discuss some of the factors that seem to mediate these effects. These include properties of the agent's behavior, dispositional factors on the part of participants, and situational factors surrounding the interaction such as if participants believe they are interaction with another participant or a computer program.

Experimental Paradigm

As discussed above, our experiments largely follow the quasi-monolog paradigm of Welji and Duncan (Welji & Duncan, 2004). As illustrated in Figure 11.3, human participants sit in front of the Rapport Agent and are prompted (either by the experimenter or by the agent itself) to retell some previously experienced situation. This situation might be a controlled experimental stimulus: in one series of experiments, participants watch a short cartoon or a video on sexual harassment and then are instructed to retell it to the agent in as much detail as possible. Alternatively, the situation might draw on real-life experience: in another series of studies, the Rapport Agent, by playing a prerecorded animation sequence, "asks" the participant a sequence of increasingly intimate questions. In either situation, the agent displays some form of nonverbal feedback while the participant speaks, with the exact nature of the feedback being dictated by the specific experimental manipulation.

In this paradigm, participant rapport is assessed through a variety of subjective and behavioral measures. Subjective measures include scales assessing rapport, social presence (Biocca & Harms, 2002), helpfulness, distraction, and naturalness. Behavioral measures include the length people speak (as a measure of engagement), the fluency of their speech (e.g., how many repeated words, broken words, and filled pauses per minute), the intimacy of their disclosure, the facial expressions produced, and amount of mutual gaze. Behavioral measures are assessed through a mixture of automatic annotation techniques and hand annotations by multiple coders.

Part of the power of this paradigm is that we can systematically manipulate aspects of the Rapport Agent's appearance and nonverbal behavior. For example, Figure 11.3 (from Gratch, Wang, Gerten, & Fast, 2007) illustrates a study that examined the impact of appearance (human vs. computer-generated human), behavior (human-generated vs. computer-generated), and contingency (carefully timed vs. random listener feedback). Going clockwise in this figure from the upper left, this experiment compared face-to-face interaction (in which a visible human participant displayed natural listening behaviors), the Rapport Agent (which exhibited computer-generated behavior and appearance), a noncontingent version of the Rapport Agent (which exhibited behaviors identical to the Rapport Agent in terms of their frequency and dynamics, but not contingent on the behaviors of the speaker), and a "mediated agent" (in which a real participant's listening behaviors were displayed on a computer-generated avatar).

Social Effects of the Rapport Agent

The picture emerging from a series of studies is that the Rapport Agent elicits beneficial social effects from human participants similar to what can be found in rapportful face-to-face interactions. Further, these benefits seem to depend on the nonverbal resonances produced by the Rapport Agent, and speaker impressions and behavior degrade when these behaviors are absent.

The presence of contingent nonverbal feedback changes participants' feelings about themselves, the agent, and the quality of their interaction. Subjective effects include:

- Greater feelings of self-efficacy (Kang, Gratch, Wang, & Watt, 2008b)
- Less tension (Wang & Gratch, 2010) and less embarrassment (Kang, Gratch, Wang, & Watt, 2008b)
- Greater feelings of rapport (Wang & Gratch, 2010)
- A greater sense of mutual awareness (von der Pütten, Krämer, & Gratch, 2009)

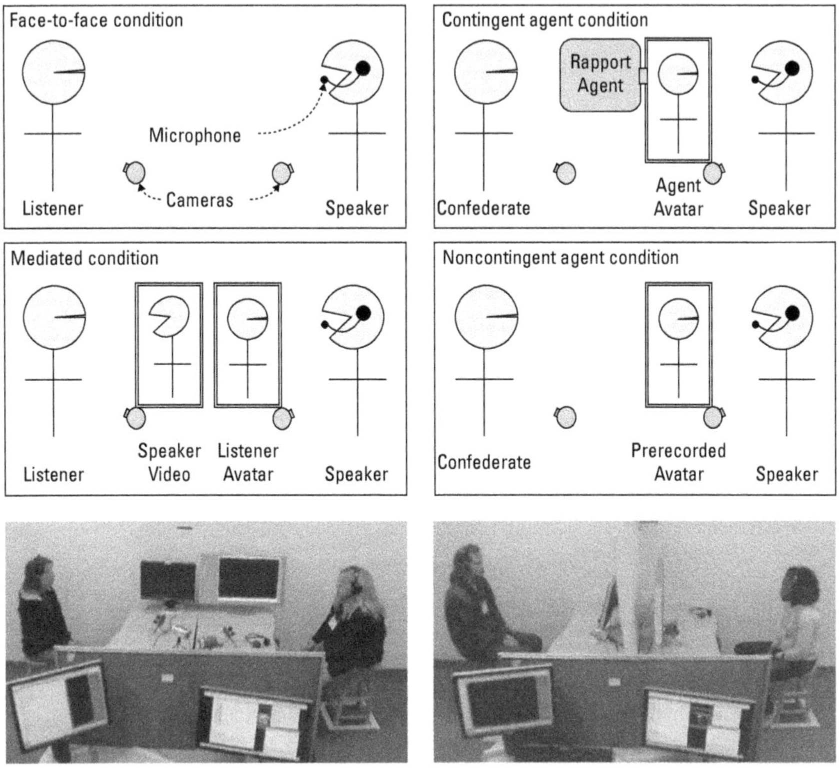

FIGURE 11.3 Graphical depiction of the four conditions. The actual face-to-face condition is illustrated on the lower left, and the setup for the other three conditions on the lower right.

- Greater feelings of trustworthiness on the part of the agent (Kang, Gratch, Wang, & Watt, 2008b)

The contingent nonverbal feedback of the rapport agent also changes participants' behavior. Behavioral effects include:

- More disclosure of information, including longer interaction times and more words elicited (Gratch et al., 2006, 2007; von der Pütten et al., 2009; Wang & Gratch, 2010)
- More fluent speech (Gratch et al., 2006, 2007; von der Pütten et al., 2009; Wang & Gratch, 2010)
- More mutual gaze (Wang & Gratch, 2010)
- Fewer negative facial expressions (Wang & Gratch, 2009b)

Factors That Influence These Effects

One focus of our empirical research has been directed at illuminating factors that mediate or moderate the observed social effects of the Rapport Agent, and more generally, explore the validity of alternative theoretical constructs for interpreting these results and guiding future agent design. We organize this discussion into three basic questions. First, what properties of the Rapport Agent are necessary or sufficient for promoting rapport? Second, what characteristics of people lead them to be more or less influenced by the agent's behavior? Finally, we consider the more general question of the usefulness of social psychological theory (which was developed to explain human-to-human interaction) as a framework for guiding the design of computer systems. Blascovich (Chapter 3, this volume) suggests that interactions might unfold very differently depending on whether people believe they are interacting *with computers* or *through computers* (i.e., the Rapport Agent might have different social effects depending on if participants believed its behavior was generated by a computer or if they believed the behavior corresponded to the movements of an actual human listener). This last question, depending on the answer, could have profound effects for the value of interdisciplinary research on social artifacts.

Characteristics of the Agent That Impact Rapport

If we adopt the former perspective and apply social psychological theory directly, Tickle-Degnen and Rosenthal's theory argues that three broad characteristic of agent behavior should promote the establishment of rapport between participants and the Rapport Agent. These factors include *positivity*, meaning that rapport will be enhanced by positive nonverbal cues, including positive facial expressions and encouraging feedback such as head nods; *coordination*, meaning that rapport will increase as the behavior of one participant is perceived as contingent upon (i.e., causally related to) the behavior of the other; and *mutual attentiveness*, meaning that rapport will increase as participants attend to each other nonverbally, for example, through mutual gaze. Thus, our empirical studies have sought to manipulate these factors independently and observe their impact on rapport.

Positivity

In face-to-face conversations, positivity is conveyed through a variety of nonverbal signals such as facial expressions and head nods. To explore the impact of positivity, we have operationalized this dimension in terms of the presence or absence of head nods generated by the Rapport Agent. Although we have yet to manipulate facial expressions (due to technical challenges in producing these at natural points in conversation), we have examined the relationship between participants' expressions and their perceptions of rapport.

Our findings illustrate that the presence of listener nods significantly enhances feelings and behavioral manifestations of rapport (Wang & Gratch, 2010). The strength of this effect seems moderated by the perceived contingency of the nods (Kang, Gratch, Wang, & Watt, 2008b) and dispositional factors (Pütten, Krämer, Gratch, & Kang, 2010) as will be discussed. We also explored whether participant facial expressions could be indicators of rapport, specifically via communicating positivity (Wang & Gratch, 2009b). We looked at participants' facial expressions, which were analyzed using the Facial Action Coding System and the Computer Expression Recognition Toolbox (see Whitehill, Bartlett, and Movellan, Chapter 6, this volume). In both of human-to-human and human-to-virtual human (Rapport Agent) interactions, more positive facial expressions were associated with greater rapport. Collectively, these findings are in line with Tickle-Degnen and Rosenthal's predictions.

Coordination

Coordination occurs when two participants' behaviors are mutually related in a timely and positive manner. Within the Rapport Agent, we have operationalized this factor by manipulating whether behaviors (such as nods or posture shifts) were generated in response to the participant's behavior (a coordinated condition) or in response to some unrelated factor (an uncoordinated condition). For example, in one study, we would create noncontingent behavior by showing a participant the same nonverbal behavior that was generated for the previous participant. This manipulation only breaks contingency while ensuring a similar frequency and distribution of behaviors are generated.

Overall, participants exhibit more subjective and behavior characteristics of rapport when coordination is present. For example, breaking the contingency of nonverbal feedback leads participants to talk less and produced more disfluent speech (Gratch et al., 2007). These effects were especially strong in participants who scored high in a scale of social anxiety as such participants, in addition to these behavioral effects, feel less subjective rapport and greater embarrassment (Kang, Gratch, Wang, & Watt, 2008b). We further explored the effects of coordination on learning (Wang & Gratch, 2009a). We hypothesized that contingent feedback would be perceived as helpful and can help students learn better. The learning task of users was storytelling interactions also used in other studies (Gratch et al., 2007; Kang et al., 2008a, 2008b]. We found that users reported higher rapport with the contingent feedback than the noncontingent one. We also discovered that rapport helped users' interaction and enhanced their self-performance, which improved learning gains. Collectively, these findings are in line with Tickle-Degnen and Rosenthal's predictions.

Mutual Attentiveness

Mutual attentiveness occurs in a conversation when both participants attend closely to each other's words or movements. In our empirical research, we have operationalized this concept in terms of gaze—for example, are participants looking at each other during a conversation? Prior research in gaze suggests there should be a curvilinear relationship between gaze and feelings of rapport. In other words, continuously staring at another person or completely avoiding his or her gaze would tend to be disruptive, but, short of these extremes, rapport should be enhanced by more visual attention.

Consistent with this, we found a similar curvilinear relationship between gaze and rapport. For example, an agent that continuously gazed at the participant without companying other timely positive gestures caused more distractions, less rapport, and more speech disfluency in storytelling interaction (Ning & Gratch, 2010). Similarly, an agent that failed to maintain gaze with the participant was equally disruptive. Collectively, these findings are in line with Tickle-Degnen and Rosenthal's predictions.

Characteristics of Participants That Impact Rapport

The previous studies and findings emphasized the impact of differences in the agent's behavior, but numerous social psychological studies emphasize that the trajectory of a social interaction is heavily shaped by the "baggage" people bring to a situation. In human-to-human interactions, people who are extroverted will more easily establish rapport than introverts, and we might expect that these dispositional tendencies will carry over into interactions with the Rapport Agent. Indeed, in a series of studies we have found that dispositional factors shape interactions with virtual humans in a similar manner to their influence in face-to-face interactions between people.

From the social science literature, we would expect that several dispositional traits might moderate the Rapport Agent's social impact. Broad personality dimensions, such as the "Big Five" (Costa & McCrae, 1992)—that is, extraversion, agreeableness, openness, conscientiousness, and neuroticism—influence many aspects of social behavior, and previous research illustrates that such effects can carry over to virtual interactions (Bickmore, Gruber, & Picard, 2005; Yee, Harris, Jabon, & Bailenson, 2010, in press). More specific personality traits also seem relevant to the study of rapport. For example, we might expect the impact of the Rapport Agent's nonverbal behavior to depend on participants' *public self-consciousness* (Scheier & Carver, 1985), which refers to their sensitivity to attend to the actions of others and adjust their own behavior to create favorable impressions. Rapport can also be impacted by one's tendency to be anxious in social situations: talking with a stranger (or an even stranger virtual human) can be threatening, and people vary in their tendency to react fearfully to novel social situations. Thus, measures such as shyness or social anxiety may illuminate mechanisms that underlie the impact of virtual humans (Cheek, 1983).

Indeed, several dispositional factors have been found to influence the effectiveness of the Rapport Agent. With respect to the Big Five, extroversion and agreeableness influence interactions in ways that are consistent with their impact in human-to-human interactions. Extroverts tend to talk more, and more fluently, and feel better about their interaction, and similar findings hold for participants who score high in agreeableness (Kang, Gratch, Wang, & Watts, 2008a; von der Pütten, Krämer, & Gratch, 2010). Social anxiety also plays a moderating role: interestingly, we found dispositionally anxious subjects felt more trust toward the Rapport Agent than in their interactions with human conversational partners (Kang, Gratch, Wang, & Watt, 2008b).

Dispositional factors don't uniquely determine the outcome of a social interaction but, rather, interact with aspects the situation. For example, someone who is confident in social situations might perform well regardless of the behavior of his or her conversational partner. However, someone who is less secure might seek constant reassurance by carefully monitoring his or her partner's nonverbal feedback: if this feedback is positive, he or she may perform well and report positive feelings; if this feedback is negative, the opposite may occur. We see similar interaction effects in our data (Kang, Gratch, Wang, & Watt, 2008a). For example, extroverts seem insensitive to manipulations that impact the quality of the Rapport Agent's nonverbal feedback, whereas participants who score high in social anxiety are quite disrupted by negative feedback (such as that produced by the noncontingent agent). We found that people having greater social anxiety felt less rapport and more embarrassment, and exhibited worse performance (e.g., more disfluent speech) when presented with noncontingent feedback.

Overall, our studies suggest that both agent behavior and dispositional factors interact to determine the overall quality of an experience with a virtual human. Further, these effects are largely consistent with predictions from the social psychological literature on human-to-human interactions. However, virtual humans are clearly different from people in many respects, and we now turn to turn to theoretical predictions that suggest these differences can profoundly shape the nature of human interactions with such technological artifacts.

Media Effects

The previous findings suggest that a social psychological theory such as rapport has some explanatory value in predicting how behaviors of an artificial agent will influence human subjective impressions and behavior. However, there are many important differences between humans and virtual humans, and some theoretical perspectives argue that these differences are crucial in determining the trajectory of a human/virtual human interaction. In Chapter 3 of this volume, Blascovich describes the threshold model of social influence within digital immersive virtual environments, which posits that a number of "media factors" can promote or disrupt the applicability of standard social psychological findings to virtual settings. For example, *agency* refers to the "perceived human sentience" (meaning the attribution of consciousness and free will) of a human-appearing agent. In the context of the Rapport Agent, *agency* would refer to whether participants believed the Rapport Agent's listening behavior corresponded to the actual movements of a sentient human participant in another room (i.e., that the Rapport Agent was an *avatar* of another participant) or whether they believed they were generated by a computer agent. The threshold model predicts that social effects of the Rapport Agent will be moderated by agency attributions. Numerous studies by different research groups show that people react socially toward both forms of representations—agents and avatars (c.f., e.g., Bailenson, Blascovich, Beall, & Loomis, 2004; Bickmore, Gruber, & Picard, 2005; Cassell et al., 2001; Gratch, Wang, Gerten, Fast, & Duffy, 2007; Krämer, Iurgel, & Bente, 2005; Nass, Moon, Morkes, Kim, & Fogg, 1997; Reeves & Nass, 1996; see Krämer, 2008, for an overview). However, it is still unclear whether people react in the same way toward agents and avatars.

We investigated whether users' belief in interacting with either an avatar (a virtual representation of a human) or an agent (autonomous virtual person) leads to different social effects in self-disclosure interview interaction (von der Püten et al., 2010). We specifically tested two dominant models of social effects in human–agent interaction: the threshold model of social influence and Nass' Ethopoeia concept. According to the threshold model of social influence (Blascovich et al., 2002), the social influence of real persons who are represented by avatars will always be high, whereas the influence of an artificial entity depends on the realism of its behavior. Conversely, the Ethopoeia concept (Nass & Moon, 2000) predicts that automatic social reactions are triggered by situations as soon as they include social cues. We found that the outcome did not demonstrate a significant difference in users' perception of agency between an agent and an avatar. On the other hand, manipulating the presence of social cues (i.e., the presence or absence of positive, contingent feedback on the part of the agent) significantly influenced users' subjective experience as well as their actual behavior: Users experienced more feelings of mutual awareness with their partner and revealed more information in the interaction when social cues of rapport were present. This outcome supports the assumption that "the more computers present characteristics that are associated with humans, the more likely they are to elicit social behavior" (Nass & Moon, 2000, p. 97). Like in face-to-face interactions, the evaluation of people is first and foremost dependent on what agents do—even if it is merely subtle differences in nonverbal behavior. In conclusion, the Ethopoeia concept by Nass and colleagues is more suitable as an approach to explain the social effects we found than the threshold model of social influences by Blascovich and colleagues.

Discussion and Conclusion

Across a wide range of studies, we have consistently shown that simple nonverbal cues on the part of a computer program can provoke a wide range of beneficial subjective and behavioral outcomes. Overall, our studies and related findings add further evidence that the nonverbal behavior of embodied virtual agents influences the behavior of the humans who interact with them in ways that are consistent with psychological findings on human-to-human interaction. Further, these effects increase as a virtual agent exhibits more human-like behavioral characteristics. More specifically, studies support Tickle-Degnen and Rosenthal's claims that rapport is promoted by social behavioral cues that are positive and contingent and convey mutual attention, and that these effects are moderated by personality traits of the human user. Interestingly, participant's belief as to whether he or she was interacting with another human or a computer program did not have much effect, reinforcing claims by Nass and colleagues that computer programs will produce social effects to the extent that they incorporate human-like social cues, and reinforcing the validity of using social psychological theory to inform agent design.

Despite the apparent success of the rapport agent, one should be cautious before concluding that people will always be so easily manipulated by simple nonverbal behaviors. According to the social inference taxonomy presented in the introductory chapter of this book (see Figure 3 of the Introduction), the Rapport Agent is leveraging social reactivity (i.e., certain behaviors such as nods or smiles might trigger automatic responses in participants) and simple social inference (i.e., by giving certain expressive behaviors at the right time, the participant is—via some process such as reverse appraisal—attributing mental state to the agent even if this state is an illusion) but is otherwise limited. Our experimental settings (storytelling and interviews) are, by design, simple for agents to navigate. The Rapport Agent conveys understanding without actual understanding, a behavior that most of us have engaged in from time to time (for example, when carrying on a conversation in a unfamiliar language or in a noisy room), but such a charade only goes so far before it ends in embarrassment. For example, in a similar storytelling paradigm, Janet Bavelas illustrated that "generic" feedback (similar to what the Rapport Agent provides) is easy to produce without actually attending to the meaning of a conversation—she had participants listen while solving complex mathematical problems—but at certain points speakers need more meaningful "specific" feedback. Bavelas et al. (2000) found that when speakers were telling personally emotional stories, they expected emotional feedback at key dramatic moments. When they failed to receive it, they felt embarrassment and had difficulty proceeding with their story. The inability for the Rapport Agent to produce meaningful feedback is a clear limitation, and its mindless feedback can easily backfire if participants realize its true nature.

Part of our research can be seen as pushing the boundary of just how far one can go with simple contingent feedback. Our early studies explored "safe" and impersonal content such as Tweety and Sylvester cartoons. We subsequently examine the more daring content such as sexual harassment. Most recently, we've been asking people to elicit very personal information such as their greatest disappointments. At each stage we continue to show robust subjective and behavioral effects of contingent positive feedback; however, we must be careful before concluding that the agent is performing well. What we've shown is that the agent performs about as well as one would when discussing personal matters with a stranger (something many people feel is a stressful experience) and better than an agent that provides no or negative feedback. While important, this is a low bar, and much can be done to improve the performance and effects of such agents.

Recently, we've been speculating that rapport can be conceptualized as a phenomenon occurring on three levels: the emotional, the behavioral, and the cognitive. Emotionally, rapport is an inherently rewarding experience; we feel liking, emotional support, and acceptance. Cognitively, we share an understanding with our conversation partner; there is a convergence of beliefs or views, a bridging of ideas or perspectives. Behaviorally (or interactionally), there is a convergence of movements with our conversational partner; observers report increased synchrony, fluidity, and coordination in partners' movements. We argue that the Rapport Agent produces effects at each of these levels (people feel liking and support; they believe they are understood; they recognize that their partner is in sync with their behavior), but only the behavioral level is truly implemented.

At the cognitive level, agent head nods merely create the illusion of mutual understanding. According to theories of conversational grounding, speakers in a conversation expect frequent and incremental feedback from listeners that their communication is understood (Nakano, Reinstein, Stocky, & Cassell, 2003; Traum, 1994). When listeners provide grounding feedback, speech can proceed fluently and presumably with a greater sense of rapport. Such feedback often takes the form of nods, such as produced by the Rapport Agent, and presumably speakers are (incorrectly) interpreting these nods as grounding cues. This illusion can be maintained to an extent, but as Bavelas' example above illustrates, it will eventually backfire and lead participants to view such feedback with suspicion. If we want to create true rapport, a major challenge in creating true rapport is how to recognize and respond meaningfully to a speaker with the rapidity seen in human dyads. Indeed, recent research in dialogue systems is making progress in this direction (Sagae, DeVault, & Traum, 2010).

At the emotional level, agent head nods are likely creating the illusion of empathy and emotional support. When a participant tells a positive story, as in a Tweety and Sylvester cartoon, this illusion is easily maintained. However, when participants are relating their fears and disappointments, they expect corresponding expressions of sympathy or empathy on the part of their conversational partner: when someone has just revealed that he or she was sexually abused, simply nodding doesn't cut it and will likely backfire. If we want to create "real" rapport, a system must not only extract meaning from a participant's speech (a prerequisite of the cognitive level or rapport) but also exhibit coherent and supportive emotional reactions to this content. Our earlier chapter on EMA (Chapter 4) illustrates how such emotional reactions could be calculated, and current efforts are aimed at integrating appraisal with the low-level behavioral feedback produced by that Rapport Agent.

Conclusion

In this book, we have argued that the study of human emotion both informs and is informed by computational methods, and the Rapport Agent is a vivid example of this relationship. By starting with a psychological theory of social processes (in this case the theory of rapport by Tickle-Degnen and Rosenthal), we are able to construct a social artifact that instantiates the theory. The resulting artifact then becomes a means for testing the theory. According to rapport theory, simple contingent behaviors could produce feelings of mutual understanding and connectedness, and more effective social interactions. But the causality of this theory is hard to confirm. Are these contingent behaviors causes or consequences of successful social interactions? Artifacts like the Rapport Agent provide the means to experimentally tease apart these factors in ways that avoid the disadvantages and potential confounds introduced by human confederates. In this chapter, we outlined a series of studies that demonstrate that, indeed, contingent behaviors cause rapport. Thus, social theory has allowed us to build a better computer and return the favor through experimental support for theory. This is a true partnership between the social and computational sciences of social emotions.

Note

1. Although we adopt the terminology and definitions of Tickle-Degnen and Rosenthal, the nonverbal patterning seen in rapport is closely related to a number of social science concepts including *interpersonal sensitivity* (Hall & Bernieri, 2001), *social glue* (Lakin et al., 2003), *interactional synchrony* (Bernieri & Rosenthal, 1991), *behavioral mimicry* (Chartrand & Bargh, 1999), backchanneling (Yngve, 1970), and *interpersonal adaptation* (Burgoon, Stern, & Dillman, 1995).

References

Adam, H., Shirako, A., & Maddux, W. W. (2010). Cultural variance in the interpersonal effects of anger in negotiations. *Psychological Science, 21*(6), 882–889.

Ambady, N., Bernieri, F. J., & Richeson, J. A. (2000). Toward a histology of social behavior: Judgmental accuracy from thin slices of the behavioral stream. *Advances in Experimental Social Psychology, 32*, 201–271.

Bailenson, J., Beall, A., Loomis, J., Blascovich, J., & Turk, M. (2004). Transformed social interaction: Decoupling Representation from Behavior and Form in Collaborative Virtual Environments. *PRESENCE: Teleoperators and Virtual Environments, 13*(4), 428–441.

Bailenson, J., & Yee, N. (2005). Digital chameleons: Automatic assimilation of nonverbal gestures in immersive virtual environments. *Psychological Science, 16*, 814–819.

Bargh, J. A., Chen, M., & Burrows, L. (1996). Automaticity of social behavior: Direct effects of trait construct and stereotype activation on action. *Journal of Personality and Social Psychology, 71*(2), 230–244.

Bavelas, J. B., Coates, L., & Johnson, T. (2000). Listeners as co-narrators. *Journal of Personality and Social Psychology, 79*(6), 941–952.

Bente, G., Kraemer, N. C., Petersen, A., & de Ruiter, J. P. (2001). Computer animated movement and person perception: Methodological advances in nonverbal behavior research. *Journal of Nonverbal Behavior, 25*(3), 151–166.

Bernieri, F. J. (1988). Coordinated movement and rapport in teacher-student interactions. *Journal of Nonverbal behavior, 12*(2), 120–138.

Bernieri, F. J., Gillis, J. S., Davis, J. M., & Grahe, J. E. (1996). Dyad rapport and the accuracy of its judgment across situations: A lens model analysis. *Journal of Personality and Social Psychology, 71*(1), 110–129.

Bernieri, F. J., & Rosenthal, R. (1991). Interpersonal coordination: Behavior matching and interactional synchrony. In R. S. Feldman & B. Rimé (Eds.), *Fundamentals of Nonverbal Behavior*. Cambridge, UK: Cambridge Univ. Press.

Bickmore, T., Gruber, A., & Picard, R. W. (2005). Establishing the computer-patient working alliance in automated health behavior change interventions. *Patient Education and Counseling, 59*(1), 21–30.

Biocca, F., & Harms, C. (2002, October). *Defining and measuring social presence: Contribution to the networked minds theory and measure*. Paper presented at the Presence, Porto, Portugal,

Blascovich, J. (2002). Social influence within immersive virtual environments. In R. Schroeder (Ed.), *The social life of avatars* (pp. 127–145): Springer-Verlag.

Brand, M. (1999, October). *Voice puppetry*. Paper presented at the 26th International Conference on Computer Graphics and Interactive Techniques (SIGGRAPH), Los Angeles.

Breazeal, C., & Aryananda, L. (2002). Recognition of affective communicative intent in robot-directed speech. *Autonomous Robots, 12*, 83–104.

Burgoon, J. (1983). Nonverbal violations of expectations. In J. M. Wiemann & R. P. Harrison (Eds.), *Nonverbal interaction* (pp. 11–77). Beverly Hils, CA: Sage.

Burgoon, J., Stern, L. A., & Dillman, L. (1995). *Interpersonal adaptation: Dyadic interaction patterns*. Cambridge, UK: Cambridge University Press.

Burns, M. (1984). Rapport and relationships: The basis of child care. *Journal of Child Care, 2*, 47–57.

Cassell, J. (2000). Nudgenudgewinkwink: Elements of Face-to-Face Conversation for Embodied Conversational Agents. In J. Cassell, J. Sullivan, S. Prevost, & E. Churchill (Eds.), *Embodied conversational agents* (pp. 1–27). Cambridge, MA: MIT Press.

Cassell, J., Bickmore, T., Billinghurst, M., Campbell, L., Chang, K., Vilhjálmsson, H., et al. (1999, May). *Embodiment in conversational interfaces: Rea*. Paper presented at the Conference on Human Factors in Computing Systems, Pittsburgh, PA.

Cassell, J., Nakano, Y. I., Bickmore, T. W., Sidner, C. L., & Rich, C. (2001, July). *Non-verbal cues for discourse structure*. Paper presented at the Association for Computational Linguistics Joint EACL - ACL Conference, Toulouse, France.

Cassell, J., & Thórisson, K. R. (1999). The power of a nod and a glance: Envelope vs. emotional feedback in animated conversational agents. *International Journal of Applied Artificial Intelligence, 13*(4–5), 519–538.

Cathcart, N., Carletta, J., & Klein, E. (2003, April). *A shallow model of backchannel continuers in spoken dialogue*. Paper presented at the 10th Conference of the European Chapter of the Association for Computational Linguistics, Budapest, Hungary.

Chartrand, T. L., & Bargh, J. A. (1999). The chameleon effect: The perception-behavior link and social interaction. *Journal of Personality and Social Psychology, 76*(6), 893–910.

Cheek, J. M. (1983). *The Revised Cheek and Buss Shyness Scale (RCBS)*. Wellesley, MA: Wellesley College.

Clark, H. H., & Wasow, T. (1998). Repeating words in Spontaneous Speech. *Cognitive Psychology, 37*, 204–242.

Cogger, J. W. (1982). Are you a skilled interviewer? *Personnel Journal, 61*, 840–843.

Costa, P. T., Jr., & McCrae, R. R. (1992). *NEO PI-R professional manual*. Odessa, FL: Psychological Assessment Resources, Inc.

Drolet, A. L., & Morris, M. W. (2000). Rapport in conflict resolution: Accounting for how face-to-face contact fosters mutual cooperation in mixed-motive conflicts. *Experimental Social Psychology, 36*, 26–50.

Forgas, J. P. (2007). The use of computer-mediated interaction in exploring affective influences on strategic interpersonal behaviours. *Computers in Human Behavior, 23*(2), 901–919.

Fuchs, D. (1987). Examiner familiarity effects on test performance: Implications for training and practice. *Topics in Early Childhood Special Education, 7*, 90–104.

Gratch, J. (2008). True emotion vs. social intentions in nonverbal communication: Towards a synthesis for embodied conversational agents. In I. Wachmuth & G. Knoblich (Eds.), *Modeling communication with robots and virtual humans* (Vol. LNAI 4930, pp. 181–197). Berlin: Springer.

Gratch, J. (2010). Emotionally-resonant media: Advances in sensing, understanding and influencing human emotion through interactive media. In K. Döveling, C. von Scheve, & E. Konijn (Eds.), *Handbook of emotions and the mass media* (pp. 370–387). London: Routledge, Taylor and Francis Group.

Gratch, J., Okhmatovskaia, A., Lamothe, F., Marsella, S., Morales, M., van der Werf, R., et al. (2006, August). *Virtual rapport*. Paper presented at the 6th International Conference on Intelligent Virtual Agents, Marina del Rey, CA.

Gratch, J., Wang, N., Gerten, J., & Fast, E. (2007). *Creating rapport with virtual agents*. Paper presented at the 7th International Conference on Intelligent Virtual Agents, Paris, France.

Hall, J., & Bernieri, F. J. (Eds.). (2001). *Interpersonal sensitivity: Theory and measurement*. Mahwah, NJ: Psychology Press.

Huang, L., Morency, L.-P., & Gratch, J. (2010, May). *Parasocial consensus sampling: Combining multiple perspectives to learn virtual human behavior*. Paper presented at the 9th International Conference on Autonomous Agents and Multiagent Systems, Toronto, Canada.

Huang, L., Morency, L. P., & Gratch, J. (2011, September). *Virtual rapport 2.0*. Paper presented at the Proceedings of the 10th International Conference on Intelligent Virtual Agents, Reykjavík, Iceland.

Kallmann, M., & Marsella, S. (2005, September). *Hierarchical motion controllers for real-time autonomous virtual humans.* Paper presented at the 5th International Working Conference on Intelligent Virtual Agents, Kos, Greece.

Kang, S.-H., Gratch, J., Wang, N., & Watt, J. (2008a, September). *Agreeable people like agreeable virtual humans.* Paper presented at the 8th International Conference on Intelligent Virtual Agents, Tokyo.

Kang, S.-H., Gratch, J., Wang, N., & Watt, J. (2008b, May). *Does contingency of agents' nonverbal feedback affect users' social anxiety?* Paper presented at the 7th International Conference on Autonomous Agents and Multiagent Systems, Estoril, Portugal.

Kang, S.-H., Gratch, J., Wang, N., & Watt, J. (2009, April). *The effect of affective iconic realism on anonymous interactants' self-disclosure.* Paper presented at Proceedings of the SIGCHI Conference on Human Factors in Computing Systems, Boston, MA.

Kopp, S., Krenn, B., Marsella, S., Marshall, A., Pelachaud, C., Pirker, H., et al. (2006, August). *Towards a common framework for multimodal generation in ECAs: The behavior markup language.* Paper presented at the Intelligent Virtual Agents, Marina del Rey, CA.

Krämer, N. C., Iurgel, I., & Bente, G. (2005). Emotion and motivation in embodied conversational agents. Paper presented at the Proceedings of the Symposium "Agents that Want and Like", Artificial Intelligence and the Simulation of Behavior (AISB), Hatfield.

Krämer, N. C. (2008, January). Social effects of virtual assistants. a review of empirical results with regard to communication. In *Intelligent virtual agents* (pp. 507–508). Springer Berlin Heidelberg.

Lakin, J. L., Jefferis, V. A., Cheng, C. M., & Chartrand, T. L. (2003). Chameleon effect as social glue: Evidence for the evolutionary significance of nonconsious mimicry. *Journal of Nonverbal Behavior, 27*(3), 145–162.

Lamothe, F., & Morales, M. (2006). *Response behavior* (No. ICT TR 01.2006). Marina del Rey, CA: University of Southern California.

Lanzetta, J. T., & Englis, B. G. (1989). Expectations of cooperation and competition and their effects on observers' vicarious emotional responses. *Journal of Personality and Social Psychology, 45*, 543–554.

McFarland, D. H. (2001). Respiratory markers of conversational interaction. *Journal of Speech, Language, and Hearing Research, 44*, 128–143.

Mead, G. H. (1934). *Mind, self and society.* Chicago: University of Chicago Press.

Morency, L.-P., de Kok, I., & Gratch, J. (2008, September). *Predicting listener backchannels: a probabilistic multimodal approach.* Paper presented at the 8th International Conference on Intelligent Virtual Agents, Tokyo.

Morency, L.-P., Sidner, C., Lee, C., & Darrell, T. (2005, October). *Contextual recognition of head gestures.* Paper presented at the 7th International Conference on Multimodal Interactions, Torento, Italy.

Nakano, Y., Reinstein, G., Stocky, T., & Cassell, J. (2003, July). *Towards a model of face-to-face grounding.* Paper presented at the Annual Meeting of the Association for Computational Linguistics, Sapporo, Japan.

Nass, C. I., Moon, Y., Morkes, J., Kim, E. Y., & Fogg, B. J. (1997). *Computers are social actors: a review of current research, Human values and the design of computer technology.* Stanford, CA: Center for the Study of Language and Information.

Nass, C., & Moon, Y. (2000). Machines and mindlessness: Social responses to computers. *Journal of Social Issues, 56*(1), 81–103.

Reeves, B., & Nass, C. (1996). *The media equation: How people treat computers, television, and new media like real people and places.* New York:. Cambridge University Press.

Roloff, M. E., & Campion, D. E. (1987). Communication and reciprocity within intimate relationships. In M. E. Roloff & G. R. Miller (Eds.), *Interpersonal processes: New directions in communication research* (pp. 11–38). Beverly Hills, CA: Sage.

Sagae, K., DeVault, D., & Traum, D. (2010, June). *Interpretation of partial utterances in virtual human dialogue systems.* Paper presented at the 11th Annual Conference of the North American Chapter of the Association for Computational Linguistics.

Scheier, M. F., & Carver, C. S. (1985). The Self-Consciousness Scale: A revised version for use with general populations. *Journal of Applied Social Psychology, 15*, 687–699.

Schröder, M., Cowie, R., Heylen, D., Pantic, M., Pelachaud, C., & Schuller, B. (2008, October). *Towards responsive Sensitive Artificial Listeners.* Paper presented at the Fourth International Workshop on Human-Computer Conversation.

Sonnby-Borgstrom, M., Jonsson, P., & Svensson, O. (2003). Emotional empathy as related to mimicry reactions at different levels of information processing. *Journal of Nonverbal Behavior, 27*(1), 3–23.

Tatar, D. (1997). *Social and personal consequences of a preoccupied listener.* Stanford, CA: Stanford University

Thiebaux, M., Marshall, A., Marsella, S., & Kallmann, M. (2008, May). *SmartBody: Behavior realization for embodied conversational agents.* Paper presented at the International Conference on Autonomous Agents and Multi-Agent Systems, Estoril, Portugal.

Tickle-Degnen, L., & Rosenthal, R. (1990). The nature of rapport and its nonverbal correlates. *Psychological Inquiry, 1*(4), 285–293.

Tiedens, L. Z., & Fragale, A. R. (2003). Power moves: Complementarity in dominant and submissive nonverbal behavior. *Journal of Personality and Social Psychology, 84*(3), 558–568.

Tosa, N. (1993, July). Neurobaby. 20th Annual Conference on Computer Graphics and Interactive Techniques (SIGGRAPH). San Diego, CA.

Traum, D. (1994). *A computational theory of grounding in natural language conversation.* (Unpublished doctoral dissertation). University of Rochester, Rochester, NY.

Tsui, P., & Schultz, G. L. (1985). Failure of rapport: Why psychotheraputic engagement fails in the treatment of Asian clients. *American Journal of Orthopsychiatry, 55*, 561–569.

Van baaren, R. B., Holland, R. W., Kawakami, K., & van Knippenberg, A. (2004). Mimicry and prosocial behavior. *Psychological Science, 15*(1), 71–74.

von der Pütten, A., Krämer, N., & Gratch, J. (2009, November). *Who's there? Can a virtual agent really elicit social presence?* Paper presented at the 12th Annual International Workshop on Presence, Los Angeles, CA.

von der Pütten, A., Krämer, N., & Gratch, J. (2010). How our personality shapes our interactions with virtual characters - Implications for research and development. In J. Allbeck, N. Badler, T. Bickmore, C. Pelachaud, & A. Safonova (Eds.), *Intelligent virtual agents* (Vol. 6356, pp. 208–221). Springer: Berlin/Heidelberg.

Pütten, A. M. von der, Krämer, N. C., Gratch, J., & Kang, S.-H. (2010). It doesn't matter what you are! Explaining social effects of agents and avatars. *Computers in Human Behavior, 6*(6), 1641–1650.

Wang, N., & Gratch, J. (2009a, July). *Can a virtual human build rapport and promote learning?* Paper presented at the 14th International Conference on Artificial Intelligence in Education, Brighton, UK.

Wang, N., & Gratch, J. (2009b, September). *Rapport and facial expression.* Paper presented at the International Conference on Affective Computing and Intelligent Interaction, Amsterdam, The Netherlands.

Wang, N., & Gratch, J. (2010, April). *Don't just stare at me.* Paper presented at the 28th Annual CHI Conference on Human Factors in Computing Systems, Atlanta, GA.

Ward, N., & Tsukahara, W. (2000). Prosodic features which cue back-channel responses in English and Japanese. *Journal of Pragmatics, 23*, 1177–1207.

Warner, R. (1996). Coordinated cycles in behavior and physiology during face-to-face social interactions. In J. H. Watt & C. A. VanLear (Eds.), *Dynamic patterns in communication processes* (pp. 327–352). Thousand Oaks, CA: SAGE publications.

Warner, R. M., Malloy, D., Schneider, K., Kooth, R., & Wilder, B. (1987). Rhythmic organization of social interaction and observer ratings of positive affect and involvement. *Journal of Nonverbal Behavior, 11*(2), 57–74.

Welji, H., & Duncan, S. (2004, August). *Characteristics of face-to-face interactions, with and without rapport: Friends vs. strangers.* Paper presented at the Symposium on Cognitive Processing Effects of 'Social Resonance' in Interaction, 26th Annual Meeting of the Cognitive Science Society, Chicago, IL.

Yee, N., Harris, H., Jabon, M., & Bailenson, J. N. (2011). The expression of personality in virtual worlds. *Social Psychology and Personality Science, 2*(1), 5–12.

Yngve, V. H. (1970, April). *On getting a word in edgewise.* Paper presented at the Sixth Regional Meeting of the Chicago Linguistic Society, Chicago, IL.

Index

www.ingramcontent.com/pod-product-compliance
Ingram Content Group UK Ltd.
Pitfield, Milton Keynes, MK11 3LW, UK
UKHW051224160926
475595UK00022B/181